Representative Rugby at Kingsholm

International, County, & Invitation Teams

MALC KING

with

DICK WILLIAMS

Malc King

GLOUCESTER RUGBY
HERITAGE

Dick Williams

First published in 2017
for Gloucester Rugby Heritage
www.gloucesterrugbyheritage.org.uk

by The Hobnob Press, 30c Deverill Road Trading Estate, Sutton Veny, Warminster BA12 7BZ
www.hobnobpress.co.uk

British Library Cataloguing in Publication Data
A catalogue record for this book is available from the British Library

ISBN 978-1-906978-46-4

Typeset in Octavian 10/11.5 pt. Typesetting and origination by John Chandler
Printed by Lightning Source

The cover illustration is by Malc King.

Contents

Foreword

Peter Ford
Gloucester, Gloucestershire and England
Former Chairman and President of Gloucester Rugby

My grandfather first took me to Kingsholm, where we stood on the Tump. I believe it was one of the wartime internationals, but I was only a young lad then and my memories of it are hazy. The first big match I remember clearly was in 1946, and the players who particularly stick in my mind from that day are Bleddyn Williams, the great Welsh international, and Johnny Thornton of Gloucester whose defence was deadly – he never seemed to miss a tackle. But their Combined Services team was well beaten by a New Zealand side, for whom Sherratt on the wing was quite outstanding. As I write this, I have a clear picture in my mind of him flipping a would-be tackler over his head and scoring a stunning try. I had experienced the passionate atmosphere of Kingsholm, I caught the bug, and I still aim to get to every match at Kingsholm more than seventy years later. There isn't anything better than Kingsholm on a big match day.

For much of my lifetime, the County match was the number one fixture of the season at Kingsholm, and if Gloucestershire were doing well there might be a knock-out match to stage there as well. But most were matches in the South West group of the County Championship, and invariably they were very hard-fought affairs against Somerset, Devon and Cornwall. Getting out of the group was often harder than subsequent games in the knock-out stages, and in many seasons replays were necessary. In 1953, it was a great honour for me to run out at Kingsholm for the first time in a Gloucestershire jersey, and even better to have my Gloucester team mates, Bob Hodge and Dennis Ibbotson, in the back row alongside me – what talented players they were. We won 8-0, which was a handsome victory in those days, when winning margins were often less. The Kingsholm crowd has always been good at building up a fervent head of steam, and these close games only served to add to the intensity of the atmosphere.

1960 saw me lead out Gloucestershire for the first time as captain, made all the better by the usual raucous Kingsholm support and an unusually wide margin of 22-0 in our favour. It helped that Peter Mitchell was playing scrum half for Cornwall, because he had made the mistake of telling me some time before that he had to protect his hands because any damage to them might curtail his profession as a jeweller. I also knew that he could only kick with one foot, so if I went for his hands and to his right hand side, I had an advantage. We still meet occasionally and enjoy reminiscing about those days. Around this time the County had a battle cry of "Timber", which Ted Parfitt came up with, and which the crowd adopted.

In the same year I had the honour of leading the Western Counties side which took on the might of South Africa at Kingsholm. We pushed them back in the first scrum, but thereafter they gave us a terrible beating, and their captain, Avril Malan, explained afterwards that they had started cautiously because they had heard that West Country scrummaging was fearsome. And we thought our front row of Dovey, Thorne and Parfitt was pretty formidable. We ended up losing 42-0 and to be honest we were lucky to get nil, but it was wonderful to have the Springboks perform on the Kingsholm stage.

Indeed, there have been a lot of memorable one-off games at Kingsholm, and I'm pleased that these have been recorded in this book. When I was captain of Gloucester in 1961, a strong International XV came to play us in a match to raise funds for the Memorial Ground in Tuffley Avenue. I treasure the memories of lining up against the likes of Bill Patterson, Peter Wright, George Hastings and Phil Horrocks-Taylor – when he managed to go past a defender, the tackler was given sympathy for letting Horrocks go one side and Taylor the other, whilst he had only got hold of the hyphen in the middle. In 1973 I was no longer playing, but was involved in organising the centenary of the Club. We had hoped to see the Barbarians play at Kingsholm, but when that fell through, Don Rutherford, by then Technical Director of the RFU, stepped in and put together a star-studded side boasting many of the best Home International players of the time. What could be better than seeing the likes of Pierre Villepreux and David Duckham weaving their magic at Kingsholm.

I have so many good memories of Kingsholm, but I'm also fascinated to hear of the history of the ground from before my time. We are fortunate that Malc King and his team of volunteers came along at the right time. They had just reached retirement when the records kept at Kingsholm came to light during the demolition of the old stand and were transferred to Gloucestershire Archives. They have since accumulated much more material and carried out meticulous research. Their hard work has brought to light the whole history of Kingsholm and Gloucester Rugby and ensured that it is there for generations to come. I thought I knew a lot about this history, but they are continually catching my interest with things I didn't know or reviving memories of things I so enjoyed. I think that what they have done is wonderful and commend this book to all those for whom Kingsholm has a place in their hearts.

Sponsors

Gloucester Rugby Heritage CIO is indebted to the sponsors shown below who have helped fund the publication of this book.

DLS Commercial Catering Equipment.
Sales, Installation, Maintenance and Breakdowns.
14 The Glenmore Centre, Jessop Court,
Waterwells Business Park,   Quedgeley,
Gloucester   GL2 2AP.
T: 01452 300 100   E: service@dlspencer.co.uk
W: dlspencer.co.uk

Gloucester Rugby Players Association
Chairman Clive Walford
Secretary Ron Etheridge

Sports Chiropractic & Rehab
The Old Barn
Daunceys Farm
Purton, nr Berkeley
Glos   GL13 9HY

The Queen's Head
Village Inn & Restaurant
84, Tewkesbury Rd, Longford
Gloucester GL2 9EJ
T: 01452 301882
E: info@queensheadlongford.co.uk
     www.queensheadlongford.co.uk

The WCD Group
Specialists in Hydration
Clearview House
Gloucester Business Park
Gloucester GL3 4BH
T: 0800 731 1491
www.watercoolersdirect.com

Introduction

THE GLOUCESTER (RUGBY) Football Club was founded in 1873, it rapidly became one of the leading clubs in the country, and Gloucester became a rugby city, which it has remained ever since. During its early seasons the Club played on the Spa, a public park in Gloucester, and when a Gloucestershire County Club was formed in 1878, the Spa became the venue for a hefty proportion of County rugby matches and trials. These early representative matches in Gloucester are recorded below for the sake of completeness, but most of this book is devoted to representative rugby at Kingsholm.

The Gloucester Football and Athletic Ground Company Limited was formed to purchase the Castle Grim estate at Kingsholm in 1891, the Gloucester Club played its first game on the new ground on 10th October 1891, and representative rugby rapidly followed. The Rugby Football Union immediately appreciated the attractions of this new rugby ground in the West of England, and organised an England trial, between Western Counties and Midland Counties, which was played on 29th October 1891, within three weeks of the opening of Kingsholm.

The County was just as keen to play at Kingsholm. The County Club reorganised itself into the Gloucester County Football Union, which held its inaugural meeting in Gloucester on 11th November 1891. Later the same day, they staged their first trial match at Kingsholm. The first full County game was scheduled for a fortnight later against Devon, but had to be postponed, and was eventually played on 17th December 1891. Thereafter the County came to Kingsholm almost every season for the next century, and for many of those years the County game was the highlight of the season.

International rugby first came to Kingsholm in 1900 with England playing Wales. Although Twickenham would become the home ground for England matches from 1910, many England representative matches at both senior and schoolboy level have been staged at Kingsholm, sometimes referred to as the "Twickenham of the West". Twenty other countries, including the big three from the Southern Hemisphere, New Zealand, South Africa and Australia, have sent representative sides to Kingsholm, culminating with four matches in the 2015 Rugby World Cup.

The passionate and febrile atmosphere generated by the enthusiastic and noisy supporters of Gloucester made Kingsholm a unique place in which to play, and has attracted representative and touring sides from far and wide. Many invitational sides have played there, including the Barbarians, who first visited in 1892 and most recently in 2015. After-dinner speeches by former players and referees are peppered with stories about performing at Kingsholm, often involving repartee with the inhabitants of the Shed. "I played at Kingsholm" or "I refereed at Kingsholm" is worn as a badge of honour around the world.

When the main grandstand at Kingsholm was demolished in 2007, many records relating to these big matches came to light in the form of programmes, documents, accounts and photographs. They are now held in the Gloucestershire Archives and became part of the Gloucester Rugby Heritage (GRH) project, which has evolved into a charity run by volunteers, with a website, www. gloucesterrugbyheritage.org.uk.

Education has been perhaps the most important part of GRH's work. There are more than a hundred lesson plans on the website, together with supporting materials, aimed at both primary and secondary schools, and tied into Key Stages of the National Curriculum. Many schools are using these educational materials and tens of thousands of local schoolchildren have been to Kingsholm and the Archives, visits which are subsidised by GRH, which has mounted interpretative displays around the ground.

Three previous books have been produced by GRH. The first is a richly illustrated but brief account of the history of the Club, entitled "Gloucester Rugby Heritage". The second is a more substantial book by Martin and Teresa Davies detailing the wartime exploits of Gloucester rugby players, entitled "They Played for Gloucester and Fought for their Country". The third, entitled "Kingsholm, Castle Grim, Home of Gloucester Rugby" concentrates on the Kingsholm ground, its acquisition and development, and those who have lovingly nurtured it over the years.

After this current volume, further books are already underway, with the next focussing on the players who have represented Gloucester Rugby, and listing every player who has represented the Club. Then will come an account of the Club's exploits in Cup competitions. And the last in the series will record the history of the Gloucester Club, covering the ups and downs of the team in every season since the Club was founded in 1873, and providing a comprehensive record of Club matches, both home and away.

This book is designed to be a lasting record, as accurate as I have been able to make it, of the many matches played by representative sides at Kingsholm. I hope that all readers will find things of interest in it, and for many readers I trust that it will serve to bring back memories, hopefully most of them fond, of big matches played in or watched at Kingsholm.

Malc King
Chairman, Gloucester Rugby Heritage Project

Acknowledgements

ALTHOUGH I HAVE had the pleasure of writing this book, there are many others who have contributed to its production. My chief collaborator has been Dick Williams, whose monumental efforts have ensured that this book is richly illustrated. He is the mastermind behind the Gloucester Rugby Heritage website, he maintains our digital library of photographs, his skill at restoring old photographs has to be seen to be believed, and he has also been kind enough to take on the task of compiling the index.

The research work behind this book and the many other Gloucester Rugby Heritage outputs has been undertaken by a core team of volunteers, who labour in Gloucestershire Archives and lunch in the Queen's Head at Longford with utter dedication. They are Chris Collier (statistician), John Cowen (cataloguer and transcriber), John Theyers (treasurer), and Malc King (chairman). Without their efforts this book would not have been possible.

We have also been fortunate in contracting John Chandler, famous locally for his work on the Victoria County History, to exercise his design and type-setting skills to produce a polished publication. Linda King and John Cowen have improved the book by exercising their editorial skills to very good effect, although the author readily confesses responsibility for any remaining errors. I am also grateful to Dave Smith, minute secretary of GRH, who is our expert on video material, and who designed the cover of this book; and to Martin Bailey for his skills in editing photographs from the Journal.

Indeed the whole Gloucester Rugby Heritage project has succeeded only because of the huge effort put in by a devoted team of volunteers, who have contributed well over 30,000 hours of their time over the past ten years. Others too numerous to mention have also contributed, but they know who they are and they have my gratitude. Many have donated material to the Gloucester Rugby

Archive - their generosity has greatly enriched our collection and added to our knowledge of the history of the Club and of rugby at Kingsholm.

GRH has also benefited enormously from the professional expertise and assistance of our partners, Gloucestershire Archives and Gloucester Rugby, and from the enthusiastic encouragement and support of a great many people who cherish Gloucester Rugby and Kingsholm. In its early years, GRH was dependent upon the financial backing of the National Heritage Lottery Fund and Ecclesiastical Insurance, and this book has benefited from the support of several sponsors whose generosity is acknowledged above – I thank them all.

Many of the details of matches and photographs in this book are drawn from the Gloucester Citizen and sister publications, and I am grateful to Jenny Eastwood, Editor of the Citizen, for permitting us to reproduce both text and images from her newspaper, and to Rob Iles and Mikal Ludlow for help in finding and copying items. I am also grateful to Phil McGowen at the World Rugby Museum at Twickenham for his expert advice and provision of material.

Last but by no means least, I owe particular thanks to Peter Ford for kindly contributing the foreword to this book. He played with distinction in many of the matches recorded in this book, earned hero status with the denizens of the Shed for his utter commitment, and then devoted himself to the Gloucester Club in almost every job from committee man to President. The blood which flows through Peter is cherry and white, and I hope he will not mind my declaring that he is truly the Grand Old Man of Gloucester Rugby.

Malc King
Chairman Gloucester Rugby Heritage

Sources

THE GLOUCESTER RUGBY Archive contains many photographs (mostly of teams), lots of notebooks giving details of matches, annual reports and accounts, ground development plans, heaps of correspondence and many legal documents. It has been the basis for the research on which this book is based, and it has provided many of the images which illuminate these pages. Whilst the hard copy originals are held in the Gloucestershire Archives, where they are publicly accessible, many items have been digitally scanned and can be accessed on the Gloucester Rugby Heritage website -www.gloucesterrugbyheritage.org.uk.

The Citizen became the daily newspaper of Gloucester in 1876, only three years after the foundation of the Club, and since then has published many column miles of reporting on Gloucester Rugby. The paper has boasted a sequence of distinguished rugby correspondents, who made it their business to get close to the workings of the Gloucester Club. Most issues of the Citizen, 1876-2004, are conveniently available on microfilm at the Gloucestershire Archives, and the book draws heavily from this source. Indeed, the Citizen has been, by some margin, the main published source of material, and, except where another source is specifically identified, all the quotes in this book are taken from the Citizen.

The Journal is also available on microfilm at the Gloucestershire Archives. A weekly publication, which preceded the Citizen by more than a century, it is a unique source on the first three years of the Gloucester Club, 1873-76, and a valuable source of photographs from the 1930s to the 1960s. Copies can be viewed on microfilm at Gloucestershire Archives up to 1992.

Likewise the Gloucestershire Echo, the Citizen's sister newspaper based in Cheltenham, regularly reported on Gloucester Rugby, but in less detail than the Citizen. Copies are available on microfilm at Gloucestershire Archives for 1930-2005, and are most useful when copies of the Citizen are missing.

The Cheltenham Chronicle and Gloucestershire Graphic was published once a week 1901-36. It did not normally cover Gloucester Club games, except for those against Cheltenham, but it did cover most of the big representative matches at Kingsholm, and is notable for being richly illustrated with good quality photographs. Every issue can be seen in bound volumes at the Gloucestershire Archives, and most of the photographs in this book from that period have been copied from this source.

The Magpie was published weekly from May 1891 to December 1893. It is available in four bound volumes at the Gloucestershire Archives. Although disappointingly short-lived, this publication reported at length on the Gloucester Club, and regularly illustrated its reports with cartoons. Fortunately it covered the period when the Club moved to Kingsholm.

In a very few cases, despite diligent searches, it has not been possible to establish conclusively whether copyright exists for certain historical images. This limited edition book has not been produced in order to make a profit, and any income resulting from sales will all be used to further the charitable work of Gloucester Rugby Heritage.

The Birth of County Rugby at the Spa

THE FIRST RUGBY matches in Gloucester between representative rather than club sides were played on what was then the Gloucester Club ground at the Spa, and followed the formation of a Gloucestershire County Club. On 28th September 1878, a meeting was held at the Bell Hotel in Gloucester, at the instigation of J F Brown, then captain of Gloucester, and J D Miller of Clifton, to put in place a structure for organising county rugby in Gloucestershire. Brown and H J Boughton attended to represent the Gloucester Club. Miller became Chairman and Captain, and Brown became Secretary and Treasurer; Brown would remain in post for five years and then be replaced by Boughton. The colours selected for the County Club were maroon jerseys with badge and blue serge knickerbockers. At the first AGM in April 1879, the Club had a balance of £5 4s 10d, and the subscription for each constituent club was set at one guinea. From 1882 the number of constituent clubs increased considerably.

The Spa ground, on a public park in Gloucester, was soon to figure prominently as the home venue for County matches. The first match organised by the new Gloucester County Football Club was a trial match at the Spa on 13th November 1878. The North of the County scored three goals against a solitary try by the South. The North side contained eight Gloucester players, with Jimmy Boughton and J Bennett of Gloucester scoring a try apiece, and Boughton kicking three conversions, known then as "placing the goals".

Jimmy Boughton, who did most of the scoring in the first County trial [Gloucester Rugby]

Gloucestershire were due to play their first fixture against another county with the visit of Devon to the Spa on 31st December 1878, but the pitch was frost-bound and the fixture had to be cancelled. So the County played its first competitive match on 2nd January 1879 at Weston-super-Mare; the result was a draw with Somerset, one try apiece. Only two Gloucester players, H J Berry and J F Brown took part.

Gloucestershire 4 goals, 3 tries Wiltshire nil
15th January 1879

THIS WAS THE first home game for the County side and was played at the Spa.

Gloucestershire: backs – J D Miller (captain, Clifton), H J Berry (Gloucester); three-quarters – R Gribble, H C Evans (Clifton); quarter-backs – J F Brown (Gloucester), G G Pruen (Cheltenham); forwards – M Cartwright, F Winterbotham (Stroud), J Bennett, J Cadle (Gloucester), J Bush, E P Warren (Clifton), T R Pakenham, E J Lamb (Cheltenham), E Hurst (Rockleaze)

Wiltshire: backs – A Christison, W W Bliss (Swindon Rangers); three-quarters - W H A Law, E Peake (Marlborough College); quarter-backs - W S Bambridge (captain), W G Roffe (Marlborough); forwards – G Cooper (Devizes), J B Backford, H D Millett, W Butler, W Haines, L Hayton, E E Haines (Swindon Rangers), J W Stanton, H E Stanton (Marlborough College)

Frank Brown, who was instrumental in setting up the County Club, and who scored in the first match [Gloucester Rugby]

It was described as "a pleasantly-contested game". The goals were kicked by Lamb (3) and Miller, with the tries scored by Evans (2), Pakenham, Bennett, Brown, Cartwright and Winterbotham; Gloucestershire also registered several "touches down".

At this time a touchdown was recorded when a team was forced to touch down behind their own goal line to prevent the attacking side from scoring a try (much like a safety in American Football today). In the modern era this results only in a scrum five or a drop-out from the 22, but in Victorian times, touchdowns were registered as part of the result of a match alongside goals and tries. However, they did not count as a score in that they made no difference to whether a match was won or lost, so they were a moral rather than a scoring advantage. It was a method used locally and adopted in the Cheltenham College scoring system and in parts of Wales, but was never included in the RFU laws. A touchdown also came to be referred to as a "minor".

A County Trial at the Spa on 26th November 1879, featured seven Gloucester players (J F Brown, J Bennett, H J Berry, W Brown, P B Cooke, G J Dewey and J F Grimes) in the North of the County team. They beat the South of the County by one goal to nil. There were due to be three

County games in the 1879-80 season, but the first against Somerset on 20th December 1879 was cancelled owing to the Spa again being frost-bound. However, games, home and away, against South Wales were played.

Gloucestershire 2 tries South Wales nil
15th January 1880

PLAYED AT THE Spa on a Thursday afternoon. South Wales failed to bring a full team, and several Gloucester players volunteered to make up their number. Even so the match was played 12-a-side.

Gloucestershire: Miller (captain), Sweet, Bennett, Ward, Cowan, Berry, Leonard, Bush, Gilmore, Cartwright, Winterbotham, Pakenham

This was described as "a not very exciting match" and therefore deemed unworthy of any detailed reporting, although the full score was recorded as "two tries and several touchdowns to nil".

A Gloucestershire side containing five Gloucester players (H J Berry, J Bennett, J F Brown, W Brown and J F Grimes) also won the return game at Cardiff by a goal and a try to nil.

In 1880-81, the fixture list was expanded. The trial game was again held at the Spa on 11th November 1880, a North of County team consisting entirely of Gloucester players lost by two tries and a drop goal to nil. The sixteen Gloucester players named in the side were: H J Berry; H Buck, R L Grist, A Hayes; W Snushall, W Boughton; J F Brown (captain), J W Bayley, H Williams, W Brown, P B Cooke, F Steele, J F Grimes, G J Dewey, A F Mann, H Birks. Five County games followed, the two home matches being played at the Spa.

Gloucestershire one goal Somerset one try
18th December 1880

THE FIRST FIXTURE between these neighbouring counties was the precursor to many hard fought encounters over the next hundred years. Both teams played with two backs and three three-quarters. "Play commenced in a storm of rain, which prevented many people from witnessing the match. Notwithstanding this, however, a goodly number assembled."

Gloucestershire : J D Miller (captain, Clifton); H J Berry (Gloucester); R A Glass (Royal Agricultural College), H L Evans, E D Evans (Clifton); W F Evans, W A Boughton (Gloucester); J F Brown, P B Cooke, G J Dewey (Gloucester), E Leonard, A D Greene (Clifton), R B Ritchie, W F Waring, W L Morgan (Royal Agricultural College)

Somerset : W H Massey (captain, St. George's Hospital), E W Corner (King's College Hospital); J Gill (Wellington), E C Saunders, H Bourdillon (late Oxford University); H G Fuller (Cambridge University), Vassall (Oxford University); J J Whiteley, H G Bryant, F E Barham (Bridgwater), W England, F E Hancock (Wiveliscombe), W G Bowyer (Weston), W H Mansfield (Yeovil)

The Somerset try was disputed. In this era, the referee's decision was by no means final. The captains were expected to reach agreement in the event of a dispute, and if they could not agree, then the decision could be referred for the authorities to rule at a later hearing. However, this dispute made no difference to the outcome. Gloucestershire won what was described as 'a fine game of football' (at this time rugby was referred to just as football rather than as rugby football).

Gloucestershire one goal Surrey one try
12th February 1881

ON A FINE day at the Spa, the crowd was estimated as 3,000. Each team played nine forwards, but they had slightly differing formations amongst the backs. Whereas Gloucestershire played two backs and two three-quarters, Surrey lined up with one back and three three-quarters; both had nine forwards.

Gloucestershire : J D Miller (captain, Clifton); H J Berry (Gloucester); H W R Gribble, W O Moberly (Clifton); W F Evans, W Snushall; J F Brown, W Brown, T B Cooke, G J Dewey (Gloucester), A D Greene, H M Hirst, E Leonard, W Strachan (Clifton), R B Ritchie (Royal Agricultural College)

Surrey : P S Clifford (Clapham Rovers); M Shearman (captain, Richmond), H A Tudor (Oxford), J Shearman (Richmond); F S Chapman (Cambridge), R F L Ross (East Sheen); A S Bryden (Clapham Rovers), F W Barnard (Harlequins), G G Hawkins (Marlborough Nomads), R H Hedderwick (London Scottish), H S Holloway (Flamingoes), A H Hurrell (Clapham Rovers), H J Rust (Arabs), J L Turvey (Lausanne), A R Gildea (West Kent)

The Gloucestershire Chronicle reported that:

For the first two or three scrimmages the forwards appeared fairly well matched, and then some fast forward play by Barnard, Hedderwick, and Shearman took the leather well in the Gloucester territory, and the home team were compelled to touch-down to relieve the attack. After the drop-out the game became fast and furious, but it was not until the first half of the game had well-nigh run its course that a determined rush of the visitors enabled Barnard to obtain possession, and, making a brilliant run, although tackled by several, he succeeded in falling over the goal-line and touched-down behind. The try, however, proved a failure [ie the kick to convert it into a goal was missed]. After change of ends the Gloucestershire men played up magnificently, but although at times somewhat pressed, they gallantly held their own. After some brilliant play in the centre of the ground, the Gloucester forwards forced the fighting within the Surrey "25 yards' flag," and Moberly dropped a splendid goal for Gloucestershire amid much cheering. Surrey strove hard to retrieve the day, but Gloucestershire ultimately retired winners by one goal to a try.

The trial match at the start of the 1881-82 season was held on 3rd November 1881 at the Spa, the North, again made up entirely of Gloucester players, scoring two tries to a goal by the South. The North team was H J Berry; R L Grist, H E Taylor, H J Boughton; W F Evans, P C Adams; J F Brown, P B Cooke, W Bayley, W Brown, H Birks, T G Smith, A C Seymour, W Stephens, N C Marris. The tries were scored by Evans and Grist.

Gloucestershire nil Monmouthshire nil
31st December 1881

MONMOUTHSHIRE TURNED UP at the Spa one short, but they enlisted the services of Tandy (Gloucester) to make up their numbers.

Gloucestershire: W Bayley; H J Boughton, G J Dewey (Gloucester), R A Glass (Royal Agricultural College); P C Adams (Gloucester), H L Evans; A D Greene (captain), H W Peck, J P Bush, H C M Hirst, J C Gilmore (Clifton), J F Brown, P B Cooke, W Brown (Gloucester)

Monmouthshire : Harding, Reynolds; Newman (captain), J. Birdie; Wood, T. Birdie; Purdon, Tandy, Clapp, Allen, Jones, Phillips,

Gould, Young, Lyne, forwards

The Gloucestershire Chronicle reported that:

> Soon the home forwards by fast play pressed their adversaries. Evans made a splendid run, and the leather getting into W. Brown's possession, he got in, but the try was disallowed upon the plea that the ball had not been thrown in straight from touch. Both sides now went to work with much determination. Many good runs were made for Gloucestershire, who on several occasions were within an ace of scoring. The Monmouth backs, however, played very energetically, and caused frequent incursions to be made well in the home quarters, but so equally did the teams appear to be matched that neither side was able to maintain any definite advantage, so that when "no side" was called the game was left drawn.

This result was regarded as controversial at the time, although probably fair enough in retrospect, since Gloucestershire felt they had scored a try which was disputed, whereas Monmouthshire had compelled their opponents to touch down three time to their once.

Gloucestershire one try Midland Counties nil
25th February 1882

THE HOME TEAM was reckoned to have a strong back division, "but being without the services of four of the best Clifton forwards, were weak in the squash".

Gloucestershire: H J Boughton (Gloucester); W O Moberly, E D Evans (Clifton), R A Glass (Royal Agricultural College); H V Jones (Gloucester), H L Evans (Clifton); J F Brown (captain), G J Dewey, P B Cooke, W J Bayley (Gloucester), H W Peck, E W Ball, W S Paul, H Dunn (Clifton), W N Jenkins

Midland Counties: R Moore (Burton); S H Evershed (captain, Burton), R Bullock (Warwick), H Phillips (Wolverhampton); W W Cassels (Burton), H A Sanders (Wolverhampton); J J Gover, C A Wright (Edgbaston Crusaders), G M Day, P Evershed (Burton-on-Trent), A S Brown, W H Rawlinson (Leamington), C A Crane (Wolverhampton), C D Curry (Stratford-on-Avon), E Worthington (Leicester)

The visitors started strongly and soon forced two touchdowns, but were then put on the defensive and conceded one of their own. Defences dominated and by half-time there was still no score. After the interval, the "splendid rushes and dribbles of the combined counties" were kept out, and:

> During the last quarter of an hour some remarkably good play was shown by both teams, Gloucestershire having decidedly the best of it. A short run by Evans, followed by a drop at goal scored a touchdown, and then a series of neat passes in which Bayley, Ball, Boughton and Moberly were engaged, completely nonplussed the visitors, and before they could recover from their bewilderment H V Jones picked up the ball and made a beautiful dodging run through his scattered opponents and scored a try close to the posts, amidst deafening applause. The place was a failure, and a scrummage was formed in front of the posts, but before any other point could be made no-side was called. Gloucestershire thus won by one try to nil, the visitors touching down twice and the home men three times.

On 11th November 1882, the County trial was again played on the Spa, this time between the XV Caps and Another XV. Gloucester players in the XV Caps were: H J Boughton, H V Jones, P C Adams, R D Cameron, F Savory, J F Brown, G J Dewey, W Brown, P B Cooke and W J

H V Jones, who scored the winning try against Midland Counties
[Gloucester Rugby]

Bayley; and in the Another XV were: H J Berry, W Brimmell, T G Smith, and H Thomas. The XV Caps won by one goal two tries to nil; the tries were scored by J F Brown, H V Jones and P C Adams, and one conversion was kicked by H J Boughton.

Gloucestershire nil Somerset nil
23rd December 1882

THESE TWO COUNTIES had already become established as fierce rivals in their annual encounter, and a stubbornly contested match was predicted, which turned out to be just the way it was. The erratic running of the trains was blamed for F Penny failing to arrive in time to take his place at half-back for Somerset, and H G Fuller was withdrawn from the forwards to play there instead.

Gloucestershire : H J Boughton; H L Evans, H E Taylor, G Coates; H V Jones, F R Little; G V Cox (captain), H C M Hirst, E Leonard, J F Brown, G J Dewey, H B Sloman, E D Trimmer, R C Cameron, H C Baker

Somerset : W M Massey (captain); R A Glass, H Rutherford, F J Hill; F H Fox, H G Fuller; A A Michell, W P Bowyer, F E Hancock, G Pruen, E McLorg, E L Strong, W A G Walter, H Baker, W Brown

H Fox (Wellington) umpired for Somerset, and J D Miller (Clifton, and normally the playing captain of Gloucestershire) was thought most satisfactory as referee.

The Gloucestershire Chronicle reported that:

> The choice of goals fell to the home county, and Massey kicked off against the wind. The forwards at once commenced a fast dribbling game, and playing hard on the ball, gave the opposing backs small opportunity to get away. The halfs especially could rarely get started, though Fox more than once made ground by his dodgy running. Before half time the ball only once crossed the Gloucester goal line, but from the maul that ensued the ball was rolled into play, and Baker, Brown, and Dewey playing up hard, carried it through the Somerset forwards and out of danger.
>
> On changing ends Cox restarted the game, and play still continued most even. A fair catch by Hill almost in front of goal, however, looked like scoring, but Glass, to whom the kick was entrusted, missed the goal, and Gloucester touched down. A fine run by Little was negatived by a fine piece of play by Hill, who throughout was most conspicuous, and this player crossed the Gloucester goal line but was pushed into touch in goal. This was the last point scored, and the call of time found the ball in neutral territory.

A stubbornly-contested game was expected and resulted, neither side being able to claim the victory, though the match was drawn in favour of Somerset, who scored a touch in goal and one touch-down to the opponents' nil, the ball never crossing the Somerset goal line.

Gloucestershire 2 goals 1 try Devon 1 try, 13th January 1883

THIS FIRST MATCH between these counties was played at the Spa. Devon selected nine players from the Tiverton club and Gloucestershire eight from Gloucester.

Gloucestershire: J D Miller (captain, Clifton); G Coates, H J Boughton, H E Taylor; H V Jones (Gloucester) F W Phillips (Newent); J F Brown, G J Dewey, P B Cooke, W Brown (Gloucester), H C M Hirst, E Leonard (Clifton), H C Baker (Bristol University), R D Cameron (Stroud), T G Myles (Bristol Medicals)

Devon: J Carpenter; A Fagan, D D Dryden (Tiverton), A E J Ellis (Exeter); V B Johnstone, E P Rooper; J Pedlar, H Pedlar, J Collier, C Collier (Tiverton), J Ellis (Exeter), F Williams (Newton), W G W Lake (Teignmouth), W H Steele (captain, Teignmouth & Clapham Rovers), H Mapleton (Exeter College, Oxford)

The Gloucester Journal reported that:

The home county kicked off, and their forwards well following up the ball, were soon busy in front of the Devon goal. Before long a touchdown was registered, and shortly afterwards Coates got over the goal line not far from touch. This score had the effect of putting Devon fairly on their mettle, and gradually they worked the ball down the field. For several minutes Devon looked like scoring, but a touchdown was the only outcome. Half time was then called, and on restarting the visitors played with great determination and gave the home men quite enough to do.

Fagan at length got the ball from a brother back, and by a strong run managed to get over the line, but the place failed. This

George Coates, who scored two tries against Devon [Gloucester Rugby]

caused Gloucestershire to play with some dash, and Coates obtaining possession of the leather tore down the field at a great pace and scored a try, which Boughton converted into a goal. Soon afterwards Baker broke through the loose and scored, Boughton again placing a goal. Nothing more was scored and at the call of time Gloucestershire were victors by two goals and a try to one try.

In the County trial on 10th November 1883, the North beat the South by one goal and one try to nil. The tries were scored by F W Phillips and J L Alexander.

Gloucestershire 1 goal Kent 1 goal 22nd December 1883

THE GLOUCESTERSHIRE TEAM contained a large contingent of Gloucester players whilst Blackheath were heavily represented in the Kent side.

Gloucestershire : J D Miller (Clifton); H J Boughton (Gloucester), S J Waterfield (Clifton), H E Taylor (Gloucester); F W Phillips (Newent), H V Jones (Gloucester); E Leonard (captain, Clifton), H C Baker (Bristol University), G J Dewey (Gloucester), H C M Hirst (Clifton), H B Sloman (Gloucester), W Baldwin (Newent), C Trimmer (Gloucester and Middlesex Wanderers), W J Pocock (Clifton), W Bayley (Gloucester)

Kent : A Stirling (Queen's); W N Bolton (Blackheath), E Hammett (Military Academy), J Bowen (West Kent); W R Parker (Queen's), A N Other; A Spurling, Arthur Spurling, R M Pattisson, G Standing, and A R Layman (Blackheath), G H Fowke, H Smith, W Matthews (Military Academy), S Ellis (Queen's)

The Gloucestershire Chronicle reported that:

After some spirited play Bayley, of the Gloucestershire team, carried the ball over the line of the Kent men, and was warmly applauded by the spectators. Hirst took the place, and landed a goal.

After half-time the visitors had for a while the best of the game; a kick by one of the Kent backs sent the ball over the home line, and a touchdown was resorted to, and this had to be repeated a few minutes later. In the succeeding play one of the visitors was hooted because he was not playing fair. A few minutes before the call of "time" Kent crossed the home line, Ellis scoring a well-earned try, and Bolton kicked a goal. The match thus resulted in a draw, each side having a goal.

Gloucestershire 1 try Midland Counties 2 tries 9th February 1884

THIS MATCH WAS played on a Saturday at the Spa. The weather was unfavourable, and the ground was in a wretched state. Gloucestershire tried a new formation for this match with the number of forwards reduced from nine to eight and with three half-backs selected.

Gloucestershire: J D Miller (Clifton); H J Boughton (Gloucester), S Waterfield (Clifton), T Bagwell; J F Brown, W A Boughton (Gloucester), F W Phillips (Newent); E Leonard (captain), M W Douglas (Clifton), H B Sloman (Gloucester), W Baldwin (Newent), H C Baker (Bristol University), W Bayley (Gloucester), T Adams (Redland Park), H A Spencer (Bristol Medicals)

Midland Counties: team not known

The play was reported to be "spirited", and the try for the home team was gained by Phillips, but Miller failed to improve on it. The home team conceded two touch downs and the visitors four.

On 1st November 1884 the North-South divide was replaced by East-West in the County Trial. There were eleven Gloucester players performing on their home ground in the East team: H E Cadenne, H J Boughton, H E Taylor, T Bagwell, G J Dewey, W Bayley, W H Fream, T G Smith, H L Broughton, W Brown and H A Sanders. Nevertheless the East lost by two goals to two goals and a try. The West's scorers were R Pocock (2 tries), J Moore (conversion and penalty goal), and for the East were T G Smith (try), H Boughton (conversion), H Osborne (penalty goal)

Gloucestershire 1 goal 1 try Somerset nil
10th January 1885

GLOUCESTERSHIRE: E D Evans (Clifton); H E Taylor (Gloucester), R J Pocock (Bristol Meds), E Moore (Clifton); H V Jones (Gloucester); F W Phillips (Newent); E Leonard (Clifton), J F Brown (Gloucester), T Adams (Redland Park), J W Rose (Clifton), R H O Bankes, J W Bayley, H V Page, W H Fream (Gloucester), H J Pocock (Clifton)

Somersetshire: team not known

The Gloucester Standard described this as:

An interesting and well-contested match. The ground was in a wretched state and rain fell at intervals during the game. There were between 3,000 and 4,000 spectators and they were rewarded for braving the elements by witnessing some of the finest play seen on the Spa this season. The passing of both teams was naturally rather uncertain, but the pretty and effective dribbling fully atoned for this.

Gloucestershire scored a dropped goal by E Moore early in the game and added a try by F W Phillips (Newent) just before the final whistle.

The County trial on 7th November 1885 resulted in a win for the West over the East by one goal to nil. The twelve Gloucester players in the East team were: J Oswell, H E Taylor, G Coates, H V Jones, T Bagwell, H E Cadenne, T G Smith, H B Sloman, R H Bankes, H A Sanders, A T Boscawen, W H Fream.

Gloucestershire 2 goals 1 try United Hospitals nil
29th December 1885

THIS MATCH ATTRACTED a crowd of 3,000 to the Spa, the numbers no doubt boosted by the selection of eight Gloucester players in the County team. It was an unusual match for the County in not being against another county side, but at the time it was considered a real feather in the cap to secure a fixture against a United Hospitals side which was highly rated, even though they arrived three or four men short and local substitutes had to be provided. Nevertheless it was reported to be "a capital game".

Gloucestershire: J Oswell; H E Taylor (Gloucester), E D Evans (Clifton), H V Jones (Gloucester); F B Budgett (Redland Park), T Bagwell (Gloucester); E Leonard (captain, Clifton), R H O Bankes, H L Broughton (Gloucester), J C Gilmore (Clifton), H Fream, H Sanders (Gloucester), J Pocock (Clifton), H J Pocock (Bristol Medicals), B S Cave (Royal Agricultural College)

United Hospitals: team not known

The Gloucester Standard and Gloucestershire News reported that:

During the first half Taylor made a fine run and obtained a try for the county, but no goal was kicked. Beyond a touchdown or two in favour of the same team this was all the scoring up to half time. On resuming Gloucestershire still had the best of the game, and Taylor and Jones got tries, which the latter converted into goals. Once or twice after this the visitors looked like scoring, but they were unable to do so.

H E Taylor, who scored two tries in the win over United Hospitals [Gloucester Rugby]

On 13th November 1886, the County Trial match included thirteen Gloucester players in the North side: J Oswell, H E Taylor, G Coates, C E Brown, R W Stoddart, T Bagwell, S Hall, T G Smith, W G Moore, H L Broughton, E Tandy, T Taylor and H A Sanders. The North won by one goal four tries to a single goal for the South, who included H Grist (Gloucester) in their ranks. The try scorers for the North were G Coates, T Bagwell, T Taylor, R W Stoddart, and C E Brown, with one conversion by H A Sanders. The sole score for the South was a goal kicked from a mark by Budgett.

Gloucestershire 1 try Somerset 1 try
22nd February 1887

THIS MATCH WAS played at the Spa on a Tuesday, but nevertheless attracted a large crowd. The Gloucestershire team was composed largely of members of the Gloucester team, which furnished the entire back division.

Gloucestershire: A F Hughes; G Coates, H E Taylor, C E Brown; T Bagwell, S A Ball; H A Sanders, H L Broughton, H B Sloman (Gloucester), H C Baker (captain), K Leonard, J W Ross, W Palmer (Clifton), J H Oakley, W H Hornby (Royal Agricultural College)

Somerset: team not known

Umpire: H J Boughton; Referee: R W Lawrence

Somerset kicked off from the Beaufort buildings end, but it was the home side which exerted all the pressure in the first half. Coates kicked the ball down to the Somerset 25, Ball passed to Hughes and on to Taylor, whose kick over the line resulted in a touchdown. Taylor was brought down five yards short, Hughes missed with an attempted drop goal and with a penalty kick, and Coates was also narrowly wide with a drop kick. The highlight was:

A run by Bagwell, who slipped through the embraces of his opponents like an eel ...Taylor getting the ball from a line-up, dashed off up the touchline, and was only brought down when about five yards from the goal-line. Bad passing lost Gloucester the advantage gained, and a series of scrimmages followed in the centre of the ground. The ball was gradually taken near the Somerset goal-line. Hughes tried to drop a goal, which did not come off, but Coates following up rolled over the line with the ball and scored a try. Hughes failed to kick a goal from the place. Some passing between Coates, Hughes, and Taylor enabled the latter to almost get round his opponents, but he was tackled in time, and Somerset forced their way to the centre flag. Gloucester rushed the ball back again to the front of the Somerset goal, a scrimmage being formed on the line. Coates, Hughes, and Taylor strove ineffectually to score and Coates narrowly missed dropping a goal, the effort resulting in Somerset touching down again.

Somerset appeared to have been revived after the break, and, having missed with a kick from a mark, "A A Glass breaking away, got over the line and scored a try, but no goal came of the kick." The visitors returned to the attack with vigour and "play if anything became faster, some of the tackling being characterised by considerable roughness". Somerset came close to scoring on two or three further occasions, with Gloucestershire relieving the pressure with clearing kicks.

On 5th November 1887, in the County Trial game, the Gloucester contingent was again thirteen in the North team: J Oswell, C E Brown, A F Hughes, G Witcomb, S A Ball, T G Smith, W Bankes-Wright, C M Blunt, H L Broughton, A Cromwell, A H Gorin, H A Sanders and T Taylor. They triumphed once more over the South by two goals and one try to nil, with tries by Horsley and Ball, a conversion by Smith and a drop goal by Hughes.

Gloucestershire 3 tries Devon 1 goal 1 try
11th February 1888

THE GROUND WAS in wretched condition, and during the first part of the match rain fell incessantly, but about 4,000 spectators still packed into the Spa. They had a while to wait. Owing to the distance some of the visitors had to travel, and their consequent late arrival, it appeared at one time that the match would not take place, but shortly after half-past three they put in an appearance.

Gloucestershire: A F Hughes; H E Taylor, T Bagwell, C E Brown (Gloucester); E L Phelps (Royal Agricultural College), W Troup (Clifton); H C Baker, E Leonard, F M May (Clifton), R Edwards (Bristol Medicals), T G Smith, H L Broughton, T Taylor, G Witcomb, H S Simpson (Gloucester)

Devonshire: D D Dryden (Tiverton); W C Paige (Newton Abbott), W G Pring (Exeter); F J Herring (Tiverton), J Challacombe (Newton Abbott); Elliott (Tiverton), T Wills (Newton Abbott), D Inch (Newton Abbott), F H Toller (Barnstaple), W S S Wilson (Dartmouth), C Mudge (Exeter), C G Stearn (Crediton), C Hawking (Torquay), H Rice (Teignmouth)

Referee: Mr. H. J. Boughton (Gloucestershire)

The conditions rendered good back play almost impossible, the players being unable to get a decent footing. The Chronicle reported that:

Troup again displayed fine dribbling powers, and Leonard continued the onward movement with a kick inside the visiting team's quarter flag, where Dryden again saved by sending the ball into touch. Troup took a pass from Phelps, and in turn handed to H. Taylor, who, when looking dangerous, slipped down, but he passed to Bagwell, who gained more ground. Troup was again to the front by stopping a forward rush, and Hughes transferred the ball into touch beyond the Devon quarter flag. Brown accepted a pass from Phelps, and by

a strong run dodged through his opponents and scored a try amidst much cheering. Hughes was entrusted with the kick, but the leather struck the posts.

C E Brown, who scored the first try against Devon [Gloucester Rugby]

Play for a time took place in neutral territory, but at length the home forwards, aided by Smith, T Taylor, and Baker, worked into Devon's quarters, where Bagwell picked up and passed to Brown, who again made a magnificent run over the line, but losing the ball Bagwell rushed up and scored a try. Hughes made another splendid shot at goal, but failed to register the major point.

After half-time Baker re-started, and Witcomb and Troup, exhibiting grand dribbling powers, took the ball in close proximity to their opponents' line. Devonshire, playing a good defensive game, removed play to safer quarters, but out of a loose scrimmage Leonard secured the leather, and making good use of his weight carried it over the line and got another try, which, like its predecessors, remained unconverted.

After these reverses Devonshire appeared to gain heart and compelled the home team to act on the defensive. Continuing to assume the aggressive their forwards, finding themselves in close proximity to the goal-line, dribbled splendidly, and eventually took the ball over, but it was kicked into touch in goal. Baker kicked out, and Devon returned to the attack. Newton, getting a clear opening, made an unsuccessful drop at goal, but Paige being on the quí vive, rushed up and touched the leather down. Dryden was entrusted with the kick, but his effort failed.

Elated with this success the visitors redoubled their efforts, and when near the centre of the field Newton got possession and transferred to Paige, who made the most brilliant run of the day, and by getting right round his opponents carried the ball behind the posts, a feat for which he was deservedly applauded. Dryden having negotiated the major point, "No side" was immediately called, and Devonshire retired the unexpected victors by a goal and a try to three tries, or four points to three, a result with which they were highly delighted after having up to a certain stage the worst of the encounter. The scoring system at this time awarded one point for a try and two for a conversion.

Boxing Day in the Provinces for Londoners

IN THE FIRST decade of the Gloucester Club, 1873-83, a lot of effort went into improving the fixture list by arranging matches against teams regarded as the strongest in England and Wales. Prominent in achieving this higher status for the Club was Frank Brown, captain 1876-83. In his last season with the Club, 1882-83, Gloucester became known as the "Invincibles", going through the whole season unbeaten, the only time this has been achieved in the entire history of the Gloucester Club. Unfortunately, at the end of that season, Frank had to give up the captaincy when his work took him away from Gloucester. He went to London but it seems that he still kept an eye open for an opportunity to help his old Club.

On 22nd December 1883, the Journal reported that:

At a smoking concert of the Kensington Football Club yesterday week, at which several London clubs were represented, it was decided to play a match on Boxing Day with a provincial team. Gloucester was selected as the best club in the West, and Mr J F Brown, the late home captain, who was present, was asked to arrange the match. A communication was received in Gloucester, and at a meeting of the team on Tuesday it was decided to play the match, which will take place at the Spa. It is understood that the visiting team are a formidable fifteen and will be composed of Kensington, Harlequins, Blackheath and LAC men.

Up to this time the Christmas period had been marked by a lengthy break in fixtures for the Gloucester Club, but the lure of a plum match against a side from London was too much to resist. They had been notoriously difficult to come by, the only previous match against a London club being when the first captain of the Club, Frank Hartley, persuaded his old club, the Flamingoes, to travel down from London for a game in February 1876. So, the arrival of the Londoners on Boxing Day 1883 was warmly greeted. Even warmer was the greeting for Frank Brown, who had also travelled down from London, and before the match kicked off he was presented with a gold watch and chain in appreciation of all he had done for the sport in Gloucester. Jimmy Boughton had been appointed as captain of Gloucester following Frank's departure, but he was injured, twisting an ankle when playing for Gloucestershire against Kent four days earlier, so Frank was persuaded to resume his former role as Club captain for the day.

Gloucester 1try, 1 disputed try London Team nil 26th December 1883

THE SIDES PLAYED in different formations. Gloucester lined up with one back, three three-quarters, three half-backs and eight forwards, whereas London had one back, three three-quarters, two half-backs and nine forwards. The London side boasted in its ranks the famous England rugby and cricket player, A E Stoddart, and his brother, H L Stoddart. They helped to attract the biggest crowd yet seen at the Spa. Spectators streamed into the 6d and 2d sides of the Spa field and £36 was taken on the gate.

Gloucester: H J Berry; H E Taylor, G W Coates, T Bagwell; J F Brown (captain), H V Jones, W A Boughton; G J Dewey, W Brown, H L Broughton, W H Fream, H A Sanders, E D Tandy, H S Simpson, C H Trimmer

London: W Douglas (Middlesex); W A Forbes (Clapham Rovers & Kent), A E Stoddart (Blackheath & Middlesex), S H Baker (Kensington); R James (captain, Kensington & Middlesex), F M Frames (Clapham Rovers & Middlesex); S C Leonard, R Leonard, E Instone (Kensington & Middlesex), W Stevenson (Kensington & Surrey), H Roberts, F L Elliot, J Elwin (Kensington), H L Stoddart, C J Kohler (Harlequins)

The London team gained more friends by appearing on the field punctually, this being an era when teams were notorious for turning out when they felt like it, sometimes so seriously late that the light had gone before the match had ended. Despite the sodden ground, both teams were reported to have played a fast game. The Londoners started the better, Baker made a strong run, and Gloucester were forced to touchdown, but their forwards responded by driving the visitors back. They dribbled the ball into the London 25 and forced a series of scrums, but were unable to get over the line.

Having conceded a second touchdown, Gloucester fought back and the Gloucestershire Chronicle reported that:

A smart run by Taylor brought the ball once more into neutral territory. Shortly after Coates stole a march upon the opponents from a line-out and amid intense enthusiasm placed the ball behind the London goal. The try was disputed, and Gloucester had to yield. At half-time nothing decisive had been obtained by either side.

At this time the referee's decision was not regarded as final — he could be overruled by the captains, and this match left plenty of room for dispute between Frank Brown for Gloucester and the London captain, R James. James won the first argument and the score remained 0-0 at half-time.

In the second half:

On kicking out Gloucester made an incursion into London territory, and after a piece of combined dribbling the ball was kicked over the visitors' goal line and Bagwell rushing up gained a try. This try was also disputed, and Gloucester, after a long dispute, kicked at goal under protest.

So, Brown insisted on winning the second argument.

Tommy Bagwell, who scored the winning try against London [Gloucester Rugby]

The kick, which was tried by Jones, was unsuccessful, it being an exceedingly difficult one. Play was fast and even for a long time, when Bagwell, by a magnificent dodgy run, and with tremendous pace, succeeded, beyond all dispute, in scoring a splendid try for the home team. The place kick, an easy one, failed. At the call of time, after a well-contested game, Gloucester were declared the victors by one try and one disputed try to three touchdowns.

In the event of disputes over scores, there was an appeal procedure, which could be invoked after the game, and which could end in a result being overturned, but this was not pursued after this match.

This match set a pattern for a few years of a team selected from London clubs playing at the Spa over the Christmas period.

Gloucester 1 goal London Team nil
26th December 1884

THE WEATHER, THOUGH cold, was fine, although rain in the morning had left the Spa heavy and greasy, and several thousand spectators turned out to watch a scratch team from London clubs. Frank Brown again turned out for Gloucester.

Gloucester: H E Cadenne; H E Taylor, G Coates, H J Boughton (captain); W A Boughton, T Bagwell; A Gorin, W Brown, W Brimmell, H A Sanders, W H Fream, H L Broughton, W G Moore, F J Brown, H V Page

London: W Douglas (Kensington); A E Stoddart (Blackheath), A E Bartrum, J Elwin; R James (captain, Kensington), F M Frames (Clapham Rovers); J T Trotman (Harlequins), R Leonard, S C Leonard, E Instone, H Roberts, J J Swainson, T D Belfield, T L Elliott (Kensington), S W Bernard (Harlequins)

Gloucester engineered the first scoring chance when a dribble by Page and a run by Taylor got into the London 25, where W Boughton made his mark, but failed with his kick at goal. Later, London came close when their captain, James, "got possession and, making a good dodgy run, succeeded in getting a try but it was disallowed", so half-time arrived with no score.

Early in the second half both teams had scoring opportunities, with Gloucester having Taylor pushed into touch near the goal line and:

H V Page, who had a good game against London, but his try was disallowed [Magpie]

Page taking the ball on well, a try was got for Gloucester, but was disallowed on the plea of off-side … H Boughton by a good kick forced London to touch down. On the kick out, a lot of loose play took place, and Taylor, rushing up, picked the ball up and ran in, gaining a try for the home team, and H Boughton kicked a goal amidst deafening applause. Gloucester thus won one of the finest and closest games played this season by a goal and three touchdowns to one touchdown.

Gloucester 1 goal 1 try R James London Team 2 goals
26th December 1885

SEVERAL THOUSAND SPECTATORS crowded into the Spa at the festive season to watch two teams playing with differing combinations, each having a back and three three-quarters, but Gloucester selecting three half-backs and eight forwards, whilst the London team lined up with two half-backs and nine forwards. J F Brown and H J Boughton, both former captains of the Club, came out of retirement to play for Gloucester. Brown captained the side and Boughton tossed for kick-off. R James, the organiser of the London side, did not play on this occasion, but acted as umpire (referee).

Gloucester: J Oswell; H V Jones, G Coates, H J Boughton; T Bagwell, H E Cadenne, J F Brown (captain); R H O Bankes, H L Broughton, W H Fream, A H Gorin, H A Sanders, H S Simpson, H B Sloman, E D Tandy

London: W Williams (Harlequins & Middlesex); A E Stoddart (Blackheath & England), H C Yockney (Kensington), R Bullock (Kensington & Midland Counties); J H Roberts (Richmond & South), E Rowsell (Queen's & Kent); C J Kohler (Middlesex Wanderers), J T Trotman, J Elwin (Kensington), W Hargreaves (Kensington & Dublin University), E Instone, A H Curnick, J J Swainson, T D Belfield, L Loy (Kensington & Middlesex)

Umpire: Mr R James (London)

Boughton won the toss and kicked off, and the play quickly became animated. Bullock gained a try between the posts, and Stoddart scored a goal for his side. When play had been resumed a try was obtained by Coates, and Jones kicked a goal. Subsequently Cadenne placed the ball behind the posts, but the kick by Jones failed.

The second half of the game was played with great spirit, and it looked as if the home team would win; but towards the close Belfield rushed through the line and passed the ball to Yockney, who gained a try, which Stoddart again converted to a goal. Thus the visitors were the victors.

Gloucester nil R James London Team 1 goal
26th December 1886

THE GROUND AT the Spa was judged to be unfit for play, but the match went ahead nevertheless.

Gloucester: J Oswell; H E Taylor (captain), E W Urquhart, G Coates; T Bagwell, S A Ball; R H O Bankes, H L Broughton, C E Brown, W H Fream, H A Sanders, J A Shirer, H S Simpson, H B Sloman, E D Tandy

London: Whiffen; H C Yockney, Theobald, C Smith; E F Rowsell, R James (captain); A H Curnick, C J Kohler, E V Gardner, J H Roberts, F L Elliott, J T Trotman, Graham, Leonard, A N Other

Referee: Mr E M Blair

Gloucester were judged, at least by the Citizen, to have had very hard lines in this match, since both Coates and Urquhart ran in tries, only to have them disallowed, one of them because there were spectators standing behind the goal line. Coates again got over the line, but was lifted back out into the field of play before grounding the ball. In the event, Yockney's try, converted by himself, was the decisive score.

Gloucester 1 try London Team (Kensington) nil
26th December 1887

THERE WAS AN even larger proportion of Kensington players in the visiting team this year. The fixture continued to attract a large crowd, although takings were reported to be a few shillings less than the previous year.

Gloucester: A F Hughes; H E Taylor (captain), T Bagwell, G W Coates; W George, S A Ball; H A Sanders, A E Healing, W Banks-Wright, E D Tandy, W H Fream, G Witcomb, H S Simpson, H L Broughton, T Taylor

Kensington: S S Wallis; H C Yockney (captain), W Higgs, W Burge; C Smith, E F Rowsell; J T Trotman, A H Curnick, E V Gardner, W Stevenson, F L Elliott, W F Lund, J K Elwin, C J Kohler, W Bligh

Gloucester had the best of the game throughout, but Kensington were a big team and defended stoutly, so that they restricted the home team to a single score. This came in the first quarter of an hour when H E Taylor rushed up and scored a try, but Hughes failed with the conversion kick from a difficult angle. Gloucester were forced to concede two touchdowns, but a score was avoided. The match was followed by tea at the Ram Inn and then a smoking concert.

Gloucester 1 try, London Team (Kensington) 1 try
26th December 1888

GLOUCESTER AND CARDIFF second teams had played on the pitch in the morning and "the turf at the Spa, already very wet,

was rendered filthy, and when the teams turned out in the afternoon the mud was so deep that it was quite impossible for the backs to do anything brilliant in the running line, the pavilion side of the enclosure particularly being a perfect mud-pool". Nevertheless the weather at the start was bright and a huge crowd, estimated at 8,000, turned out, the pavilion being packed, chiefly with ladies, and £33 being taken on the gate.

It was agreed that the match would be played as 16-a-side, but the Londoners only had 15 until Marshall of Newent was added to their numbers. Although largely drawn from the Kensington club, they did boast a number of star guest players including two internationals in Stoddart and Jeffery.

Gloucester: E Smith; H E Taylor (captain), T Bagwell, G W Coates, R Grist; S A Ball, W George; A H Brown, A Cromwell, R C Jenkins, E D Tandy, T Collins, W Taylor, J Williams, T Taylor, H S Simpson

Kensington: S H Baker (London & Middlesex); C H Knight (Kensington), A E Stoddart (England), H C Yockney (Middlesex), Marshall (Newent); Mackenzie, Easterbrook (Kensington); G L Jeffery (England), L F Elliott, W Hargreaves (Surrey), E V Gardner (Kensington), A H Curnick (London), W Bligh, J Elwin (Kensington), J T Trotman (Middlesex), E E Wilbe (Kent)

A game confined almost entirely to the forwards was dominated by the Gloucester pack. The individual talents of the London players may have been greater but the cohesion of the home team more than made up for that, pushing the visitors back in the scrums, dribbling well, and tackling fiercely, overwhelming Stodddart every time he got the ball. Nevertheless, Yockney was not as closely marked as Stoddart and he brought off several dashing runs, one of which resulted in a try after splendid dodging through his opponents. The scorer of the Gloucester try is not recorded, but Cromwell missed four kicks at goal, any one of which would have won the game for Gloucester, but none was easy and the conditions made them more difficult.

This was the last visit to Gloucester by a London select XV, but Boxing Day matches at Kingsholm continued. This slot was filled by Penygraig in 1889, but from 1890 onwards Old Merchant Taylors, a London club, were the opponents and came every year thereafter for some sixty years.

A Political Match

Conservatives 1 try Liberals 1 goal 3 tries
27th March 1886

THIS MATCH BETWEEN Conservative and Liberal members of the Gloucester Football Club was played at the Spa to raise money for the relief of the unemployed in the City and drew a large crowd.

The Gloucestershire Chronicle reported that:

Great interest centred in the encounter, and party spirit ran high during the progress of the match, the excitement being such as is seldom witnessed at the Spa. Both sides having got together the best teams possible there was every expectation of a keen struggle, and anticipations were fully realised; the betting at the commencement of hostilities was in favour of the Conservatives to the extent of 6 to 2. As both teams emerged from the pavilion they were loudly cheered by their political friends. Hubert Boughton led the "Blues" and T G Smith the "Yellows.

Tom Graves Smith, who captained the Liberals [Gloucester Rugby]

Liberals: O H Jones, back; G Coates, H V Jones, S A Ball, three-quarter backs; T Bagwell, H E Cadenne, half-backs; T G Smith (captain), C E Brown, W H Fream, H S Simpson, H B Sloman, A H Gorin, T Taylor, V Rowles, S S Starr, forwards

Conservatives: J Oswell, back; H J Boughton (captain), H E Taylor, G F Dere, three-quarter backs; W A Boughton, E D Tandy, half-backs; W C Bailey, R H O Bankes, W J Bayley, A T Boscawen, A H Brown, H L Broughton, E Kilminster, W G Moore, T Hatherall, forwards

Umpires: A W Vears, A J Barnes
Referee: E Lawrence (Cheltenham)

Smith kicked off from the Beaufort end, the "ballot" ball falling into the hands of Dere, who returned it to the centre of the field, where some slight scrimmaging took place. Hubert Boughton made a fair catch almost in front of the Liberal goal, but the shot failed, and a touchdown resulted, the Tories thus registering the first "vote" in their favour.

For some time afterwards the wearers of the "mustard and blacking" were compelled to act on the defensive, until at length Coates obtained possession of the ball and got over the line of the Blues, but the try was disallowed amidst a scene of excitement. The Liberals still "hung" round the polling-booth of their opponents, where H V Jones got the ball and passed to Coates, who made a splendid run in and scored a try, and Jones, taking the place-kick, placed a goal. H Boughton kicked off from the centre of the field, and the ball being badly returned the Tories took the game to the other end of the ground, and, aided by a huge punt by Oswell, the leather was taken over the line by Boughton, but H Boughton failed at a rather easy place.

The teams having crossed over, each side was encouraged on by their partizans. Jones and Coates between them carried the leather into their opponents' territory, where the former attempted to drop a goal, but failed, and Starr, following up, crawled into the polling-booth and recorded a second vote in favour of the Liberals; the shot for goal was a failure. Shortly afterwards Jones grounded the ball over the line, but he failed to register it into a goal. These reverses fairly aroused the spirits of the Tories, and for a time they played up with great determination, but they did not exhibit the same amount of dash and combination as their Radical friends, although H Boughton, Tandy, and W J Bayley put in a lot of hard work. "The People's Tommy Bagwell" was the next to record a success in the Radical interest, but not without a protest by Taylor, who collared him over the line, and after a sharp maul Bagwell succeeded in touching down, no goal, however, resulting from the kick by Jones.

Give-and-take play followed, and when the whistle sounded for the close of the poll the Liberals had a majority of one goal and three tries to one try. Had the Tories played with the precision which characterised their opponents, who also had the great advantage of playing more men in touch with each other, the match would have been of a much more even description, but after half-time some of them appeared to lose spirit, and there was a perceptible falling off when their efforts were most required. Owen Jones, as goal-keeper for the Radicals, proved an utter failure in that position, whilst Oswell, for the Conservatives, played a splendid defensive game throughout, his safe collaring and huge punts being most invaluable to his side."

On the following Monday the Mayor stated at the police-court that he had received a cheque for £18 11s 10d from the Football Club, as the result of the receipts of the match. "As the funds of the poor-box were rather low, only 26s being in it, he thought he could not do better than place £5 of the proceeds of the cheque in the box, as a considerable portion of the funds from it had been used for the benefit of the unemployed." He decided to give another £5 to the Charity Organisation Society, and the balance of £8 11s 10d to the Soup Kitchen.

The First International Side to Play at Gloucester

Gloucestershire 1 try
New Zealand Maoris 1 goal 1 try
2nd February 1889

THE FIRST INTERNATIONAL touring team to visit the British Isles, the New Zealand Maoris, consisted of players born in New Zealand rather than just players of Maori extraction. They played an incredible 74 matches on their tour during the 1888-89 season, winning 49, losing 20, drawing 5, and scoring 394 points against 188. Played on the Spa, this match remains the only appearance by an international side in Gloucester at anywhere other than Kingsholm. The Citizen reported:

It has been a source of great satisfaction and pleasure to lovers of the game here, to know that our winter pastime has so spread in our colonies that New Zealand can furnish a combination who can compete with a good measure of success with some of our best fifteens. When the team first arrived in this country, they relied principally upon their dribbling tactics and the strength of their forwards for success, but constantly coming into contact with, and experiencing the effectiveness of the passing game, they have adopted it, and their backs have succeeded in working themselves into a high state of efficiency at this branch of the game, and the brilliancy of their passing now equals that of their dribbling and forward play.

The managers of the team endeavoured to cancel their matches in this part of the country, on the ground that they did not anticipate sufficient gate money to defray their expenses, but the local authorities refused to allow them to break off the engagements, and we think their misgivings in this direction were somewhat premature, for under the improved circumstances there was every prospect of a "gate" the like of which has not previously been heard of in Gloucester.

This match, the event par excellence of the football season at Gloucester, came off before an immense concourse of spectators, the weather being bitterly cold. Special permission had been obtained from the Corporation of the City to enclose the ground for the occasion, and accordingly the match was shut off from the view of outsiders by canvas, and the thousands who usually obtain a good view of the Gloucester matches "on the cheap", either had to pay for the entertainment in common with the more practical supporters of the club, or put up with the only alternative of missing one of the most interesting and important matches of the season.

Gate takings, notoriously difficult to collect at the Spa, where canvas screens had to be erected to deny a view of the match from elsewhere in the park, amounted to about £193. The Gloucester Club provided the whole of the County back division.

Gloucestershire – A F Hughes; T Bagwell, G W Coates, C E Brown, R Grist; S A Ball, W George; James Faulkner, H C Baker, E Leonard, R Edwards, H V Page, G J Witcomb, T Collins, R C Jenkins.

Maoris – W Warbrick; McCausland, W Wynyard, F Warbrick; Keogh, Gage, Smiler; Ellison, Taiaroa, G Wynyard, G Williams, Rene, Maynard, Anderson, H Lee.

R Grist, who scored the only Gloucestershire try against the Maoris
[Gloucester Rugby]

Both teams had chances to score during the first half, and the deadlock was only broken when a dodging run by Keogh resulted in a try for the Maoris, which McCausland failed to convert from close to the posts. This was the only score of the first half. Early in the second half:

Keogh received a pass from Gage and with one of his feints at passing got off and running strongly and at a tremendous pace seemed certain to score, but was just hauled down on the line by Hughes and Brown. He was, however, rewarded for his effort for immediately after he got the ball again and crossed the line, scoring a try, which McCausland converted into the major point with a magnificent kick.

The game having been returned to the centre, Ball got a "free" and Baker took a place kick at goal, but, though he put in a good kick the goal proved a little too far off. Ball picked up from a scrum, and passed out to Coates, who ran well and passed to Grist, who took the ball, and putting on top pace, dodged several opponents and got over in the corner, scoring after a maul in goal. This was the first opportunity he had had, and he was loudly cheered. Baker made a creditable shot at goal.

Both sides had further chances, but none were taken, and the Maoris won by one goal, one try, and two minors, to one try and one minor.

The Start of the County Championship

THE COUNTY CHAMPIONSHIP was started in 1888-89, but, for the first two seasons, counties made their own fixtures, and the Rugby Union then looked at all the results and declared a County Champion. In each season this was Yorkshire, because they won all their games. The Gloucester Club was generally supportive of the County Club, and indeed recommended that the County Secretary write to all clubs in the County asking them to join, but believed that there was a time and a place for County rugby which had to fit in with Club commitments. In March 1890, the Club Committee voted to continue its membership of the County Club only on the understanding that County matches would be played on weekdays, and that Saturdays be reserved for Club fixtures. In December 1890, Jimmy Boughton drafted a list of rules for the County Club, which were approved by the Gloucester Club Committee before being circulated to other clubs, and then accepted at a County Club meeting in Bristol.

The 1888-89 County Trial pitched the Gloucester Club side against the Rest of the County. Sixteen players were named in the Gloucester side: E Smith; T Bagwell, G W Coates, R Grist, G Witcomb; W George, S A Ball; T G Smith, A H Brown, T Collins, A Cromwell, R C Jenkins, E D Tandy, T Taylor, W Taylor, J Williams. Another Gloucester player, S G Simpson turned out for the Rest of the County. Gloucester gained an emphatic victory on their home ground by 1 goal 9 tries to nil. Tries were scored by G W Coates (3), G Witcomb (2), R C Jenkins, A Cromwell, T Bagwell, R Grist, and E Tandy, and T G Smith kicked a conversion.

Gloucestershire nil Somerset 1 goal
12th January 1889

ABOUT 5,000 SPECTATORS assembled at the Spa to witness this encounter. The ground was in a wretched condition, and rain and snow fell during the greater part of the game. The Gloucester Club supplied no fewer than eleven of the home side, including the entire back division.

Gloucestershire: A F Hughes; G Coates, T Bagwell, C E Brown; W George, S A Ball; A Cromwell, G Witcomb, T Collins, W Taylor, R C Jenkins (Gloucester), F M May, R Edwards (Clifton), J Faulkener (Royal Agricultural College, Cirencester), S W Brown (Bristol)

Somersetshire: C E Winter; S Escott, F C Duckworth, C J B Moneypenny; R Escott, F H Fox; J E Aldridge, H T Gillmore, P F Hancock, E Hancock, W H Mansfield, R M P Parsons, F Soanes, C J Vernon, Hancock

From the outset it was apparent that the game would be a forward one, and both sides were evenly matched. The Chronicle reported that:

George secured the ball, and after a run, passed to Coates, who looked dangerous, until he was grassed in fine style by Winter. Neither side could claim any advantage before half-time, except that Gloucester touched down once from a long kick by Duckworth.

After changing ends, and a new ball having been provided, the contest became more fierce and furious, and the excitement of the spectators was intense. The leather travelled up and down the field at a great pace, both goals in turn being placed in jeopardy, until within ten minutes of time, when the Somerset men gradually worked to near the home line, and E Hancock succeeded in registering a try, which S Escott converted into the premier point.

With a goal against them the home team played in splendid fashion, and once Bagwell and Coates dribbled to within a few yards of their opponents' citadel, but Winter fell on the ball and

prevented further progress. Gloucester were unable to equalise the score, and had to retire beaten. Although defeated the point scored against them was the result of a misunderstanding on the part of the home team, as they were appealing to the umpire for a pass forward when Hancock planted the ball behind the goal posts.

On 30th November 1889, the County Trial was held at the Spa between the Stripes, who scored two tries to win against the Whites with only one try. There were fifteen Gloucester players selected for this trial, but on this occasion they were split between the two teams. Those playing for the Stripes were C E Brown, R Grist, E J Ward, S A Ball, T Phelps, H V Page, C Williams, J Williams, T Collins jnr. For the Whites were A F Hughes, T Bagwell, R W Stoddart, W George, A Cromwell, T Collins. Collins, Grist and Cromwell scored the tries.

Gloucestershire 2 tries Devon 1 try
11th January 1890

THE JOURNAL REPORTED that Gloucestershire had experienced considerable difficulty in raising a side for this, their second fixture, "and when at last their efforts were successful in placing 15 men on the field, the team was not one which might be expected to strike terror to the hearts of the visitors". Tommy Bagwell declined to play and watched from the side lines because he had taken offence at not being selected as first choice at centre. So Witcomb, the Gloucester forward, was pressed into service as a three quarter, alongside H George who was normally amongst the forwards in the Gloucester 2nd XV; Phelps was another Gloucester 2nd XV player.

There had been wet weather throughout the previous week, and the rain resumed on the morning of the match, which rendered the ground very heavy. The home side's prospects were not rated highly:

George Witcomb, the Gloucester forward, who found himself on the wing for the County [Gloucester Rugby]

Putting against this so-called Gloucestershire team the full strength of Devonshire, the former's chance of success appeared a little shady before the match, and had they not played up in surprising fashion they would undoubtedly have had a severe reverse to put up with instead of a highly-meritorious victory to compliment themselves upon. Notwithstanding all the deterring influences a fine game resulted from the meeting, a deal of interest in the encounter being denoted by the splendid attendance, whilst the excitement during a large portion of the game ran very high.

Gloucestershire: A F Hughes; C E Brown (captain), H George, G Witcomb; T Phelps, S A Ball (Gloucester); S W Browne (Bristol), H V Page, A Collins, T Collins, A Cromwell, R C Jenkins (Gloucester), J Smith (Cambridge University), Lockey (Bristol), Edwards (Bristol)

Devon: C G Middleton; H Holme-Davies, M H Toller, J Willcox; J Davies, W Sayer; G Body, H Toller, C Hawkins, W Ashford, W M Ball, G Williams, G Bennett, C Collier, L H Biddle

The Journal reported that:

Not many minutes from the kick-off, some clever passing, in which several forwards took part, gave T. Collins an opportunity, and he fell over the Devon goal line with a try, amidst tremendous cheering. The place was close to the touch-line, and Hughes could not convert the point; but the home men, not to be denied, continued to press their opponents, and a minor was quickly followed by a second try, T. Collins again distinguishing himself by taking the leather in a line-out a few yards from the goal line, and scrambling over close to touch. Hughes could not send the ball over the cross-bar, and, after another minor point had been gained, the visitors worked out to safer quarters, and Willcox, making a brilliant run, passed to Body, near the home goal, enabling the latter to score an easy try, which was not improved upon.

At half-time Gloucestershire had scored two tries and two minors to their opponents' try, and after the usual "breather," the game was so stubbornly contested that a couple of minors to Devon were the only points added, the play being most exciting and interesting, so that when the time arrived for the suspension of hostilities, the score stood in favour of the Gloucestrians, the margin being one try. The Devon three-quarter backs were far superior to the home trio, their kicking being more serviceable, whilst in running there was no comparison. But the visitors failed utterly to take advantage of this fact.

Gloucestershire nil Midland Counties nil
20th February 1890

THIS MATCH WAS played on the Spa on a Thursday afternoon in front of a good-sized crowd. However, the ground was in a dreadful condition. Gloucestershire went into this game having already won against Devon and Somerset.

Gloucestershire: Hughes; Brown, Bagwell, (Gloucester), Kent (Cheltenham); Parlane (Cirencester), George (Gloucester); C. Williams, J. Williams, Witcomb, Simpson (Gloucester), Baker (captain), Edwards, Lockey (Clifton), Wolfenstein, Druce (Cirencester)

Midland Counties: Bennett (Crusaders); Sully, Marsden (Burton), Harrison (Rugby); Slatter (Crusaders), Rogers (Moseley); Mayne, Lycett, Morris, Burgess, Sturges, Richardson, Deykin (captain), Evershed, Laurie

Midland Counties made most of the early running, and the Chronicle reported that:

Brown was called upon to stop an ugly rush by Evershed, Mayne, and Deykin. Soon after Evershed got clear, but was brought down by George in the nick of time. Hughes got in a kick, from which Evershed secured a "free," nothing, however, coming of it. C. Williams relieved by a fine dribble to the centre, where Witcomb carried on the ball, and was not stopped until well within the Counties' twenty-five. The home team strove hard to score, but were repulsed, and half-time arrived with no point registered on either side.

On the teams crossing over, Bagwell was again prominent by cleverly dribbling to the visitors' twenty-five flag. Several scrimmages were now formed, but neither side could gain any material advantage, the teams being splendidly matched.

Harrison got a "free" in an easy position, but the heavy state of the ball frustrated Sully's attempt to cover the goal-post, and Hughes very pluckily kicked into play. First one side got the advantage and then the other, and so the match was contested; and at the call of time no score had been obtained by either side, and the game was left drawn slightly in favour of the Midland Counties, who scored a touchdown.

T B Powell, who scored a hat trick of tries in the County trial [Magpie]

On 11th December 1890, the City, composed entirely of Gloucester players, but only thirteen in number, were again pitted against the Rest of the County for the County Trial match at the Spa. The City side was: A F Hughes, T B Powell, W Jackson, S A Ball, T Bagwell, W George, J Osborne, A E Healing, A Cromwell, A Collins, R C Jenkins, J Williams, C Williams. By this time points scoring had been introduced and the City beat the County 16-0 made up of four goals and four tries, with a try worth one point and a conversion two. The tries were scored by T B Powell (3), A Collins (2), W Jackson (2), and C Williams, A F Hughes kicked three conversions and T B Powell one.

In 1890-91, the Rugby Union organised the counties into groups, and the winner of each group went into the knockout stages to decide the Champion. Gloucestershire was grouped in the South West with Somerset, Devon and Midland Counties. The weather played havoc with the fixture list. Gloucestershire's opening match against Devon was cancelled due to frost, and so they moved on to the Spa against Midland Counties.

Gloucestershire 5 Midland Counties 0
15th January 1891

THE MATCH WAS originally scheduled to be played at Coventry, and then at Burton, but, with each of these grounds being judged unfit, it was at the last moment decided that the fixture should be played at Gloucester. Out of the fifteen home players the local club furnished no fewer than thirteen.

Walter George and Sammy Ball, the half-back pairing against Midland Counties
[CC&GG]

Gloucestershire: A F Hughes; T Bagwell, W Jackson, W H Taylor (Gloucester), C A Hooper (Cambridge University & Gloucester); W George, S A Ball; H V Page (captain), A E Healing, G J Witcomb, R C Jenkins, A Cromwell, C Williams (Gloucester), W H Birch (Clifton), W Thomson (Bristol)

Midland Counties: J F Moore; W W Auster, W P Nicholll (Old Edwardians), A Rogers, Dr Robertson (Moseley); A Rotherham, R A Rotherham (Coventry); J H Rogers, W N Mayne (Moseley), W A Marris (Old Edwardians), E R Lycett (Moseley), W H Sturgess (Leicester), F Arblaster (Old Edwardians), W N Greenwell (Burton), T Horton (Moseley)

Walter Jackson, who scored the first try against Midland Counties
[Gloucestershire Archives]

The first half of the game was evenly contested; the Chronicle reported:

> The combination of the home backs was much better than that of their opponents, as after a brilliant bout of passing Jackson cleverly scored a try near the corner, which Hughes successfully converted into a major point. This was the score at half-time, although some superb play between the Midland backs almost culminated in Dr Robertson getting over the home line, Hughes saving by conceding a minor.

The second half of the game was characterised by some magnificent cork-screw runs by Hooper, whose play throughout was somewhat sensational, as his opponents were unable to cope with him, and he had exceptionally hard lines in not scoring on several occasions. Taylor also registered a try after one of his well-known sprints, as did Bagwell, but in each case Hughes failed at the place-kicks.

Although nobody realised it at the time, this was to be the last match played by the County at the Spa. By the start of the following season, the Kingsholm ground had been purchased and was made ready for rugby just in time for the County's first match.

Meanwhile, Gloucestershire went on to draw against Somerset at Bristol, before winning the replay 3-0 with three tries at Bath, and thus becoming Champions of the Western & Midlands division of the County Championship for 1890-91. As such, they progressed to a semi-final against Lancashire at Whalley Range, Lancashire, where 13 Gloucester players were in the team, which was well beaten, 0-14.

With this national structure in place, the County Championship soon became the stepping stone from club to international rugby. County caps came to be treasured by the players, and for the best part of the next century, the County game was often the biggest match of the season at Kingsholm.

The First England Trial at Kingsholm

*left: W.H. Taylor, who came closest to scoring against Midland Counties [Magpie]
right: George Witcomb, who impressed for Western Counties [Magpie]*

THE RUGBY FOOTBALL Union committee was impressed by the new facilities available at Kingsholm and keen to make use of them, so an international trial was organised there within three weeks of the ground being opened.

Western Counties 0 Midland Counties 8
29th October 1891

THE SIX GLOUCESTER players selected for the Western Counties ensured plenty of local interest and over 3,000 spectators attended. The Midland Counties team included five Burton players paying a quick return visit to Kingsholm, having turned out for their club against Gloucester in the first match on the ground on 10th October.

Western Counties: G C Middleton (Devon); J M Wilcock (Devon), W Jackson (Gloucester), W H Taylor (Gloucester); W George (Gloucester), Seth Steel (Devon); G Witcomb (Gloucester), A E Healing (Gloucester), J Mayo (Gloucester), W Manfield (Somerset), P F Hancock (Somerset), F Soane (Somerset), G H Allington (Devon), F J Sellicks (Devon), B H Wallis (Devon)

Midland Counties: F J Byrne (Moseley); A Rogers (Moseley), G A Marsden (Burton), A H Frith (Coventry); R H Cattell (Moseley), F C Duckworth (Burton); F Evershed (Burton), A W Gorton (Burton), W Greenwell (Burton), J H Rogers (Moseley), E R Lycett (Moseley), W D Ludlow (Moseley), W A Marris (Edwardians), W Rice (Coventry), A Williams (Northampton)

Referee: Mr H Vassall (RFU), with Rowland Hill as one of the touch judges.

The referee deserved sympathy, in that Midland Counties turned out in all white, although some wore a maroon or blue sash, whereas the Western Counties appeared in jerseys of various hues, the Gloucester players wearing their club colours (red, yellow and black at the time), except for Jackson who sported a deep maroon jersey.

J Mayo was brought into the Western Counties side two minutes after the match had kicked off, because A Collins (Gloucester) had failed to put in an appearance. There was no score in the first half, during which "as the game had commenced, so it continued – extremely fast, first one side and then the other gaining a slight advantage." George Witcomb was prominent with his dribbling, and there was "a splendid round of passing by George, Jackson, and Taylor, followed by a grand run by the latter". Healing, with a splendid dribble, gained considerable ground, but most of the pressure came from the Midland Counties, who appeared far heavier and more powerful and made it count.

In the second half, Witcomb again impressed, but "the prettiest bit of play during the whole game was when from a scrum near the grand stand Jackson had a pass from George, returned it to the latter again when pressed, George in turn passing over to Taylor, who, having an opportunity of showing his speed, did not fail to embrace it, racing in a grand style right up the field, and taking the leather to within a few feet of the Midland goal line before he was brought down."

Western Counties were "roused to greater exertion by the cries of the multitude to "Play up Westerns," varied occasionally with the query, in a stentorian voice, "Will you please play up, Gloucester?" which caused considerable laughter." But their forwards were outclassed by their opponents, and the Midland Counties took advantage late in the game to run in two tries. They added a drop goal just before the final whistle to complete their victory by one drop goal, two tries and ten minors (8 points) to three minors (0 points).

The Gloucestershire Magpie described the occasion as follows:

It was only natural to expect that an unwonted amount of interest would be taken in the grand trial match between representative teams of the Midland and Western Counties, which was played on the new ground at Gloucester on Thursday; and as none but the best of players would take part – so far at least, as the committees or representatives of the various clubs could judge – a well-contested game was inevitable. In fact, one of those very much becoated and becaped individuals who haunt football and athletic grounds who always wear brown boots and tweed caps, and who always know before hand what the result of any event will be, assured me on the way to the ground that the game would end in a draw, no point being scored by either side. "Mark my words," said he, in accents peculiar to his class "both sides will be so good that the one will not allow the other to score." I did mark his words; but I came away from the ground sorrowing in a subdued manner. For with the majority of my fellow citizens I take a pride in the orange and red stripes [the Gloucester Club colours at the time], and not only a pride, but I feel assured that the side on which they play must be victorious.

Nature proved remarkably kind to players and spectators; the sun shone brilliantly from a clear blue sky, the air was sharp and crisp, and the turf, while extremely greasy in places, was soft and yielding. There was but one objectionable feature connected with the ground, and that was the abominable smell of pigs wash and decaying vegetables which assailed the olfactory organ near the entrance. Yes, I forget, there was one other matter which requires remedying. Small boys and youths have a practice of getting under the ropes, and running out when play moves down the touch line, to their own danger and the annoyance of other spectators, and some means should be taken to prevent their doing so.

The Rugby Union selectors met after the match and selected Jackson, George, Ball and Witcomb of Gloucester for the Western and Midlands Counties team to play London in the next trial match, with Taylor and Collins amongst the reserves.

The First County Matches at Kingsholm

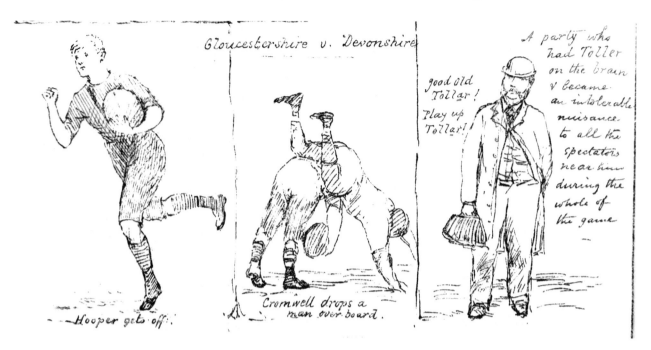

A cartoon of scenes during the first County match at Kingsholm [Magpie]

THE GLOUCESTER COUNTY Football Club was wound up with a deficit of £7 10s 2d at the end of the 1890-91 season. It was replaced by the Gloucester County Football Union, the first general meeting of which was held at the Spread Eagle Hotel, Gloucester, on 11th November 1891. Clubs represented were Gloucester, Clifton, Royal Agricultural College, Bristol, Cheltenham, Lydney, and Sharpness and Dursley. Also member clubs were Stroud & Gordon Wanderers (Gloucester). H J Boughton (Gloucester) was elected as Chairman and President, H V Page (Gloucester) as captain, and T G Smith (Gloucester) as secretary. Having had their meeting, they then went off to Kingsholm, which had opened only a month previously, to see and play in the County Trial match. H V Page's XV scored three tries without reply from T Bagwell's XV and thus won 6-0.

A Referees Association was also set up with H W Bennett (Gloucester) as secretary. Twelve referees were appointed, 8 of them from Gloucester – H J Boughton, T G Smith, H S Simpson, C E Brown, S S Starr, G W Coates, H V Page and W C Bailey. In 1892, 10 more referees were added to the list, 6 of them from Gloucester – S A Ball, H Brown, G Evans, F Tandy, W G Roberts and C Jones.

Gloucestershire 9 Devon 0
17th December 1891

ORIGINALLY ARRANGED FOR 25th November 1891, this match was postponed because of the death of the secretary of the Devonshire County Club. Unfortunately the rearranged date turned out to be a cold and foggy day and despite the selection of eleven Gloucester players and it being early closing day in Gloucester, few spectators turned out to watch and those that did take the trouble were unable to see most of the game.

Gloucestershire: A F Hughes; C A Hooper, T Bagwell, W Jackson (Gloucester), E Fenner (Bristol); W George, J Watts; H V Page (captain), A E Healing, A Cromwell, C Williams, R Jenkins (Gloucester), A Whitley (RAC), W Thomson (Bristol), E P Press (Clifton)

Devon: J Causey (Aller Vale); J M Wilcocks (Exeter), G H Harding (Torquay Juniors), M H Toller (Barnstaple), Lieut Bigge (Albion); Penny (Barnstaple), J Davies (Torquay); F H Toller (captain, Barnstaple), R J Lawson (Paignton), H May (Albion), R Biddell (Exeter), H Osmond (Exeter), S H W Brooking (Torquay), G Cox (Tiverton), H Vallance (Sidmouth)

Referee: Mr H J Boughton (Gloucester)

Devon had the much the better of the game territorially in the early stages, but then lost Penny to a head injury, and Gloucester came back into it. The Magpie reported that:

Hooper, getting hold of the leather, conveyed it through his opponents and the fog to the Devon side of the field. Here he was collared, and Wilcocks by a dashing run, transferred to the home quarters, Toller, the Devon captain, and other players, following up well, and the Gloucester full back kicking the ball out. After the kick out play was still confined to the Gloucester end, until Bagwell, by some especially smart dodging, took it through the Devon pack, and almost immediately afterwards Page, Hooper, and Jackson also put in some good work, but neither side was able to score during the first half.

On changing ends, however, Gloucester soon recorded a try – W. George obtaining possession, passing on to Jackson, the latter turning it over to Fenner, who scored in a fairly good position, but Jackson was unable to convert. Then Cox for Devonshire took the game into Gloucester territory and being followed up by the forwards, Gloucester was for a short time hard pressed. Bagwell again got the leather, and passed to Hooper, but a minor only resulted. Again Cox dribbled well up the field, and again Bagwell came to the rescue. Eventually Jackson got the ball and passed it on to Bagwell, who in turn handed it on to Hooper, the latter scoring. The angle was a difficult one, and the kick failed. Subsequently Page scored in an easy position, and this was converted, leaving Gloucestershire the winners by a goal and two tries to nothing.

During this first season of the County Union, the players complained that the woollen jerseys were too heavy and at the end of the season in April 1892 the committee addressed the issue, but lighter alternatives were judged too expensive.

The County Trial match featured the Probables 22 against the Possibles 4 on 19th October 1892.

Gloucestershire 0 Somerset 0
29th October 1892

WITH THE MIDLAND Counties having been transferred to another group, this was seen as the critical game in the South West,

the Citizen declaring that "the result practically decides which of the two counties is to hold the championship of the south-western group for this season, there being little to fear to either team from the other two counties – Devon and Cornwall".

Despite heavy rain earlier in the week, the Kingsholm ground was in good condition for what had become an important derby match for the respective supporters. The Magpie was effusive about the anticipation of this encounter:

The match between Gloucestershire and Somersetshire, which was played at Kingsholm on Saturday, attracted a larger number of

Scenes at the Somerset game [Magpie]

spectators than I can remember to have seen at any county match played in the city before, and the widespread interest taken in the event was evident from the fact that among the large number which passed the turn stiles were contingents from all parts of this and the adjoining county. It has been stated that the match was so attractive to the members of the Cinderford club that they journeyed to Gloucester instead of staying at home to keep their engagement with Dursley. I don't know whether this is so or not, but I know a great number came in on the chance of witnessing a stiff tussle and were duly rewarded.

The large crowd was reported to be particularly dense on the sixpenny side. The gate money amounted to £64 13s. 6d. The Chronicle was a bit suspicious about one selection for this match, commenting on:

"E. Hancock," who took the place of Duckworth on the visiting side. A certain amount of mystery surrounded this player, and who for reasons best known to himself wished to conceal his identity, although he had frequently appeared in the ranks of the Somerset team.

Gloucestershire: A F Hughes (Burton); E Fenner (Bristol), W Jackson, T Bagwell (Gloucester), H B Turner (Bristol); W George, S A Ball; H V Page (captain), R C Jenkins (Gloucester), W H Watts (Newport), A Lewis (Cardiff), W Thomson, W H Birch, A W Ford (Bristol), H L Norrington (Clifton)

Somersetshire: H B T Boucher; S M J Woods (Taunton), F H Fox, E Hancock (Wellington), T England (Newport); H Merry (Wellington), T N Parham (Bath); P F Hancock, C J Vernon (Wellington), F Soane (Bath), B Morris (Taunton), W H Manfield (Yeovil), J E Aldridge (Weston), J Roman, H Rouse (Bridgwater)

Referee: Mr M E T Gurdon; Touch judges: Messrs T G Smith, G Fox

As regards the game itself, the Magpie was utterly dismissive, reporting that " the game would have been more interesting if more open, but it wasn't, and there's an end on't." The Chronicle rather agreed: "of the game itself I cannot say that it was particularly interesting from a spectator's point of view. Its chief characteristics were of a forward nature; but, perhaps, the Somerset men knew where their strength rested, and they played accordingly". Missed chances were the order of the day.

As the game wore on, the massive Somerset pack, led by an England international in P F Hancock, threatened to power their way to victory. The Citizen reported that: "the Somerset forwards screwed a scrum capitally, and "baby" Hancock got away with the leather at his feet, but Jackson picked up smartly and kicked into touch". The Chronicle agreed that "they were certainly a heavy lot of forwards, and consequently endeavoured to keep the ball well smothered; but what the home forwards lacked in bulk they made out in trickiness", but used a different epithet in describing how ""Jumbo" Hancock made some of the home players look mere Lilliputians, and despite this disparity the little ones, nevertheless, buzzed round him with deadly effect". At the death Gloucestershire made one final rally and "some neat passing between the backs nearly enabled Bagwell to get over. He was brought down, however, and a scrum was shortly afterwards formed within a yard of the Somerset line, where it remained until the call of no side, a stubbornly-contested game thus ending in a draw."

The Barbarians Put in an Appearance

Gloucester 10 Barbarians 9
28th March 1892

THE BARBARIANS HAD first offered to come to Gloucester during their Easter tour in 1891, when the Club was still playing at the Spa. Unfortunately Easter fell after the ground had been handed back to Gloucester Cricket Club for the summer season, and no alternative ground could be found. They came the following season, and by then the new Gloucester ground had been opened at Kingsholm. The weather was fine, but a cold north wind blew from the St Mark's end (during the first season at Kingsholm, the ground was aligned north-south with a St Marks end and a City end). The Barbarians were advertised in the Citizen as "15 members of some of the crack combinations of the country", including three internationals and six each from Blackheath and Cambridge University. The Gloucester team was depleted by the loss of Taylor, Page and Poole from their first choice side. The Barbarians lined up with three three-quarters and nine forwards.

Gloucester: A F Hughes; W Gough, T Bagwell (captain), W H Jackson, C A Hooper; S A Ball, W George; A Cromwell, R C Jenkins, A Collins, F W Mugliston, D Phelps, C J Click, J Mayo, G F Jones

Barbarians: A S Johnstone (Blackheath); W Neilson, C M Wells, E P Biggs (Cambridge University); H Marshall (Blackheath), A Rotherham (Coventry); A Allport, J Hammond, W P Carpmael (Blackheath), C B Nicholl (Cambridge University), A A Surtees (Harlequins), W H Manfield (Somersetshire), W E Newbigging (Middlesex Wanderers), P Maud (Blackheath), W Cope (Cambridge University)

Referee: Mr Budd

Mr Budd, referee for the Barbarians match [Magpie}

The Citizen described the first try by Gloucester as follows:

George and Cromwell did some good foot-work, and the latter bothering Johnston at the centre, Ball picked up and ran into the visitors' quarter. Here he was overtaken, but, passing to Cromwell (the Barbarians unsuccessfully appealed for "forward"), the latter got over under the posts. Jackson easily converted.

The correspondent of the Magpie waxed lyrical about Gloucester's second try, which

was partly the result of as fine a specimen of combination between Hooper and Jackson as I have ever seen. Both are possessed with good dodging abilities. Jackson first received from a scrum at half-way, and dodging well through numerous opponents, took it into the visitors' 25; here finding himself pressed he passed neatly to Hooper, who in turn again transferred to Jackson, enabling him to score in a capital position. It need scarcely be recorded that, as in the previous try gained by Cromwell, who broke away from outside the twenty-five and scored near the posts, shouts loud and long were sent up by the delighted spectators, which were increased when Jackson sent the oval sailing beautifully over the centre of the cross-bar.

Walter Jackson, who converted both tries against the Barbarians
[Gloucester Rugby]

Matters looked decidedly rosy for the home team at this point – half-time nearly reached and a score of two goals in their favour. Their success had made them less watchful than before, and they allowed the visitors to get a firm footing within a few yards of their goal line, and then successively gave Neilson "the softest try imaginable" and Wells the opportunity to walk over beside the posts, the latter try being converted.

The second half according to the Magpie:

On resuming the game waxed additionally fast and furious; both teams worked exceedingly hard and once or twice it looked doubtful whether Gloucester would not after all be vanquished – especially when Wells, by a capital run, got away, and handed to the Scotch international, Neilson, who put on another try for the Barbarians. This was not converted, and Gloucester still led by the small majority of a single point, which the visitors tried in vain during the remainder of the game to wipe out. Time after time individual Barbarians broke away, but in each case were safely held – though they took a great deal of holding, and caused play to be a trifle rough. Towards the conclusion of the game they looked extremely dangerous, dribbling well up from midfield, where the struggle had been maintained for some time, to near the Gloucester line; but Hughes, equal to the occasion, saved in grand style, and the game was again transferred to the centre. It was nevertheless a decided relief to the partisans of the Gloucester team when the referee's whistle sounded "no-side", and left their favourites winners by a point.

One member of the Barbarians who had played a first-class game, stuck his hands in his pockets at the conclusion of the game and sang "Never again, my darling" in a perfectly happy manner as he walked from the field; and this a friend or two of mine interpret to mean that they will not again try conclusion with the city boys; but I think just the opposite construction may be put upon it – if it is worth anything at all.

In fact it was eight years before the Barbarians next came to Gloucester. The points system at this time, with two points for a try and three for a conversion, had secured a narrow victory for Gloucester. Although outscored by three tries to two, the home side kicked both conversions whilst the visitors managed only one. The Magpie declared that the game "was the best played on the new ground up to date", but this was very early days and there was a lot of history at Kingsholm yet to come.

A F Hughes, who presented a sound last line of defence against the Barbarians
[Gloucester Rugby]

The Tykes come to Town

Gloucestershire Scratch 9 Yorkshire Scratch 7
13th April 1893

THIS MATCH WAS originally organised and advertised as being against Halifax, but that club had an important cup match coming up, so the selection was widened to produce a Yorkshire side containing four internationals. What was described as "an immense and record crowd for Kingsholm" paid more than £100 to come through the turnstiles. The spectators were not best pleased that the teams did not appear until four o'clock, although it was not unusual in that era for games to kick off late. They were eventually rewarded with a fast and exciting game. Yorkshire played in black, and Gloucestershire in Gloucester Club colours.

Arthur Cromwell, who scored against Yorkshire [Gloucester Rugby]

DON'T FORGET THE GRAND MATCH

ON

KINGSHOLM FOOTBALL GROUND,

THURSDAY Next, April 13.

HALIFAX

(Winners of the Yorkshire Challenge Cup)

VERSUS

A GLOUCESTERSHIRE TEAM

Assisted by A. J. Gould (Welsh International),
R. E. Lockwood and D. Jowett (English Internationals,) &c.

Admission 1s. and 6d.; Grand Stand 6d. extra. Cheap trains from all parts.

Advertisement for the match [Magpie]

Gloucestershire: A F Hughes; W H Taylor, A J Gould, W Jackson, K Fenner; J Eliott, T Bagwell; R C Jenkins, F O Poole, A Collins, A Cromwell, J R Price, A E Henshaw, E Leighton, J Hanman (captain)

Yorkshire: J Nash; J Dyson, J Smithies, B Sharp, I Rawnsley; H Barker, H Varley; J Toothill (captain), J Thewlis, A Dywie, H Lodge, W Knowles, A Hartley, F Wood, A Wellings

Referee: Mr H J Boughton (Gloucester)

Both teams came close to scoring before Toothill gained the first points with a try for Yorkshire, but then, the Magpie reported "the Gloucester team played up finely, and after a grand passing bout, in which Eliott, Gould, Jackson and Fenner took part, the latter was enabled to go over in the corner after a dashing run". It was a try apiece at half time.

The Gloucestershire team [Gloucestershire Archives]

Toothill again opened the scoring in the second half with a try under the posts which Smithies converted. This gave Yorkshire a five point lead, with the current scoring system awarding two points for a try and three for a conversion, and they narrowly missed extending it when many thought Smithies had kicked a drop goal, but the referee ruled that it had dipped under the bar. Gloucestershire struck back: "Fenner got hold from a kick by Smithies. The Bristolian put in a fine punt, and following up again, secured the leather, and dashing past several opponents, forced himself over the line with two visitors on his back."

The home side had to resist several scrums close to their line, but made their way up to the Yorkshire 25, where they won the ball at a lineout. "Eliott threw to Cromwell, who took the ball finely, and dashing past the back, planted the ball near the uprights amidst a hurricane of cheers. Arthur Gould [a Welsh international] this time took the kick, and landed the premier point, the applause on this success being renewed with even more vigour." And rightly so, he had won the game, "and one of the best matches ever witnessed at Kingsholm ended in a perfectly satisfactory manner – certainly to Gloucestershire". The takings amounted to about £130, and after the match, both teams were entertained to a smoking concert at the Ram Hotel, with many recitations and songs to make the evening go with a swing.

John Hanman, captain of Gloucestershire against Yorkshire in 1893, but not allowed to play in 1894 [Gloucestershire Archives]

The County Trial was staged at Kingsholm on 23rd October 1893 and ended Probables 13 Possibles 0.

Gloucestershire & South Wales 19 Yorkshire 0
26th April 1894

YORKSHIRE WERE THE reigning County Champions, and a wealth of internationals took to the field, which drew in a crowd estimated at 4,500. The match was organised to help make up for the loss of revenue resulting from the closure of Kingsholm the previous month by the Rugby Union. Gloucester had been found guilty of contravening the laws on transfers and professionalism by selecting a player still registered with the Stroud club. The Gloucester captain, John Hanman, was credited with working indefatigably to ensure the fixture came off, although he was not able to play because he was suspended until the end of the season. It was surely no coincidence that Yorkshire and South Wales came to Gloucestershire's aid, since it was these clubs which were to the forefront in the dispute with the Rugby Union over the laws on professionalism. This would soon result in the breakaway of many northern clubs to form the Rugby League.

Gloucestershire & South Wales: A F Hughes (Gloucester); Norman Biggs, J Elliott, D Fitzgerald (Cardiff), W H Taylor; T Bagwell, A Stephens (Gloucester); J Bowley, H Day, Wallace Watts (Newport), C Williams, W Leighton, A Collins (Gloucester), F O Poole (Oxford University, captain), W H Birch (Bristol)

Yorkshire: A Ward (Bradford); Stephenson, A Chorley, W Jackson, F Firth; A Rigg (Halifax), R Wood (Liversedge); J L Toothill, W Sugden (Bradford), H Speed (Castleford), R Mellor, R Winskill (Halifax), A Wellings, O Walsh (Hunslet), A Barraclough (Manningham)

Referee: Mr E B Holmes (Midland Counties)

The game kicked off at 5pm on a Friday, and the home pack soon established the upper hand, but play flowed from end-to-end. "Norman Biggs, taking the ball beautifully from a kick by Ward, raced down the touch-line in grand style. The Cardiffian was grassed by the Yorkshire custodian, but he managed to pass to Bowley, who obtained the first try amidst tumultuous applause." Another Biggs run put Wallace Watts into the corner for the second try, and the home side turned round ahead by two tries to nil.

They kept up the pressure in the second half, and "from a line-out the ball became loose, and Collins getting the leather at his feet dribbled over very cleverly near the posts, scoring a capital try", before "Stephens initiated another round of passing, and after the whole of the backs had had possession Taylor secured and, leaving Ward practically standing still, scored behind the posts." Before the end, another burst away from a line-out enabled Bowley to score his second try, and stretch the winning margin to two goals and three tries.

After the match, both teams dined at the Ram Hotel, before going on to a variety entertainment in the Corn Exchange, presided over by Sir Lionel Darell. This featured John Hanman boxing three exhibition rounds against Morgan Crowther, the 8st 10lb Boxing Champion of England. Since Hanman insisted on seeing this through despite being in obvious pain from a sprained ankle, it was described as "an example of British pluck under difficulties". All the proceeds went to the Gloucester Club.

Pat Marshall, chief rugby writer of the Daily Express, recorded advice from a Yorkshireman on playing in the early days at Kingsholm:

Advice from my Yorkshire granddad who played a season with Swansea: "T' game I best remember were agin Gloucester. Lot of they Dean Forest men in t' side, too. Hard? You could kick 'em an hack 'em till your toes ached. They never said owt; but they didn't half clip you a good 'un if you didn't watch out. Now, lad, if tha ever get to playing those lads from t' Forest I'll give thee some good advice – get thi blow in fust, then watch it! And watch crowd, too! Reckon they'll know more about t' game than thee and referee put together. If they find thi a bit short in skill or heart, they'll let thi know reet enough, lad. And happen they'll be reet, too. They know what game's all about. But they're fair, mind. If thi takes their fancy with skill or guts, they'll communicate. And they'll give opponents a reet good cheer at end if thi's played game to their liking.

County Matches 1894-99

Gloucestershire 8 Cornwall 3
8th December 1894

THE WEATHER WAS beautifully fine and the ground was in good condition considering the heavy rain of the previous day, Cornwall had a strong fifteen out, including three Oxford University players, and Gloucestershire were almost at full strength. But this was the fight for the wooden spoon in the South-West championship group, as both teams had previously succumbed to Devon and Somerset, and this probably accounted for the attendance being below that of an ordinary Gloucester club fixture.

Gloucestershire: B Daunter (Cinderford); W H Taylor (captain, Gloucester), D H Haines (Stroud), R Whitehead (Lydney), E Fenner (Bristol); W J Lias (Clifton) W T Pearce (Bristol); W Leighton, J R Price, A Wellings (Gloucester), J Bowley, W H Birch, T Q Davis, W Jarman, P Lockyer (Bristol)

Cornwall: T Eathorne (Redruth); J C Nunn (St. Bartholomew's Hospital, London), W Thomas (Redruth), Hosking (Camborne), A G Chapman (Falmouth); A Paull (captain, Redruth), E L Hammond (Keble College, Oxford); T Tarbutt, C A P Tarbutt, E Campbell, F Johns (Camborne), R Triggs (Penzance), J Hammond (Blackheath), M Kitson (Keble College, Oxford), Olivey (Redruth)

Referee: Mr A C Crane (Midland Counties)

The Chronicle reported that it was:

one of the most uninteresting football matches that has taken place in Gloucester for some time past. Dash was completely out of the question, while combination and open play was conspicuous by its absence. The match was characterised by plenty of grovelling on the ground, and was utterly devoid of running and dribbling, which one is expected to witness in a county match. The game was a mere farce, more especially so on the part of Gloucestershire, and a few more such exhibitions would lower the reputation of any third-rate club to the depths of mediocre. As it was Gloucestershire just managed to struggle home by a goal and a try to a penalty goal after a miserable exhibition.

The Citizen was a little more forgiving in its reporting of the game, describing how:

From a line-out near the centre the Gloucestershire men got possession, and after some running and passing Bowley got over near the posts, Haines kicking a goal. After the re-start play became very fast, the Gloucestershire backs exhibiting some neat exchanges. Fenner tried hard to get through, but he was safely held, and then one of the Cornishmen intercepting a pass ran to Daunter, who, however, pulled his man down splendidly. The visitor, however, managed to pass the leather to a confrère, and the home lines were in danger. A general scramble ensued in front of the Gloucester goal, ending in the home side being penalised. From the easy place the visitors scored a goal.

Gloucestershire commenced the second half, and play immediately settled in the visitors' end. Taylor, receiving from Haines, nearly got in, and then Taylor with a run and kick sent the ball to within half a dozen yards of the goal-line. From the line-out Lockyer received, and with a good dash succeeded in grounding the ball over the line. Haines essayed the kick at goal, which, however, proved abortive. Ensuing play was mostly in favour of Gloucestershire, but was generally of an uninteresting character. Occasionally the monotony of scrambling scrimmages would be relieved by a creditable effort.

On 24th October 1895, it was Reds 8 Stripes 5 in the County Trial.

Gloucestershire 5 Devon 18
30th November 1895

HEAVY RAIN IN the preceding week had left the ground sodden and heavy, and there was a large bare patch in front of the grandstand, but the weather for the match was bright. About 2,000 spectators turned up and were kept waiting, the teams not taking the field until gone 3pm for a 2:45 kick-off.

Gloucestershire: J B Smithson (Bristol); W H Taylor (Gloucester), W T Battye (Clifton), E H Searle (Drybrook), L Smith (Stroud); C W James (Clifton), A Stephens (Gloucester); J Bowley, W H Birch, H Hale, W Jarman (Bristol), C Hall, F M Stout (Gloucester), W Leighton (Cinderford), G E Mitchell (RAC)

Devonshire: H Gloyns (Devonport Albion); E G Pallett (RNEC), M H Toller (Barnstaple), W E Bildings (Devonport), F J Salter (Exmouth); H C Nicholay (Barnstaple), E Down (Devonport); C Thomas, F H Toller (Barnstaple), A May, G H Allington, F Long (Devonport), R M Hayman (RNEC), J Bond (Torquay Athletic), R Shaw (RNE College)

Referee: Mr G Rowland Hill (English Rugby Union)

The Citizen reported that Devon started well, but:

Gloucestershire having obtained a footing in their opponents' end pressed severely, and from a dangerous rush by the front rank they were almost over. A moment later Searle almost crossed after a grand burst. Gloucestershire continued to have much the best of the game, but they could not score. Devon, however, followed up this effort by attacking severely, and following some loose scrimmaging near the Gloucester line, Bildings dashed over near the goal posts. Salter kicked a fine goal. The visiting forwards heeling out, Down sent out cleverly to Toller, who handed to Bildings. The latter after going a few yards passed to his wing, Salter. The Exmouth player took the ball beautifully, and after a grand dodgy run finished up by scoring behind the posts. The same player easily landed a goal. However, just before the interval, James once more got off, and running through the Devon three-quarters and dodging Gloyns, scored a fine try, amidst enthusiastic applause. Searle landed a particularly fine goal.

At half time Devon led by two goals to one. Thereafter:

Nicholay, intercepting a pass, dodged splendidly, and though Smithson checked him a little it was not sufficient to stop his opponent, and the Barnstaple half-back completed his effort by scoring about ten yards from the goal-post. Salter failed with the place kick. In the last few minutes Devon made strenuous efforts to add to their score, and Bildings receiving the ball from Nicholay brushed aside several opponents, and, eluding Smithson, obtained the visitors' fourth try. Salter essayed the kick at goal, which proved successful.

Gloucestershire 6 Cornwall 0
7th November 1896

GLOUCESTERSHIRE WENT INTO this game as clear favourites, having won all four previous encounters between these counties, with Cornwall having only a solitary penalty goal to show for their efforts. The visitors broke their journey, spending a night in Bristol, before moving on to the Ram Hotel in Gloucester. An hour before kick-off the heavens opened and, although special arrangements had been made for cheap railway trips from the surrounding districts and Hinton's Band played on to provide pre-match entertainment, only about 200 spectators braved the elements. And they were kept waiting to greet the teams onto the field 15 minutes after the scheduled start, when the mist hanging over the ground gave it a depressing appearance. The gate money amounted to £51 2s.

Gloucestershire: J B Smithson (Bristol); W H Taylor (Gloucester), A F Hailing (Cheltenham), H Williams (Cinderford), Lewis Smith (Stroud); C W James (Clifton), W Needs (Bristol); F M Stout, C Rose, C Hall (Gloucester), W Leighton (Cinderford), C E Miller, P Smith (Stroud), W Gwynn (Clifton), J W Jarman (Bristol)

Cornwall: E Jasper (Penzance); C F Mermagen (Falmouth), R Thomas Redruth), W D Lawry (Penzance), T Wright (Cambridge); W Paul (Redruth), Z Rusden (Falmouth); E Collings, R C Lawry, O Triggs, R Trembath (Penzance), R Smith (Falmouth), W Wheeler (Camborne), C Pollard, R Jenkins (Redruth)

Referee: Mr A J Gould (Newport)

Cornwall had the best of it in the early stages, but both sides came close to scoring, each conceding a minor when touching down behind their own line, before:

Percy Smith was again prominent with an individual burst which gave Gloucester a footing in the Cornishmen's half. Here the home forwards heeled out nicely, and Needs sending out smartly to Williams, the latter ran across to Taylor's wing. Ignoring Hailing, the Cinderford man threw the ball out wide to the Gloucester captain. Taylor took the oval nicely, and sailing round his opponent scored a fine try, amidst great enthusiasm. Smithson made a fine attempt to convert, but just failed.

In the second half, both sides missed with penalty kicks before:

Useful kicking enabled Gloucester to relieve their lines, and then a splendid loose rush by the home forwards, in which Stout, Percy

W H Taylor, try scorer against Cornwall [Gloucester Rugby]

Smith, and Hall were prominent, transferred play right to the other end. Buckling to, Gloucestershire tried hard to add to their score, and eventually their efforts were crowned with success, Hailing running over prettily after receiving a pass from James. Smithson was unsuccessful with the kick at goal. The last five minutes was particularly exciting, being very fast and full of incidents. The forwards on either side were particularly noticeable for dashing play, and once or twice Cornwall looked like going in. The defence of the home men, however, was sound, and when the whistle sounded a final cessation of hostilities Gloucestershire had won by six points to nil.

Gloucestershire 16 Midland Counties 0
28th October 1897

PLAYED AT KINGSHOLM in fine weather, and before a good gate, this was a friendly match which did not form part of the County Championship. The visitors were late arriving, so the match did not kick off until past 4 o'clock. Gate takings were £50.

Gloucestershire: B Hipwood (Gloucester); Lewis Smith (Stroud), A F Hailing (Cheltenham), Percy Stout (Gloucester), R G Parsons (Bristol); W. Needs (Bristol), T. Willstead (Cinderford); W Leighton (captain), W Mudway (Cinderford), J W Jarman, H B T Bingham (Bristol), Frank Stout, C Hall, A Pitt (Gloucester), P Smith (Stroud)

Midland Counties: W Comrie (Coventry); R B Sparrow (Wolverhampton), J F Byrne (captain), F A Byrne, G Birtles; J C Hall (Moseley), W H Goodman (Old Edwardians); A St G Cummins (Wolverhampton), A O Dowson, C Marston (Moseley), D P Millar (Stratford), B J Ebsworth, B. H Cattell, R Challoner (Moseley), H B Carslake (Old Edwardians)

Referee: Mr A J Davies (Glamorgan)

The Citizen recorded that the home team created several good chances in the first half, but the first score was not registered until a couple of minutes before half-time, when:

from out of some loose play Jarman gathered smartly in his own 25, and passing neatly to Hailing, the Cheltenham captain got off with a fine sprint. Being pressed Hailing handed to Needs, and the latter subsequently yielded up to Percy Stout, who put the finishing touches on a magnificent bit of combined play by scoring a try. The same player failed to convert, though the shot was well directed.

At the start of the second half Gloucestershire held the advantage and:

heeling out nicely Needs got a chance of distinguishing himself, and feinting to pass the Bristolian made a good opening for Percy Stout. The city club's centre made off at full speed, and beating several opponents cleverly, he got to the full back. Comrie went for his man, but the Gloucestrian knocked him off, and continuing his journey, concluded a fine effort by scoring behind the posts, loud and continued cheering greeting what was an exceedingly splendid performance. Stout easily goaled.

Some loose play gave the Midlanders an opening, but Frank Stout, with a bit of superb individual play, not only relieved his side, but dribbled to his opponents' quarter before being stopped. In his effort Stout came into collision with Comrie, and was laid out for a minute or two. On resuming the game hovered near the centre until Willstead initiated an onward movement towards the visitors' goal. Here out of some loose play Frank Stout got possession, and with a smart dash managed to get over with a try about twenty yards wide of the posts. Percy Stout failed to convert.

In being tackled by Hailing, Fred Byrne got hurt, and was carried off the field. A short stoppage ensued. From the first scrum on resuming Willstead got away smartly, and passing to Needs the latter made a grand opening. Being pressed the Bristol half-back handed the ball to Hailing, and the latter went over with another fine try in the corner. Percy Stout this time landed a brilliant goal from near the touch-line.

Gilbert Collett, who scored a brilliant try against Glamorgan and converted it himself [Gloucester Rugby]

Frank (on left) and Percy Stout, brothers who both scored against Midland Counties [Gloucestershire Archives]

Gloucestershire 8 Glamorgan 0
6th January 1898

THIS FRIENDLY FIXTURE was the first meeting between these sides at Kingsholm, and fine weather drew a large crowd, who paid £46 on the gate.

Gloucestershire: B Hipwood (Gloucester); R Parsons (Bristol), F M Luce (Oxford), G F Collett (Cheltenham College), E Hussey; W Needs (Bristol), Car Cummings; Bert Lewis, C Hall (captain), F Goulding, A H Click (Gloucester), H R T Bingham (Bristol), W Leighton, W Mudway (Cinderford), P Smith (Stroud)

Glamorgan: T Jones (Penygraig); W Llewellyn (Llwynypia), D Rees (Swansea), L Deere (Mountain Ash), I Edmunds (Llwynypia); Dan Jones (Aberavon), E Lewis (Treherbert); D Evans (Penygraig), F Vigors (Neath), W H Alexander (Llwynypia), W F Rees (Pontypridd), J Jenkins (Treherbert), T Madden (Aberavon), Hopkin Davies (Swansea), J Matthews (Bridgend)

Referee: Mr F H Fox (Somerset)

Glamorgan mounted numerous attacks in the early stages of the game and Deere looked the most dangerous player, but successive tackles by Hipwood, Luce and Collett kept him out. However, the home side also had chances, Luce getting clear but losing the ball, and Collett and Needs both coming very close. However, half-time arrived with no score.

When play resumed, the Citizen described it as "fast and furious, and there was some really clever play exhibited on both sides. The home men were lucky to escape a score by kicking dead, after several futile attempts by players on both sides to touch down." Towards the end of the game:

Cummings got the ball from a scrum and passed to Needs, who made off down the touch-line. When confronted by Llewellyn the Bristolian handed inside to Hall, who subsequently re-passed to Needs, for the latter to run over with an exceptionally clever try, amidst loud cheers. Collett failed at goal, though the attempt was a good one. Just

previous to no-side some loose play opened at the centre, out of which Luce secured and passed to Parsons. The latter immediately handed to Collett, who was in close attendance on his right, and the old Cheltenham College captain went off at a good pace. Beating the full-back cleverly, Collett, though closely pressed from behind, continued on his journey, finishing up an exceptionally brilliant run by scoring behind the posts. Collett himself took the place kick and covered the cross bar neatly, at which success the cheering was loud and prolonged. Directly after the referee sounded a cessation of hostilities.

Gloucestershire 0 Glamorgan 23
6th April 1899

RAIN COMMENCED TO fall at one o'clock, and continued with increased severity till the time of the kick-off. These conditions affected the attendance, which was under 2,000; £93 was taken on the gate.

Gloucestershire: G Romans (Gloucester); W H Taylor, J Cook (Gloucester), F Fry (Cheltenham), A M Ricketts (Cardiff); G. Hall, B Parham; Frank Stout, C Hall, F Oswell, F Goulding, G H Smith, J Lewis (Gloucester), B L Watkins (Bristol), H B T Bingham (Clifton)

Glamorgan: Joe Davies (Neath); V Huzzey, W Jones (Cardiff), G Davies, W Trew (Swansea); G Hughes (Cardiff), J Hopkins (Tondu); W H Alexander (Llwynypia), F Miller, Rev T Davis (Mountain Ash), H Jones (Penygraig), J Thomas (Neath), V Jones (Aberavon), F Kirby, W Gibbs (Penarth)

Referee: Mr E B Holmes (Midland Counties)

Early in the game there was cut and thrust in both directions, and Gloucestershire were pressing when:

the home front rank indulged in some smart footwork, but a kick by George Davies sent the leather to Romans. The latter fumbled in gathering, with the result that the Glamorgan forwards secured, and after a couple of passes Thomas practically walked over under the posts. Joe Davies easily converted. Gloucestershire resumed, and immediately the home team showed up with a splendid burst. The ball was kicked to Taylor, who got in a sharp return. The leather struck an opponent in its transit and put several Gloucester forwards on-side. There was a splendid chance of scoring, but Huzzey nipped in and spoiled it, a minor only resulting.

And so it was one goal to nil at half-time. Glamorgan started the second half in fine style and "a brilliant bit of combined work by the

Glamorgan pack took the ball close to the Gloucestershire line. Alexander lifted it nicely over Romans' head, but Cook ran back and punched the ball dead." But they were not to be denied for long and "George Davies securing from Hopkins, the Swansea centre ran clean through the opposition and scored a brilliant try." The flood gates had opened when " a passing bout by Hopkins, Jones, and Huzzey saw the latter punt over the line near the goal. Fry received, but the Cheltonian let the oval drop through his hands and a Glamorgan forward obtained one of the softest tries imaginable." Then a clearance kick was marked by Huzzey, who calmly kicked a long range drop goal from the mark. The comprehensive victory was rounded off when a couple of Glamorgan forwards broke away from a lineout and passed to Alexander, who scored a try behind the posts.

Gloucestershire 13 Midland Counties 9
19th October 1899

THIS FRIENDLY FIXTURE was played on a Thursday in beautiful summer-like weather, but Gloucestershire were by no means at full strength and there were eight changes to the Midland team; the attendance was described as fair.

Gloucestershire: G Romans (Gloucester); F Lewis (Cinderford), J Cook, C Smith (Gloucester), R Parsons; W Needs (Bristol), R Goddard; F Goulding, C Hall, A H Click, F Oswell (Gloucester), B J Watkins, F Shannon (Bristol), F W Harrison (Stroud), B H Bingham (Clifton)

Midland Counties: A O Jones (captain); H Wilkinson (Leicester), H S Nicol (Old Edwardians), A H Frith (Coventry), E H Gausson (Burton); J Braithwaite (Leicester), A C Andrews (Nuneaton); R N Campbell, M S Scott, J W Garner, S Matthews (Leicester), C M Clive (Handsworth), C W Wright (Wolverhampton), A J Currington, F Cleverley (Coventry)

Referee: Mr W M Douglas (Cardiff)

Early in the match Watkins was injured and had to be carried from the field, but it was Gloucestershire who then applied the pressure. They forced a minor and from the resulting drop-out "Whacker" Smith made a clever run and passed to Needs, who put Harrison over the line for a smart try, which Goddard converted. Though a man short in the scrum, the Gloucestershire forwards worked manfully, remained on the front foot and the home side came close to scoring twice, Parsons getting over the line, but the try was disallowed. Numbers were equalised when Currington suffered a broken ankle and had to retire to the Infirmary.

In some loose play which followed Goddard picked up and transferred quickly to Needs. The Bristolian darted away in smart fashion, and secured a lovely opening. Feinting to pass when he reached Jones he put the Midland custodian completely off his guard, and finished up a splendid effort by scoring behind the posts. Goddard easily converted.

The Midlands were first on the scoreboard in the second half when their captain, Jones, kicked a splendid goal from near the halfway line. Needs came close with a drop goal, but Gloucestershire then had to defend stoutly to keep the Midlands out. A combined rush by the home forwards put the Midlanders on the defensive, and a neat pick up and pass by Goddard to Goulding enabled the latter to score. Before the finish Jones landed another penalty goal and Wilkinson scored a try for the Midlands, but it was too little too late.

Fred Goulding who scored the final try against Midland Counties Gloucester Rugby]

The First International Match at Kingsholm

England 3 Wales 13
6th January 1900

THE AWARDING OF this match to Kingsholm was regarded as a considerable feather in the cap of the Gloucester Club, and they put enormous effort into ensuring its success. However, the lack of any local players in the England team selection and bad weather on the day conspired to keep the crowd down. Up to 30,000 had been hoped for, but in the event only 14,600 turned up.

England won the toss, and decided to play with the wind from the Deans Walk end; Wales kicked off and had the better of it in the early stages of the game. The game was stopped for an injury to Dick Hellings, but he played on in great pain and with one arm not functioning properly (there were no substitutes allowed) – after the match it was found to have been broken just above the wrist. The Welsh pack gradually gained the upper hand, and most of the play settled down in the England half of the field. They resisted successfully for some time, but eventually the pressure told, and none other than the injured Hellings crossed for the first try to

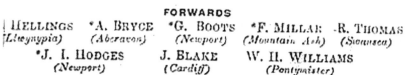

England v. Wales.

International Match, Gloucester, Jan. 6. 1900.

W. J. Bancroft (Captain of Welsh Team)

Welsh Team.

SCOER } Half-Time Result

BACK
*W. J. BANCROFT
(Swansea)

RIGHT   LEFT

THREE-QUARTERS
*W. LLEWELYN   D. REES   G. DAVIES   W. TREW
(Llwynypia)   (Swansea)   (Swansea)   (Swansea)

HALF-BACKS
*G. L. LLOYD   L. A. PHILLIPS
(Newport)   (Newport)

FORWARDS
HELLINGS   *A. BRYCE   *G. BOOTS   *F. MILLAR   R. THOMAS
(Llwynypia)   (Aberavon)   (Newport)   (Mountain Ash)   (Swansea)
*J. I. HODGES   J. BLAKE   W. H. WILLIAMS
(Newport)   (Cardiff)   (Pontymister)

O

FORWARDS
J. BELL   R. W. BELL   W. COBBY   A. COCKERHAM   J. JARMAN
(Northumberland)   (Yorkshire)   (Bristol)
S. REYNOLDS   U. T. SCOTT   J. BAXTER
(Richmond)   (Cambridge)   (Cheshire)

HALF-BACKS
*R. H. CATTELL   G. MARSDEN
(Midland Counties)   (Yorkshire)

THREE-QUARTERS
NICHOLSON   A. BRETTAGH   G. G. SMITH   S. F. COOPER
(Cheshire)   (Yorkshire)   (Blackheath)   (Devon)

BACK
*H. T. GAMLIN
(Somerset)

SCORE } Half-Time Result

English Team.

Names, Age, Height, Weight of Players

WALES	Age.	Height	Weight
BANCROFT ...	28	5 6½	11 0
LLEWELLYN...	21	5 8	10 12
REES ...	21	5 9	11 11
DAVIES ...	24	5 9	11 2
TREW ...	21	5 8	10 12
LLOYD ...	22	5 6	10 6
PHILLIPS ...	21	5 6	10 13
HELLINGS ...	26	6 0½	14 1
BRYCE ...	27	5 11	13 10
BOOTS ...	25	5 10	12 9
MILLAR ...	30	6 0	14 0
BLAKE ...	24	5 11	13 4
HODGES ...	22	5 10	12 8
THOMAS ...	26	5 8	12 10
WILLIAMS ...	25	5 11½	12 12
ENGLAND			
GAMLIN ...	21	6 0	12 10
COOPER ...	21	5 8	11 2
SMITH ...	23	5 8½	11 10
BRETTAGH ...	21	5 9	11 4
NICHOLSON ...	21	5 9	11 11
CATTELL ...	27	5 8	11 4
MARSDEN ...	21	5 9	11 0
BELL, F. J. ...	21	5 10	11 12
BELL, R. W. ...	22	5 9	12 2
COBBY ...	24	5 10	11 10
COCKERHAM ...	20	6 0½	12 13
JARMAN ...	28	5 8½	11 10
REYNOLDS ...	21	5 7	12 0
SCOTT ...	21	5 8½	12 0
BAXTER ...	28	5 10	12 2

The match programme; note that the tallest player was 6ft 0 ½ ins, and the heaviest was 14st 1lb [Gloucester Rugby]

The England team [Gloucestershire Archives]

The Wales team [Gloucestershire Archives]

Action during the match [World Rugby Museum, Twickenham]

Wales, Billy Bancroft converting. Although the England backs showed some promise, there was no further score before half-time.

England went onto the attack after the resumption, and narrowly missed one scoring chance before they took another. Dick Cattell passed out to George Marsden, who sold a dummy and drew the fullback before passing out to Elliot Nicholson, who sprinted over in the corner. The wind took Herbert "Octopus" Gamlin's attempt at a conversion just wide of the posts. England came close to two further tries, and Wales were hanging on as the speed of the game increased, but back they came, and nearly all the Welsh backs handled in a move which put Billy Trew over for a try behind the posts, which Bancroft converted. Play went from end to end, but the Welsh finished the game the stronger. Shortly before the final whistle they were rewarded with a penalty kicked by Bancroft, and thus ran out comfortable winners.

The Press Association representative at the game was H V Jones, the former Gloucester player; he summarised the game as follows: "It must be confessed that the game was a little disappointing, the play for the most part being only moderate. The Welshmen quite deserved their victory, but with a little luck the game might easily have gone the other way."

Everyone in Gloucester was proud to have staged the match, but for the Gloucester Club, which had invested so much in making the event a success, it was a financial disaster, from which the Club's finances took several years to recover. A few years later the RFU opened their new ground at Twickenham and from 1910 onwards home internationals were played there. So, more than 90 years had passed after the 1900 international before the full England team played again at Kingsholm.

The Barbarians Return

Gloucester 13 Barbarians 0
12th April 1900

THE BARBARIANS ADDED this fixture at Kingsholm onto the start of their Easter tour, so it was played on the Thursday afternoon before Easter. It was arranged in order to help alleviate the financial problems of the Gloucester Club following the huge losses made when hosting the England v Wales international match three months earlier. The Barbarians brought a strong team, including several international players, and the home side, anticipating a stiff test, turned out at full strength. The match was played in a steady drizzle, which, together with a 5:25pm kick off, doubtless contributed to the modest attendance, and the gate receipts amounted to a paltry £35.

Gloucester: G Romans; W H Taylor (captain), G F Clutterbuck, J Stephens, C Smith; R Goddard, G Hall; C Hall, A H Click, J Lewis, H Manley, F Oswell, G H Smith, A Hawker, J Gough

Barbarians: F W H Weaver (Birkenhead Park); R Forest (Blackheath & England), R F Cumberlege (London Harlequins), J Kynaston Jones (Birkenhead Park), H G Alexander (Newport); J C Marquis (Birkenhead Park & England), P D Kendall (Birkenhead Park); T Drysdale (London Scottish), R I C Thompson, R C Galloway (Marlborough Nomads), C Witt (Rosslyn Park), W P Scott (West of Scotland & Scotland), J G Franks (Trinity, Dublin & Ireland), G R Gibson (Northumberland), C S Edgar (Birkenhead Park)

Referee: Mr Gil Evans (Swansea)

The Barbarians got off to the better start and only fine defence by "Whacker" Smith and "Nobby" Hall kept them out until:

a splendid touch-kick by Romans enabled Gloucester to reach the centre, where, from some loose play, the ball got to "Whacker" Smith, who put in a sharp punt. The ball in its transit touched a visitor, and the City forwards being put on side, Lewis picked up and ran and passed to Click, who romped over with a good try. Romans converted with a splendid kick. After this Stephens, Taylor, and Clutterbuck combined in a movement which took play to the Barbarians end. The ball was punted to Weaver, who essayed a flying kick. "Whacker" Smith ran and fielded the ball nicely, and running round scored in the corner. Romans made a grand effort to convert, the ball hitting the cross-bar and rebounding into the field of play.

In the second half, the Barbarians:

opening out the game a bit, Marquis executed a fine run up the field, and a series of transfers which ensued apparently left the line at their mercy, but Gloucester got round and saved in a wonderful manner. The Barbarians still attacked, but they could not score. Operations, however, were principally confined to the forwards, and lacked interest. Gloucester more than held their own, and gradually they found a footing in their opponents' end. Once or twice the home men looked dangerous, but the situation was saved. At length G. Hall fairly caught the opposition napping, and running clean to the full-back he passed to Lewis, who went over under the posts. Romans easily converted.

A H "Fred" Click, who scored the first try against the Barbarians [Gloucester Rugby]

Whacker Smith, who scored the second try against the Barbarians [CC&GG]

County Matches 1900-01

Gloucestershire 18 Durham 6
11th January 1900

Five days after the first international match at Kingsholm, Durham visited as part of a tour of the West Country. A greasy ball kept the score down in a game which rarely raised the pulse rate of the small crowd. Spectators were doubtless discouraged by the fact that Gloucestershire had already been eliminated from the County Championship at the group stage, and the game being played on a Thursday afternoon, although this was early-closing day in Gloucester. Because the colours of the two counties were almost identical, Gloucestershire played in the City Club's cherry and white jerseys.

Gloucestershire: G Romans (Gloucester); P L Nicholas, F M Luce (Oxford University), A S Dryborough (Bristol), C Smith (Gloucester); W Needs, S H Foster (Bristol); C Hall (captain), F Oswell, J Lewis (Gloucester), F Channon, M Courtney (Bristol), F W Harrison (Stroud), T Downing (Lydney), Claude Smith (Stroud).

Durham: Hector (South Shields); Taylor, Gordon (Tudhoe), Cox (Sunderland), Irvine (Hartlepool Old Boys); Allison (Penarth and Tyne Dock), Oughtred (Hartlepool Rovers); Stitt, Frater, Carmedy (Tudhoe), Peat (South Shields), Smith (Hartlepool Old Boys), Summerscale (Durham City), Thornton (Tyne Dock), Wreford-Brown (Sunderland)

Referee: Mr G Harnett (Kent)

Gloucestershire opened the scoring when they pounced on a Durham error; Hall, Lewis and Harrison dribbled the ball down the field, and "Nobby" Hall scored a try, George Romans adding the extra points. More was to follow as "the Northerners eased the pressure a little, but Needs, with a clever feint, made a capital opening. The ball was transferred at the right moment to Luce, and the Oxonian feeding Smith the Gloucestrian jumped the full-back and scored a capital try. Romans converted with a good kick."

So Gloucestershire turned round two goals to the good, and added to their lead when Needs put Channon in for a try in the corner early in the second half. Durham fought back with a try of their own by Taylor, before "Nobby" Hall broke away from a line-out to feed Channon for his second try, which Romans converted with a lovely kick. Just before the end of the game, Peat took a cross kick from Irvine and struggled through a tackle to register Durham's second try.

Frank Luce, who set up a try against Durham [Gloucester Rugby]

Gloucestershire 0 Glamorgan 27
13th December 1900

HALF OF THE players originally selected by Gloucestershire were unavailable, whereas Glamorgan brought a strong side including ten international players. The weather was fine, and there was a fair sized crowd.

Gloucestershire: J Oates (Bristol); W H Taylor, J Cook, J Stephens (Gloucester), G F Collett (Cambridge University); A Goddard, T Brick (Cheltenham); F M Stout, C E Miller, A Hawker (Gloucester), T L Horton (Stroud), J Sweet, A Harris, F Channon (Bristol), T Downing (Lydney)

Glamorgan: H B Winfield (Cardiff); H G Alexander (Newport), Dan Rees, G Davies, W Trew (Swansea); J Jones (Aberavon), W H Jones (Mountain Ash); A Bryce (Aberavon), F Miller (Mountain Ash), J Blake (Cardiff), F Scrines, R Thomas, H Davies (Swansea), W H Alexander (Llwynypia), Howell Jones (Neath)

Referee: Mr Coles (London).

Gloucestershire started the game in fine style and Glamorgan had all their work cut out to defend, but the home side could not force a score, their backs passing wildly at the critical moment. The Glamorgan forwards relieved the pressure and, after some clever passing, Trew raced over for a try, which Winfield converted. The play went back to the other end and Taylor almost scored but was hauled down by Winfield and Gloucestershire maintained the pressure for a time, but some rapid passing by the Glamorgan three-quarters bamboozled their opponents and Trew scored his second try. The visiting forwards were now controlling the game, and the precision of their backs set up Trew to complete his hat trick before half-time, when the score was 13-0.

The second half saw more of the same with play confined to the home half of the field:

> After repeated attempts to score, the efforts of the visitors were at length rewarded by Trew running round behind the posts from a pass by G. Davies. Winfield added the extra points. The game continued fearfully one-sided, Gloucestershire having no chance whatever. From a feeble punt out by Oates, Scrines made his mark, and Winfield placed a lovely goal; whilst shortly after Davies scored behind the posts, after an exceptionally smart effort. Another goal resulted.

Gloucestershire 26 Midland Counties 3
10th October 1901

GLOUCESTERSHIRE WARMED UP for the 1901-02 season with a friendly match against Midland Counties.

Gloucestershire: G Romans; C Smith, J Cook, G Clutterbuck (Gloucester), E Watkins Baker (Bristol); G Hall, R Goddard; C Hall (captain), J Lewis, T Spiers, C E Miller (Gloucester), J Wilcox, J Claridge (Bristol), F M Stout (Richmond), C Harris (Lydney)

Midland Counties: A C Butlin; H Wilkinson (Leicester), Rev W H Goudge (Moseley), W Orton (Coventry), J H Miles; J Braithwaite (Leicester), H Lovatt (Old Edwardians); G V Evers (Moseley), G H Maddocks, B Beasley (Handsworth), J Woodward, W Merry (Nuneaton), G G Yeld, D Atkins (Leicester), B C Newbould (Burton)

Referee : Mr. T. Williams (Llwynypia)

The first half was a tale of missed chances:

Whacker Smith, the England international, who scored and butchered tries against Midland Counties [Gloucestershire Archives]

Goddard was early prominent with a dodgy run, but his pass went astray ... G Hall initiated a pretty passing movement, which resulted in Cook and Smith making considerable headway, but the latter's final pass inside to Goddard was adjudged forward ... Goddard attempted a screw kick across the ground, but the ball went over the line, and a dead ball resulted ... from just outside the quarter flag Miller burst away in fine style, and passing between Lewis, C. Hall, Baker, Cook, and Smith looked certain for a try, but the International was rolled into touch just outside.

Shortly before the break, "Whacker" Smith finally scored following a clever bout of passing initiated by Goddard, and Romans kicked a splendid conversion. There was just time for Yeld to reply with a penalty before half-time, when the score was 5-3.

The second half started with a penalty from near the half-way line by Romans. Play then fluctuated to and fro before "Goddard worked a pretty opening for Smith, but the International knocked on badly with no one to beat. A couple of minutes later, however, after a dash by G Hall, his brother scored a neat try." This opened the floodgates and Gloucestershire ran in further tries by G Hall and Baker. To round things off "immediately after the kick-off Cook executed a marvellous run from his own line, and passing to Baker the latter ran and handed to G. Hall, who completed a wonderful effort by scoring in a good position. Romans added the extra points" to extend the final margin to four goals, one penalty and one try to one penalty.

George Hall, who made and scored tries against Midland Counties [Gloucestershire Archives]

The First County Championship Final at Kingsholm

Gloucestershire 3 Durham 9
5th April 1902

GLOUCESTERSHIRE SOMEHOW MANAGED to win the group stage of the 1901-02 County Championship competition. First they squeaked home in Cornwall by two tries to one. Then, away to Somerset, the referee declared a draw at three points apiece, but on appeal later the penalty awarded to Somerset was disallowed and the match was awarded

to Gloucestershire. Devon were beaten 16-3 in a brilliant performance at Bristol, and Gloucestershire were through to the semi-final. This was against Middlesex at Richmond, and proved to be another closely fought affair, with Gloucestershire scoring on the stroke of time to win 13-10. Before the final, a County Trial was played at Kingsholm on 20th March 1902, which resulted in Gloucester beating the Rest of the County 8-3.

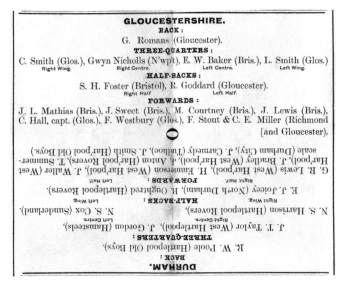

[Mark Hoskins]

The final against Durham was played at Kingsholm. Despite home advantage, Gloucestershire did not start as favourites. This was the third year in succession in which Durham had appeared in the final, whereas Gloucestershire's only previous appearance had been in a substantial defeat by Lancashire eleven years previously. More than 5,000 spectators were in the ground when a heavy storm swept through just before the kick-off and rendered the playing surface very greasy.

Gloucestershire: G Romans; C Smith (Gloucester), Gwyn Nicholls (Newport), E W Baker (Bristol), Lewis Smith; R Goddard (Gloucester), S H Foster (Bristol); C Hall (captain), F Westbury (Gloucester), C E Miller, F M Stout (Richmond), J Lewis, M Courtney, J Sweet, W Claridge (Bristol)

Durham: R Poole (Hartlepool O B); N Harrison (Hartlepool Rovers), J T Taylor (West Hartlepool), J Gordon (Hamsteels), N S Cox (Sunderland); B Oughtred (Hartlepool Rovers), E J Joicey (North Durham); G H Lewis, J Waller, R Bradley, J J Emmerson (West Hartlepool), J Auton (Hartlepool Rovers), T Summerscale (Durham City), J Smith (Hartlepool Rovers) J Carmedy (Tudhoe)

Referee: Mr Adam Turnbull (Scotland)

Gloucestershire came close to scoring first when Lewis had a clear run to the line, but passed to Sweet who knocked-on. Another tremendous storm then burst over the ground, left the pitch in a shocking state, and was responsible for a succession of handling errors. However, "Gradually Gloucestershire worked down to their opponents' goal, where from a scrum the ball came prettily from the Gloucestershire halves. Nicholls came across the ground and passed at the right moment to Baker, who, feinting to pass, cut inside Taylor and Harrison and scored a beautiful try amidst tremendous cheering." The ground was now "a veritable mud-pool in places, and the players experienced the utmost difficulty in keeping a footing", and there was no further score before the teams changed ends with Gloucestershire 3-0 ahead, but now facing the wind and rain.

[Mark Hoskins]

The Gloucestershire team [CC&GG]

The Durham team [CC&GG]

Consequently they spent much of the second half defending their line, which led to a scrambled kick under pressure from their line being caught by a Durham forward only 12 yards out, and Taylor kicked a drop goal from the mark, which put Durham ahead, 4-3. Attacks by the home side were repelled with huge relieving kicks, and from a scrum the Durham forwards swept all before them. The ball went over the goal line near the corner, and Joicey was credited with a try, which Taylor converted with a magnificent kick, given the conditions. The rest of the game was played out with Gloucestershire defending desperately.

To=Day's Great Football Match
AT GLOUCESTER
(Final for the County Championship—Gloucestershire v. Durham).
Four of the Leading Gloucestershire Officials.

T. GRAVES SMITH, President.

J. H. TRATT, Hon. Treasurer.

C. E. BROWN, Hon. Secretary.

C. HALL, Captain.

The great and the good of Gloucestershire rugby attending the match [CC&GG]

Charity Matches

Gloucester 8 Rest of County 3
20th March 1902

THIS SPECIAL MATCH was arranged by the Gloucester Club for the benefit of T Collins.

Gloucester: G Romans; C Smith, F Rooke, J Stephens, Lewis Smith; R Goddard, G Hall; C Hall, A H Click, F Westbury, W Johns, J Jewell, Bert Parham, G H Smith, E Essex

Rest of County: B Blanch (Stroud); C Clifford, J Cook (Cheltenham), C Goddard, S S Harris (Gloucester); R S V Dyas (Cheltenham), A Hall (Gloucester); T Gillmore, G Cossens (Cheltenham), H Penney, B Fisher (Stroud), Brown (Cinderford), J Lewis (captain, Bristol), A Purton, J Merchant (Gloucester)

Harris came close to scoring first when he dashed down the line, only for Romans to get across to bring him down, but from the good position which this set up for the Rest of the County, Harris received the ball again and this time crossed for a try. Gloucester struck back when Rooke took a pass from Goddard and cut between the opposing centres before passing back to Goddard who ran between the posts to give Romans an easy conversion and establish a 5-3 lead at half-time.

In the second half, the Rest pressed hard and forced Gloucester to concede two minors, but the defence held out and indeed both full-backs were credited with particularly fine performances. The final score came when Lewis picked up a loose ball and, following some neat exchanges with Westbury, went over for a try.

George Roman's Gloucester XV 5
Samuel Aitken's Cardiff XV 13
14th April 1904

THIS MATCH WAS organised at the end of the 1903-04 season to raise money for the Gloucester Royal Infirmary. There was a good crowd in the ground by the time of the 5:30 kick-off and £62 12s 6d was taken on the turnstiles. The selected sides were:

Dicky Goddard, who scored for Gloucester [CC&GG]

Roman's XV: G Romans (captain, Gloucester); A Lewis (Lydney), J Stephens (Gloucester), E W Baker (Clifton), D W Smith (Bristol); D Gent, G Williams; B Parham, F Goulding, A Hawker, W Johns, G Matthews (Gloucester), G Denley (Stroud), T Hussey (Lydney), N Moore (Bristol)

Aitken's XV: H B Winfield (Cardiff); C E Lewis (Newport), Dr Timms, R T Gage, Cecil Biggs (captain); F David, P F Bush; A Brice, W Neill, E Rumbelow, W Ham, A Spackman, J Brown, F Smith, H Harding (Cardiff)

Referee: Mr S A Ball (Gloucestershire)

There were late substitutions including Harrison and Vears in Roman's XV and Gunstone in Aitken's XV, but it is not known who was replaced; Mr Phelps took over as referee.

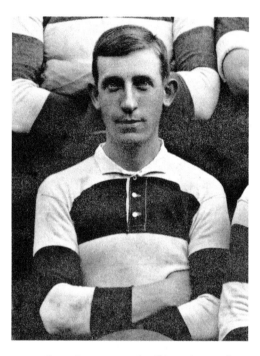

George Romans, captain of his XV [CC&GG]

Harrison made an early break for Gloucester, but the ball went loose and the chance was lost before Cardiff won the ball at a scrum and a loose rush took it beyond Romans for David to score. Gloucester struck back when Gent passed the ball out from a scrum and a brilliant bout of passing saw the ball handled by Williams, Stephens, Harrison, Vears and finally back to Williams, who scored behind the posts. Romans converted and thereby gained a 5-3 advantage at half-time.

The second half started in similar fashion to the first with Gloucester pressing strongly and coming close but failing to get over the line, only for a Cardiff forward to secure the ball at a lineout and walk over for a try by the posts, which was converted. Gloucester continued to attack, but Harrison failed to take a scoring pass from Williams, Austin Lewis made a sensational run up to the Cardiff full-back only for his pass to be intercepted, and Romans missed an easy penalty to equalise. Superior Cardiff finishing was demonstrated when Gunstone scored a fine try, converted by Biggs. Gloucester attacked furiously, but Vears was stopped on the goal line and the game was lost.

County Matches 1903-04

Gloucestershire 3 Devon 7
7th November 1903

THE WEATHER WAS gloriously fine, the ground was in grand condition for a fast, open game, and the crowd was estimated at 4-5,000 by kick-off.

Gloucestershire: J Oates; R S Vaughan, G A Lamond (Bristol), E W Baker (Clifton), A Lewis (Lydney); J Stephens (Gloucester), W Vincent (Bristol); F M Stout (captain, Richmond), F Goulding, A Hawker, B Parham (Gloucester), J L Mathias, T Webb, E Meyer (Bristol), G Matthews (Stroud)

Devon: S Irvin (Devon Albion); P L Nicholas (Exeter), E J Vivian (Devon Albion), T Mills, W Beasley; F Lee, J Peters (Plymouth); C Thomas (captain, Barnstaple), S Williams, R Gilbert, S G Willcocks (Devon Albion), L Tosswill, A Brock (Exeter), J Evans (Devon Albion), A Avery (Plymouth)

Referee: Mr F W Nicholls (Leicester)

Play started with a succession of kicks to establish position, but defences held secure. The game was finally enlivened by:

A brilliant bit of play by the Gloucestershire backs. Stephens started the movement and Vincent and the whole of the three-quarters in turn received. Lewis had a possible chance of running round, but he preferred to cross-kick, and Devon saved. Gloucestershire carried the succeeding scrum, but Lee again got off-side, and Oates, taking a shot for goal from near the centre, landed the ball beautifully over the cross-bar amidst tremendous cheering.

Gloucestershire created further scoring opportunities, but none were taken and the Devon defence was solid, so at half-time only a penalty separated the sides.

Devon restarted strongly, but dropped a scoring pass and had a dropped goal attempt charged down, from which Gloucestershire raced away but fluffed the chance when they had the Devon full-back outnumbered.

Several scrums followed right on the home line, but at length the home forwards relieved with a wheel. A Devonian, however, picked up and passed out to Vivyan, who swung out a wide transfer to Mills. The latter handed to Beasley, who, seeing he was likely to be cut off, dodged back, and with a nice kick dropped a lovely goal from a difficult angle. In the last few minutes Devon made desperate efforts to score, and just before the end a try came as the result of a magnificent effort by Vivyan. Fielding a kick in the open, the Albion centre beat several opponents in clever fashion, and going right up to Oates passed to Thomas, who completed the movement by scoring near the posts. The goal-kick failed, but the score definitely settled all doubts as to the ultimate winners.

Gloucestershire 3 Glamorgan 6
13th October 1904

THERE WERE ABOUT 2,000 present for this first County match of the season played on a beautiful Thursday afternoon. There were multiple changes to both teams from the original selections.

Gloucestershire: G Romans (Gloucester); A A Lewis (Lydney), J Harrison (Gloucester), E W Baker (Clifton), D Smith (Bristol); W V Butcher (Richmond), D. R. Gent (Gloucester); F Goulding, A Hawker, G Matthews, W Johns, B Parham (Gloucester), L Cook (Cheltenham), T Huzzey (Lydney), A J Gardner (Clifton)

Glamorgan: F Young (Cardiff); F Gordon, W Arnold (Swansea), Cecil Biggs (Cardiff), H T Maddocks (London Welsh); W Hopkins (Bridgend), R M Jones (Swansea); A Smith (Swansea), W Taylor (Bridgend), G Vicary (Aberavon), D Davies (Swansea), W Galloway (Treherbert), Matthews (Penygraig), Price (Mountain Ash), Owens (Treherbert)

Referee: Mr J B Minahan (East Midlands)

Unfortunately for Glamorgan Taylor had to retire in the first few minutes with an injured leg, but the Chronicle told its readers that "with only seven forwards the Welshmen were much too good for the home eight, and much more frequently got the ball out". Although the Citizen reported occasional bright moments, much of the play in the first half was described as uninteresting and the break was reached with no score.

The second half resumed in similar vein until "Jones put in a splendid run down touch, and passing at the right moment to Biggs, the latter ran round behind the posts with a good try; the same player failed at the easy place." Glamorgan continued to press and despite some heroic defence by Gent "Jones worked out a nice opening, and Arnold sending to Biggs, the Cardiff captain scored his second try; the place-kick failed". Gloucestershire struck back when "Gent, passing out to Butcher, the latter fed Baker, who in turn sent to Smith. The Bristol flier at once put on his best pace, and beating Young scored a fine try. Romans made a poor attempt at conversion." Whilst Glamorgan remained on the attack until the final whistle they had to be content with a 3-point victory in what was reckoned to be overall a disappointing game.

The Southern Hemisphere comes to Kingsholm

NEW ZEALAND

Gloucester 0 New Zealand 44
19th October 1905

THE FIRST ALL Blacks tour to Great Britain in 1905 included a match against the Gloucester Club at Kingsholm. The visitors were a fearsome proposition; this was the tenth match of their tour, and they rolled into town having won the previous nine by an aggregate of 341 points to 7. They would finish their tour with 32 wins from 33 matches, only Wales lowering their colours, and with 868 points scored against a meagre 47 by their opponents.

Under the headline "The Colonials at Kingsholm", the Citizen reported that "in football circles the game had been keenly anticipated for weeks past, not that it was thought Gloucester had any chance against their opponents, but everybody was anxious to see the wonderful team that had pulverised all and every combination pitted against them."

The weather was fine and anticipation was keen, with a large crowd waiting for the gates to open. The Gloucester Selection Committee decided to play only seven forwards, their judgement being that an extra half-back would be more useful to the side than a wing forward. The wisdom of this decision was debatable, but whatever formation had been chosen is unlikely to have altered the outcome of the match. There were other differences in positioning and nomenclature which are shown in the team lists.

Gloucester: L Vears (back); C Smith, E Hall, J Harrison, A Hudson (three-quarters); J Stephens, A Wood, D Gent (half-backs); W Johns (captain), A Hawker, F Pegler, G Vears, B Parham, H Collins, G Matthews (forwards)

New Zealand: G Gillett (back); G W Smith, R J Deans, W Wallace (three-quarters); J Hunter, W Stead (five-eighths); F Roberts (half-back); F Glasgow, W Glenn, W Cunningham, G Nicholson, J O'Sullivan, C Seeling, W Johnstone, D Gallagher (forwards)

Referee: Mr F Nicholls (Leicester)

Billy Johns leads Gloucester out to take on the All Blacks [CC&GG]

The New Zealanders appeared on the field five minutes before kick-off to an enthusiastic reception. It was a thing of note that they wore large numbers on the backs of their jerseys to enable spectators to identify them by reference to their programmes; this was not generally the practice in England, but Gloucester also wore numbers for this match. The home captain won the toss, about the only thing which Gloucester were to win all afternoon, and elected to defend the Deans Walk end.

New Zealand had an early chance to score when Wallace marked a Gloucester kick ahead, but his attempt to kick a goal from the mark fell short. The Gloucester forwards then had the upper hand for a spell, and when Wood intercepted, he whipped out a wide pass to Hudson, who dashed down the touchline. Gillett not only got across to tackle him, but Hudson was knocked out in the process and had to be taken off. Despite this setback, Gloucester came close to opening the scoring when Gillett had his clearance kick charged down, but Roberts managed to prevent a try by kicking the ball over the dead ball line.

After twenty minutes, New Zealand broke the deadlock when a slick passing movement put Glenn over near the posts and Wallace kicked the easy conversion. This led to relentless pressure by the visitors and, having twice narrowly failed to get over the line, Smith sprinted over on the left for their second try. The flood gates were open and immediately after the resumption, Roberts passed to Stead, who burst clean through before giving the scoring pass to Deans.

It went from bad to worse for Gloucester when "G Vears picked up and tried to clear, but he was tackled, and though he let the ball go he was badly kicked by an opponent, the spectators shouting in indignation. Vears had to receive the attention of the ambulance men, but was fortunately able to continue." From a scrum, the New Zealand pack drove over the line and Seeling was credited with the try. Before half-time, a brilliant series of exchanges ended with Wallace beating Vears and racing round behind the posts, and Hunter scored another after brilliant passing and inter-passing. These last three tries were converted by Wallace (2) and Gillett for an interval lead of 26-0 (four goals and two tries).

Hudson returned after the break and quickly relieved the pressure with a kick to the visitors' 25, and from another long kick by Hudson, the ball went over the line and Gillett was forced to concede a minor. Hudson also tackled Wallace when he was racing at full speed towards the Gloucester line. Wood was also heroic in defence, twice saving apparently certain scores with decisive tackles, but he was then caught off-side and Gillett had a shot at goal, but only a minor resulted. Gloucester came close when Collins, Parham and Matthews got possession and dribbled down the field, but Wallace got back to stop them. Gloucester were just not quick enough to take advantage of their chances.

With ten minutes to go, a wonderful sweeping move ended with Deans scoring under the posts. As in the first period, so in the second half New Zealand then put in a whirlwind finish, again taking advantage of Gloucester playing a man short through injury, when Wood tackled Gallagher to stop another attack, but twisted his ankle and had to be carried off. New Zealand drove forward relentlessly in his absence, Wallace dodging over for a clever try, which he converted, before tries right at the death by Seeling and Deans, both converted by Wallace, added the icing to the cake. The final score was an overwhelming 44-0, made up of seven goals and three tries (which would convert to 64-0 in today's scoring values).

Although Gloucester conceded all but one of their opponents' ten tries when they were a man short, there were no complaints about the result. WB reported in the Citizen that:

Scenes from the All Blacks game [CC&GG]

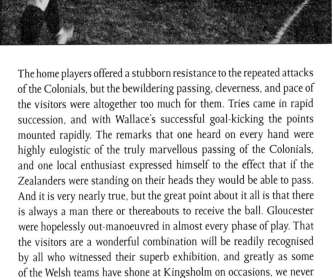

The home players offered a stubborn resistance to the repeated attacks of the Colonials, but the bewildering passing, cleverness, and pace of the visitors were altogether too much for them. Tries came in rapid succession, and with Wallace's successful goal-kicking the points mounted rapidly. The remarks that one heard on every hand were highly eulogistic of the truly marvellous passing of the Colonials, and one local enthusiast expressed himself to the effect that if the Zealanders were standing on their heads they would be able to pass. And it is very nearly true, but the great point about it all is that there is always a man there or thereabouts to receive the ball. Gloucester were hopelessly out-manoeuvred in almost every phase of play. That the visitors are a wonderful combination will be readily recognised by all who witnessed their superb exhibition, and greatly as some of the Welsh teams have shone at Kingsholm on occasions, we never remember any side reaching the perfection attained by the All Blacks.

Reminiscing in 1924, Dai Gent wrote:

Of course, the most memorable match in my day was that against the New Zealanders in 1905. We had a very fine side indeed at that time, but we were too light. In the all-important middle of the field were Stephens, Harrison, Hall, and myself, not one of us as much even as 11 stone in weight, whilst my own "fighting" weight was, to be exact, 9st 4lbs! That was the chief reason why they beat us by a cricket score - they simply trod on us and went on!

SOUTH AFRICA

Gloucestershire 0 South Africa 23
3rd November 1906

LESSONS HAD BEEN learned from the regular maulings which club sides had suffered at the hands of New Zealand the previous season and the Springboks were confronted by county sides as they travelled the length and breadth of the country. So it was Gloucestershire they faced at Kingsholm, where they arrived with an impressive record to date of played 11, won eleven, points for 246, points against 13, quite similar to the All Blacks at this stage of their tour. The weather was gloriously fine,

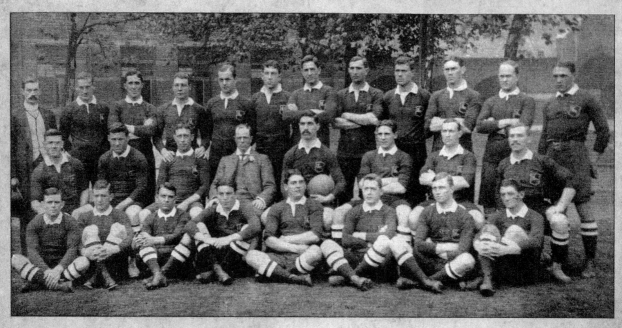

" THE SPRINGBOKS," 1906=7.

BACK ROW:—A. F. Marsburg, A. Stegmann, J. Krige, D. Morkel, H. Reid, J. Raaff, D. Brink, H. Daneel, D. Brookes, S. Morkel, D. Mare.
SECOND ROW:—H. Carolin, W. A. Burger, W. C. Martheze, J. C. Carden (Manager), Paul Roos (Captain), P. Le Roux, J. A. Loubser, H. A. de Villiers.
BOTTOM ROW:—F. J. Dobbin, Andrew Morkel, S. de Melker, W. Millar, J. Le Roux, A. R. Burmeister, D. C. Jackson, J. G. Hirsch.

Copyright—Halftones Ltd.   Printed by Chance & Bland, Gloucester.

The 1906 Springboks, above, and the teams in the match programme, opposite [Mark Hoskins]

SOUTH AFRICAN TOUR 1905-06

THE ORIGINAL SPRINGBOKS.

Autographs of the South African tourists [Gloucester Rugby]

the Kingsholm pitch was in perfect condition, the teams took to the field on time and the ground was packed to capacity.

Gloucestershire: A Wood (Gloucester); A Hudson (Gloucester), W Hyam (Devon Albion), T Wild (Lydney), C Smith (Gloucester); J Stephens (Gloucester), F Niblett (Cinderford); W Holder (Gloucester), G Matthews (Gloucester), J D Bedell-Sivright (Cheltenham), J Watkins (Cinderford), J L Mathias (Bristol), T Webb (Bristol), T J Richards (Bristol), W Bale (Bristol)

South Africa: A F Marsberg; J Le Roux, J G Hirsch, J Krige, J A Loubser; H Carolin, F J Dobbin; W A Burger, H Daneel, W C Martheze, W S Morkel, H Reid, D Mare, W Miller, D Brink

Referee: Mr F W Marsh (South Shields)

The South Africans were the first to score as the Citizen reported: "the Colonials got away with a lovely bout of passing, and Loubser sailed away in grand style. Wood only partially checked the dashing right wing, but "Whacker" Smith got across, and brought off a superb tackle. The visitors immediately got the ball out again, and following some clever exchanges Le Roux ran in and scored behind the posts. Mare failed at the easy place."

They kept up the pressure, but heroic defence, particularly by Wood and Hudson, kept them at bay until "from a mark by Krige, Carolin made a grand attempt at goal from near the centre, the ball just going wide. Following the drop-out the South Africans attacked strongly, and a lovely series of exchanges resulted in Le Roux beating Smith and crossing the line. Hudson came across and collared him, but failed to stop the try. Carolin's kick for goal was a fine one, but it just missed."

It was not long before "the Springboks indulged in a brilliant bout of passing, and Loubser, the last to receive, ran over with the third try, the Gloucestershire men being left standing. Carolin landed a goal, and at the end of 25 minutes' play the South Africans had a lead of 11 points." The score remained thus until half-time thanks to good tackling by the home defenders – "on the one wing Loubser was grandly tackled by Wood, and "Whacker" Smith stopped Le Roux when he looked all over a scorer."

Early in the second half, the South Africans twice kicked ahead over the try line, but Wood won the race for the ball to concede minors. The Citizen reported:

Scenes from the South Africa match [CC&GG]

The Colonials were now giving the ball plenty of air, and they indulged in some clever handling, but could not quite clear the opposition ... then Krige cut out a lovely opening for Le Roux, after being checked by Wood, but the latter knocked on. Wood was injured in this last tackle, and had to receive attention. He was, however, able to resume after a two or three minutes' delay ... just outside the 25 line the South African halves were at fault, but Carolin recovered marvellously, and running round the scrum dropped a lovely goal with his left foot. Resuming, the Springboks were soon under way again, and following a lovely round of passing Le Roux notched a very fine try, which Carolin converted.

Later Hudson and Loubser went for the ball near touch, and coming in contact with the touch-judge all three came down together, to the amusement of the spectators. In the next few minutes the Gloucestershire forwards distinguished themselves, and Matthews and Sivright dribbled over the line, forcing a minor... just before the end the visitors intercepted a pass and Krige, getting possession inside his own half, ran clean home with a try behind the posts.

South Africa had won 23-0, scoring two goals, one drop goal and three tries. The performance of the Springboks was summarised in the Citizen as follows:

The accounts of previous matches had led the spectators to expect great things from the "Bokken". And they were in no wise disappointed. It was a game fit for the gods. There was not the "slimness" of the All Blacks, perhaps, but it was the real old Rugby game played in the old style by a set of the finest exponents of the game anyone could wish to see. The brilliancy of the backs' movements and their magnificent pace made the County men look quite out of it at times; but let credit be given where credit is due, and it must be said that though badly beaten the home defenders were in no way disgraced. The visitors are immensely strong – they are conscious of their strength, and certainly give no quarter. When a man's collared by the Colonials there is no mistake about it – down they go, "planted deep". The visitors get rid of the ball in marvellous fashion, and it is no exaggeration to say that it takes "three to one to hold them". One great mistake the County men made was that they repeatedly tried to collar too high, which against men of such speed and strength, proved generally futile. The game was truly a great one, and must ever live as a brilliant event in local football history.

AUSTRALIA

Gloucestershire 0 Australia 16
1st October 1908

THIS WAS ONLY the second match of the Australian tour of the British Isles, even though the team had departed Sydney by ship on 8th August. The British press initially referred to them as the Rabbits, but the Australian players objected to this label and took a vote on what they would prefer. Wallabies won against alternatives such as Waratahs, Wallaroos and Kookaburras, and Wallabies it has been ever since. There was not the same excitement surrounding the visit of Australia as there had been for New Zealand and South Africa, and there was some resistance to the price of tickets for a mid-week game. However, there was local interest not only in the home side but also in Tom Richards, who had played at Kingsholm two years earlier for Gloucestershire against South Africa, when he was a Bristol player, and about 8,000 turned up to watch.

Gloucestershire: B Davy (Cheltenham); A Hudson (captain), M Neale (Gloucester), V F Eberle, E F Eberle (Clifton); D R Gent, T Elliott; W A Johns, H Berry (Gloucester), A Teague, A Redding, J Hyndman (Cinderford), W W Hoskin (Clifton), W Stinchcombe (Lydney), F W Feltham (Bristol)

Australia: P P Carmichael (Queensland); D B Carroll (St George), E F Mandible (Sydney), J J Hickey (Glebe), C J Russell (Newtown); F Wood, C H McKivat (Glebe); Dr H M Moran (captain, Newcastle), T S Griffen (Glebe), J T Barnett (Newtown), C A Hammond (University), P A McCue (Newtown), S A Middleton (Glebe), T J Richards (Queensland), N E Row (Eastern Suburbs)

Referee: Mr T D Schofield (Welsh Union)

Spectators in front of the grandstand at the Australia match – in the front row hat off is J Hart, Treasurer of the Gloucestershire Club – on the extreme right of the front row are Tom Graves Smith (Gloucester and Gloucestershire), W S Dorme (Somerset) and C A Crane (president of the Rugby Union) [CC&GG]

A lineout during the match against Australia [CC&GG]

A lovely passing move with the ball going all along the line and a beautiful opening being made by Woods, Russell went over on the right wing to open the scoring for Australia; Carmichael converted. Gloucestershire fought back and the Citizen reported that:

Hudson was given possession, and the City captain tried hard to work out an opening for Neale, but threw forward. In the next minute the Gloucester forwards broke away, but a good tackle checked them, one player having his garments torn, and there was a wait in the game. However, another score soon came, Russell running in at the corner after a series of short passes. The goal-kick failed. After a spell of even play the Colonials took up the running again, and Barnett was credited with a try, though the final pass appeared to be a forward one. No goal resulted.

At half-time the Wallabies led 11-0. Early in the second half Berry was injured and had to retire for a while for attention by the ambulance men, but:

With only seven men in the pack Gloucestershire played up strongly, and Gent by smart work fed Hudson, who sent to Neale. The latter brilliantly eluded his opponents and cross-kicked, but V Eberle just failed to get up in time. Another pretty movement gave Neale possession, and the ex-Bristolian put in a dashing run down touch, but succumbed to Carmichael, who knocked his opponent out in the tackle. There was a stoppage whilst attention was given to Neale, who was unable to resume. Berry came out to three-quarter when play was continued. The Colonials at once made headway and in quick succession two players were laid out with heavy tackles. Both were able to continue after a slight delay.

One or two of the referee's decisions were unfavourably received:

In the Gloucester 25 a visitor broke away cleverly, and secured a nice opening for Wood, who ran over behind the posts. The transfer looked perilously like forward, and there was a loud shout from the spectators as to the legitimacy of the point, but it was allowed and a goal resulted. The visitors called forth shouts from the crowd for a foul of Gent, when the little half-back was dribbling, but the referee took no notice of the incident.
Just after Gloucestershire started an attack, in which several players took part, but at the critical moment the passing failed. Gloucestershire continued to hold their own splendidly, and were lasting quite as well as their opponents. Elliott, V Eberle and Hudson took part in a smart movement which led to the Wallabies being forced to defend. Encouraged by this effort the home team played desperately and Johns nearly succeeded in doing the trick. The Colonials tried hard to relieve, but they were beaten back and Russell just saved in the nick of time. For lying on the ball Russell was penalised, but Elliott failed with a shot at goal, a minor resulting.

The crowd groaned at him missing an easy kick and that proved to be Gloucestershire's last chance. The Morning Post summarised the game as follows:

As a rule the luck of the game goes with the winning team, and Gloucestershire had to mourn the unkindness of fortune. The side had to put up with the worst of the luck in official decisions, and then, in the second half, Neale, the right three-quarter back, was injured and had to be carried off the field. Neale had been playing quite a fine game on the right wing outside to Hudson, the English International; and to make good this vacancy on the three-quarter line Gloucestershire brought Berry, a very fine forward, from the scrummage. It was the Hudson and Neale wing that had occasionally promised to turn the game against the Australians; and Neale's loss was irreparable. The other wing - V F and E F Eberle – was the weak point in the Gloucestershire game; it was weak alike in attack and defence; and Elliott, the outside half to Gent, was also poor. It was this left wing that let in Russell for the first two Australian tries. There was a bout of passing that led up to the first try; but otherwise the lack of organised movement was always obvious. Gloucestershire, apart from the scoring of points, had little the worse of the play in the first half and in the second half the county had again a good share of the football, though it lost Neale as well as having Berry off the field for some time with a cut head. In tackling the Gloucestershire men were not nearly so efficient as the Australians. Otherwise there was not much to choose between the two packs. Gloucestershire stuck to their game to the very end, and on the hot afternoon the men were no more punished than were the Australians.

During their tour the Wallabies played 31 matches, winning 25 and losing 5. They also won gold medals for rugby at the London Olympic Games of 1908, beating Cornwall, the reigning English County Champions, 32-3 in the only match of the competition. All the other nations had either declined or withdrawn, leaving these two to play out the final on a pitch beside the Olympic swimming pool at the White City stadium, with mattresses alongside and netting over the pool to prevent injury and drowning.

First Rendition of the Marseillaise

Gloucestershire 39 Racing Club de France 0
24th December 1908

RACING CLUB DE France, opened their Christmas tour with the first appearance by a French team at Kingsholm. The weather was favourable, and a large crowd greeted the teams. The Frenchmen, kitted out in pale blue and white striped jerseys, came onto the pitch to the strains of the "Marseillaise".

Gloucestershire: F Welshman (Gloucester); F Smith, W Hall (Gloucester), L W Hayward (Cheltenham), L Vears (Gloucester); W Dix, J Stephens (Gloucester); G Vears (captain), W Johns, H Berry, D Hollands, B Parham (Gloucester), W H Williams (Cheltenham), J Hyndman, J Watkins (Cinderford).

Racing Club de France: Burgen; H Combemale, M Combemale, Gaulard, Martinet; Decamps, Baudouy; Borchard (captain), Dedeyn, Guillem, Gommes, Gaudermen, Tricot, Bertbet, Vincent.

Referee: Mr F Abbey (Gloucester).

Racing Club soon showed that they were capable in the scrums and not afraid to give the ball plenty of air. However, Gloucester made early headway with loose footwork, before "Father" Dix, fielding cleverly, made a fine opening for Leslie Hayward, who received the ball on half way and raced home behind the posts. The second score was some time coming, but eventually Jim Stephens opened out, and Hayward found an opening for Lindsay Vears, who brushed off the full back and notched a fine try. Then Dix, "dodging and jumping several opponents cleverly, cleared all opposition and scored a good try". Just before half time, Stephens pounced on a loose ball and went over near the posts; Welshman converted to give the County a 14-0 lead.

In the second half, Gloucestershire turned up the heat. Although out-scrummaged, their forwards continually threatened in the loose, and their backs clicked well as a unit. The irrepressible Dix jumped over the French full back to score, Frank Smith intercepted and beat the full back for a try, and then Willie Hall put him in for another, before Dave Hollands crossed for the eighth. The Frenchmen tried desperately to break their duck before the end, but their only reward was to see Smith snapping up the ball and racing away. Burgen got a hand on his leg and brought him down, but could not hold him and Smith jumped up again and scored. Welshman landed his sixth successive conversion, and Gloucestershire had won by 6 goals and 3 tries to nil.

Scorers against the French: top left, Lindsay Vears; bottom left, Frank Smith; top right, "Father" Dix; bottom right, Dave Hollands [Gloucester Rugby]

County Matches 1907-10

Gloucestershire 6 Cornwall 13
5th January 1907

GLOUCESTERSHIRE HAD TO make four late changes to their line-up and Cornwall one. The Citizen reported that "the weather was dull, but the rain kept off. The attendance was rather disappointing, and was not up to the record of a good club fixture. The reason was not far to seek, for the County Union are not in the good books of the Gloucester crowd just now. The ground was in good condition, a drying wind aiding it considerably."

Gloucestershire: F Johnson (Stroud); A Hudson (Gloucester), W Hyam (Devon Albion), M E Neale (Bristol), F Smith (Gloucester); A Goddard (Cheltenham), J. Spoors; J L Mathias (Bristol), G Matthews, W Holder, G Vears (Gloucester), J Watkins (Cinderford), W Spiers (Devon Albion), A Teague (Cinderford), A J Gardner (Clifton)

Cornwall: E J Jackett (Leicester); B Bennetts (Penzance), Bert Solomon (Redruth), F Dean (Devon Albion), B W Lee (Old Leysians); F Brice (Falmouth), F Richards (Plymouth); R Jackett (Falmouth), J G Milton (Camborne School of Mines), H Roberts (Falmouth), N Tregurtha (St. Ives), N Howe-Brown (Oxford University), Rev J G Bussell (Camborne Town), J Thomas (Devon Albion), D Brown (Penzance)

Referee: Mr F W Nicholls (Leicester)

Cornwall monopolised the ball in the scrums, and only a forward pass prevented them from scoring, but almost immediately:

Brice sent out neatly to Dean, who ran to Johnson and handed to Bennetts, who raced over in the corner; Jackett failed at goal. Operations continued in the home 25, and following a passing movement Solomon received and dropped a lovely goal. In the home 25 Spoors broke away from a pass by Goddard, and transferred to Hyam, who came through and handed to Hudson. The Gloucestrian ran to Jackett and re-passed, and the ball coming back to Hudson,

Arthur Hudson, who scored a try against Cornwall [John Hudson]

the latter completed a brilliant movement by scoring in a favourable position. Johnson failed at goal. Exciting play followed in the visitors' 25, and Neale gathering cleverly made a brilliant attempt to score, but was stopped in the nick of time. Gloucester still pressed, but a big effort by Cornwall took them to near the centre. Here Hudson took a short line out, and putting in a short kick the ball was taken over the Cornwall line and Hyam touched down for a try.

Leading 7-6 at half-time, Cornwall restarted by battering away at a resolute Gloucestershire defence, as a result of which Spiers was laid out and had to be carried off the field. Thus advantaged, Jackett took the ball from a forward burst and scored in the corner. Play continued to be mostly in the home half and when Gloucestershire lost possession, Milton picked up and went over near the posts. Dean missed the easy conversion, but Cornwall had won the game.

Gloucestershire 3 Cornwall 15
20th February 1908

HAVING STARTED THE 1907-08 County Championship campaign unusually well, with good wins over Devon and Somerset, Gloucestershire suffered a heavy defeat, 10-34, at Redruth against Cornwall. This meant that a three-way play-off was required to determine the winner of the South West Group. Gloucestershire were awarded the advantage of playing at home this time against Cornwall, and chose Kingsholm as the venue. Just before kick-off a message was received from Neale that he could not get to Gloucester, and G Cook was drafted into the home side.

Gloucestershire: A E Wood (Cheltenham); A Hudson, G Cook (Gloucester), V F Eberle, E F Eberle (Clifton); A Hall, F Niblett (Cinderford); W Johns, D Holland, H Quixley (Gloucester), J L Mathias (Bristol), F Teague (Cinderford), J Nelmes (Lydney), A Redding, J Hyndman (Cinderford)

Cornwall: R Eathorne (Plymouth): F J Jackett (Leicester), F Dean, R Bennetts, J Jose (Devon Albion); T Wedge (St Ives), J Davey (Redruth); J G Milton (School of Mines), R Jackett (Falmouth), F Jackson (Leicester), J Thomas (Devon Albion), N Tregurtha (St Ives), R Lawry (Redruth), R J Wilson (School of Mines), R Davey (Redruth)

Referee: Mr T D Schofield (Welsh Union)

The ground was in excellent condition, and favoured a fast and open game, but the tackling proved deadly. Both sides missed kicks at goal, Deans dived for the line for Cornwall but was held up short, and Johns crossed the line for Gloucestershire, but was pushed back into play. Cook was knocked out for a couple of minutes, and Wood injured his shoulder, but both carried on, and Wood narrowly failed with a drop at goal before half-time arrived with no score registered.

The home side started the second half strongly, but Cornwall broke clear and Wood found himself facing three opponents – Jose scored and Jackson converted. The Gloucestershire wall had finally been breached, and two further Cornish tries soon followed, scored by Davey and Bennetts; Jackson converted both. A penalty by Wood with the last kick of the game was Gloucestershire's only reward. Cornwall, nicknamed "the Pasties", thoroughly deserved becoming South West Champions for the first time.

Alfie Wood, who kicked Gloucestershire's only points against Cornwall
[Ken Daniell]

Somerset were re-invigorated after the break and were rewarded when Ascott intercepted and put Timmins in at the corner. The momentum of the game had swung right round, and within five minutes they had scored again when Mapledorain secured the ball at a lineout and, although tackled, managed to plant it over the line. However, Gloucestershire struck back when "Gent, Stephens and Hayward combined in an effort which gave Eberle an opening. With a splendid dash the Cliftonian made no mistake and, beating Dyte cleverly, notched a splendid try." The game

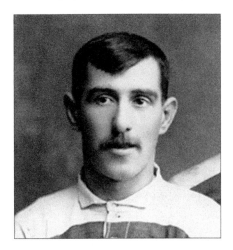

Jimmy "Jummer" Stephens who orchestrated the win against Somerset
[Gloucester Rugby]

was rounded off with a further try apiece. Moore passed to Stephens who scored in the corner and Hancock ran round to score behind the posts, but still Dyte was unable to land a conversion. So Gloucestershire finished winners by one goal, four tries and a penalty to three tries.

Gloucestershire 20 Somerset 9
5th December 1908

GLOUCESTERSHIRE STARTED THE 1908-09 campaign with a seemingly disastrous loss, 3-32, to Devon, but then played Somerset at Kingsholm and things started to look up.

Gloucestershire: F W Welshman; F Smith, W Hall (Gloucester), L W Hayward (Cheltenham), E F Eberle (Clifton); J Stephens, D R Gent; W Johns, H Berry (Gloucester), J Hyndman, J Wright, J Watkins (Cinderford), W Stinchcombe (Lydney), J L Matthias (captain), N Moore (Bristol)

Somerset: D Dyte (Taunton Albion); R Ascott, J T Timmins (Bath), L Marshall, P Fear (Weston-super-Mare); J Larcombe (Taunton), C O D Carey (Oxford University); F Dibble (Blaenavon), T Woods, E E Hancock (Bridgwater Albion), C Perkins (Weston-super-Mare), H Mapledorain (Taunton Albion), H Cunningham (Taunton), W Roman (Bridgwater)

Referee: Mr J H Miles (Leicester)

Gloucestershire started brightly and applied early pressure on the Somerset line, with Hayward prominent and Smith twice coming close to scoring, and Somerset were forced to concede two minors, before "from a line-out Johns gathered, and after a short dash passed to Berry, who brushed past Dyte and scored a fine try. Welshman converted with a splendid kick… In some loose play Watkins cleared and threw to Berry, who transferred to Mathias for the captain to score smartly." Berry had to be moved out from hooker onto the wing for a while when Hall was knocked out in a tackle, but he returned before half-time. By then Somerset had been caught off-side, from which Welshman kicked the penalty, and then "the Gloucestershire forwards rushed through in fine style. Stephens was following up and picking up cleverly threw the ball to Hall, who fed Smith at the right moment and the latter crossed in the corner." Half-time arrived with the score 14-0.

Gloucestershire 16 Devon 8
21st January 1909

A 14-6 WIN AGAINST Cornwall in the first County match to be played at Stroud, caused a three-way tie in the South West group, thus demanding replays. There were plenty of changes from the first encounter against Devon, and a foggy morning at Kingsholm turned into a beautiful afternoon for this first replay match.

Gloucestershire: F Welshman (Gloucester); E F Eberle (Clifton), L W Hayward (Cheltenham), F Holbrook (Bristol), F Smith; D E Gent, J Stephens; W Johns, H Berry (Gloucester), J Hyndman, J Wright, J Watkins (Cinderford), N Moore (Bristol), W Stinchcombe (Lydney), G Denley (Stroud)

Devon: F Lillicrap (Devon Albion); E Butcher (Plymouth), D W Twining (London Devon), G L Gibbs (Naval College), M Matthew (Oxford); S Kerswill (Exeter), J Peters (Plymouth); W H Pope, E Gardner, W Mills (Devon Albion), J Sandford, F Knight (Plymouth), Lieut Charig (Royal Navy), J S Huggins (Paignton), W Mann (Exeter)

Referee: Mr A O Jones

Devon had the first good chance to score, but one of their forwards fumbled the ball when a try seemed certain, and a penalty kick fell just under the Gloucestershire bar, Errors led to a fast and even half ending scoreless.

Eventually Gloucestershire broke the deadlock when Hyndman gathered the ball and passed to Berry, who rounded Lillicrap and scored a fine try; Welshman kicked the conversion. Devon responded immediately, and within three minutes were level through a try by Charig, and a conversion by Butcher. The home side started to apply more pressure, a Devon man was caught off-side, and Welshman earned the points with

F Welshman, who kicked seven points against Devon [Gloucestershire Archives]

a lovely kick. Desperate defence by Devon kept Gloucestershire out for a long period, until Butcher broke out, kicked over Welshman, and Mann scored to bring the scores level again. The Gloucester pack prevailed towards the end of the match, and late tries by Eberle and Smith saw Gloucestershire home.

However, the second replay, lost 0-11 to Cornwall at Redruth, saw Gloucestershire eliminated from the competition.

Gloucestershire 16 Somerset 8
20th January 1910

THE SOUTH WEST group of the County Championship had once more resulted in a three-way tie in 1909-10, so play-offs were again

required. Gloucestershire having already beaten Somerset 21-14 at Weston in their group match, the teams met again at Kingsholm. Played on a Thursday, the match coincided with a general election, but fine weather brought out a sizeable crowd.

Gloucestershire: W Egerton (Gloucester); C Kingston (Bristol), V Eberle (Clifton), J Spoors (Bristol), W J Vance (Gloucester); D R Gent (Gloucester) captain, J Stephens (Gloucester); W Johns, H Berry, D Hollands (Gloucester), A Teague, E Kilby, J Wright (Cinderford), J Nelmes, W Stinchcombe (Lydney)

Somerset: E Hartell (Bath); A Kitching, J T Timmins (Bath), H Shewring (Bristol), Lieutenant Wade-Gery (Bridgwater Albion); A Norville (Weston) A Hatherill (Bath); W H Thomas (Bath, E Cambridge (Bath), W Gibbs (Weston), P Down (Bristol), T Bailey (Bridgwater Albion), R Gilbert (Home Fleet), P Beard (Taunton), F Dibble (Blaenavon)

Referee: Mr Jones (Bridgend)

Good defence and final passes going astray caused several scoring chances to be missed before the Gloucestershire half-backs combined to put Eberle in for the first score, but Somerset soon responded with a try from Wade-Gery, and the conversion by Hartell put Somerset ahead 5-3 at half time. The game turned when:

Berry and Wright led Gloucester in a good rush, which was checked at mid-field. Gent here fed Stephens smartly, and the ball came along nicely to Spoors, who punted. Vance raced up, but the ball bounced the wrong way for him. Still, the Gloucester forwards came up and smothered Hartell, and the visitors were hotly pressed. Inside the Somerset 25, Gent and Stephens worked out a pretty opening, and Eberle receiving he dashed through and handed to Kingston, who completed a lovely movement by scoring a try. Egerton added the goal points, and Gloucestershire regained the lead.

Tries were then exchanged by Eberle and Gilbert, before Spoors followed up a kick by Kingston and scored under the posts. Hartell broke his collar bone trying to prevent the score. Egerton converted with the last kick of the game.

County Champions for the First Time

Gloucestershire 23 Yorkshire 0
9th April 1910

THIS WAS THE first time that these two sides had played one another in a full county fixture. In the early years of the County Championship, Yorkshire had been an almost irresistible force, but the schism in rugby in 1896 between the amateur Union game and the professional League game had robbed them of most of their best players. It took them more than ten years to recover, but they made it to the final again in 1910, having seen off Northumberland in the semi-final after a replay.

Gloucestershire had a very different record – since they had lost to Durham in the final at Kingsholm in 1902, they could boast only three wins in their group. Indeed they had a real struggle to progress in 1909-10; the South West group resulted in a three-way tie, which necessitated replays. The first was played at Kingsholm, where Somerset were defeated 16-8 (see previous chapter). Having won this match, Gloucestershire then faced another play-off against Cornwall, who had won the group game 11-0. Gloucestershire won a surprising and nail-biting victory at Redruth, 12-11, and thus set up a semi-final against Kent at Blackheath, which was also won narrowly, 6-3. The prize was a home draw for the final, which the County decided to play at Gloucester. In order to free up Kingsholm for the match, the Gloucester Club had to cancel their match with Plymouth.

During the run-up to the final, the Yorkshire club champions, Headingley, travelled down to Kingsholm to take on Gloucester, who were themselves the Gloucestershire club champions, having beaten Lydney 18-0 to win the county cup. Headingley triumphed 15-8, which did not augur well for the forthcoming county final.

A large crowd was anticipated, and nearly a thousand seats were provided inside the ropes. These proved a popular attraction at 2s 6d, but there was customer resistance to the 4s charged for seats in the grandstand. Later in the week the rows at the back were reduced to 3s, but even then there was not much demand. Yorkshire travelled down the day before the match and based themselves in the Ram Hotel. The weather was fine, this was the match of the season, the excitement around Kingsholm was intense, and the teams were greeted rapturously when they ran out.

Gloucestershire: W R Johnston (Bristol); A Hudson (Gloucester), V F Eberle (Clifton), J A Spoors (Bristol), M E Neale (Bristol); D R Gent (captain, Gloucester), J Stephens (Gloucester); W Johns (Gloucester), H Berry (Gloucester), D Hollands (Gloucester), G Halford (Gloucester), J Wright (Cinderford), G Bowkett (Cinderford), A Redding (Cinderford), H Uzzell (Newport)

Yorkshire: T W L Strother (Harrogate OB); J L Fisher (Hull & E R), F W Hinings (Headingley), W R Brown (Headingley), K Duncan (Otley); H Willey (Sheffield), F Hutchinson (Headingley); A H McIlwaine (Hull & E R), A Clarke (Skipton), H A Motley (Headingley), F Trentham (Otley), D Hellewell (Shipley), E Gaille (Headingley), N Ellis (Otley), Rev A Thompson (Headingley)

Referee: Mr T Schofield (Welsh Union)
Touch-judges: Mr S Tattersall (Yorkshire), Mr C E Brown (Gloucester)

Although Gloucestershire started wth a knock-on from the kick-off, they soon recovered, Jim Stephens threw out wide to Spoors, who cut through beautifully to the full-back, and Eberle was up to receive the scoring pass; Johnston converted and Gloucestershire were five points up in about as many minutes. The pack, ably led by Billy Johns, started to gain the upper hand up front, and Johns himself led a forward rush with Harry Berry, Wright and George Halford, which established a good position. This led to

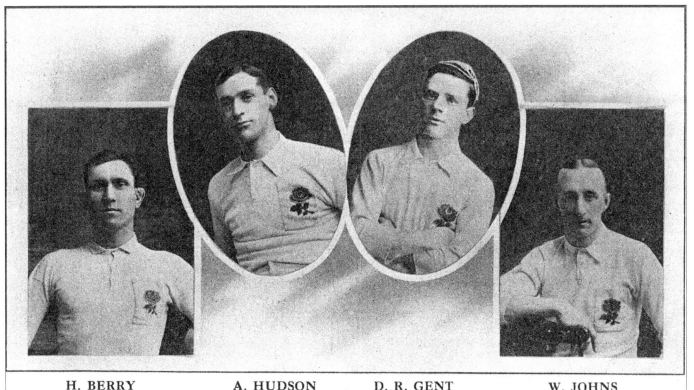

| H. BERRY | A. HUDSON | D. R. GENT | W. JOHNS |
| (Forward). | (Three-quarter). | (Half Back). | (Forward). |

Gloucester's four England internationals who helped Gloucestershire win a first County Championship [Gloucestershire Archives]

A commemorative collection of photographs, which was framed for display at Kingsholm:
1. Johnston, the Gloucestershire back, clears with a fine line kick after Neale had passed back to him on the line
2. A line-out in Gloucestershire territory
3. Mr E Temple Gordon (English Rugby Union), Mr Richardson (ERU), Mr C Craddock (Cheltenham), and Mr T Schofield (Welsh Rugby Union), the referee, have a chat at half-time
4. The Gloucestershire team and committee
5. The Yorkshire team
6. Spectators in the grandstand
7. A Gloucestershire forward tries to win the ball in a line-out
[CC&GG]

some smart handling by the backs, which left Arthur Hudson, the last to receive, with three men round him in the corner. Twisting and turning, he slipped over the line and scored a splendid try, which Johnston converted. At half-time Gloucestershire thus led by two goals to nil.

Early in the second half, Eberle made a brilliant break, and, faced by the Yorkshire full back, passed wide to Hudson, who did well to catch the ball with one hand, but this unbalanced him and he stumbled and fell with the line at his mercy. Gloucestershire kept up the pressure, and Stephens, who showed sound judgement throughout in his management of the game, dashed through, before passing wide to Spoors, who got into his stride, zigzagged past the last defenders, and raced round behind the posts; Johnston again added the goal points. Soon after the resumption Gloucestershire were penalised for pushing in the lineout, and the visitors had a shot for goal, but the kick was charged down.

Dai Gent was the lynch pin for Gloucestershire in attack and defence, and he cheekily pinched the ball from the Yorkshire forwards and fed Spoors, who beat Brown before handing on to Neale; he rounded Strother with a lovely run to score the fourth try. Gloucestershire were now playing magnificent football, the backs doing almost what they liked, and this led to the final try by Hudson, who had been playing in his very best international form – "keen, dashing and ever ready to make headway" – he sprinted in at the corner and then ran round behind the posts to make Johnston's conversion easy. Gloucestershire had won the game 23-0, and thereby secured their first County Championship. The win was hailed as "a brilliant wind-up to a season full of good things".

After the match, more than 100 sat down for dinner at the New Inn as guests of the Mayor of Gloucester. Sixteen speakers ensured that there was no shortage of toasts to be drunk.

County Matches 1910-13

Gloucestershire 13 Cornwall 17
3rd December 1910

THE FINAL MATCH of the group stage was played in front of a disappointingly modest crowd at Kingsholm and ended in defeat for the reigning County Champions. J Lane (Gloucester) received his one and only county cap as a late replacement for Wright (Cinderford).

Gloucestershire: W R Johnston (Bristol); A Hudson (captain, Gloucester), L W Hayward (Cheltenham), V Eberle (Clifton), M E Neale (Bristol); D R Gent (Plymouth), W Hall; H Berry, G Halford, J Wyburn, W J Pearce, J Lane (Gloucester), J Hyndman, G Bowkett, A Redding (Cinderford)

Cornwall: E J Jackett (Leicester); R Bennetts (Redruth), G Rice (Camborne), F Gilbert(Devon Albion), T Barrett (Redruth); T Wedge (St Ives), A Martin; R Jackett, F J Jones (Falmouth), A J Thomas, C Marshall (Devon Albion), N Tregortha, E White (St Ives), F Dean, A Elliott (Plymouth)

Referee: Mr Nicholls (Leicester)

Gloucestershire started brightly, with the lively Gent getting his back division moving, and both Johnston and Neale came close to getting across the line. But, against the run of play, Gilbert intercepted a pass from Eberle intended for Hudson, and raced away for the opening try; Jackett converted. Gloucestershire responded quickly; Eberle broke away and when confronted by the full-back passed out to Hudson, who raced round behind the line, but as he tried to get behind the posts the ball was punched out of his grasp and a glorious try was thrown away. Hudson soon made up for this blunder when he next received the ball and again used his pace to streak clear. Feinting to pass inside he utterly deceived Gilbert, then dodged past other defenders, raced round Jackson and scored a magnificent try, which Johnston converted. The home pack now rampaged down the field, and Hayward put Neale over for another try, which Johnston converted. But better still was to come:

From the next scrum the crowd were treated to a bit of the real unadulterated Gent. He beat Wedge and racing to Jackett kicked over his head, and catching the ball again before it dropped, scored a brilliant individual try on his own in the corner. It was great and the crowd rose to it to a man.

Gilbert struck back with a try on the stroke of half-time to reduce the deficit to 13-8, a sign of what was to come in the second half. A cross-kick by Dean gave Gilbert his second try in the corner, and a reinvigorated Cornwall created "a fierce and desperate game, the men playing like tigers". Total commitment led to Tregortha being attended to by the ambulance men and Neale being dazed by a kick to the head. But it was Tregortha who revived to dash over for a try, which put Cornwall one point ahead. Johnston was so badly injured that he had to be carried off, the referee assisting, and it was backs to the wall for Gloucestershire, but their defence was eventually breached when Wedge dodged over for a try.

Gloucestershire 8 Monmouthshire 5
12th October 1911

THIS FRIENDLY MATCH was advertised as a trial for County Championship selection, and the teams put on a fine display in splendid weather. It was noted that:

The teams had not met since 1881-2, when at Gloucester and Newport the games ended in pointless draws. The Monmouth side was considerably disorganised, and arrived one short, Λ. Robbins, of Cinderford, a budding player, turning out as substitute. The Gloucestershire side was something in the nature of an experimental one, for seven of the players were making their initial appearance in county football.

Gloucestershire: B Davy; H Hughes (Cheltenham), V F Eberle (Clifton), L Hamblin (Gloucester), C Kingston (Bristol); W Hall, W Dix; W Johns, S Smart (Gloucester), J Wright, A Redding, G Bowkett (Cinderford), B W Onslow, L H Peckever (Cheltenham), S A Dommett (Clifton)

Monmouthshire: T Norris (Abertillery); J James (Brynmawr), R Edwards (Newport), A Robbins (Cinderford), H Hirst (Newport); T H Vile, W J Martin (Newport); Jim Webb (Abertillery), H Uzzell (Newport), L Trump (Newport), E Stephens (Pontypool), Jim Foley (Brynmawr), F Hathaway (Pill Harriers), M Blackwell, W Hall (Abertillery).

Referee: Mr A J Parkes (Coventry)

Gloucestershire won, but:

It was questionable whether they were the superior team. The scorers for the winners were Kingston and Dix. The former got over after an exceedingly good passing movement, but the sensation of the afternoon was the try scored by Dix. Vile, the visitors' International scrum-half, got the ball from a scrum, and passed to Martin, only to find the leather intercepted by Dix, who scored brilliantly with it. Davy, who played at full-back for Gloucestershire, was not so good as usual, and it was through his slowness that Martin scored a very soft try for the visitors. The Cheltonian made a great mistake in waiting until the ball had bounced.

Eberle played a grand game for Gloucester at three-quarter, as did also Hirst of the losers. The Gloucester halves, Dix and Hall, combined extremely well, the latter delighting the spectators by his clever defence and overhead kicking under difficulties. Of the visiting halves, Vile was the better. Johns led the Gloucester forwards in his usual inimitable style, being well backed up by Redding, Bowkett, Onslow, Wright and Smart. Uzzell was the pick of the Monmouth forwards.

Gloucestershire 15 Cornwall 11
14th December 1912

GLOUCESTERSHIRE ARRIVED AT Kingsholm having already drawn 8-8 with Devon at Devonport, beaten Somerset 21-9 at Cheltenham, and beaten Hampshire (newcomers to the group) 9-8 at Portsmouth. Cornwall, referred to in match reports as the Pasties, were also undefeated, so this was effectively the group final. Heavy cloud threatened rain, but it held off to the relief of the crowd of 4,000, although there was a blustery wind.

Gloucestershire: W R Johnston (Bristol); W Washbourne, L Hamblin (Gloucester), S Cook (Gloucester and Cheltenham Training College), C Kingston (Bristol University); J Baker (Cheltenham), A Hall (Bristol); G Vears, N Hayes (Gloucester), C Merry, A Redding, G Bowkett (Cinderford), L H Peckover (Cheltenham), S Smart (Gloucester), W Bradshaw (Bristol)

Cornwall: M Lee; D Bailey (Camborne), R M Gent (Trinity College, Oxford), B Smith (Redruth), W Eustace (Camborne); R J Martin

Lionel Hamblin scored the try of the match against Cornwall [John Hood]

interval. Somerset struck early in the second half with another try, but Hamblin responded with the try of the match — he picked up a loose ball, punted high, chased hard, robbed the Somerset fullback, and fought his way over the line. A second try by Washbourne extended the lead, but Cornwall had the better of the latter stages of the match. Rich scored under the posts to reduce the deficit to four points, but the home defence then resisted everything thrown at them. This win took Gloucestershire into the semi-final, for which they chose to return to Kingsholm.

Gloucestershire 6 Midlands 0
30th January 1913

GLOUCESTERSHIRE AND THE Midlands were both undefeated in their respective groups of the county championship, and met in this semi-final to decide which of them would play Cumberland in the final. The match was played on a Thursday, but aroused a lot of interest and attracted a large attendance, who paid around £127 on the gate. With the kick-off at 3:30 pm on a rainy day, the latter stages of the match were played in semi-darkness. Only Johns and Redding survived from the Gloucestershire side which won the Championship in 1910.

Gloucestershire: W R Johnston (Bristol); W Washbourn, L Hamblin (Gloucester), Stanley Cook (Cheltenham Training College), C H Kingston (Bristol); A Hall (Bristol), J Baker (Cheltenham); W Johns, G Vears, S Smart, N Hayes (Gloucester), A Redding, J Watkins (Cinderford), W Bradshaw (Bristol), F Hopkins (Cheltenham)

Midlands: G E G Assinder (Old Edwardians); P W Lawrie, F N

(Redruth), F Rule (Camborne); R Jackett, W Rich, H Gray (Redruth), N Tregartha (St Ives), S J Kenley, E Gardiner (Devonport Services), C Lovelock (Camborne), C Marshall (Devon Albion)

Referee: Mr G I Evans

Gloucestershire played with the wind behind them in the first half. They took the lead with a penalty, Somerset levelled the scores with a try, but tries by Kingston and Washbourne built a 9-3 advantage at the

Scenes from the semi-final:
1. Mr V H Cartwright (English selection committee) has an umbrella over his knees, with Charles "Nobby" Hall, the former Gloucester and England player next to him
2. A lineout with Midlands nearest the camera
3. The Midlands scrum half breaks away from a scrum for a move which almost resulted in a try
4. Another lineout, with Sid Smart nearest the camera at the front of the Gloucestershire line, Billy Johns third and Hopkins fourth]
[CC&GG]

Tarr (Leicester), H J Pemberton (Coventry), S Farmer (Leicester); G W Wood and F M Taylor (Leicester); H Lawrie, W J Allen, G Ward, F Taylor, A Dalby (Leicester), W L Oldham, S G Wolfe (Coventry), F H Deakin (Moseley)

Referee: Mr L Bulger

Rather confusingly for the Kingsholm crowd, the Midlands played in cherry and white hoops. A greasy pitch and a slippery ball raised the error count, and several chances had gone begging before Gloucestershire opened the scoring on the stroke of half-time. Taking possession of the ball near half-way, Baker gave a clever reverse pass to "Tart" Hall, the ball then passing through the hands of Lionel Hamblin and Cook on its way to Kingston. The Bristol man cut inside Assinder beautifully, and running hard for the line, scored a brilliant try.

The Midlands pressed hard at the start of the second half, but the home defence held and when Tarr attempted to kick, the ball was charged down by Hall. Cook came through at pace, kicked past Assinder, raced to gather the ball again on the bounce, and with a determined burst got over the line and scored near the posts amidst tumultuous acclaim. Although the Gloucestershire pack were outplayed in the tight, they showed better footwork and speed in the loose, with Sid Smart to the fore and Billy Johns notable for his splendid dribbling. The ability of Cook to prise open the Midlands defence and the side-stepping of Kingston were constant threats, but it was perhaps the defensive quality of the backs which did most to win the game. The Midlands had the better of the exchanges in the latter stages of the game, and tested the Gloucestershire defence severely, but they were unable to force a score, and the whistle blew for a hard-earned but deserved win for the home side.

A month later, Gloucestershire travelled to Carlisle for the final. A couple of players were unable to travel because of work commitments, and two more missed the train after the overnight stop in Leeds. The kick-off was delayed in the hope that Gloucestershire could make a complete team, but they had to start one short and, playing into the wind, were soon under pressure, which was only relieved when Watkins finally arrived to make up the numbers. At half-time the score was 3-3 but with a full complement and the wind behind them in the second half, Gloucestershire gradually got on top. "Tart" Hall, who was to join Gloucester later that year, had a wonderful game, repeatedly gathering the ball from the feet of the Cumberland pack and breaking through to set his own three-quarters away, but several chances were spurned before two tries were scored in the last ten minutes, by Peckover and Kingston. Gloucestershire thus became County Champions for the second time, and it was very much a triumph for team work. Despite their success, this side contained only one current international, Billy Johns, and only one other, Sid Smart, who would later go on to win an England cap, but that also has to be seen as a comment on the London- and Oxbridge-centric international selections of this era.

Gloucestershire 3 Devon 3
1st November 1913

BOTH SIDES AWARDED first county caps to several players. Gloucestershire showed six changes from their Championship-winning team of the previous season and Devon brought Jago out of retirement to captain their team. The pitch was in very good condition on a fine afternoon and a large crowd attended.

Gloucestershire: W R Johnston; C Kingston (Bristol), A Lewis, L Hamblin, W Washbourn; J Baker (Gloucester), A Robbins (Pontypool); G Halford, S Smart, N Hayes (Gloucester), A Redding, F Russell (Cinderford), A Saunders (Bream), Private Nash (1st Glo'ster Regiment), Gus Carr (Pontypool)

Devon: Holman (Exmouth); E G Butcher, W R Lyle (Devon Albion), P Hodge (Newton Abbot), G Bickley (Exeter); R Jago (Devon Albion), W Mogridge (Exmouth); T Woods, J Wright, E Lee, W P Pope (Devon Albion), R Sharp (Newton Abbot), S Mogridge (Exmouth), R Jones (Exeter College), W Goff (Cardiff)

Referee: Mr T D Schofield (Welsh Union)

Baker was caught off-side at a scrum early in the game and from the resulting penalty Butcher put Devon ahead with a fine kick. A Devon forward soon reciprocated by straying off-side, but Johnston made a poor attempt to drop a goal. Robbins then made a good mark, but his shot at goal failed. The first score came when:

From a line-out Hayes broke away grandly, but was tripped, and Gloucester were deservedly awarded a free. Hamblin this time was given the ball, and with a superb drop kick equalised the points with a goal. Then Baker forced a minor with a kick to touch-in-goal. It was all forward work, however, and as a spectacle the match was keenly disappointing. At the interval nothing further had been scored.

Here followed some very erratic play, the ball being thrown about with a reckless abandon seldom seen in a championship. There was little of real interest, however, the backs scarcely getting a sight of the ball. Butcher failed to land a goal, and Robbins took a left foot drop for goal, the ball just dropping short and going over the line for a minor. The last five minutes were very exciting. In the Gloucester half Lewis snapped up a pass from Jago and secured a good opening. A pass to Kingston sent the right winger away, but though making a splendid effort, the Bristolian could not clear Holman. This was the last item of interest, and the game ended.

The Start of Schools Rugby

THE GLOUCESTER SCHOOLS Football Union was founded in 1897 and initially played Association Football, but in 1904 it switched to the Rugby code and rapidly flourished, making a mark both locally and nationally. A founder member was Eric Keys, who became the moving force behind schools rugby for fifty years. The first schoolboy match played at Kingsholm was a semi-final in the County School's Competition.

Gloucester Boys 0 Bristol Boys 5
12th January 1910

THE CROWD WAS described as a "fair attendance, in which the juvenile fraternity predominated". The Gloucester Boys played three half-backs and seven forwards and on their wing was a young Tom Voyce.

Gloucester Boys: Gough; Voyce, Baldwyn, Smith, O'Niell; Mullings, Pugh, Langford; Groome, Rigby, Gough, Hough, Mans, Melling, Morgan

Bristol Boys: Corbett; Dawe, Wilkins, Pollett, A. Vallis; Houghton, Williams; Pickard, Downs, Cossens, F. Vallis, Schonberg, Smith, Seager, Dite

Referee: Mr F Abbey

Gloucester started brightly, but the Bristol boys had the advantage in weight, and this told as the first half wore on. However, despite touching down behind their own line to concede two minors, the Gloucester defence held firm and fierce tackling kept the score sheet clean up to half-time.

The second half was largely a forward contest played in the Gloucester half of the pitch until:

Eventually after a good burst Pickard picked up and scored, himself placing a goal. Resuming, Bristol again attacked, and Vallis had a good dash for the line, but was upset, being injured in the neck in falling. He had to retire, and Bristol continued one short. Gloucester did better in subsequent play, but Smith twice failed to take his pass when there was a prospect of an opening. Bristol came again before the end, but there was no more scoring.

There were to be many more Gloucester Boys matches played at Kingsholm over succeeding years, but details of them are not included in this book.

West 9 East 3
4th February 1911

THE ENGLISH SCHOOLS Rugby Union organised this international trial match at Kingsholm. The teams and Committee were entertained to luncheon before the match, and tea after the match, in the Gymnasium at Kingsholm by Mr. H Terrell, KC, MP. There was a good attendance. The Citizen gave details of the four Gloucester boys selected to play in this match:

Thomas Voyce, centre, "of Gloucester National, was born in 1897. He stands 5ft 3 ½ ins, and weighs 7st 8lbs, and is, in all respects, a player representative of the good old City and the Gloucester National. He played for the City in 1909-10 against Cheltenham and Bristol. A strong as well as clever three-quarter; plays on the wing or centre. Has won prizes in swimming, and also gained a life-saving certificate. It is the hope of all Gloucester schoolboys that he will gain his cap this year." Tom went on to play for Gloucester, England and the British Isles as a

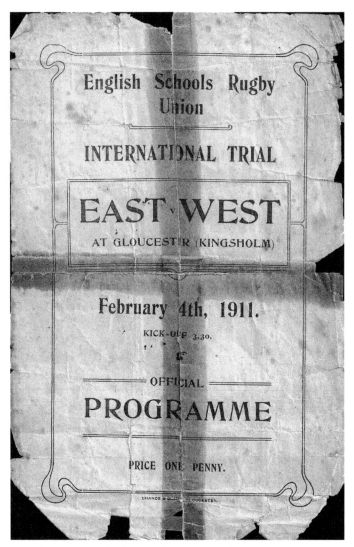

wing forward at senior level, and is arguably Gloucester's greatest ever player.

Sid Brown, left wing, "of the Gloucester Linden Road School, is a capital runner. He was born on May 7th 1897, stands 4ft 11 ½ ins, and turns the scale at 6st 6lbs. He played for Gloucester v Cheltenham, 1909-10, and was first reserve in 1908-09. He has won prizes in local sports, and in swimming has gained a life-saving certificate." Sid went on to enjoy a very successful senior career, scoring many tries for both Club and County, but tragically died of injuries received whilst playing for Gloucester at Kingsholm in 1926.

Albert Langford, "scrum half for Gloucester National School since 1908. He played in this position for Gloucester versus Bristol and Cheltenham. He stands 5ft 3½ ins, and weighs 8st. He is possessed of plenty of pluck and, with a good knowledge of the game, he is one of the best boys Gloucester has ever found. Very strong both in defence and attack, and can open up the game well. He is a Gent on a small scale. If there is a better scrum half in England then he is a downright good one."

Harry Terrett, forward, "a Gloucester Linden Road Schoolboy, for which school he has played for three seasons Born February 7th 1897; height 4ft 11½ ins; weight 7st 6lbs. Has represented the City at Cheltenham, where he scored. An exceedingly clever forward, with plenty of dash and pluck."

West: Corbett (Bristol); Wood (Plymouth), Wilkins (Bristol),

Voyce, Brown (Gloucester); White (Bristol), Langford; Terrett (Gloucester), Down, Francis (Bristol), Tovey (Cheltenham), Page, Toghill (Exeter), R Smart (Cheltenham), H Best (Torquay)

East: Norman (Leicester); Reading, Meisenheimer (Coventry), Tedds (Leicester), Holme (Rugby); Howkins, Butler (Rugby); Starkey, Fletcher, A Jaynes (Leicester), Mildenhall, Gilbert, Jolly (Birmingham), Coleman (Coventry), Gamble (Rugby)

Referee: Mr S R Carter (Rugby)

The match kicked off at 3:30pm, rather late for a February afternoon, but the West started the match with a bang, Brown feeding Wood who very nearly got over in the corner. "The West were working desperately now, and, going over in a bunch, Down was credited with a try far out." Terrett nearly succeeded with a drop goal for the East, but half-time was reached with the West ahead 3-0.

Langford punted ahead, but Reading just won the race to touch down. The East came back strongly, Jolly leading a forward rush to the far end, and Howkins nearly got clear, but Voyce floored him, only for Starkey

to gain possession, shake off a couple of tacklers, and score wide out.

The West, however, were not to be denied, and Down, receiving in the lineout, went over in the corner after a good burst. The West had the better of succeeding exchanges for some time, but it was too dim a light to distinguish individuals. Just before the end the West gave a real taste of their quality, showing passing that would have done credit to men many years their seniors. White and Langford opened out, and Wilkins and Voyce handled and passed out to Brown on the wing. The Gloucester boy beat his man very smartly, and running well, he got over with an admirable try far out.

Voyce, Brown and Langford were subsequently selected to play for England against Wales at Leicester on 4th March 1911. Langford kicked the drop goal which secured a 4-3 victory, England's first at this level against Wales. It was not until 1954 that the RFU first designed to allow the use of Twickenham for a schoolboy match.

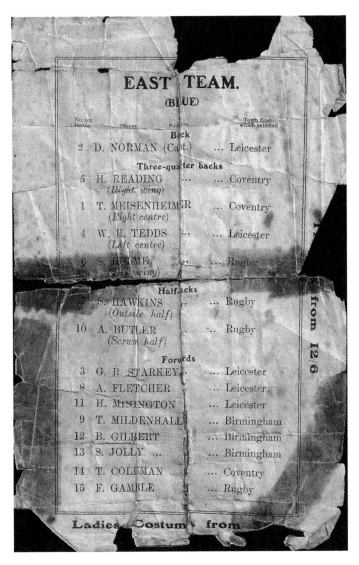

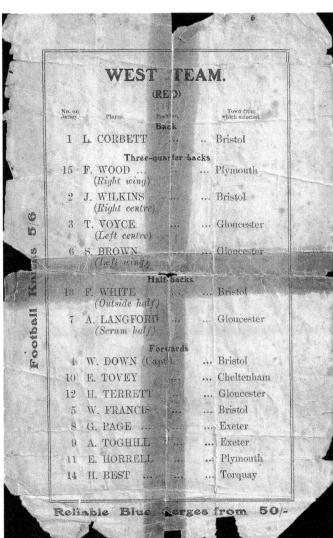

[Gloucestershire Archives, above and previous page]

The Great War

GREAT BRITAIN DECLARED war on Germany on 4th August 1914. All men on the Special and National reserves were immediately recalled to their regiments, quickly followed by the Territorials. A recruitment frenzy swept the country and most players from the Gloucester Club, and many of their supporters, signed up. There was also moral pressure put on sports clubs to cancel fixtures, and plans for the coming season were quickly abandoned. However, one match was played at Kingsholm between local military units.

5th Glo'sters 25 Gloucestershire Hussars 4
17th October 1914

THE ROYAL GLOUCESTERSHIRE Hussars (Yeomanry) challenged the 5th (Reserve) Battalion of the Gloucester Regiment to a game. Both units were based in Gloucester at the time, undergoing training. The Club made no charge in granting use of Kingsholm for the encounter. Admission was free, but the grandstand was reserved for ladies, officers of both regiments, and members of Gloucester RFC. Ladies carried boxes round the ground, making a collection from the crowd in aid of the Belgian Refugees' Fund, and a collection was also made for the Soldiers' and Sailors' Families Association. The 5th Battalion borrowed a set of Gloucester cherry and white jerseys and wore them proudly as their superior passing and running led to a comfortable victory.

5th Glo'sters: Lt Badcock; Privates Newman, Harris, Lane, Merrett; Cooke, Moore; L Smith, Lt Rickerby (captain), Privates N Angell, H Lippett, Bathe, Yeend, Bartlett, W S Robertson

Royal Gloucestershire Hussars: Troopers Baker; Norton, Corporal Smith, Troopers Church, R E Henley; Dickson, Purcell; Issitt, Grant, Davis, Bennett, Hopkins, Hayward, Huggett, Kelly

The military training which the players had been undergoing was thought to have improved their fitness for rugby. Both sides certainly threw themselves into the fray and the standard of play was really good. The Hussars had the better of the early exchanges, but the Glo'sters began to show better cohesion and scored first when Cook went over in the corner from a line-out. They soon added a second try, Badcock fielding the ball at the back and running strongly to beat several opponents before bringing the rest of the line into the move for Newman to score wide out. Badcock then made a fine sweeping run to beat all the opposition and score by the posts; Angell converted. There was still time for Cook to add another try to make the half-time score 14-0.

Early in the second half, this lead was extended when Moore broke away and, a couple of passes later, Lane went over. This was followed by a fine forward rush by the Glo'sters which took them over the line; Smith was credited with the try. By now the Glo'sters were having things very much their own way and from a scrum Moore broke away and passed to Lane who cut inside beautifully to score, Angell converting. However, the Hussars had the final word, C Bennett grasping the ball in loose play and dropping a neat goal.

Although many Gloucester players were in the 5th Glo'sters and continued to play rugby, most notably as members of a very strong battalion XV, none of these games were played at Kingsholm, although the team was proud to advertise its origins by playing in cherry and white jerseys.

Wounded Soldiers 9 Hospital Orderlies 3
22nd April 1916

ALTHOUGH RUGBY AT Kingsholm essentially came to a standstill for the duration of the Great War, this match was allowed in order to raise money for the Red Cross and to provide a bit of light relief in hard times. It featured wounded soldiers at the Western Road hospital in Gloucester and the Red Cross orderlies who looked after them. The Wagon Works Silver Band was there to entertain the crowd, and the Boy Scouts

The 5th Glo'sters team [CC&GG]

The Hussars in possession of the ball [CC&GG]

made a collection at half-time, which added to the ticket sales ensured that a substantial sum was raised.

The Soldiers team included George Halford, the former Gloucester Club captain. On the day their ranks were also supplemented by F Abbey, a leading Gloucester player, and Dr Arnold Alcock, a former international who would later become the Gloucester Club President. The Orderlies were also boosted on the day by the substitution of Arthur Hudson, the England and Gloucester wing. The Mayor of Gloucester kicked off in front of a large crowd, who enjoyed an entertaining game.

Wounded Soldiers: Cpl Morris (2nd Dragoon Guards); Pte Sheldon (RGA), Pte G Halford (1st Glos), Pte Bryant (2nd Lon San Sec), Pte Toombs (MTASC); Cpl. D E Blackwell (RE), A N Other; Pte Walding (RNL), Pte Starling (1st Glos), Bom Blakemore (RFA)(T), Pte Lloyd

(RWF), Pte Cook (1st Glos), Pte Berry (6th Welsh), Pte Davis (ASC), Pte Hughes (captain, Welsh Horse)

Hospital Orderlies: H T Shewell; H J Hodgetts, A Lander, J Tippin, J Carter; J Limbrick W Meek; J Jewell, A Blunt, T Barrow, A Margrett, F Simpson, W Drinkwater, W Gallen, E Tidmarsh, W Parsons

Referee: Rev O E Hayden

The teams were evenly matched and cancelled one another out in the first half, so there was no score at the interval. The deadlock was broken when Hudson made a strong run and, with the defence beaten, he passed and an easy try was scored. The Soldiers quickly equalised and a few minutes later added a second try. Before the end they scored a third try to seal victory.

Royal Naval Depot Matches

A SLIGHT RELAXATION OF the restrictions on rugby as the war dragged on, led to a series of matches against a side representing the Royal Naval Depot, Devonport. Arthur Hudson served in the Navy, mostly on submarines, but when ashore, he was based at Devonport, played rugby for various naval sides and organised the Depot XV which would play naval XVs every time a ship came into dock. He brought his side to play on his home ground at Kingsholm on three occasions to raise money for the Gloucester Royal Infirmary.

Gloucestershire 11 Royal Naval Depot 21
3rd March 1917

THE RND TEAM had played together for some time and this told against a scratch Gloucestershire side. However, the home side boasted three internationals amongst their three-quarters, Arthur Hudson, Fred Birt and Reg Plummer, whilst the RND ranks included several rugby league players. Fine weather ensured an excellent crowd, which included a large contingent of wounded soldiers. They were entertained by the Wagon Works Silver Band, and the Mayor of Gloucester, Sir James Bruton, kicked off. The match raised £45 0s 6d for the Royal Infirmary.

Gloucestershire: J Hall (Cinderford); A Hudson (captain, Gloucester & England), T Stone (Bream & County), F Birt, R Plummer (Newport & Wales); A Hall, J Baker (Gloucester & County); G Halford, N Hayes (Gloucester & County), A Redding, G Bowkett, G L Jones (Cinderford & County), A Ward, W Robbins, A Hewlett (Cinderford)

Royal Naval Depot: J Jarvis; A Hoar (Somerset), W A Davies (captain, Wales), S G Tovey (Monmouthshire), A W Ackroyd (Halifax, Northern Union); J Brittain (Leeds, NU) S J Budd (Bristol); H Snell (South & Devon), J Atkinson (Aberavon), T Williams (Swansea), E J Davies (Neath), H Reynolds (Stroud), J Urquhart, D Keift, W Luddington (United Services)

Referee: Mr A Brown (Gloucester)

Within the first two minutes, the RND kicked ahead, the ball was fumbled and Hoar dribbled over the line and beat Plummer to the ball to score a try, which Luddington converted with a fine kick. Hoar would have quickly scored a second but for a foot in touch. Gloucestershire fought back and exerted a period of pressure on the RND line, but stout defence held them out until the home forwards broke through en masse and carried the ball over for a try attributed to Hayes. Play was confined to midfield for a while until Hoar seized on a loose ball, dashed down the touch-line, exchanged passes and raced over for a splendid try. He was soon back on the attack and was brought down just short, but from the subsequent line-out, the RND forwards drove over for a try. Luddington converted and the RND led 16-3 at half-time.

The RND team had to play the second half without an injured Tovey, and Gloucestershire came back into the game, their forwards, with Redding prominent, dribbling deep into the opposition half, the ball being kicked over the goal line and Halford narrowly failing to touch down before it went over the dead ball line. Whilst the home forwards continued to win plenty of possession, their backs had achieved little until Baker, Hall and Stone worked the ball out to Hudson, who was off in his distinctive high-stepping style to beat Jarvis cleverly and score a try, converted by Birt. Then:

A kick down the field sent the ball to Jarvis, who ran across and started a passing bout. The ball quickly got out to Hoar, who, putting on full speed, rounded the defence and scored wide out. The visitors continued to press on the restart, and following a smart effort by Brittain, Hoar received and ran over with his fourth try, which Luddington goaled. A smart bit of combination between Hall, Birt, and Plummer, ending in the latter racing over for the final score.

The Gloucestershire team [CC&GG]

Scenes from the 1917 match:
1 – Baker gets the ball away for Gloucestershire
2 – In the front row are the RND team manager, Rev O E Hayden, George Romans, Sir James Bruton, and a wounded soldier
3 – A line out
4 – Spectators in front of the stand, including old County players A Joe Cromwell and B Bill Leighton
5 – Sir James Bruton kicks off
6 – A line out
7 – Old Gloucester players in Navy – A Pegler was touch judge
[CC&GG]

The RND team in 1918 [CC&GG]

Gloucester 3 Royal Naval Depot 29
26th January 1918

THE CITIZEN DESCRIBED this as "the most important Rugby match of the season". The Wagon Works Band played through the city as well as at Kingsholm to add to the sense of occasion. Arthur Hudson brought a strong side, containing several Rugby League stars, which had sustained only one defeat in twenty matches so far that season. Arthur played for his RND side on this occasion and they proved far too strong for a scratch Gloucester team.

Gloucester: A E Wood (Gloucester, England & Oldham); Capt Alec Lewis (Gloucester & County), E Hall (Gloucester & Coventry), W Hall (Gloucester & Oldham), J Stone (Bream & County); A E Elton (Coventry & Midlands), A Hall (Gloucester, Cinderford & County); Hayes, G Halford (Gloucester & County), A Redding, W Robbins, J Weaver, H Edwards (Cinderford), J Lane, Sgt Lee

Royal Naval Depot: T Campbell (Cornwall & Services); H Buck (Yorkshire & Hunslet, Northern Union), Rev T J Williams (Llanelly & Glamorgan), A Hudson (Gloucester & England), J W Todd (Wakefield NU); J Brittain (Leeds NU), S G Tovey (Bristol); D Hollands (Gloucester, Oldham & England), J Edwards (Plymouth), A Lawton (Services), G Reynolds (Stroud), A Nesbitt (Plymouth), A Cutler (Services), F Urquhart (Services), Eng-Lieut T T Murphy (Monkstown & Ireland)

Referee: Mr J B Minahan (Northampton)

The home team showed up well in the early stages of the game and pressed hard on the RND line, but "from a scrum Brittain broke away on the short side, passing neatly to Buck, who returned the ball to Hollands for the latter to race over easily with the first try". Gloucester got close again with both Lewis and Stone held up just short of the line, but the naval men continued to give the ball plenty of air, and were rewarded with three further tries. First Buck touched down when the ball went over the line from a loose scrum, then Buck and Nesbitt chased a kick ahead for the latter to score, and finally Stone was knocked over as he went to touch the ball down over his line and Brittain followed up to score. At half-time RND were 12-0 ahead.

After the teams had turned round, Gloucester again started brightly, Stone being brought down just short and Wood missing with a penalty kick. But E Hall was then knocked out in a tackle and had to leave the field, which caused Robbins to move out to centre. The disruption opened the floodgates and Hollands started a move which ended in a try

for Buck. Gloucester revived briefly when Stone charged down a kick by Buck and chased the ball over the line to score, but play soon returned to the other end where Hudson, feinting to pass, slipped through and scored his side's sixth try. The pace of Todd brought him a brace of tries and Buck went over for his side's ninth try to complete an easy victory, the margin of which would have been greater but for only one conversion kick succeeding.

Gloucester 5 Royal Naval Depot 14
15th February 1919

ON THIS OCCASION, the Depot were not allowed to play their Northern Union men (Buck Beames, and Robertshaw) owing to a ruling by the Rugby Union barring rugby league players from appearing against civilians, even though they were allowed to play against Union military teams.

Gloucester: L Marmont; Sgt-Maj Pugh, L Hamblin, Lieut MacMullen, Cpl Bishop; A Hall, R C Cook; N Hayes, A Redding, L Robbins, A Ward, J H Webb, J Reynolds, L Taylor, J Lee

Royal Naval Depot: Evans; Holt, Hudson, Jenkins, Mitchell; Budd, Hathaway; Roberts, Woods, Kieft, Atkinson, Nesbit, Vineer, Luddington, Edwards

Early on Hamblin appeared to have repulsed RND with a good relieving kick, but "the visiting forwards broke away, and Roberts receiving brought off a strong run and scored well out." Gloucester pressed hard but twice errors near the line denied them. "At length, however, the ball was got away to Hall, and the latter serving Hamblin, the old City centre dodged his way through and over the line with a good try. Pugh converted." RND came back strongly "and the Gloucester line narrowly escaped. Marmont and then Hamblin brought relief with fine touch-finders, and some fast play ensued. Cook serving Hall, the latter handed to Pugh, who ran and punted over Evans' head. Racing on, the Gloucester man again secured, but he knocked on in picking up, and thus lost a certain try." So, Gloucester led 5-3 at half-time.

Gloucester restarted in promising fashion, and held their own well for a while, but:

From a scrum Budd broke away and passed to Jenkins, who slipped past the defence and scored near the posts. The goal points were

The Gloucester team in 1919 [CC&GG]

A line out during the Gloucester v RND game in 1919 [CC&GG]

added, and the Depot regained the lead. The visitors were not long ere they added to their score. From a forward rush Marmont was hard pressed, and getting his kick charged down the ball dropped over the line, and Kieft was credited with a soft try. Gloucester struggled hard to effect a score, and twice the Depot line only just escaped, but just before the end, from a mistake by Gloucester near the visitors' line, the Depot backs broke clean away and Mitchell scored easily.

The Commonwealth and the Services

Australian Trench Team 50
Australian Flying Corps 0
15th February 1919

THIS MATCH WAS played as a curtain raiser before the Gloucester v Royal Naval Depot game reported above. It was also a trial match for the Australian team which was about to be selected to play in the Empire Services League Competition for the King's Cup, which included a match against the RAF the following month at Kingsholm. The Trench team had been very successful since coming to England from France and boasted Stenning, an Australian international wing who proved to be the star of the show with six tries. Up to this time, the Australian Flying Corps team was unbeaten and was drawn from units stationed at the nearby Leighterton and Minchinhampton Aerodromes in Gloucestershire. No record of the team lists has survived.

Stenning with the ball [CC&GG]

The game continued to go all in favour of the Trench team, and from a scramble near the line Quinn added an unconverted try; whilst a little later Stenning, after a splendid dodgy run, scored under the posts, the same player kicking a goal. Before the interval Stenning scored two further tries, the Trench team leading at half-time by 28 points to nil.

The Trench team attacked strongly on the re-start, and early on Stenning nearly scored after a splendid round of passing. From the right wing the ball came along to the left, and Hickey giving the "dummy" ran over cleverly, Stenning missing the goal points. The game continued one-sided, and further tries were added by Hickey (2), Suttor, Watson, Carpenter, and Stenning.

The Australian Flying Corps team [CC&GG]

Action from the game with the Australian Trench team in striped jerseys [CC&GG]

The Australian Trench team [CC&GG]

The Trench pack were noticeably more hefty than their opponents and secured a stream of possession, which was soon put to good use when Auglerzark initiated a passing movement, which resulted in Stenning scoring a try. Although the Flying Corps made a brief foray into their opponents' 25, the Trench soon got the ball back to Stenning, who scored another try and kicked a fine goal from a mark, all within the first ten minutes. The Trench pack then took over and Suttor picked up to run over beside the posts.

A line out during the Australian game [CC&GG]

Gloucester 12 New Zealand Army 15
22nd March 1919

ON A FINE but cold afternoon, a large crowd enjoyed a well contested match with plenty of open play. The New Zealand Army were running two first-class fifteens, one of which was playing Australia in the

Scenes from the New Zealand match:
1 – Some New Zealanders at half-time
2 – Hudson lies injured, having been kicked on the nose
3 – Spectators
4 – Spectators applaud Hudson's try
5 – The forwards wait for an injured man to receive treatment
6 – Reynolds coming across to tackle a New Zealander who kicks
7 – More spectators
8 – A rush for the ball, secured by a Gloucester player who kicks
[CC&GG]

Empire League, while the other played Gloucester. However, the side which appeared at Kingsholm was almost the same selection as had defeated the Royal Air Force earlier in the week in a friendly, and also disposed of the Canadians in the Empire League.

Gloucester: T Miller; C F Webb, L Hamblin, W Stone, A Hudson; A Hall, W Dix; G Halford, N Hayes, A Redding, J Reynolds, L Robbins, W Davies, W F Ward, L Taylor

New Zealand Army: H Capper; E Ryan, E Watson, G Owles; R Roberts, G Yardley; D Sandman; F Arnold, M Cain, S Standen, E Naylor, J Douglas, P Allen, A West, A Bruce

Referee: Mr A Brown (Gloucestershire)

Both sides missed a number of scoring chances in the initial exchanges, and each was forced to touch down behind their own line, but Gloucester generally had the better of it and deserved to take the lead. The score finally came when:

Intercepting an opponent's pass in the visitors' 25, Hudson raced to the line when he passed to Halford, who, however, was at once upset and the ball got loose. A Colonial picked up and raced back, but his pass went astray, and Hamblin, gathering beautifully, ran down and scored wide out amidst great cheering.

With half-time looming, the "Colonials" struck back with two quick tries, the first by Arnold after a loose dribble, and the second by Cain in the corner. Overall Gloucester could count themselves unlucky to be behind at the break.

In the second half, Gloucester started well, but were under pressure when

Well inside the home half Dix opened out, the ball in turn was handled by all the backs. Hudson was the last to receive, and the Old International, putting on his best pace, raced away in fine style. He cut inside the full back beautifully, and beating another opponent who had come across the field finished up a great effort by scoring behind the posts.

Hamblin landed the conversion to put Gloucester two points ahead. This lead was soon lost to a penalty by Capper, but the crowd was reported to be in a high state of excitement, and the home players responded with unremitting pressure. Hamblin dropped a goal ten minutes from the end for a 12-9 lead, but New Zealand were not finished. Two late tries by Capper and Ryan enabled New Zealand to win a thriller in the last few minutes by 15 points to 12, but the moment which lingered longest in the memories of the spectators was the magnificent run and score by Arthur Hudson. The game as a whole was described at the time as "one of the finest matches ever played on the Kingsholm ground".

RAF 7 Australia 3
29th March 1919

THIS MATCH WAS played as part of the Inter-Services competition organised by the Army Rugby Union between the "Mother Country", New Zealand, South Africa, Australia, Canada and the RAF for the King's Cup. Australia were clear favourites in the only game played at Kingsholm, having won one and lost one previously, whereas the RAF side had lost all three of their previous games. There had been a heavy snowfall the night before the match, but strong sunshine had melted most of it before kick-off.

RAF: Lieut W F Seddon; Capt G B Crole, Lieut G M Wrentmore, Maj L H T Sloan, Lieut W F Warner; Lieut H W Taylor, Lieut L Randles; Capt W W Wakefield, Capt G Thom, Lieut R S Simpson, Lieut D H Malan, Capt E F Turner, Capt Greer, Lieut Bates, Lieut H H Thesen

Australia: Capt N Beith; Sgt Egan, Gnr J Bosward, Lieut H R Pountney, Sgt D Suttor; Lieut S Ryan, Pte T Flannagan; Lieut W T Watson, Q-M-S J Bond, Pte A Lyons, Sgt R Bradley, Cpl V A Dunn, L Cpl Thompson, Sgt J Murray, Sgt G See

Referee: Mr R Pollock (Wales)

Australia threatened to score first when a forward rush carried the ball over the line, but Seddon kicked the ball dead before it could be touched down. However, they were not to be denied long and, following a sharp run by Suttor, he managed to release the ball as he was tackled, and Watson picked it up and went over for a try. The forwards then kept the ball to themselves for a long period, before the Australians opened out and a kick ahead resulted in a race between Suttor and Seddon, which the latter just won to clear. Ryan and Egan also came close, before a couple of good runs by Crole set up chances for the RAF which were squandered by handling errors to leave the score 3-0 at half-time.

The RAF passing improved in the second half and they equalised when "Crole galloped hard for the line. He tried a short punt, but the ball went into touch near the corner. The Australians cleared a few yards, but the ball being kicked into the open, it went to Seddon, who dropped a lovely goal from 40 yards range." Thus taking a 4-3 lead encouraged the RAF and when Crole was tackled near the line as he was about to gather the ball, Wrentmore converted the resulting penalty with a fine kick to settle the match.

Gloucester 8 RAF 18
5th April 1919

SEDDON, FULL-BACK FOR the RAF in the Empire League the previous week, was not allowed to play in this game against a club side because he had previously played Rugby League. A large crowd bathed in strong sunshine.

Sid Smart, who played his first game for Gloucester against the RAF after 4 ½ years of Army Service, having just been demobilised from the Royal Munsters, with whom he had been in Italy for 16 months, followed up with a try against Canada. [Gloucestershire Archives]

Gloucester: T Miller; A Hudson, L Hamblin, W L Stone, F Webb; W Dix, A Hall; G Halford, S Smart, Lieut T Voyce, W Davis, A Redding, L Robbins, W F Ward, J Reynolds

Royal Air Force: Capt I L Hamilton; Lieut W G Clarke, Maj Fuller, Lieut L Randles, Lieut W F Warner; Capt C Lawton Moss, Lieut H W Taylor (captain); Capt W W Wakefield, Capt G Thom, Lieut D H Malan, Capt E F Turner, Lieut R S Simpson, Lieut H H Thesen, Capt J P Findlay, Capt Copeland

Referee: Mr P R Clauss (Cheltenham College)

Gloucester were immediately under pressure and, when Miller misjudged his fielding of a kick, the ball went loose and was fed out to Clarke who dashed into the corner, but failed with his conversion. The RAF had the upper hand in the scrums but it was more even in loose play. Gloucester kicked out of defence, only for Fuller to catch the ball and drop a splendid goal with his left foot.

Restarting, the Air Force attacked strongly, the backs indulging in some good passing. Near the centre Dix got the ball away to Hall, who cut through and sent out wide to Hudson. The latter ran down to Hamilton and then passed inside to Hamblin, who completed the remaining distance and thereby put the finishing touch to a fine movement. The game was being keenly contested in the home half when Dix smartly fed Hall, who sent a quick pass to Hamblin. The latter cut through and handed to Stone, who raced away, and though tackled by the legs just outside the line managed to get the ball over — a very fine try indeed. Hamblin added the goal points, and Gloucester gained the lead. The Air Force soon got on the attack following the restart, and the Gloucester defence was sorely tried. It held out for a time, but Taylor, gathering in the loose, passed out quickly, and the ball travelled out to Clark, and the latter scored his second try.

This gave the RAF a 15-8 lead at half-time. Early in the second half, Hudson injured his leg and Warner his face and both had to leave the field for a while. Play continued vigorously, but fine tackling and errors prevented any further scoring except when "faulty play in the open by Gloucester allowed the visitors to dribble right away, and the home side was placed in danger. The position was saved for a moment, but another forward dash took the visitors over the line and Thesen was credited with a try."

Gloucester 21 Canada 6
19th April 1919

THIS WAS THE first of the Easter holiday fixtures, and a splendid crowd turned out. The Canadians, noted for "having several hefty men in their ranks", had been taking part in the Empire league, but were looking for their first victory in this country.

Gloucester: L Mormant; F Webb, L Hamblin, A Hudson, Sgt-Maj Pugh; W Dix, W D Stone; Lieut Voyce, A Redding, A Hall, H Robbins, W F Ward, S Smart, J Harris, F Mansell

Canada: Cpl Holland; Lieut McGrugan, Sgt-Maj D J Davies, Capt Grimmett, Capt Leall; Cpl Lee, Sgt-Maj S T Davies; Pte Hall, Sgt Light, S-Q-M S Shine, Lieut Wakefield, Sgt Macdonald, Sgt-Maj Nesbit, Lieut Wilson, Q-M-S Yeoman

Gloucester struck early when "Dix broke away cleverly, and passing to Mansell, the old Gordon Leaguer opened the scoring with a try behind the posts. Gloucester were soon off again, and after clever combination Hudson scored a good try". Hamblin converted both. "Subsequent play was very scrambling, the bustling tactics of the Canadians somewhat upsetting the intentions of the home players. Both teams appeared to be affected with the hot weather," and the score remained 10-0 at half-time.

There was no improvement in the standard of play on the restart until "the ball getting loose the Canadians dribbled away to the other end, where from a line-out one of the forwards secured and dashed over with a try." Gloucester responded through their forwards, with Robbins and Smart both scoring following a dribble and a line-out respectively. One of the Canadian forwards then scored from a forward rush which carried him over the line, but the game degenerated into a scramble, and the only further score came when Hamblin kicked a fine penalty.

The First Golden Age of Gloucestershire Rugby

WHEN THE COUNTY Championship resumed after the Great War, it ushered in the first Golden Age of Gloucestershire rugby. The intense atmosphere at Kingsholm inspired many of the heroics performed by the County team in this era.

THE 1919-20 CHAMPIONSHIP

THE SOUTH WEST group reverted to a foursome of Gloucestershire, Somerset, Cornwall and Devon. Gloucestershire's first match was a 3-3 draw against Devon at Torquay, which did not augur particularly well, but their two remaining group matches were played at Kingsholm, and things started to look up.

Gloucestershire 18 Cornwall 8
13th December 1919

A SIZEABLE CROWD INCLUDED the Mayor and Mayoress of Gloucester and the City High Sheriff. A surprise selection was Coventry in the centre for Gloucestershire, since he had played only one game of first-class rugby beforehand, when he had appeared for Bristol against Swansea the previous week, and clearly made an immediate impression.

Gloucestershire: B Davy (Cheltenham); F Webb (Gloucester), R C W Pickles, F J Coventry (Bristol), A Hudson; W Dix, L Hamblin; G Halford, S Smart, A Hall, T Voyce (Gloucester), M Shaw, J S Tucker, J Leahy (Bristol), F Fletcher (Lydney)

Cornwall: Floyd (Newlyn); Ham (Redruth), Williamson (Camborne School of Mines), Hammer (Camborne), Trewarthen (Redruth); Gibson (Hoyle), Rule (Camborne); Rickards, Harris (Redruth), Dunbar (Penryn), Harvey, Martin (Camborne School of Mines), Rogers (Camborne), Ellis (Hoyle), Wakeham (Camborne)

Referee: Mr W H Brown (Somerset)

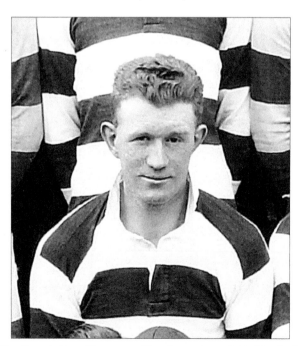

Tom Voyce, in his maiden season of first-class rugby, made his debut for the County against Cornwall in this match [Gloucester Rugby]

Cornwall proved to have a good pack, but were rather let down by their backs, who kicked continually and failed to create a single scoring opportunity. It was the Gloucestershire backs who won the game, with the Gloucester wings, Arthur Hudson and Fred Webb, at the heart of most of their best efforts. Tries from Lionel Hamblin and Hudson put the home side ahead, but a dreadful error let Williamson in for Cornwall before half-time.

Early in the second half, the Gloucestershire pack rumbled over and Smart was credited with the try. A couple of minutes later:

> Just inside the Cornwall half Dix got the ball away, and Pickles receiving cut through in brilliant style. Racing right away, he reached Floyd, when he yielded to Hudson, who scored in the corner – a very fine movement … Gloucester were in a dangerous position for a moment, but the forwards heeling, Dix and Hamblin opened out. Coventry getting possession, the young Bristolian brought off a fine run and pass to Hudson. The latter, however, being pressed, kicked across to the goal mouth, and Smart being well up scored the fifth try for the side … The ball was dropped and immediately snapped up by Pickles, who was through in a moment. There was a clear field with the exception of Floyd, but the Bristol captain putting on his best pace cleared the visiting custodian, and maintaining his lead, finished a glorious effort by scoring in the left corner.

There was much complaint amongst the spectators about the late kick-off, further delayed by the team photographs, which meant that this last try was scored in near darkness. Gloucestershire tried four different kickers during the game with a uniform lack of success, but it mattered not.

Gloucestershire 7 Somerset 5
24th January 1920

ALTHOUGH THE GATE takings of £370 exceeded those at the Cornwall match, they were less than those at the Club match between Gloucester and Llanelly a few weeks earlier.

Gloucestershire: G Welshman; S A Brown, A Hudson (captain, Gloucester), R C W Pickles, H Feltham (Bristol); W Dix, L Hamblin; S Smart, T Voyce, G Halford, A Hall, A Ward (Gloucester), M Shaw, J S Tucker, J Leahy (Bristol)

Somerset: C J Whittaker (Bath); R Quick (Bristol), J Jarvis (Bridgwater), N H Coates (Leicester), J Davidge (Taunton); H Vowles, S Considine (Bath); R Dibble (Newport), F Spriggs, A Spriggs, C Hawkes, W Fowler, J Reed (Bridgwater), T G Parkes (Taunton), J Pope (Bath)

Referee: Mr F W Jeffery (Plymouth)

Gloucestershire won the toss and elected to defend the Deans Walk end with a strong wind at their backs. They used the conditions to put early pressure on Somerset, and were duly rewarded when "Dix opening out cleverly the ball was handled beautifully by all the backs ending in Brown dashing over on the left - a fine try." The game was keenly contested without further score until close to half-time, when "there was a sharp pass out to Dix who, taking cool aim, dropped a lovely goal amidst tremendous cheering."

The lead of seven points scarcely seemed enough when the teams turned round, and after some heroic home defence Somerset broke through for Parkes to score near the posts. The successful conversion brought the lead down to two points, and Gloucestershire had to withstand wave after

Scenes from the match against Cornwall: 1. Three Gloucester forwards, from left, "Tart" Hall, Tom Voyce and "Biddy" Halford
2. Gloucester dignitaries in the front row of the pavilion - on the left of the post is the Sheriff and on the right is the Mayor
3. The Gloucestershire forwards in white dribbling the ball forward
4. Spectators probably on the Tump
5. Gloucestershire turning the Cornwall defence
6. Spectators between the pavilion and the gymnasium
7. Spectators in front of the pavilion
8. A lineout with Worcester Street in the background [CC&GG]

wave of attacks – Somerset "made prodigious efforts to score. The last few minutes were contested amidst great excitement, but the home defence rose to the occasion, and there was no further scoring."

Gloucestershire thus won the South West Group, and their reward was a semi-final against East Midlands at Northampton, which resulted in a fine away win, 16-11. Nine Gloucester players – A Hudson, F Webb, W Dix, T Millington, G Halford, S Smart, A Hall, F Ward and F Ayliffe – were selected for the final at Bradford against Yorkshire. Tom Millington made his debut for the County, Arthur Hudson was captain but sustained an injury during the match which ended his playing career, and Fred Webb injured his knee, but remained on the field because replacements were not allowed. Despite these difficulties, Gloucestershire dominated the match and ran out 27-3 winners. Fred Webb even managed to score a try on his one good leg. County Champions for the third time, Gloucestershire had a winning combination of skilful and speedy backs and a fearsomely strong pack. Unlike the 1913 side, it contained seven present or future internationals, which was a clear sign that the Great War had caused some change in attitudes and weakened class and geographic prejudice in terms of selection for the national team.

Gloucestershire, the 1920 County Champions, outside the New Inn, Gloucester
[Gloucester Rugby]

THE 1920-21 CHAMPIONSHIP

Gloucestershire 15 Devon 3
6th November 1920

THE WEATHER WAS gloriously fine, the ground was in perfect condition, and eight Gloucester players were selected for the reigning champions, all of which bolstered the gate takings to £477.

Gloucestershire: B Davy (Cheltenham); H Feltham, R C W Pickles (captain), L J Corbett, T Spoors (Bristol); W Dix, T Millington (Gloucester); G Halford, S Smart, A Hall, W F Warde, F W Ayliffe, T Voyce (Gloucester), J S Tucker, P F Williams (Bristol)

Devon: Knapman (Torquay Athletic); E Butcher (Plymouth Albion), Weir (United Services), Bickle (Plymouth), F Bradford (Exmouth); Smith (Teignmouth), Fast (Plymouth Albion); Wright, Sloman, Boddy (Plymouth Albion), Edwards (United Services), Bawden (Brixham), Ball, Gempton (Teignmouth), Lawes (Torquay Athletic)

Referee: Mr H J Burge (Somerset)

"The visitors, a big-looking lot, took the field first", but it was Gloucestershire who took the lead with a goal kicked by Voyce, when Devon were penalised at a scrum. The home side added two tries before half-time, the first coming from smart work by Dix, who transferred quickly to Millington, who handed on to Pickles, who scored in the corner after a strong burst. Several further promising attacks just fell short, before Dix was gifted a try when Corbett kicked across to the opposite wing, where a defender missed the ball and Dix was left to stroll over. Thus the lead was 9-0 at half-time.

A brilliant burst by Voyce carrying the ball for thirty yards was carried on by Halford, who threw the ball wide to Feltham, who sprinted over for a fine try in the corner. Dix then bamboozled his opponents and fed Spoors on the left wing; he raced clean away, but the referee's whistle went for a forward pass and another scoring chance was lost for an off-side decision. However, Dix soon set his backs in motion again, Pickles made a brilliant break, and Corbett was on hand to score a sparkling try. An off-side decision against a Gloucestershire forward allowed Butcher to kick the goal which prevented a whitewash.

Next came two tricky away fixtures. There were nine Gloucester players in the team against Somerset, who were seen off fairly easily, 20-0, at Bath. George Halford scored a try; Tom Voyce added another and kicked a conversion. Next up were Cornwall at Camborne, a tough proposition. In a dramatic finish to the game, Gloucestershire scored a magnificent try right on the stroke of time to snatch victory, 9-6. This won the South West Group, and secured a semi-final against the winners of the South Group, which was played at Kingsholm.

Gloucestershire 21 Surrey 3
17th February 1921

ALTHOUGH THE TWO counties had met previously in friendlies, this match was the first time that they had confronted one another in the County Championship. Gloucester again supplied nine of the home team, with W F Warde left out, and Stanley Cook brought in at centre. It was largely a case of the Gloucester pack and half-backs providing the ball to the Bristol backs. Great pride was taken in the fact that all fifteen players were born and bred in Gloucestershire, except for Reg Pickles, the captain, who was born in Somerset. This contrasted with the Surrey team, in which not one of their star international players, drawn from all four home nations, had been born in the county, and qualified only by reason of residence.

The match was played on a Thursday afternoon, which was seen as an advantage, with half-day closing of shops in the City allowing many to attend who could not get to Kingsholm on a Saturday. The match was seen as such a major event that the major works in Gloucester closed for the day. Fine weather also helped to boost the attendance, which was estimated at over 10,000, and £850 was taken on the gate. The spectators were entertained before kick-off by the Wagon Works Silver Band.

Gloucestershire: R C Pickles (captain); H Feltham (Bristol), S Cook (Gloucester), L J Corbett, T Spoors (Bristol); W Dix, T Millington; G Halford, A T Voyce, S Smart, F Ayliffe, A Hall, J Harris (Gloucester), J S Tucker, P J Williams (Bristol)

Surrey: H van Heerden (Guy's Hospital); C N Lowe (Blackheath), A R Aslett (Army), A L Gracie (Harlequins), W C Wilkins (London Welsh); V G Davies (Harlequins), J R B Worton (RMC Sandhurst); W D Doherty, A H Shelswell (Guy's Hospital), C Shaw (St Bartholomews Hospital), L G Brown (Blackheath), C L Marburg (London Scottish), C F Hallaran (United Services), E H Fouraker (Harlequins), C W R Francis (Streatham)

Referee: Mr A E Freethy (Neath)

Early in the game Millington fed Cook, who whipped out a long pass to Spoors on the wing to run in the first try for the home team. Cook proved to be an inspired selection, and was soon in action again, when he received a pass, sold the dummy, and cut inside to score a lovely try, much appreciated by the enthusiastic crowd. He then made a smother tackle to snuff out a Surrey threat, before making a wonderful run which took him so far ahead of his support that his pass went to ground. Gloucestershire kept up the pressure, but there was no addition to their

A scene from the Surrey match: Feltham has the ball and is about to pass to Voyce [CC&GG]

10-0 lead before half-time.

In the second half, Gloucestershire stayed on the front foot, and a sweeping attack by their backs was halted only five yards short. Surrey heeled the ball at the ensuing scrum, but little "Father" Dix darted round, picked up the ball under the nose of his opposite number, and plunged over the line for a try. The crowd went wild for their local favourite, who continued to entertain them, and baffle the opposition, with a series of reverse passes. Stanley Cook continued to have a big influence in the game, and was instrumental in Gloucestershire gaining good position, from which Tom Millington got over the line but was called back for an infringement.

However, the home side was now in full flow, and a beautiful combined movement by the backs put Spoors over in the corner. Even better was to come when the Surrey defence was shredded as the ball went from Dix, via Millington, Cook and Corbett to Feltham on the wing, who then slipped the ball back inside to Corbett for the final try. The backs may have monopolised the scoring, but the match was won up front, where the home pack shone in the loose, and also dominated in the scrums against a Surrey pack which had started the match with a high reputation.

Gloucestershire 31 Leicestershire 4
10th March 1921

WITH HOME ADVANTAGE, Gloucestershire chose to return to Kingsholm for the final, which attracted tremendous interest. All the seats in the grandstand were snapped up within a day of going on sale, and all reserved accommodation was sold well before match day. Complimentary tickets were issued to every former player with a County cap. Civic leaders from across the County booked their places, including the Mayors of Gloucester and Cheltenham, and the Lord Mayor of Bristol. In response to the overwhelming demand for tickets, the County Secretary, Mr R A Roberts of Gloucester, made extra provision at the ground, including additional banking at the Deans Walk end, which squeezed in another 3,000 spectators. The official attendance was 10,701, although over 12,000 were reckoned to have made their way into the ground by one means or another. The gate takings were £1,041, a record for Kingsholm. The match was again played on a Thursday afternoon, it was blessed with fine, summer-like, weather, and the spectators were again entertained by the Wagon Works Silver Band.

Leicestershire, winners of the Midlands group, had defeated Yorkshire, winners of the North group in their semi-final, although many critics thought them lucky to do so. This was Leicestershire's first

season in the Championship as an individual county, having previously participated as part of the Midlands Counties side. Gloucestershire stuck with their winning combination of Bristol backs and Gloucester half-backs and forwards. The Leicestershire team needed no introduction to one another, being drawn entirely from the Leicester club, and included six England Internationals to Gloucestershire's three.

Gloucestershire: R C W Pickles (captain); T Spoors, L J Corbett (Bristol), Stanley Cook (Gloucester and Cambridge University), H Feltham (Bristol); W Dix, T Millington; G Halford, T Voyce, S Smart, F W Ayliffe, A Hall, J Harris (Gloucester), J S Tucker, P J Williams (Bristol)

Leicestershire: J Wilkinson; E Haselmere, Norman Coates, P W Lawrie, A M Smallwood; G W Wood, F M Taylor; G Ward, F Taylor, W J Allen, C W Cross, D J Norman, Walter Buckler, J Wickson, William Buckler (Leicester)

Referee: Mr Helliwell (Yorkshire)

As in the semi-final, it was the threat posed by Stanley Cook in the centre which stood out early in the game, and he was involved in the first try: "Dix again opened out in clever style, and Millington taking a low pass in wonderful style, there was a nice opening. Cook ran strongly, but when within half a dozen yards of the line he was pounced upon from behind. He, however, let the ball go, and Feltham gathering neatly ran over and behind the posts amidst loud cheers."

Williams of Bristol soon added a second, catching the ball in a line-out, and bursting forward, side stepping the full back, and charging over the line. The 10-0 half-time lead was well deserved.

The second half almost started in sensational fashion, Frank Ayliffe running straight up the centre of the field, with Voyce alongside, but the scoring pass was dropped. However, within four minutes of the restart, Gloucestershire had scored again when "Dix got the ball away sweetly to Millington, who sent to Corbett. The latter missed Cook, and transferred wide to Feltham, who being hemmed in, passed to Cook. The latter seized upon an opening at once, and, never being touched, scored behind the posts."

Gloucestershire were now doing all the attacking. Voyce pounced on a loose ball, which was quickly passed out to the wing, where Feltham raced round behind the posts for his second try. Reg Pickles' conversion hit the upright but bounced over. Leicester now looked a beaten side, and it was not long before Hall opened out, and, after some slick passing, Stanley Cook scored the fifth try. Pickles' conversion was disallowed because a Leicester man was judged to have touched the ball in its transit over the bar. Bristol and England's Len Corbett added another try, before Leicestershire finally made it onto the scoreboard with a dropped goal. But there was still time for Spoors of Bristol to run in a final try to complete a resounding victory. Gloucestershire had retained

Gloucestershire on the attack towards the Deans Walk end in the 1921 final; Stanley Cook has just been tackled, but released the ball to Feltham, who is shown outflanking the Leicestershire defence before running round behind the posts to score the first try of the match; note the dapper dress of the touch judge [CC&GG]

The Gloucestershire pack on the rampage against Leicestershire; from the left the Gloucestershire players in white are J Harris, J S Tucker, P J Williams, S Smart, F W Ayliffe and T Voyce [CC&GG]

the County Championship, and Kingsholm was the place to be.

For many years matches in the South West group often proved harder to win than some of the later encounters in the knock-out stages of the County Championship. So it proved at the start of the 1921-22 campaign, as Gloucestershire endured a very hard game to win 9-6 against Devon at Torquay, before beating Somerset slightly more comfortably 16-6 at Bristol. The deciding match in the group was played at Kingsholm against Cornwall.

A commiseration card produced to commemorate the thumping win [John Hudson]

Stanley Cook scores a try in the second half of the 1921 County final at the Worcester Street end; he is shown standing on his head as he completes a somersault after touching the ball down [Gloucester Rugby]

Gloucestershire 34 Cornwall 3
10th December 1921

GLOUCESTERSHIRE NEEDED ONLY to avoid defeat to progress from the group, and were criticised for selecting a team of old stagers, but a crowd of about 10,000 saw them run in nine tries.

Gloucestershire: R C W Pickles; T Spoors, L J Corbett (Bristol), Stanley Cook (Gloucester & Cambridge), H Feltham (Bristol); W Dix, T Millington (Gloucester); Major Roderick, A Hall, F W Ayliffe (Gloucester), P F Williams (Bristol), J F Lawson, G Halford (captain), A T Voyce (Gloucester), J S Tucker (Bristol)

Cornwall: E Wills (Camborne); A Gregor (Redruth), C Paul (Camborne School of Mines), L Hammer (Camborne), E Holman (Redruth); A Gibson (Hayle), H Ham (Redruth); W H Taylor (Guy's Hospital), J Campbell (Paignton), A C Groves (Redruth), W Biddick, T Harvey, J Boase, R H Selwood (Camborne), W Peake (Newlyn)

Referee: Mr R Fear (Somerset)

Gloucestershire lost the toss, but that was just about their only setback for the whole match. Early play was confined to the Cornish half, where Millington gathered a difficult pass beautifully and passed on to Corbett, who handed to Cook. He sold a dummy and cut through before feeding Feltham, who dodged finely, and finished a lovely movement by scoring a try within four minutes of the start. Dix soon initiated another delightful movement by the Gloucestershire backs, and when a pass failed to go to hand, Voyce was up in support to pluck the ball from the ground and dash over behind the posts. Cook then came into the picture with a superb run and pass to Corbett, who dashed ahead, but his transfer to Spoors went astray, and Ham gathering he passed to Hammer, who raced away along the touch-line for half the length of the

field and scored a great try for Cornwall in the corner.

When Corbett was held up near the line, the home forwards took over and rushed in a body for the line, the result of which was a try to Roderick. Voyce and Millington were temporarily laid out in quick succession, but they were able to resume. Pickles added a penalty, and just before the break a succession of scrums on the Cornwall line led to Dix gathering the ball and beating Gibson and Ham to go over for a glorious

Frank Ayliffe, the Gloucester forward, who scored against Cornwall [Gloucester Rugby]

try, which built the lead to 17-3.

In the second half Cornwall were well beaten forward and unable to cope with the home backs, but Gloucestershire errors resulted in several spurned chances until a pretty spell of passing put Feltham over in the corner. With the home side continuing to give the ball plenty of air, Pickles added another try in the corner and then Voyce rampaged forty yards and the ball went via Lawson to Ayliffe, who went over behind the posts. Before the end Lawson and Voyce added further tries for a massive win, which would have been even greater with more accurate kicking – Millington and Pickles managed only one conversion each and Pickles one penalty.

This earned Gloucestershire a semi-final against Surrey at Richmond. In front of only about 2,000 spectators, the two teams slugged out a draw, 8-8. Kingsholm hosted the replay.

The Gloucestershire team being led out from the changing rooms in the gymnasium by their captain, Corbett [CC&GG]

University & Gloucester), H Feltham (Bristol); W Dix, T Millington; G Halford, T Voyce, F W Ayliffe, A Hall, S Smart, Major Roderick (Gloucester), J S Tucker, P J Williams (Bristol)

Surrey: R H King (Harlequins); E M Saunders (Rosslyn Park), C A Williams (Streatham), E Hammett (Blackheath & England), D B Anderson (Old Millhillians); V G Davies (Harlequins & England), J B Worton (Harlequins); G T Cockerill (Old Blues), E S Francis (Streatham), A F Blakiston (Blackheath & England), J C Connell (Harlequins), G G King (London Scottish), G E Middleditch (Old Blues), J A Rowe (Streatham), J E Cummings (London Scottish)

Referee: Mr E Roberts (Llanelly)

Gloucestershire put the first points on the board when Dix got the ball away on the short side of a scrum to Evans, who dashed up the touch line and punted ahead. Racing up he beat King to the ball and scored. Voyce and Halford were prominent in forward rushes which made plenty of ground, and they gained position from which Sam Tucker, the Bristol and England hooker, gathered from a line-out and tore away, before slipping a pass to Voyce, who had a clear field ahead of him, shook off a would-be tackler from behind, and dashed over the try line wide out. Surrey briefly threatened, but Gloucestershire soon struck again, Halford, Tucker, and Ayliffe combining in a brilliant passing move, before Dix and Millington broke away from a scrum thanks to quick inter-passing, and Dix dived over to loud acclaim from the jubilant crowd. Half-time arrived with the home side nine points to the good.

Gloucestershire cut loose in the second half. After Surrey had missed with a penalty kick in front of the posts, Dix and Millington combined to send Corbett over for a try. Then Cook darted clear, beat the defence with a marvellous run, and finished up scoring a great try behind the posts amidst terrific cheering, which was renewed when Dix added the goal points. The game was now won, but there was no letting up, and Dix, Millington, Cook and Corbett whipped the ball out to Evans, who rounded King to score again. The spectators were in heaven when superb movements led to further tries for Dix and Cook, both converted by Dix, and Gloucestershire had won a famous and resounding victory.

Gloucestershire had to travel to Villa Park for the final against North Midlands. This was the first time a Rugby Union game had been played on the ground. The Gloucestershire side were hugely more experienced in playing rugby at this level, and won easily, 19-0, with tries from Spoors, Ayliffe, Corbett and Dix, a conversion by Millington, and a conversion and a penalty by Pickles. Gloucestershire were the Champion County for the third season in succession.

Three England Internationals who played in this match; Blakiston and Hammett on either side of Voyce [CC&GG]

Gloucestershire 30 Surrey 0
16th February 1922

SURREY HAD TO travel without three of their international stars, but brought in two others, Hammett and Blakiston. They played for Blackheath, but qualified by virtue of residence in an adjoining county.

Gloucestershire: A J Kerwood (Gloucester); D Evans (Bristol University), L J Corbett (Bristol captain), Stanley Cook (Cambridge

Scenes from the replay against Surrey:
1. "Father" Dix is receiving the pass from Tom Millington, from which he scored the final try of the first half at the Deans Walk end;
2. Tom Voyce is shown with the ball shortly before scoring the second try of the match [CC&GG]

Gloucestershire, crowned 1922 County Champions at Villa Park [CC&GG]

All Blacks Tested

Gloucestershire 0 New Zealand 6
25th September 1924

WHEN NEW ZEALAND returned to these shores, it was decided to offer stiffer resistance by playing the County against them rather than the Club side, which had been well beaten in 1905. However, the Gloucester pack, which had scrummaged the County to so much glory after the Great War, was no more, and their replacements seemed to lack weight as well as experience. On the same day as this match, the British Isles team played the last fixture of their tour of South Africa, which denied Gloucestershire the services of Tom Voyce.

Gloucestershire selected only seven forwards in a formation which more closely resembled that adopted by New Zealand at the time. Every commentator predicted that the home side was doomed against an All Blacks side which had impressed from the start of their tour. This was their fourth match and they had already beaten Devon, Cornwall and Somerset without conceding a point. Rain fell incessantly for 12 hours before the match and the weather continued to be foul during it. The Kingsholm surface cut up badly and the ball was greasy and heavy, which greatly detracted from the standard of play and ensured forward domination.

The New Zealand team [CC&GG]

The Gloucestershire team [CC&GG]

Gloucestershire: T Millington (Gloucester); S A Brown (Gloucester), L J Corbett, R C Pickles, T Spoors (Bristol); G G C Taylor (Gloucester), C B Carter (Bristol) G Thomas (Gloucester); M V Shaw, A S Prowse, A T Hore (Bristol), S Preece (Bream), G Dubberley (Cinderford), S Bayliss (Gloucester), A R Rickards (Cardiff)

New Zealand: G Nepia; G Hart, R W Brown F W Lucas; N P McGregor M Nicholls; W Dalley, C G Porter; M Brownlie, J Richardson, R Stewart, G Donald, L Cupples, W R Irvine, L H Harvey
Referee: Mr R Fear

The All Blacks perform the haka before the kick-off [CC&GG]

The misgivings about the prospects of the home side were reinforced soon after kick-off, with New Zealand soon on the attack. Millington was swept aside as the ball went over the home line and Donald fell on it for a try wide out; Nepia's attempt to convert failed. Donald soon turned from hero to villain, when he received a stern lecture from the referee for a heavy tackle on Shaw. Gloucestershire were forced into spending almost all their time and energy in tackling, which they did heroically, but play was confined to their half. On the rare occasions when they managed to mount an attack, they found Nepia immaculate in his defence at the back, often returning kicks with added interest. The All Blacks came close to a second score when Nepia had a penalty shot which appeared to clear the cross-bar, but it was disallowed for reasons which were not immediately apparent, although it was presumed that the referee judged it to have been touched in flight. New Zealand dominated the lineouts and had a stream of possession, but a forward pass and a dropped ball came to Gloucestershire's aid when tries seemed certain. The Gloucestershire men managed not a single foray into the New Zealand 25 in the first half, but New Zealand failed to play the right game for the conditions – they over-elaborated and were called back for several forward passes. When the teams turned round one half of the pitch had been turned into a quagmire while the other half was still virgin grass.

The Gloucestershire team at half-time; note M V Shaw's tattered jersey…
[CC&GG]

...so Tommy Bagwell brings him a new one and something to drink [CC&GG]

Although New Zealand had the bigger pack, and Gloucestershire looked out-weighed and slow by comparison, they were winning the scrums and showed more fight after the break. The level of excitement rose, especially when Pickles kicked over the New Zealand defence and forced Nepia to concede a minor. It was "a hot and strong battle between the forwards", with the home forwards holding their own and winning a much better share of possession. However Nepia continued to put on a master class at the back with safe catching, quick clearances and long and accurate kicking, all the more remarkable given the conditions. `As the game wore on, a break in the rain seemed sure to help the All Blacks, but Millington made a fine tackle when a try seemed certain, and the New Zealand wings showed a remarkable propensity to knock the ball on rather than catch it when put clear. A couple of minutes from time, the All Blacks finally found a gap in the defence, which Donald was quick to exploit, the forward scoring his second try. Nepia again failed with the conversion, which was not surprising given that the ball must by then have absorbed so much water as to resemble a lead weight.

In the evening the Mayor of Gloucester, Mr Charles Gardner, hosted a dinner for players and officials in the Guildhall, before the visitors performed their war cry and dance, and were taken off to see a performance of "The Belle of New York" at the Hippodrome.

The match in progress [CC&GG]

The Jubilee Match

Gloucester 11 Capt W S Donne's XV 9
13th November 1924

THE PRESIDENT of the RFU, Captain W S Donne sent the following message to the Gloucester Club to mark its 50th anniversary:

A Club which has had an honoured career for 50 years, which has furnished its Country and its County with a host of great players, and which, for the best part of such period has been able, year in and year out, to hold its own with any opponents in the British Isles, deserves the heartiest congratulations of all the Rugby Football fraternity. Such a Club is the Gloucester FC.

He also brought a team of international and county players to Kingsholm on a Thursday afternoon for a jubilee match to celebrate the anniversary. There was a reunion of old players and officials at Kingsholm before the match, which was watched by a crowd numbering about 5,000, and the weather turned fine in time for the kick-off.

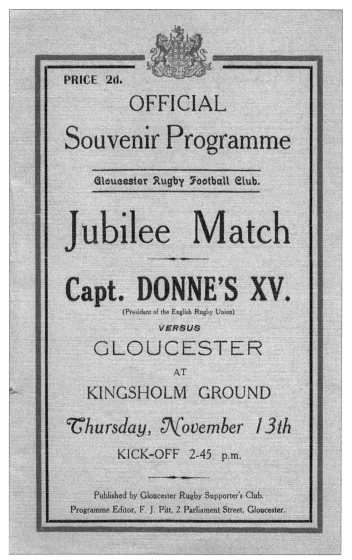

PRICE 2d.

OFFICIAL
Souvenir Programme

Gloucester Rugby Football Club.

Jubilee Match

Capt. DONNE'S XV.
(President of the English Rugby Union)

VERSUS

GLOUCESTER

AT

KINGSHOLM GROUND

Thursday, November 13th

KICK-OFF 2-45 p.m.

Published by Gloucester Rugby Supporter's Club.
Programme Editor, F. J. Pitt, 2 Parliament Street, Gloucester.

Gloucester: T Millington; S A Brown, G Beyers, H D Mackay, C E Macintosh; R Milliner, Dr Taylor; T Voyce (captain), F W Ayliffe, A Hall, F Ford, S Duberley, H Roberts, A Rea, W Hemmings

Capt W S Donne's XV: L C Sambrook (North & Leicester); H C Catcheside (England & Northumberland), L J Corbett (England & Gloucestershire), R Hamilton Wickes (England & Harlequins), R Quick (Bristol & England Trial); E Myers (England & Yorkshire), E J Massey (North & Leicester); W R F Collis (Ireland & Cambridge University), R Armstrong (North & Northumberland), H B L Wake (Bath & Somerset), F D Prentice (Leicester), J C R Buchanan (Scotland & Devon), H G Rew (Devon), J S Tucker (England & Gloucestershire), M V Shaw (South & Gloucestershire)

Referee: Mr A D Stoop (England & Harlequins)

Capt Donne kicked off and once his side had settled down, they looked the more threatening. The Citizen reported:

The City reached mid-field, but from a passing movement Corbett secured, and sent Catcheside away. Facing Millington the Northumbrian cross-kicked beautifully, and gave Prentice the first try under the posts. Armstrong missed the easy place. Resuming the Scratch side were soon on the attack again, and Quick ran and punted to near the line, where a knock-on occurred. From the ensuing scrum, however, Myers passed to Quick, who scored in the corner, the place kick failing.

Six points down, Gloucester restarted strongly, and near the centre Taylor intercepted cleverly, and ran to Sambrook, who tackled him. The Gloucester half-back, however, got the ball away to Ford, who dashed over with a fine try, which Millington converted, the success of the home side being loudly cheered.

Later the City pack heeled, and Milliner got the ball away to Taylor and Mackay and Beyers in turn handled. A final pass to Macintosh saw the Oxonian race past Quick, and go strongly for the line. Voyce had dashed up the centre, and the International taking the ball over the line, touched down for a splendid try. Millington failed at goal, but Gloucester had gained the lead, and the crowd cheered vociferously. Encouraged by this success, the Gloucester forwards resumed with great dash, and rushed their opponents right to the line. Milliner once scrambled over, but was called back, and Voyce was similarly treated a moment later."

Half-time was reached with Gloucester ahead 8-6. Voyce restarted the game and:

Mackay found touch a yard from the line. Gloucester tried hard to pierce the defence, but could not succeed, though Mackay, in a drop for goal, sent the ball under the cross-bar. From the drop out the Scratch broke away, and Catcheside brought off a strong run. This led to a sharp attack on the home line, and following a series of transfers Quick, though tackled by Millington, managed to place the ball over the line. Sambrook failed at goal.

Taylor, who was seen limping, now left the field, and Voyce came out to partner Milliner. The ball getting loose, the Scratch had a fine opening with Corbett away and Quick unmarked. The Bristolian, however, essayed the "dummy," which was not taken, and a certain try was lost. Dashing forward work gained relief for Gloucester, who were putting up a fine contest despite the loss of Taylor.

The end was near, and Gloucester put forth great efforts to save the game. Success came right at the finish, and was a fitting climax to a splendidly contested game. On the 25 line Macintosh was given possession, and the Oxonian, putting on tremendous speed, went straight for the corner. Corbett and one or two others tried to cut Macintosh off, but with a superb finish the Gloucester wing got the ball safely over the line amidst a tremendous outburst of cheering. The referee consulted Mr Gordon Vears (linesman) before giving his decision, but the "all right" was signalled, at which the crowd cheered lustily again. Millington missed the goal kick – a difficult one – but the score was sufficient to give Gloucester a two-points victory. Immediately the whistle sounded "No side" the crowd rushed into the field of play, and some of the more excited surrounded Macintosh and shouldered him to the Gymnasium amidst great enthusiasm.

The crowd had certainly enjoyed a fast and open game and the result. In those last minutes the whole Gloucester team had risen to the great occasion, which was reported to be "one of the finest exhibitions of the handling code ever witnessed in Gloucester.

A line out during the second half [CC&GG]

County Matches in the 1920s

Gloucestershire 24 Cornwall 6
8th December 1923

IN 1923-24, GLOUCESTERSHIRE started with a narrow win away to Devon, but then lost to Somerset at Bristol, and the selectors made wholesale changes to the Gloucestershire team for this last group match at Kingsholm. Cornwall started as clear favourites, having already beaten both Devon and Somerset. It was played in front of a disappointingly small crowd, but they were rewarded with a fast open game.

Gloucestershire: T Millington (Gloucester); H Feltham, L J Corbett (Captain), R C W Pickles, B S Chantrill (Bristol); E Hughes, W Collins (Gloucester); M V Shaw, E A Richardson (Bristol), A S Prowse (Bristol University & Bristol), A T Voyce, A Coulson, S Bayliss (Gloucester), W Preece (Bream), W Dubberley (Cinderford)

Cornwall: Ham (Redruth); Beckerleg (Penzance), Hammer, Collins (Camborne), Jago (Penryn); Pearce (St Ives), Adams (Camborne); A Andrew (Falmouth), Biddick (Camborne), Young (Army & Harlequins), Thomas (Camborne), Curnow (Newlyn), Mayne, Warren (Camborne), Welsh (Penryn)

Referee: Mr J Frost (Plymouth)

Tom Millington, who was selected at full-back, rather than his usual stand-off position, at the request of the England selectors [Gloucester Rugby]

Gloucestershire dominated from the start, and scored first when Chantrill chased his own punt, regathered and ran in for a try. Within the first ten minutes, Cornwall had strayed offside, Millington kicked the penalty, and Gloucestershire were six points to the good. Before half-time, from a scrum inside the Cornwall half, the home pack heeled, Hughes picked up and cut through, beating several opponents and almost making it to the line, before offloading to Voyce who scored the easiest of tries. The teams turned round at 9-0.

There was a sensational start to the second half. From the kick-off by Cornwall, Prowse gathered and burst up the field. Richardson, Bayliss and Voyce all handled, before Coulson scored. Feltham was pushed into touch a yard short, but more pressure was applied and Corbett went over. Cornwall now looked a beaten team, and from a lineout Prowse gathered and dropped over the line for Gloucestershire's fifth try. Another fine move with the irrepressible Hughes to the fore led to Prowse's second try. The only blot on a fine performance by the home side was their place kicking. They had tried three different kickers in Millington, Chantrill and Pickles, but none of them managed a conversion. Towards the end of the match, the light faded badly, but through the gloom it was determined that Collins had added another try after clever work by Pickles and Hughes, before Cornwall finished with a late flourish, notching a penalty by Jago and a try by Beckerleg. A fine victory was too little too late for Gloucestershire to progress in the Championship.

Gloucestershire 10 Middlesex 9
7th February 1925

GLOUCESTERSHIRE CAME THROUGH their group of the County Championship in 1924-25, after the usual keenly contested games. They enjoyed a comfortable home win against Devon at Bristol, 33-6, and two narrow away wins, 18-11 against Somerset at Bridgwater, and 6-5 against Cornwall at Redruth. This set up a semi-final, which was played at Kingsholm.

Gloucestershire: T Millington (Gloucester); S A Brown (Gloucester), L J Corbett, R C W Pickles, T G Spoors (Bristol); R Milliner, Dr G C Taylor (Gloucester); M V Shaw, J S Tucker, A T Hore (Bristol), A T Voyce, S Duberley, F Ayliffe (Gloucester), W Preece (Bream), F Coombes (Cinderford)

Middlesex: D N Rocyn Jones (Old Leysians); R H Hamilton-Wickes (Harlequins), R G Hopkins (Blackheath), C C Bishop (U C S Old Boys), C

The Gloucestershire forwards bursting through against Cornwall [CC&GG]

A lineout in the Middlesex match [CC&GG]

H L Wynne (Blackheath); H McGregor (St Bart's Hospital), J A Farmer (U C S Old Boys); W W Wakefield, H C Brodie (Harlequins), R Cove-Smith, R K Maclennan (Old Merchant Taylors), R J Hillard (Oxford University), R H Betting (St Bart's Hospital), G Macdonald (London Hospital), A C McLeod (Middlesex Hospital)

Referee: Mr W J Llewellyn (Welsh Union)

The reports of the match are unanimous in declaring Middlesex the stronger team in a lively and exciting game, although they concede that most of the polish came from Gloucestershire, at least while Dr G C Taylor of Gloucester was orchestrating their back division. He played a blinder, "his handling, running and dodging were very clever, and he was mainly responsible for both of the tries scored by his side, though Corbett was the man who crossed the line on each occasion. Taylor, perhaps, is a tall man for the position (stand off), yet he has the physique and cleverness and speed requisite for a great player." Unfortunately he was injured early in the second half and had to leave the field for ten minutes. It was enough to change the balance of the game.

Towards the end Middlesex had an overwhelming superiority, which resulted in two late tries, but they made a dreadful hash of the easy conversions, and that lost them the match. With Millington converting both the Gloucestershire tries, they squeaked home 10-9 (2 goals to 3 tries). The final was played at Bristol, where Leicestershire won the title, 14-6.

Gloucestershire 9 Monmouthshire 8
1st October 1925

GLOUCESTERSHIRE STARTED THE season with an experimental selection and a friendly fixture against Monmouthshire at Kingsholm, although as ever "friendly" turned out to be a misnomer for a match against a Welsh side. The attendance at the match was somewhat disappointing and the gate receipts amounted to only £57, but the main purpose of the match, to identify candidates for the County Championship side, was thought to have been well served. Hughes, Reed, Short and Prowse were picked out as fresh talent.

Gloucestershire: J Davies (Lydney); F Fellows (Cheltenham), E H Hughes (Gloucester), R Probert (Lydney), R Warner (Stroud); F Fields (Cinderford), C A Watkins (Stroud); J Reed, M Short (Gloucester), P C Taylor (Lydney), E C Dymond, A S Prowse (captain, Bristol), T Harry (Cheltenham), J Willis (Lydney), P G Waters (Stroud)

Monmouthshire: L Williams (Crumlin); A J Prosser, E Kitson (Tredegar), E Kirton (Ebbw Vale), W Rhodes (Blaenavon); H Bates (Cross Keys), F Clarke (Pill Harriers); S Morris, R Herrera, A Green (Cross Keys), W Morris (Abertillery), C Pritchard (Pontypool), R Parker (Blackwood), B Watkins (Blaina), "Duff" Lewis (Newport Police)

Referee: Mr H Locke (Somerset)

The main talking point of the match concerned the place kicks:

A S Prowse, who captained the Gloucestershire team, had a remarkable experience as regards goal kicks. He converted his first try, but had the points disallowed because the ball was touched in its flight over the cross-bar. For his second try there was no goal kick taken. Kicker and placer were not in accord as to when the ball was down; the Monmouth men ran out, and the ball being left on the ground it was casually kicked away. But the third instance — and I never remember three incidents of the kind happening in one match — was even more extraordinary, and left many spectators in doubt as to the actual result of the match. "No charge" was ruled by the referee, and the ball was placed for the Bristolian. Just as he took the kick the referee blew his whistle owing to a visitor being over the mark, and another shot was ordered. The ball was on the ground and Prowse altered its position, an infringement of the rule, which states: "A kicker and a placer must be distinct persons, except in the case of a penalty kick, and the kicker may not under any circumstances touch the ball when on the ground, even though the charge has been disallowed." The referee had his back to the kicker when the infringement took place, but he was apparently acquainted of it, for after the match it was announced that the goal had not been allowed.

The match was won by a try at the death:

R Probert, who was always doing something useful at centre, came into the limelight with a spectacular try at the finish, which enabled Gloucestershire to snatch a victory just as time was about to be blown. An intercepted pass at midfield saw Probert clear to the full back. Without checking his speed he punted over his opponent's head, re-gathered the ball on the bounce, and scored between the posts — a cleverly engineered and meritorious effort.

As a result Gloucestershire squeezed home by three tries to one goal and one try. The County Championship campaign started well with an 11-5 win against Devon at Exeter, and a 20-10 win over Cornwall at Bristol, which left the deciding tie to be played at Kingsholm. However, it had to be postponed because of a frost-bound pitch.

Teek's view of the postponement [Citizen]

FOR A SECOND TIME THE MEN OF SOMERSET MADE THE JOURNEY TO KINGSHOLM TO SEE THE BEST TEAM WIN — AND ON THIS OCCASION THEY GOT SOMETHING FOR THEIR MONEY.

MR. JEFFERY THE REFEREE. A RUGGED AND GRANITE. FACED MAN OF DEVON

THE FIERCE AND DETERMINED ATTITUDE OF THE SOMERSET LADS WHILE WAITING FOR THE START SUGGESTED TROUBLE COMING ALONG FOR SOMEBODY

EARLY IN THE GAME, WITH SOMERSET SOME 7 POINTS AHEAD, A LOYAL LITTLE GLO'STER DOG CAME ON TO THE FIELD AND OFFERED TO PLAY FOR HIS COUNTY —

THE REFEREE WOULDN'T HEAR OF IT — PICKLES SAID "HOP IT" AND MILLINGTON ACTUALLY SCOOTED HIM OFF THE GROUND — BUT, IN

RURAL CELEBRATIONS IN SOMERSET THAT NIGHT.

VIEW OF WHAT HAPPENED LATER, IT MIGHT HAVE BEEN BETTER FOR US IF MILLINGTON HAD ACCEPTED THE LITTLE DOG'S OFFER OF HELP.

TEEK 1925

Gloucestershire 9 Somerset 10
28th December 1925

WHEN THE MATCH was eventually played, incessant rain on top of a thawed pitch made for very tricky conditions, but 9,000 spectators braved the weather.

Gloucestershire: T Millington; S A Brown (Gloucester), L J Corbett, R C W Pickles, T G Spoors (Bristol); Dr G C Taylor, R Milliner (Gloucester); J S Tucker, M Shaw, A T Hore, J K Morman (Bristol), A T Voyce, F Ayliffe, M Short, J Hemmings (Gloucester)

Somerset: W F Gaisford (St Bart's Hospital); R G B Quick (Bristol), J W Bruford (Taunton), N C Partridge (Sherborne), W J Gibbs (Bath); M J Turnbull (Cambridge University), A V Twose (Wellington); H B L Wake (Bath), T Rose (RAF), A Spriggs (Bridgwater), C S Barlow (Cambridge University), W G Francis, Dr H L Shepherd (Bristol), G A H Roberts, L W Bisgrove (Weston-super-Mare)

Referee: Mr F W Jeffery (Devon)

This was a typical West Country battle with the forwards and half-backs spoiling to their hearts' content in the mud, and the backs unable to do more than make a few furtive passes, but more often having to kick to elude the pressure. Partridge slipped through the defence very cleverly and, although collared from behind, he scrambled over the line beside the posts to notch the first try for Somerset; Gaisford converted. Back came Gloucestershire and a reverse pass from Milliner to Taylor created space, but a wild pass eluded the grasp of Pickles, Bruford picked up the ball, and Twose was on hand to run in behind the posts. Gaisford again converted and Somerset were ten points up. The home side fought back strongly, but tremendous tackling kept them at bay until Milliner and Taylor started a move, the ball went wide to Sid Brown, who sprinted away and got close to the line before passing inside to Corbett, who finished off a fine try. 3-10 at half-time.

The second half saw Gloucestershire battering away at the Somerset line, but they again met stubborn resistance until another forward rush swept the opposition aside and Hemmings was credited with the try. Gathering darkness made play difficult to follow in the latter stages of the game, but the Gloucestershire forwards broke away in a body and drove the ball over the line, where it was reported that Milliner touched down for a try. The conversion was an easy one, but Millington was having an off day with his kicking and he missed it. This was to prove crucial, because, even though Gloucestershire monopolised possession and field position for the last few minutes, and the forwards came close to scoring on two or three occasions, the luck was with Somerset and they held out.

This left the group tied, so a play-off between Gloucestershire and Devon was required; and having home advantage, Gloucestershire chose to stage it at Kingsholm.

Gloucestershire 10 Devon 3
28th January 1926

GLOUCESTERSHIRE WERE BESET with selection problems and their line-up, which included seven reserves, was only decided a few minutes before kick-off. Tom Voyce was one of the absentees, and was replaced by Stan Weaver, the Cinderford captain, who played the game of his life and was declared the man of the match.

Gloucestershire: B S Chantrill (Bristol); R C Thompson, E H Hughes, T Millington, S A Brown (Gloucester); C A Watkins (Stroud), R Milliner (Gloucester); M V Shaw (captain), J K Morman (Bristol), F W Ayliffe, M Short, J Hemmings (Gloucester), F Carpenter, S Weaver (Cinderford), P C Taylor (Lydney)

Devon: W Pritchard (Torquay Athletic); H Smith (Barnstaple), J Hanley (Plymouth Albion), A B Knapman, T S Lee (Devonport Services); E Richards (Plymouth Albion), S B Barrington; W G E Luddington, A B Paddon, Mog Davies (Devonport Services), F Rew (Exeter), L R Stephens (Plymouth Albion), J Williams (Barnstaple), C Gummer, E Stanbury (Plymouth Albion)

Referee: Mr R Fear (Weston-super-Mare)

Devon opened the scoring with a cleverly worked try by Smith, and threw the ball about in a way which kept threatening more. They looked all over the winners, as had been predicted. However, the home side gradually worked their way back into the game with the pack getting the upper hand over a hefty set of opponents as "their irresistible rushes, clever footwork and deadly tackling set one's pulses tingling. Devon felt the full weight of these smashing tactics and fairly crumpled under the continued onslaughts." A forward rush led to a try by Taylor, converted by Millington, which gave Gloucestershire a lead of 5-3 at half-time.

Soon after the resumption, "from a kick by Chantrill the home county attacked, and Weaver, seizing on an opening, dashed ahead and passed to Shaw. The latter threw out a wide pass to Thompson, who took the ball nicely, and going all out scored a fine try. Millington converted, the ball striking the upright and bouncing over the cross bar." Even when temporarily reduced to thirteen men, injury causing Brown and Watkins to have to leave the field, Gloucestershire held out.

They were the deserved, if surprise, winners of "a game in which there was plenty of unrestrained vigour and crudity, but in which the winners displayed the more intelligent use of their forces". This victory put Gloucestershire into a semi-final against Hampshire, which was lost 6-16 at Southampton.

Gloucestershire 14 Yorkshire 4
23rd September 1926

YORKSHIRE CAME TO Gloucester for a friendly fixture as part of an early season tour of the West Country, going on to play Somerset two days later. The gate receipts were £210. The profits made at the Gloucestershire and Somerset games was pooled and devoted to the encouragement of rugby in junior clubs. Gloucestershire unusually played in blue and black jerseys.

The match was overshadowed by a dispute between the Gloucester and Bristol clubs. At the end of the previous season, Bristol had cancelled future fixtures with Gloucester after an acrimonious 3-8 loss at Kingsholm. At the start of the new season, Gloucester proposed that the clubs meet once that season, on a neutral ground if necessary, but this suggestion was rejected. Some Bristol players said that they would be prepared to play for the County at Kingsholm, but the Gloucester players, led by Voyce and Millington, announced that if they would not play in a friendly game between the clubs, then they could not play together in the same side since it would be impossible to generate the proper team spirit. The County committee decided to pick a team with no Bristol players.

Gloucestershire: R D Evans (Clifton); R N Loveridge (Gloucester), Probert (Lydney), C A Watkins (Stroud), S R Crowther; R Milliner, T Millington; A T Voyce, M Short, F J Seabrook, G McIlwaine (Gloucester), P C Taylor, J Willis (Lydney), F Carpenter, H Roberts (Cinderford)

Yorkshire: D T Thomas (Otley); H Moore (Harrogate Old Boys), F T Adams (Halifax), E G Rycroft (Ilkley), F Hickson (Bradford); H Fletcher (Bramley Old Boys), H Thompson (Otley); S R Whitfield (Batley), H Bottomley (Headingley), J H Eastwood (Halifax), Lieut C K L Faithfull (Halifax), S Winkley (Hull and East Riding), H Wilkinson (Halifax), R C Hart, H E Proctor (Headingley)

Referee: Mr A J Locke (Somerset)

Gloucestershire made a spirited start and within five minutes

The Gloucestershire team: standing: F Carpenter, M Short, F J Seabrook, P C Taylor, J Willis, H Roberts; seated: G McIlwaine, R N Loveridge, A T Voyce, T Millington (captain), S R Crowther, W Probert, R D Evans; in front: C Watkins, R Milliner [CC&GG]

The Yorkshire team: standing: E G Rycroft, H Moore, H Wilkinson, R C Hart, H L Proctor, Lieut C K L Faithfull, F Hickson, D W Thomas, P S Wade (Vice President); seated: R F Oakes (Hon Secretary), H Eastwood, E Winkley (captain), S R Whitfield, F T Adams, H Bottomley, H C Harrap (President); in front: H Fletcher, H Thompson [CC&GG]

Sidney Crowther scored the first try in the corner. Yorkshire struck back with a fine passing move, and only a great tackle in front of the goal posts denied them a try. The Gloucestershire forwards did good work in the loose, but Yorkshire were faster and more entertaining, and looked more likely to score. Only determined tackling continued to keep them out. However, a handling mistake by the visitors allowed Watkins to snap up the ball and run clear through to the full back, when he gave a beautiful pass to Voyce in centre field. The International galloped away in his characteristic style and, although hotly chased, he kept his lead to score beside the posts for Millington to add the goal points. Before half-time, Yorkshire threw away a golden chance to score when one of their forwards hung on to the ball too long, and Voyce got over the line at the other end but lost the ball before he could touch it down. So the teams turned round at 8-0.

The second half continued the pattern of Yorkshire attacks stopped by resolute tackling, especially by Watkins and Evans, but forward rushes by the home pack, with Seabrook, Short, Willis and Taylor to the fore were a handful for the visitors. A neat combination between Crowther and Millington put the latter over the line, but the final pass was judged forward. After several fruitless Yorkshire attempts to cross the line, the ball was passed out to Adams, who converted a good dropped goal. The pace of the game was fierce, and Probert came close when following up a punt ahead, but it took a moment of magic to produce a score. Dick Loveridge received a pass near the touch-line, beat three opponents and scored wide out. Gloucestershire were now on top and missed two further opportunities to score before Seabrook got over to seal the victory. Millington kicked a penalty goal before the end, but it was disallowed because a Yorkshire player had touched the ball in flight.

Mrs Stanley Smith provided a fine dinner after the match at the Spread Eagle, and the Yorkshire party were taken on a tour of the Wye valley the following day.

A lineout forms during the Yorkshire match [CC&GG]

Gloucestershire 3 Cornwall 3
3rd December 1927

ALREADY DEFEATED BY Devon and Somerset, there was nothing in this game for Gloucestershire, but Cornwall were playing to win the group. The crowd numbered around 5,000 and gate receipts amounted to about £320.

Gloucestershire: T W Brown (Bristol); R James (Gloucester), H M Locke (Bristol), W Richards (Lydney), H Baldwin (Stroud); L J Corbett, C B Carter; M V Shaw (captain), F J Coventry, W G Bryant, B Parsons (Bristol), L E Saxby, J F Evans (Gloucester), R Ling (Clifton), S Weaver (Barnstaple)

Cornwall: C H Gosling (Keyham Naval College); L Roberts (Redruth), P Collins (Camborne), R Jennings (Redruth), J Jago (Penryn); J Andrew (Redruth), F Rogers; W Biddick (Camborne), J Hollow (Redruth), J Evans, J Carter (Camborne), N Peake (Penzance), F Sellwood (Camborne), E Maddrell (Penzance), R Matthews (Camborne)

Referee: Mr J Adams (Cumberland)

Part way through a generally uninspiring first half :

There was a stoppage owing to a Cornwall player being laid out and having to go off. Resuming, Gloucestershire gained ground with a passing run and punt by Locke. Play veered to the other wing from an attack initiated by Carter, but Richards' pass went wide of James. Gloucestershire had the better of the exchanges, and Gosling missing the ball from a short punt on the blind side of the scrum, Evans dashed up and, gathering the ball neatly, dashed over in the corner with a good try. Brown failed at goal ... Richards, the young Lydney centre brought off a brilliant run through the Cornish defenders, but after travelling half the length of the field he was tackled from behind in trying to beat a Cornishman, and a great effort ended.

At half-time Gloucestershire were one try to the good.

The Cornish pack started to exert some pressure in the second half and when Gloucestershire were penalised, Jennings kicked a lovely goal from 40 yards out. The play was described as vigorous and when

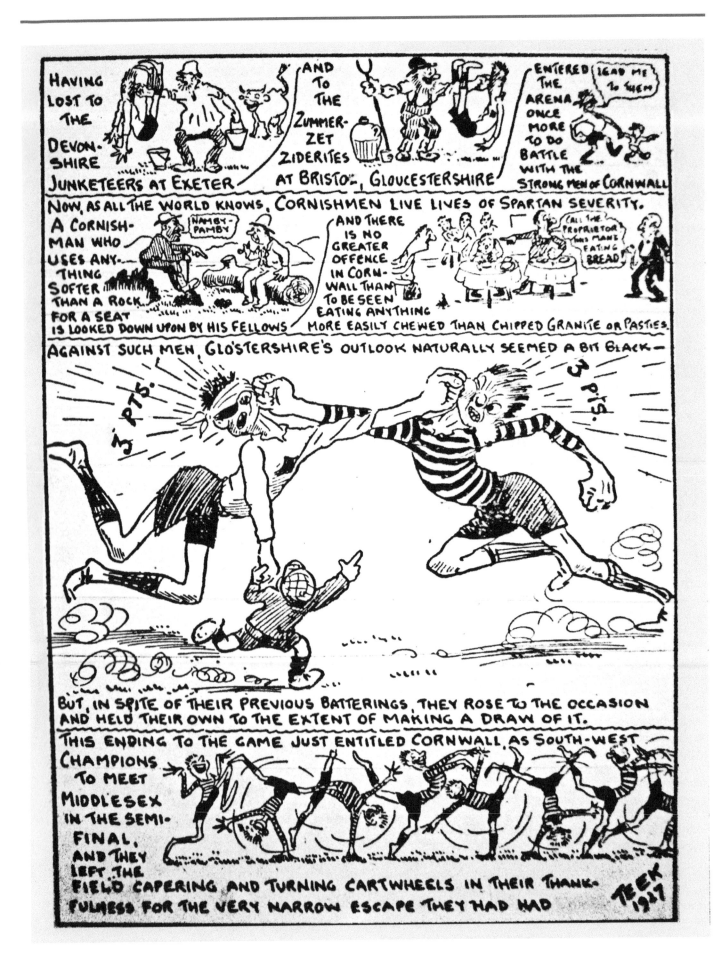

"Biddick tried to check the Cornishman was knocked out" before "Ling was laid out in a tackle, and had to leave the field." Gloucestershire came close when Brown had a drop for goal which missed by a yard, and the last few minutes were hotly contested, but both sides lacked scoring ability. The draw was considered a fair result and Cornwall went through to face Middlesex.

Gloucestershire 13 Devon 0
27th October 1928

INCESSANT RAIN ON the Friday continued on match day, so that the match was played in conditions which were thoroughly unpleasant for players and spectators alike, with rain driving across the ground in a strong cross wind. The weather had a considerable effect on the attendance, which was less than 3,000, who packed into the limited covered accommodation leaving the terraces largely deserted. The takings were a severe setback to the finances of the County Union, especially since this was the only home game in the Group stages. Local interest was also reduced by the inclusion of only three Gloucester players, and two of those, James and McCanlis, were played out of position on the wings.

Gloucestershire: T W Brown (Bristol); R James (Gloucester), H M Locke, D Burland (Bristol), M A McCanlis (Gloucester); C B Carter (Bristol), W Thomas (Lydney); J S Tucker (captain), F J Coventry, W Bryant, J N Hazell (Bristol), R N Williams (St Bart's Hospital), J Willis (Lydney), L E Saxby (Gloucester), G Jones (Bream)

Devon: T Scourfield (Torquay); J L Dalrymple (Devonport Services), T Evans (Plymouth Albion), Gwyn Richards (Torquay), W Bell (Barnstaple); J Merchant, E Richards (Plymouth Albion); E Stanbury, R H Sparkes, A H Brigstoke (Plymouth Albion), H Rew (Exeter), A Wells (Exmouth), I Thomas (Torquay), R Hooper (Teignmouth), M Wilson (Plymouth Albion)

Referee: Mr Devine (Yorkshire)

Both sides missed chances before Gloucestershire opened the scoring when Devon were caught off-side, and Burland kicked the penalty. Given the weather, it was no surprise that the match settled down into a keen forward contest, but Gloucestershire did manage to create some attacking positions, only for their backs to spill the greasy ball. James missed a drop goal, Scourfield was tackled on his line but Devon managed to clear the danger, and McCanlis got away but was tackled short by Bell.

The Devon pack had much the better of it up front, even when they had a man off the field in the second half, but Gloucestershire seemed to enjoy all the luck. Tries by Hazell and Bryant, converted by Brown and Burland respectively, eventually saw them home, but the margin of victory was flattering. Dai Gent reported on the match for the Sunday Times and thought Gloucestershire deserved to win but that the margin was flattering. However, Devon got their just desserts when the teams met in the group play-off at Exeter the following February, winning 11-0.

Tom Voyce's Special Matches

A T Voyce's XV 8 Newport Borough Police 0
6th April 1932

GLOUCESTER RUGBY AND Cricket Clubs had been closely associated for some fifty years, the Rugby Club having played on the Spa as a sub-tenant of the Cricket Club from 1874 to 1891, and there having been many players and officials in common across the years. So, when the Cricket Club found itself in financial difficulty at the start of the 1922 season, a match was organised at Kingsholm to raise funds to alleviate the situation. George Boots, who played for Newport and Wales, pulled together the opposition, which included four Welsh internationals – their names are listed below as being in the selected XV, but none of the four turned out and the policemen who replaced them are not known. Prices of admission were set at 2s for reserved seats and 1s entrance, but 6d tickets were also issued by the Labour Exchange to the unemployed. The match raised £125, which not only covered the Cricket Club's deficit of £35, but also allowed them to start their new season in a healthy financial position.

A T Voyce's XV: J C Collett (Gloucester): Lieut Bloxham (Army & Stroud), R James, E H Hughes (Gloucester), C H L Ewing (Clifton & Bristol University); W Dix, T Millington; T Voyce, F W Ayliffe, Smart, A Hall, H W Collier, J Harris (Gloucester), T R K Jones (Cambridge University), H T Stephens (Cheltenham)

Newport Borough Police: F Birt; Reg Plummer (Newport &

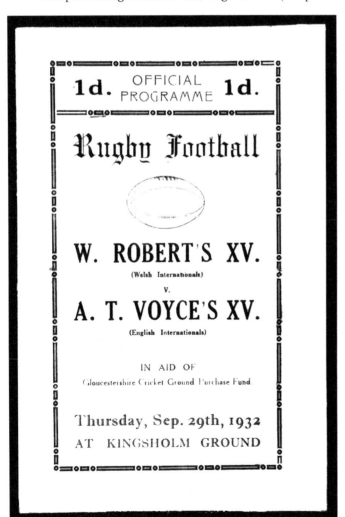

Wales); Ebb Wetter (Newport), Dowling (Risca), Towigg; T H Vile (Newport & Wales), C Jermain (Newport); H Uzzell (Newport & Wales), Williams, Collins (Newport), Friend (Wales trial), G Thomas (Pill Harriers), Birch, Hogg, and McHugh.

Referee: Mr. George Romans (Gloucester)

It was a keen, hard game, but with little that was spectacular. The Police were strong forward, and with the backs tackling well Voyce's XV were seldom able to finish off the numerous attacking movements initiated. However, Jones scored for Voyce's side in the first half, Millington missing the goal points. The Police had one or two good chances of getting level after the change of ends, Meredith making one fine opening, but his pass went astray. Dowling and Rose, too, made a couple of strong efforts on the right wing, but Hughes saved a score with some determined tackling. Collett started the move which led to a try in the second half, Wetter failed to gather a high punt, Voyce dribbled on, and the ball was gathered by Collier, who scored behind the posts, for Dix to convert. The teams enjoyed dinner at the Wellington Hotel afterwards.

A T Voyce's XV 42 W Robert's XV 6
29th September 1932

THIS MATCH, PLAYED at Kingsholm, between English and Welsh teams, was to raise money for the Gloucestershire Cricket Club in aid of their Ground Purchase Fund. Gate receipts amounted to about £230. B H Lyon, the Gloucestershire Cricket captain, kicked off, and W W Wakefield, the former England Rugby captain, officiated as referee.

Voyce English XV: T W Brown (Bristol & England); J S R Reeve (Harlequins & England), J B D Chapman (Harlequins), Don Burland (Bristol & England), C C Tanner (Gloucester & England); Don Meadows (Gloucester), B C Gadney (Leicester & England); P Hordern, A Carpenter (Gloucester & England), R J Longland, E Coley (Northampton & England), A J Rowley, R S Roberts (Coventry & England), C Webb (Navy & England), D H Swayne (Oxford & England)

Roberts Welsh XV: J Bassett (Penarth & Wales); A T Thomas, A H Jones (Cardiff), V G. Jenkins (Oxford), R Jones; M J Turnbull (Cardiff), H M Bowcott; R Barrell (Cardiff and Wales), T Day (Swansea & Wales), A Lemon (Neath & Wales), F A Bowdler (Cross Keys & Wales), K. Salmon (Cross Keys & Gloucestershire), C Thompson (Cross Keys), T L Tanner (Oxford)

Some 5,000 spectators witnessed a fine exhibition of running rugby, with the English backs dominant. It resulted in a handsome win for Tom's team by seven goals and three tries to two tries. Try scorers for the English side were J R Reeve (3), D Burland (2), R J Longland (2), Don Meadows and "Kit" Tanner; R Barrell (Cardiff) scored both Welsh tries. After the match, the teams enjoyed dinner at the Bell Hotel.

A T Voyce's XV 18 W W Wakefield's XV 11
23rd November 1940

THIS MATCH WAS organised as the climax of Gloucester's War Weapons Week. Tom Voyce and his old England captain, Wavell Wakefield, persuaded many rugby stars to turn out. Match receipts and a collection totalling some £900 went to the Gloucester War Charities Association.

A T Voyce's XV: H Boughton (captain, England); Lt C V Boyle (Ireland), Lt N J Daly (Ireland), Flt Lt Adams (New Zealand), Lt H

Voyce's XV (in cherry and white): back row: Collison, Fosse, Coutts, Voyce, White, Hudson, Jones, Moreland; front row: Boyle, Brook, Murphy, Carpenter, Boughton, Daly, Travers, Adams [Journal]

Wakefield's XV: back row: Thornton, Morgan, Mould, Young, Wakefield, A'Bear, Day, Twidie, Upham; front row: Gough, Jenkins, Mahoney, McKibben, Williams, Pollock, Hughes [Journal]

F Collison (Lancs); G A White (English Trials), Pte W H Moreland (Gloucester); Bbr W T Travers (Wales), A Carpenter (England), Pte W G Jones (Wales), Cpl G Hudson (Gloucester), Rev P W P Brook (England), Sgt C R Murphy (English Trials), L/Cpl F H Coutts (Scottish Trials), K Fosse (English Trials)

W W Wakefield's XV: Ivor Williams (Great Britain); J Young (RAF & Scotland), Lt M R McKibben (Great Britain), F Off Mould, R C Upham (Gloucester); Lt J S Pollock (Ireland); F Gough (Gloucester); J G Jenkins (RAF & Surrey), Rev H M Hughes (Welsh Trials), Pte T Mahoney (Somerset), J H A'Bear (Great Britain), J Thornton (Gloucester), Cadet R

The two captains, Boughton and McKibben lead their teams out [Journal]

A Twidie (Ireland), Lt T D G Morgan (Wales), T Day (Gloucester)

Referee: Mr W W Wakefield

Wakefield's team opened the scoring in unexpected fashion when "Upham took the ball almost off his feet, and long passes to Mould and Hughes brought the ball to Gough in the centre. The defence evidently thought he was going for the line, but he stopped dead in his tracks and hooked the ball round just skimming the bar for a dropped goal." Travers responded with a try for Voyce's XV, but Mould with a high kick landed Wakefield's second dropped goal, and half-time was reached at 3-8.

The second half started excitingly, when a cross-kick from Boughton was taken by Boyle, who set off down the wing at high speed, only to put a foot into touch. As the half wore on, Voyce's XV gained the upper hand, and inter-passing amongst their forwards resulted in a try for Jones, which Boughton converted to level the scores. A penalty by Boughton, put Voyce's XV ahead, but a Gough try levelled it again. A dropped goal restored Voyce's lead, and the win was assured when "Boughton, pouncing into the fray like a terrier, immediately started his forwards in a rush to the other end. They carried the ball to the line, and with four or five men all falling on the ball it was difficult to see whether Boughton or Murphy scored".

A T Voyce's XV 16
G Cryer's Old Centralian XV 8
20th April 1953

MAJOR GUY CRYER was the rugby master at Central Secondary Technical School, Gloucester, and all his side had learned their rugby under him. Some 3,000 spectators attended and all proceeds went into the Memorial Ground Fund.

A T Voyce's XV: T Halls (Gloucester); D Taylor (Lydney), J Taylor, M Baker, M Sutton; W Nield, W B Cartmell; G Hastings, K Taylor (Gloucester), D White (Clifton), P G Marriott (Stroud), J Watkins (Lydney), G Hudson (captain, Gloucester), R C Hodge (Gloucester), C Price (Lydney)

G Cryer's XV: E Sherwood; R Amos (Old Centralians), B Russell (Rotol), D Hill (Spartans), K Daniell (Gloucester); J Brinkworth (Rotol), D Jones; A Wadley (Gloucester), J Fowke (Spartans), J Varney, G Gough (Old Centralians), R Owen (Spartans), D Ibbotson (Gloucester), D Nyland (Old Centralians), P Ford (Gloucester)

Referee: Mr E Roberts (Gloucester)

Cryer's XV held their own for much of the match and took the lead when Brinkworth dodged through between the posts and converted his own try. Mike Baker kicked a penalty in reply and then scored a try in the corner from a move which swept the length of the field. Bob Hodge, Voyce's captain, then snapped up a chance and touched down behind the posts for Baker to convert, and his side went further ahead when John Taylor crossed the line and Baker converted. Cryer's XV revived as the game wore on and Amos burst through for a try in the corner.

The match was followed by a dinner at the New Inn. Major Cryer was presented with an engraved clock and Arnold Alcock, President of Gloucester Rugby Club, commented that "the number of rugby footballers Guy Cryer has trained in the 27 years since his school was founded is extraordinary and includes twelve schoolboy internationals".

Second England Trial

Probables 16 Possibles 12
21st December 1929

HAY AND STRAW had been laid on the ground to counter the threat of frost earlier in the week, and heavy rain the night before the match made its removal a messy job. But the sun came out on the morning of the match, and Engineer-Commander S F Cooper, RN, the Secretary of the Rugby Union, who had played on the wing for England against Wales at Kingsholm in 1900, pronounced himself greatly impressed with the state of the ground and the match arrangements.

Most of the local and district rugby clubs had cancelled matches so that their players could go to Kingsholm, and the crowd numbered around 7,000 by the time that the match kicked off, although spectators were still coming into the ground. There was some disappointment that no Gloucester players had been selected, although Maurice McCanlis, Joe Davies, and Fred Wadley were asked to stand by as reserves. There was some local interest in the Bristol and Gloucestershire players who were selected. Sam Tucker captained the Probables (who played in white), and Don Burland and A W Lillicrap were included in the Possibles side (in blue). When one of the original selections at centre had to withdraw, it was hoped that McCanlis would be brought in, but the selectors thought otherwise, shuffled positions and moved Novis from the wing to centre. McCanlis was given a job as touch judge.

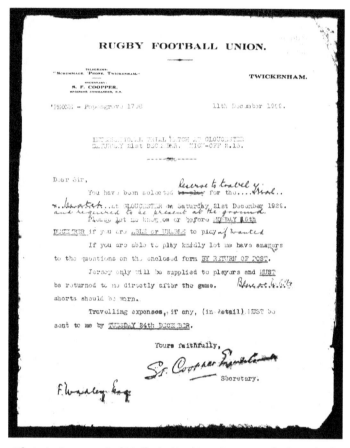

The invitation sent to Fred Wadley inviting him to be a reserve for the England trial [Gloucestershire Archives]

Probables: E C P Whiteley (Old Alleynians); B D Butler (Fylde), F W S Malir (Otley), A L Novis (Headingley), J C Gibbs (Harlequins); W H Sobey, R S Spong (Old Millhillians); H Rew (Exeter), J S Tucker (Bristol), H C S Jones (Manchester), P McD Hodgson (Northern), B H Black (Oxford University), G S Seward (Woodford), W W Wakefield (Harlequins), W E Tucker (Blackheath)

Possibles: J G Askew (Cambridge University); A W Lillicrap (Bristol), R Jennings (Redruth), D Burland (Bristol), R G Turnbull (Old Merchant Taylors); A Key (Old Cranleighans), J R Cole (Harlequins); A H Bateson (Otley), D J Norman (Leicester), N W Matthews (Bridgwater), D Turquand-Young (Richmond), J W Forrest (United Services), A G

Fred Wadley [Gloucester Rugby]

The Probables team [CC&GG]

The Possibles team [CC&GG]

Sobey about to receive the ball from Spong for the Probables [CC&GG]

Cridlan (Oxford University), P D Howard (Oxford University), G Townend (Devonport Services)

Referee: Mr T J Bradburn (Lancashire)

The Possibles started the stronger, and opened the scoring when Cole dropped a lovely goal, but the Probables struck back with their first attacking move, when Novis broke through and fed Gibbs to score in the corner. This led to a lengthy period of pressure by the Probables, which ended with a try under the posts for Malir, converted by Black. Before half-time, errors by the Probables allowed the Possibles to counter-attack, and twice Lillicrap raced away for tries, the second of which was converted by Jennings for a 12-8 lead.

During the interval, the selectors decided to make some changes to the teams. Joe Davies of Gloucester replaced W E Tucker in the Probables pack, J A R Reeve (Harlequins) replaced Lillicrap, and J C Hubbard took Askew's place. To the frustration of most in the ground, McCanlis was still left waving his touch flag.

The second half was keenly contested and fairly even until Wakefield suddenly shot out from a crowd of players to score a splendid try, and Black's conversion gave the lead to the Probables. An attempt by Gibbs at a drop goal resulted in Davies flopping over the line, but the score was disallowed. Spong was injured and replaced by Collison, before Novis was tackled on the line but managed to release the ball to Gibbs who concluded the scoring with his second try.

It had been a surprise that the Possibles pack had the upper hand forward, but Sobey made the most of any Probables ball to put his back division on the attack, and this was judged to be the main reason for their narrow victory. Tony Novis, Roger Spong and Wilf Sobey stood out as the best players on view. Gate receipts were £700-800.

Inter-War Schoolboy Rugby

West 6 East 8
17th February 1923

FOR THIS SECOND England Schoolboy trial at Kingsholm, five Gloucester boys were selected. There was a good attendance, but the ground was very heavy after several days of rain.

West: Powell (Bristol); Borlase (Plymouth), Hall, Poole, Cole (Gloucester); Jones (Bristol), Meadows (Gloucester); Williams, Hollister, Burman (Bristol), Grinter, Howard (Bath), Stevens, Curry (Plymouth), Smith (Gloucester)

East: Bates; Clark, Blake (Coventry), Raven, Timson (Leicester); Giles, Whitehead (Coventry); McReadie (Rugby), Harris, Hilyard, Cooke (Leicester), Romeley, Trickett, Wheatley (Coventry), Walker (Rugby).

Referee: Mr W Thomas

The East had the better of the first half, their backs showing better co-ordination, but all they had to show for it was a minor, until just before half-time. Then:

By robust work in the loose the West forwards pressed to the East quarter, where a keen struggle took place. The West tried hard to score but were thrust back, and in the course of a three-quarter movement Blake broke through and punted over Powell's head for Raven to score. Blake easily converted.

On the resumption the West forwards made a short burst, but they were quickly forced back and had to defend desperately. What chances came to them of clearing they missed, until Borlase gathered in the loose and put in a run three-parts the length of the field. He lost the ball, but Meadows carried on to the line, where a scrum was ordered. From the ensuing melee Williams fell over with a try, but the kick at goal failed.

This seemed to encourage the West, and they played up well for a time, but after combined pressure Timson scored an unconverted try for the East. Time after time the East backs made for the West line, but Meadows, Borlase and Powell worked indefatigably and the defence held. Just on time a change came over the game, and after the West forwards had rushed to the East line Borlase picked up and scored an unconverted try.

Of the Gloucester boys, Don Meadows impressed sufficiently to be chosen as England's stand-off in the subsequent international against Wales, with Hall selected as a reserve.

Gloucester Schoolboys played at Kingsholm several times each season, with Bristol being regular opponents, and occasionally drawing the attention of Teek for his weekly cartoon in the Citizen.

England Schools 0 Wales Schools 22
19th March 1927

THE GLOUCESTER CLUB provided the Kingsholm ground free of charge for this schools international, the arrangements being left in the hands of Eric Keys and his Gloucester Schools RU committee. The enclosure and stands were well filled with a crowd estimated at 8-9,000.

England: Strong (Bristol); Lockyer (Bristol), Cutts, Boswell (Coventry), Drake (Gloucester); Littlewood (Coventry), Dix (Gloucester); Murphy, Smith (Bristol), Bone (Redruth), Smith (Gloucester), Jarvis (Leicester), Harper, Clarke (Coventry), Badhams (Leicester)

Wales: Barnes (Aberavon); Jenkins, Parker (Neath), Loosemore (Pontypridd), Jones (Swansea); Squires (Newport), Stevens (Neath); Evans (Newport), Banfield (Neath), Anthony (Llanelly), Hughes (Llanelly), Meyrick (Aberavon), Daniels (Neath), Ransome (Cardiff), Price (Bridgend)

Referee: Mr Scott (Scotland)

The English started brightly and put the Welsh line in danger, but they failed to break through and Murphy missed with a shot at goal from a penalty. Cutts opened out and the ball was passed along the line, but Drake missed the ball, and Loosemore seized on it for Wales, ran down the line and passed inside to Jones, who raced away for a glorious try. Wales now dominated play for a period, but failed to add to their lead, and both sides missed with penalty kicks. Littlewood missed a glorious chance for England by failing to take the ball in front of the posts, and the mistake allowed Wales to break away. Jones started the move by punting ahead to catch the English defence out of position. Strong was a long way out of position and could not field the ball. Parker slipped the defence nicely, fed to Loosemore and he handed to Jones, who easily beat Strong and crossed for the try which made the half-time score 6-0.

Wales were soon on the attack in the second half, and appeared to have scored two tries, but both were disallowed by the referee, before a fumble on the England line gave Jones the chance to touch down for his hat trick. Squires then gained more possession for Wales, and Jones showed everyone a clean pair of heels to score under the posts; Barnes converted. The compliment was returned when Jones made another sparkling run to set up the position from which Squire scored down the blind side of a scrum. Jones looked set to score his fifth try but lost the ball when already over the try line. However, Wales did not have to wait long to complete the rout with a final try by Squire. Jones, the star of the game, was carried off the field on the shoulders of his teammates.

After the match the teams and officials were entertained to dinner at the Old Corn Exchange in Southgate Street, Gloucester. There were speeches galore, a surfeit of toasts, and "Land of my Fathers" sung in Welsh.

Gloucestershire Schools 3
Midland Counties Schools 0
5th January 1928

GLOUCESTERSHIRE: Church (Gloucester); Webb, Haddocks (Bristol), Watkins, Jelf (captain, Gloucester); Cooke (Bristol), Budding; Hawkins, Fletcher, Dainty, Maysey, Davies (Gloucester), Blackmore, Rogers, Jackson (Bristol)

Midlands: Castle (Bedworth); Watson, Hammonds (Leicester), Brooks (Coventry), Root (Leicester); Venn (Coventry), Clark (Leicester); Sanders, Wall (Coventry), Kent (Burton), Roberts, Cobley, Draper (Leicester), Duncan (Nuneaton), Doe (Rugby)

Referee: Mr J Holder (Gloucester)

The Midlands had the wind behind them in the first half and used it to good effect to keep pressure on the home side. They missed the first opportunity to score when the ball fell short from an attempted drop goal by Brooks, and the same player broke clear on two occasions and seemed certain to score, only to be brought down short. So half time arrived with no score.

The Midlands domination continued in the second half. Dainty prevented a score by dragging Root down a couple of yards short of the line, and occasional forays by Gloucestershire into the Midlands half were

nipped in the bud by Church. The Midlands missed several more chances to score, and were made to pay in the closing stages when Budding picked up in the loose and threw himself over the line to score a try. Jackson could not convert, but it was enough to gain a somewhat fortunate victory.

England 44 The Rest 3
9th March 1935

WITH SEVERAL LOCAL players included in the teams, there was a good deal of interest in this boys' international trial at Kingsholm, but the attendance of less than 2,000 at kick-off suffered owing to the bitterly cold weather, although more came along later.

England: Startin (Nuneaton); Telford (Carlisle), Hall (Hexham), Thompson, Cartwright; Preece (Coventry), Evans (Bristol); Roberts (Gloucester), Steele (Cleator Moor), Daniells (Bristol), Fornear (Morpeth), Hamilton (Plymouth), Wallis (Bristol), Hill (Rugby), Couldrey (Gloucester)

The Rest: Vernon (Bristol); Upham (Gloucester), Hick (Redruth), Wanklyn (Coventry), Kerswell (Barnstaple); Arch (Gloucester), Braunton (Barnstaple); Townsend (Gloucester), Martin (Redruth); Bramley (Leicester), Weston (Coventry), George (Bristol), Batten (Cornwall), Colmer (Plymouth), Ison (Coventry)

Referee: Mr J Holder (Gloucester)

England proved to be much better organised than the Rest, and scored early on when Evans passed out for Cartwright to race over. He was soon in action again when he was fed the ball well inside his own half and finished a fine run by scoring his second try under the posts. The Rest fought back, Townsend threatened with a good dribble, and Vernon

kicked a penalty, but they were too often caught in possession. They held out for a while, but Evans picked up from a loose scrum and burst through to score by the posts. Fornear kicked his third conversion for a 15-3 lead at half-time, when the fullbacks were swapped over.

In the second half a strong wind contributed to some scrappy play before Cartwright ran in easily for his third try. Hall then ran thirty yards for another and the Rest started to wilt. By the end England had scored five further tries through Telford, Hall (2), Cartwright and Fornear, who finished with seven conversions.

After the match the teams and officials were entertained to tea at the Mercer's Hall and subjected to a series of speeches.

England Schools 0 Wales Schools 29
6th March 1937

THERE WAS LOCAL interest in the England team with two boys from Gloucester, G J Locke (Central) and H Hiam (Archdeacon); and two boys from Cheltenham, J Simmonds (Grammar) and F M Long (Naunton Park). Locke was regarded as the "babe" of the team, whilst the other three, who were forwards, contributed plenty of Gloucestershire beef, their combined weight being over 36 stone, which was remarkably hefty for boys of that age in that era. J Hussey came into the England side at the last minute, when it was discovered that G B Smailes (Newcastle) was one day too old to qualify as a schoolboy.

England: J H Kirkby (Kendal); N Furgusson (Carlisle), D Paul, J Oxley (Bristol), G J Locke (Gloucester); N Dent (Burton-on-Trent), L Irish (Hale); J Beach (Leicester), G Bantoft (Tynemouth), J Hussey, R Bushnell (Coventry), H Hiam (Gloucester), H J Simmonds, F M Long

Murray scores a try for Wales in the north-east corner in front of a huge crowd which included spectators perched on the roof of the Worcester Street stand [Journal]

(Cheltenham), W A Trask (captain, Plymouth)

Wales: B L Williams (Cardiff); K R Thomas (Swansea), E Stockford (Bridgend), K Jones (Abertillery), W L Murray; T R J Gravell (captain, Aberavon), T A Whitfield (Newport); T N Masters (Penygraig), D K Hatton (Abertillery), D R Thomas (Mountain Ash), L M C Hale (Newport), W D Lewis (Ogmore Valley), G L Garnham (Swansea), A E Minty (Abercarn), W K Rees (Maesteg)

Referee: Mr R J Jones (Cross Keys)

Kingsholm was packed with 20,000 fans, who did not have to wait long for Wales to score their first try, although the second came only just before half-time, when the score was 0-8. Kirkby suffered concussion and could not resume after half-time, which damaged the English cause, but they were completely and utterly outclassed, and the second half turned into a rout, Wales winning by four goals and three tries to nil. Whilst this was a crushing defeat for England, Kingsholm as a venue had again been a winner – the attendance record at a boys' match had been smashed and never had such a profit been banked by the English Schools RU.

Trevor Wellington (Sheriff of Gloucester), greets W A Trask (English captain) at the Civic Reception after the match; on the left is Eric Keys and fourth from right is T R J Gravell (Welsh captain) [Journal]

Gloucestershire & Somerset Schoolboys 35 Cornwall & Devon Schoolboys 0 5th February 1938

THIS MATCH WAS staged as an English schools trial.

Gloucestershire and Somerset: Cullen (Bristol); Locke (Gloucester), Sara (Weston), Parkes (Bristol), Davis; Bircher (Gloucester) Hawkins; Daniels, Neal, Price (Bristol), Holt (Weston-super-Mare), Jones (Forest of Dean), Bastable (Bridgwater), Knight (Cheltenham), Hopkins (Gloucester)

Devon and Cornwall: Uren (Camborne); Godbeer (Exeter), Pulling (Barnstaple), Garland (Plymouth), Woolcock (St Ives); Irish (Hayle), Harvey (Newlyn); Heather, Williams (Redruth), Elson, Pomeroy, Parkin (Plymouth), Husbands (Barnstaple), Lander (St. Ives), Shear (Exeter).

Referee : Mr. J. H. Holder (Gloucester).

The game opened with forward rushes by each side before Davis and Locke showed their speed with fine runs down their wings, and it was Davis who got away again and out-stripped his opponents to score an unconverted try in the corner. G&S kept up the attack and with the forwards heeling cleanly almost every time, their three-quarters got plenty of work, which allowed Sara to cut through on his own to score an unconverted try wide out and Daniels to score a runaway try under the posts, which Price converted. G&S kept up the pressure and just before half time Daniels flopped over for another unconverted try for a 14-0 lead.

G&S opened the second half with a try when the D&C full-back fumbled and Knight dribbled through. Davis followed this up with a

brilliant try, running from halfway with a fine turn of speed and side-stepping the full-back to score under the posts. Price converted. G&S were having things very much their own way, and Jones got over for an unconverted try from a line-out. Locke secured possession in the loose, cut in towards the centre with a side-step, and scored under the posts, and then Knight broke away to send in Price, who converted both.

Gloucestershire Boys 21 Somerset Boys 0 21st January 1939

GLOUCESTERSHIRE BOYS WORE black armlets in memory of the late Mr J T Brookes, Chairman of the Gloucester Club and two minutes silence was observed before play began. The ground was very slippery, and not at all helpful to open play.

Gloucestershire made the first attack with a forward rush, and after a tussle near the Somerset line A Jones forced his way over for an unconverted try. Gloucestershire kept up a steady pressure, and a neat combination on the left wing brought a try for Edwards, who swerved cleverly past two opponents, before Ferris added a third in the right-hand corner. Just before half-time Daw added a fourth.

After the interval, a good touch-finder by A Jones and a forward rush, soon put Gloucestershire on the attack again. After Somerset had touched down twice behind their own line, Gloucestershire got the ball out cleanly from a loose scrum and L Jones shook off all tacklers to score a good try. Ferris added another by pouncing on the ball when it came loose behind the Somerset line. Towards the end Somerset showed some improvement and kept play in the Gloucestershire half for some time, but they were unable to get close enough to be dangerous, and just before no side Gloucestershire rushed to the other end and Franklin scored their seventh try.

After the match, L Jones, D Ferris, R Franklin, R Price and F Cook of Gloucester were selected to play for Gloucestershire and Somerset against Devon and Cornwall in an English trial.

Gloucestershire Boys 21 Northern Home Counties Boys 3 1st April 1939

IT WAS THE visitors who opened the scoring soon after the start with a penalty goal by their captain, Till. Gloucestershire retaliated almost immediately, with a penalty goal by Wellington. The home side had the better of the first half and Ferris, on the right wing, made several promising runs, but it was Jones who put the home side ahead by breaking through and scoring an unconverted try near the posts. Till nearly levelled the scores with another penalty shot, which one linesman actually signalled as a goal, but the referee ruled otherwise. So the home side reached half time with a narrow 6-3 lead.

Edwards, the home captain, put Gloucestershire further ahead just after the interval with an unconverted try in the corner. Then Jones, following up a punt ahead by Franklyn ran through to score his second try, which was also unconverted. Gloucestershire continued to attack, and several times opened out nicely, but still were not passing quickly enough. Eventually Heath got over from a line out on the visitors' line, and Sherwood added another in the other corner. The Home Counties had hardly been out of their own half, and Gloucestershire launched attack after attack on their line. Eventually a punt by Waters gave the Counties a lot of ground but Jones retaliated with a dodging run, and Clark followed this up by scoring a final try for Gloucestershire.

The Second Coming of Gloucestershire

Gloucestershire 20 Somerset 11
9th November 1929

AFTER DRAWING THEIR first group game 8-8 at Exeter, Gloucestershire knew that their season would effectively be over if they failed to win the second at Kingsholm. Perfect weather greeted a crowd of about 6,000, which included John Daniell and Admiral Percy Royds of the English Selection Committee, although attendance on the side with the cheapest entry charge of 2d was disappointingly less than had been hoped for.

The Gloucestershire team against Somerset – standing: S Weaver, H Boughton, R N Williams, J Davies, F Wadley, L E Saxby, W Bryant; seated: Roy James, George Davies, A Carpenter, J S Tucker, D Burland, T Babington, R A Roberts (Hon Sec); in front: I C Bendall, C Carter [CC&GG]

Gloucestershire: H Boughton; Roy James (Gloucester), D Burland (Bristol), T Babington (Leicester), George Davies (Cheltenham); C Carter (Bristol), I C Bendall (Cheltenham); L E Saxby, J Davies, A Carpenter, F Wadley (Gloucester), J S Tucker, W Bryant (Bristol), R N Williams (St Bart's Hospital), S Weaver (Cinderford)

Somerset: J E Connelly (Weston-super-Mare); W Hancock (Bath), R A Gerard (Taunton School), A W Lillicrap (Bristol), A V Twose (Wellington); D J Snooks (Bridgwater), D W Pickles (Bristol); A J Spriggs (captain, Bridgwater), W Hale (Bristol), H G Clayton (Weston-super-Mare), E J McIntyre, E M Bovill (Tank Corps), G G Gregory (Taunton), T D Corpe (Clifton), T Masters (Wellington)

Referee: Mr E Langham (Leicester)

Play was fairly even in the first half, but Gloucestershire took their chances, opening the scoring when Roy James raced down the left touchline before cross-kicking to Weaver who dashed over next to the posts. Don Burland converted, and then George Davies dropped an unlikely goal from an oblique angle. Just before half-time, Bendall made a clean break, and put Roy James away – he was tackled as he went over the line, and was knocked out in the act of scoring.

Gloucestershire turned round 12 points to the good, but had to resist a determined comeback by Somerset which resulted in two tries. However, a second from Weaver and one from Burland saw the home side run out comfortable winners in the end. Harold Boughton was the man of the match, with his excellent positioning, several strong runs, and most of all his siege-gun kicking, which regularly relieved the pressure.

Boosted by this result, Gloucestershire went on to beat Cornwall and to win the group. They then defeated Middlesex 12-6 at Twickenham in the semi-final, and Lancashire 13-7 at Blundellsands in the final. In

Don Burland about to score a try in the second half [CC&GG]

doing so, they secured their sixth Championship title.

In 1930-31 Gloucestershire did not play any of their group games at Kingsholm, but a successful campaign brought them to Gloucester for a semi-final against Hampshire.

Gloucestershire 9 Hampshire 6
5th February 1931

HAMPSHIRE QUALIFIED FOR the semi-final as winners of the South group, and included a strong military contingent in their ranks. Les Saxby took over the captaincy of Gloucestershire when Sam Tucker was a late withdrawal, replaced by Ernest Comley to form an all-Gloucester front row. The attendance of between 5,000 and 6,000, and gate receipts of £650, were reckoned to be quite good for a Thursday fixture. All five England selectors were in attendance.

Harold Boughton missed an early penalty chance, 40 yards out in front of the posts, and although Hampshire then had a very good spell, surprising the home side with their vigour, they conceded another penalty wide out. Boughton made a grand attempt, but the ball just grazed the underside of the cross bar. However, when Hampshire were again penalised at a scrum after half an hour, Burland kicked the goal. Hampshire soon equalised with a penalty by Gosling, but had a narrow escape when Dowling and McCanlis came close, and again from a Burland drop goal attempt. Back in their own half, the home side kicked clear, but the ball was passed out to Lane, who raced hard, punted ahead, and won the chase to touch down the ball over the line, which put the visitors ahead 3-6 at half-time.

Gloucestershire were hanging on in defence for much of the second half, repeatedly trapped in their own 25. Hampshire looked more likely to score, but the pace was frenetic and mistakes abounded. Eventually Hampshire started to tire, and the home pack, led by Les Saxby, finished the stronger. This pressure told with two late tries. First McCanlis put Dowling away, and the left wing ran hard for the corner and scored. And then came a gem of a try started and finished by Burland. After a splendid effort by Osborne, who cut inside, Burland looped round outside him and took the well-judged return pass to cross in the corner. Boughton just missed the conversion, and there was a very exciting last five minutes, with Gloucestershire pressing hard for another score, but both Dowling and Osborne were stopped in the nick of time. So the Champions had prevailed, but their lack of finishing had made it a below-par performance.

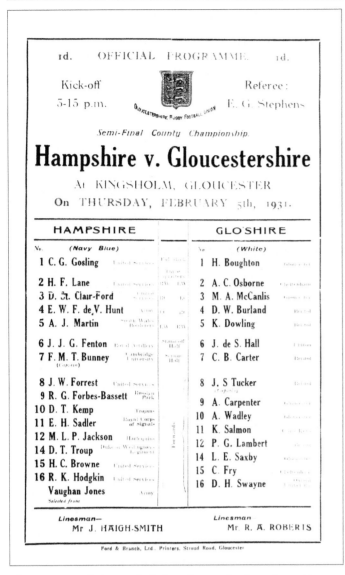

id. OFFICIAL PROGRAMME id.

Kick-off
3-15 p.m.

Referee:
E. G. Stephens

Semi-Final County Championship.

Hampshire v. Gloucestershire

At KINGSHOLM, GLOUCESTER

On THURSDAY, FEBRUARY 5th, 1931.

HAMPSHIRE		GLO'SHIRE	
No.	(Navy Blue)	No.	(White)
1 C. G. Gosling	United Services	1 H. Boughton	Gloucester
2 H. F. Lane	United Services	2 A. C. Osborne	Cheltenham
3 D. St. Clair-Ford	United Services	3 M. A. McCanlis	Gloucester
4 E. W. F. de V. Hunt	Army	4 D. W. Burland	Bristol
5 A. J. Martin	South Wales Borderers	5 K. Dowling	Bristol
6 J. J. G. Fenton	Royal Artillery	6 J. de S. Hall	Clifton
7 F. M. T. Bunney	Cambridge University	7 C. B. Carter	Bristol
(Captain)			
8 J. W. Forrest	United Services	8 J. S. Tucker	Bristol
			(Captain)
9 R. G. Forbes-Bassett	Rosslyn Park	9 A. Carpenter	Gloucester
10 D. T. Kemp	Trojans	10 A. Wadley	Gloucester
11 E. H. Sadler	Royal Corps of Signals	11 K. Salmon	Gloucester
12 M. L. P. Jackson	Harlequins	12 P. G. Lambert	Gloucester
14 D. T. Troup	Duke of Wellington's Regiment	14 L. E. Saxby	Gloucester
15 H. C. Browne	United Services	15 C. Fry	Cheltenham
16 R. K. Hodgkin	United Services	16 D. H. Swayne	Gloucester
Vaughan Jones	Army		
Selected from			

Linesman—	Linesman
Mr J. HAIGH-SMITH	Mr R. A. ROBERTS

Ford & Branch, Ltd., Printers, Stroud Road, Gloucester.

The programme, which was a single sheet of paper printed on only one side; note that both teams declined to use unlucky number 13 [Gloucestershire Archives]

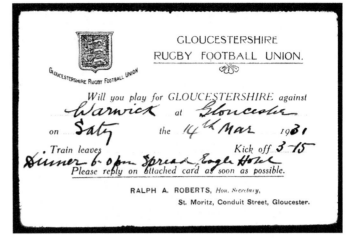

GLOUCESTERSHIRE RUGBY FOOTBALL UNION.

GLOUCESTERSHIRE
RUGBY FOOTBALL UNION.

Will you play for GLOUCESTERSHIRE against *Warwick* at *Gloucester*
on *Saty* the *14th Mar* 1931.
Train leaves
Dinner 6-0pm Spread Eagle Hotel
Please reply on attached card as soon as possible.

Kick off 3-15

RALPH A. ROBERTS, *Hon. Secretary*,
St. Moritz, Conduit Street, Gloucester.

*The invitation sent to Fred Wadley to play against Warwickshire
[Gloucestershire Archives]*

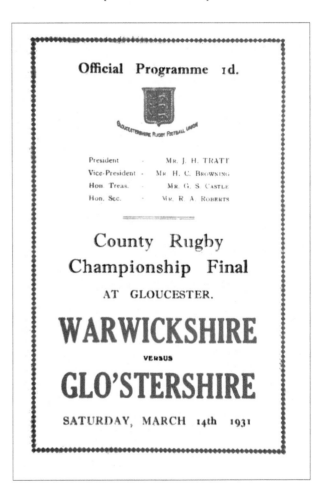

Official Programme 1d.

President	-	Mr. J. H. TRATT
Vice-President	-	Mr. H. C. BROWNING
Hon. Treas.	-	Mr. G. S. CASTLE
Hon. Sec.	-	Mr. R. A. ROBERTS

County Rugby
Championship Final
AT GLOUCESTER.

WARWICKSHIRE
versus
GLO'STERSHIRE

SATURDAY, MARCH 14th 1931

Gloucestershire 10 Warwickshire 9
14th March 1931

THE COUNTY CHOSE to return to Kingsholm to play against Warwickshire, who were making their first appearance in a county championship final, but had the confidence gained from a semi-final victory over Lancashire, and the advantage of the team cohesion which came from the selection of eleven Coventry players. The gates were opened early and 6,000 were inside Kingsholm an hour before kick-off, but swarms of spectators continued to descend on the ground, with men with megaphones trying to control them. 17,000 were crammed into the ground and the gate was £1,400. Warwickshire played in white and Gloucestershire in cherry and white.

Gloucestershire started with a whirlwind attack, but Davies bravely threw himself on the ball at the feet of the home forwards as they dribbled through to thwart the chance, and a counter-attack saw Smith almost score in the corner. Warwickshire gradually built an ascendancy, their forwards getting most of the possession from the scrums and their backs looking the more lively. They were rewarded after twenty minutes when Gascoigne burst through and passed to Ford, who scored to the right of the posts. Warwickshire:

swept down the field in a beautifully conceived passing movement. The ball travelled from left to right in the most electrifying style, and when Harriman passed out to Mayo in Gloucestershire's 25 there was a great roar of cheering. Mayo drew Boughton and passed out to Smith, who ran in to score in the corner. It was all Warwickshire and Smith went over again only to be called back for a forward pass.

Warwickshire were very good value for their 6-0 lead at half-time, and went off at a terrific pace again on the restart, but Boughton managed to stop Bonham when he looked all over a scorer. The Gloucestershire forwards dribbled out and:

Warwickshire		Referee: Mr. E. HOLMES (Dolham)		Gloucestershire	
NO	White Jerseys, with Crimson Badge.			NO	Cherry and White
1	H. J. Davies	Rugby	Full Back	1	H. J. Boughton	Gloucester
			Three-Quarters			
8	H. E. W. Smith	Rugby	R. Wing L. Wing	2	K. Dowling	Bristol
4	T. P. Mayo	Coventry	R. Centre L. Centre	3	M. A. McCanlis	Gloucester
3	G. Harriman	Coventry	L. Centre R. Centre	4	D. W. Burland	Bristol
2	S. H. Bonham	Coventry	L. Wing R. Wing	5	C. A. Osborne	Cheltenham
6	W. E. Lole	Coventry	Stand-off Half	6	W. Thomas	Lydney
7	A. Gascoigne	Coventry	Scrum Half	7	C. B. Carter	Bristol
8	T. Coulson, Capt.	Coventry		8	J. S. Tucker, Capt.	Bristol
9	F. Ford	Coventry		9	P. Wadley	Gloucester
10	A. Walker	Coventry		10	A. D. Carpenter	Gloucester
11	R. S. Roberts	Coventry		11	R. N. Williams	St Bart's Hospital
12	H. Wheatley	Coventry	Forwards	12	P. G. Lambert	Bristol
13	N. C. Marr	Rugby		14	L. E. Saxby	Gloucester
14	A. J. Rowley	Coventry		15	J. Davies	Gloucester
15	P. E. Dunkley	Harlequins		16	K. Salmon	Cross Keys
	Linesman—J. H. BURTON		Kick-off 4·30 p.m.		Linesman—R. A. ROBERTS	

from a scrum Carter passed to Thomas, who cut through and passed out to Burland. The Bristol man drew Davies and then passed out to McCanlis, who raced through unchallenged to score behind the posts. Boughton converted.

With their lead suddenly reduced to a single point, Warwickshire looked rattled, but Bonham raced away on the left and had his opponents beaten when he put a foot in touch. The Warwickshire forwards then battered away on the Gloucestershire line for a lengthy period, but the defence held firm.

McCanlis heading for the line to score Gloucestershire's first try [Citizen]

From a drop out, Burland raced away and, although tackled, he managed to pass out to Osborne. The Cheltenham winger went down on the right and passed in to McCanlis, and the latter, although tackled by Coulson, threw the ball out to Saxby, who scored under the posts. Boughton converted amidst great enthusiasm. Warwickshire fought back and Bonham missed an easy penalty kick. With 15 minutes to go there was an exhilarating struggle for supremacy, and the excitement was intense when Dunkley kicked a penalty goal for Warwickshire.

Gloucestershire held on for the narrowest of wins. As in the semi-final, they had been outplayed for three-quarters of a thrilling game, played at high speed. Much of their success was down to their stout defence, and their greater stamina told at the end of the game. National newspapers carried headlines such as "Gloucestershire Not The Better Team", whilst even the Citizen conceded that the victory was rather lucky, although WB thought it the best County game he had seen in almost fifty years of viewing.

1. The victorious home team – back row: T P Barrow, A W Chapple, E S Bostock Smith, J T Brookes (all County committee members); second row: E Holmes (referee), R A Roberts (County Secretary), M A McCanlis, F Wadley, J Davies, R N Williams, G S Castle (County Treasurer); seated: W T Pearce (President, Rugby Union), J H Tratt (County President), H Boughton, D W Burland, L E Saxby, J S Tucker, A Carpenter, P G Lambert, K Salmon, H W Browning (County committee); in front: C A Osborne, C B Carter, W Thomas, K Dowling
2. Former Gloucester and Gloucestershire players – George Clutterbuck, Arthur Hudson, George Romans, "Father" Dix, Stan Weaver, Dai Gent, "Biddy" Halford, Tom Voyce, Arthur Cromwell and "Tart" Hall
3. Ford and Coulson (former Gloucester players in the Warwickshire team)
4. A breakaway in the second half by Warwickshire, with Gascoigne, the scrum half on the right, about to take the ball [CC&GG]

A commiseration card issued following the defeat of Warwickshire [Gloucester Rugby]

Scenes at the Cornwall match:
1. A line out with Gloucestershire in the white jerseys
2. The Gloucestershire team run out from the gymnasium, led by Carter and McCanlis
3. Carter about to get the ball away from a scrum
4. Spectators in front of the pavilion
5. Saxby, the Gloucestershire captain, jumping for the ball
6. The crowd in the cheap enclosure on the Tump [CC&GG]

Gloucestershire 28 Cornwall 3
12th December 1931

GLOUCESTERSHIRE STARTED THEIR 1930-31 campaign with a heavy loss in Devon, which would normally have settled their fate for the season. However, boosted by a win over Somerset at Bristol, Gloucestershire started as favourites against Cornwall at Kingsholm, further strengthened by the introduction on their right wing of "Kit" Tanner, who turned out to be the hero of the match. He joined three other England internationals in the side – Tom Brown, Don Burland and Maurice McCanlis. More than 5,000 spectators cheered the teams onto the field.

Gloucestershire: T Brown; K Dowling (Bristol), M A McCanlis (Gloucester), D W Burland (Bristol), C C Tanner; R James (Gloucester), C B Carter (Bristol); A D Carpenter, E Comley(Gloucester), A D Allen (Bristol), K Salmon (Cross Keys), P G Lambert (Bristol), L E Saxby, J Hemming (Gloucester), C Fry (Cheltenham)

Cornwall: R Jennings (Redruth); J S Walsham (RNE College and Devonport Services), H Curnow (Redruth), P Collins (Camborne), G A P Moorhead (Camborne School of Mines); F Rule (Redruth), H Richards (Penrhyn); F Sellwood (Camborne), E Smith (Falmouth), L Buckingham (Redruth), C Webb (Devonport Services), W Rowe (Penzance), C G H Penny (Camborne School of Mines), C Roberts (Falmouth), C Triniman (Redruth)

Referee: Mr F C Stephens (North Midlands)

Gloucestershire took an early lead when the ball was passed to the right from a scrum; Burland fed Tanner, who was challenged by two opponents, but with a strong hand-off he beat both and scored a fine try in the corner. Tanner continued to look dangerous, but it was Burland who ran in the next two tries, the second scored under the posts after McCanlis, who scored under the posts himself. The favour was soon returned when Burland fed McCanlis to score under the posts. Cornwall pressed from the re-start, but lost the ball, and the Citizen reported:

> From their own goal Gloucestershire opened out, and Tanner was given possession ten yards from the line. Putting on full speed the old Cambridge Blue beat immediate opponents and clearing Jennings scored one of the finest tries ever seen on Kingsholm or elsewhere. The whole crowd rose en masse to cheer Tanner on his effort, which was well deserved.

Gloucestershire turned round 23-0 ahead. After the break, Cornwall scored first with a penalty, before Tanner raced round to complete a memorable hat trick of tries on his first appearance for the County. Many of the Kingsholm faithful reckoned Tanner to be the most beautiful player they had ever seen, his sweeping runs at high speed regularly setting their pulses racing.

This result meant that Gloucestershire had to travel to Bridgwater for a replay to decide the outcome of the group. They somehow squeaked through 10-6, and did so again in the semi-final at Portsmouth, beating Hampshire 9-6, for the second year in succession. The final was also played away, against Durham at Blaydon, but a season which had started so disastrously finished with Gloucestershire County Champions again after a 9-3 win. For the second time in their history the County had won the title for three seasons in succession.

County Matches in the 1930s

HOLDERS OF THE Championship for the past three years, Gloucestershire started their 1932-33 campaign at Kingsholm against Devon, having lost to them at Exeter the previous season, and minus three internationals from their Championship-winning side – Saxby, Tanner and McCanlis.

Gloucestershire 6 Devon 11
22nd October 1932

RAIN HAD FALLEN on Gloucester for about thirty hours up until noon on the day of the match. However, the weather cleared and was bright and fine for the afternoon; the ground was soft but in good condition. About 5,000 was regarded as a disappointing turnout for a County Championship match.

Gloucestershire: T W Brown; K Dowling (Bristol), G Davies (Cheltenham), D W Burland (Bristol), Roy James; D. Meadows (Gloucester), C B Carter (Bristol); F Wadley, A Carpenter, E Comley (Gloucester), K Salmon (Cross Keys), A D Allen, P G Lambert (Bristol), P T James (Clifton), B Parsons (Bristol)

Devon: T Scourfield (Torquay); G W F Bell (Barnstaple), W Webber (Teignmouth & Blackheath), W Jarvis (Salcombe), J P Kirkby (R.N.E. College); E E Richards (Plymouth Albion), W J Delahay (Torquay); R H Sparks, A Brigstocke, M Wilson (Plymouth Albion), W Paddon (Devonport Services), W H Northcott (Newton Abbott), W Nixon (RNE College), H Rew (Exeter), C Lewis (RAF)

Referee: Mr R E Holmes (Durham)

Both sides fashioned early chances, but Devon were the first to come close with:

A reverse pass from Richards to Delahay sending the latter away. Jarvis progressed by the aid of a "dummy," but Bell, the next to receive, was finely collared by Burland. From inside their 25 Gloucestershire opened out, and the ball was got across quickly to James. The Gloucester wing ran with great resolution for 60 yards, and then cross-kicked. The ball was partially checked. Jarvis thinking he was over the goal line touched down, but he was yards inside the field of play, and was promptly upset. There was a scramble, and Gloucestershire rushed the ball over the mark. There was a shout as Burland apparently gained the touch, but only a minor, however, was given.

It was Devon who took the lead when Northcott went over for a try, with an opponent clinging to his back, following a dashing run by Lewis. This proved to be the only score in the first half

Soon after the restart, Gloucestershire equalised when Burland picked up a loose ball, sold a dummy to Scourfield, and cut through for a fine try. They then went ahead as "Burland gathered and sent to James, who took an awkward pass nicely. He only had to beat Scourfield, but with a characteristic side-step he had the Devon custodian well beaten, and completed a nice effort by scoring a try. Davies' kick for goal hit the upright." Delahay put in a powerful run, handing off Burland and beating Brown, to put Webber in for a fine equalising try, and another from Bell, which Sparkes converted, proved to be the match-winner.

Gloucestershire 14 Somerset 7
11th November 1933

THE GLOUCESTERSHIRE TEAM appeared in a new strip – white jerseys and shorts and red and white stockings.

Gloucestershire: H Boughton; C C Tanner (Gloucester), D W Burland (Bristol), J C Brooks, R James; D Meadows, C Fifield; E Comley, A D Carpenter (Gloucester), F W Tucker (Bristol), K Foss (Clifton), C A L Richards (Clifton and Oxford University), Ivor Williams (Gloucester), C Murphy, A T Payne (Bristol)

Somerset: K C Kinnersley (Bristol); A E Merrett, S Williams, W H Moncrieffe (Bath), K G Harvey (Bristol); T J M Barrington (Bristol), P S Luffman (St Thomas's Hospital); N W Matthews (Bath), G G Gregory (Bristol), F W Williams (Weston-super-Mare), J Price (Taunton), R V Watkins (Devonport Services), J W R Swayne (Bridgwater), F C Goddard (Taunton), B Barber (Bath)

Referee: Mr J H Bott (London)

Kit Tanner (left) and John Brooks (right), heroes of the hour against Somerset [Gloucester Rugby]

A scrappy game suddenly burst into life when Gloucestershire heeled the ball from a scrum just inside the Somerset half, Brooks passed to Burland who shot through to the Somerset fullback, and found James up to take his pass before sprinting hard to race over behind the posts. The home side then put together another gem of a try from their own 25 – the forwards burst clear, Meadows made a beautiful run, and the ball then went via Brooks to Tanner, who drew the full-back before returning the ball to Brooks to score. Merrett replied for Somerset to make the half-time score 8-3.

The home backs continually threatened in the second half, and scored two glorious tries:

Fifield picked up in the loose, and started passing, and the ball was handled in turn by Meadows, Burland and Brooks, who fed Tanner immediately. The captain beat Merrett with his speed, and went straight for the corner. Here he was met by Kinnersley, who went for a low tackle. Tanner, however, jumped his man, and planted the ball over the line for a glorious try amidst deafening applause.

Inside their own half, Fifield swung out a nice pass to Meadows, who sent on to Burland. The Bristol centre cleared his opponent and handed to Brooks. The ball went out to the wing and back to Brooks, who went over with another glorious try. More excitement and continued cheering, and the movement deserved it.

Gloucestershire went on to win the group, and then beat Hampshire 10-9 at Boscombe in the semi-final, before losing 0-10 to East Midlands at Northampton in the final.

Gloucestershire 29 North Midlands 6
18th October 1934

THIS FRIENDLY FIXTURE was arranged as a warm-up for the County Championship campaign and attracted little interest, drawing a crowd estimated at 1,000.

Gloucestershire: H Boughton (Gloucester); T B H Burroughs (Clifton), L C Watkins, F G Edwards (Gloucester), W V Sheppard (Leicester); M Hobbs (Bristol), D Meadows (Gloucester); A D Carpenter, R Morris (Gloucester), A Jones, R G Hurrell, D Cummins (Bristol), Ivor Williams (Gloucester), W Woodward, C Murphy (Bristol)

North Midlands: J A M Tierney (Bromsgrove). P A Feeney (Moseley), T B Rigby (Birmingham University), H Kenyon (Birmingham University), C H Elgood (Old Edwardians); R J West (Handsworth), Lieut H P L Glass (Army); J T Merriman (Moseley), W G Bird (Old Edwardians), J Pritchard (Walsall), J MacDowell, B A Thomas, S E A Anthony (Old Edwardians), H R K Broughton, C G Trentham (Moseley)

Referee: Mr F Spill (Bristol)

Sloppy handling by the visitors allowed Edwards to gather the ball and put Watkins over behind the posts, which gave Boughton an easy conversion. Soon after Edwards and Watkins combined to hand an easy run in to Burroughs, so that Gloucestershire were eight points to the good in as many minutes. Burroughs scored his second try racing over in the corner, before Rigby gathered the ball on the bounce and passed to McDowell, who scored to register the Midlands' first points. But from the restart Watkins made an opening for Burroughs to complete his hat trick and Boughton converted to give the home side a 16-3 lead at half-time.

The second half opened with scrambling play, and a succession of mistakes in handling. Play was mostly in the Midlands half, but it was aimless sort of football and devoid of incident. The monotony was relieved by Kenyon effecting a smart clearance run to midfield,

Harold Boughton, who kicked eleven points against North Midlands
[Gloucester Rugby]

where Feeney continued the movement. The attack was beaten off, and then Meadows darted away, beat the immediate defence, and on reaching Tierney, gave to Watkins, who had an open line and an easy try behind the posts. Boughton goaled.

Kenyon picked up and, racing away, scored a fine try for the Midlands, but Gloucestershire responded with a try by Sheppard after a strong run. Boughton converted and completed the scoring with a late penalty.

Gloucestershire 5 Cornwall 7
14th December 1935

THIS WAS THE final match in the South West group, and with both teams arriving at Kingsholm with two wins under their belts, it would decide who faced Hampshire in the semi-final. It was 25 years since Cornwall had last won at Kingsholm. Owing to the threat of mist thickening, the teams kicked off 15 minutes early in front of 5,000 spectators.

Gloucestershire: H Boughton (Gloucester); W Claridge (Bristol), F G Edwards, J C Brooks (captain, Gloucester), W O Wood (Stroud); M S Hobbs, Ron Morris (Bristol); A D Carpenter, C Harris (Gloucester), W H Woodward (Bristol), J G A'Bear (Gloucester), R G Hurrell (Northampton), Ivor Williams (Gloucester), A T Payne, C R Murphy (Bristol)

Cornwall: F Pappin; L Roberts, Roy Jennings, K Williams, H Curnow; F Bone (Redruth), A P Steele-Perkins (Exeter); L Semmens,

F Gregory (Redruth), F Richards (Penryn), H Williams, F Roberts (Redruth), Marine Webb (Devonport Services), P Rogers (Redruth), C Selwood (Camborne)

Referee: Mr L H Sanderson (London)

In a fierce encounter, the play was not of the highest quality and Gloucestershire were criticised for contributing to their own downfall through a lack of thrust, judgement and finish behind the scrum. When Bone kicked an early dropped goal, his success was greeted by a cacophony of bells and rattles from the away supporters. Morris appeared to have replied in kind, but was called back for an earlier offence. However, sustained pressure brought a try by Payne, which was converted by Boughton for a one point lead for the home side at half-time.

WB reported in the Citizen that :

> Wood made the best individual run of the afternoon, a glorious effort in which he beat some half-dozen opponents and which only just failed in a try. He got the ball outside the 25 line and at that moment I thought his best policy was to run for the corner, where his speed would have carried him over. But Wood cut inside and exhibited amazing dexterity in clearing the opposition at a fast pace. He looked a scorer until a Cornishman grabbed him from behind and he was pulled down in sight of the coveted mark.

The climax to the game came in the last ten minutes, when Edwards made a fatal error in not passing the ball to Wood, who had a clear run to the posts. So, a penalty by Bone remained the solitary score in the second half and settled the issue.

Gloucestershire 6 Devon 3
24th October 1936

THIS WAS GLOUCESTERSHIRE'S first game of the season, and only about 2,000 came through the gates to see it. It proved to be the first of two very narrow wins at Kingsholm, which would eventually lead to the County being crowned Champions again.

Gloucestershire: G W Parker (Gloucester); T G N Baynham, R R Morris (Bristol), F G Edwards, Rev E L Phillips (Gloucester); E Day, D Meadows; T Price, A D Carpenter, C Harris, J G A'Bear (Gloucester), Lt V Tarrant (Bristol), Ivor Williams (Gloucester), A Payne, C Murphy (Bristol)

Devon: G R Knapman (Devonport Services), G R Matthews (Torquay Athletic), W M Hopkins (Aberavon), B Marsh, R Hurden (Devonport Services); R J P Madge (Exeter), J Merchant (captain, Torquay); J Pannell (Exmouth), W Sanders (Plymouth Albion), Lieut N L Evans (Devonport Services), W M Jones (Plymouth Albion), E J Wright (Newport), Paymaster-Lieut L Lyddon (Devonport Services), W White (Torquay Athletic), A Brigstoke (Plymouth Albion)

Referee: Mr D E Ellwood

Hurden opened the scoring for Devon early on with a try down the right wing, but Gloucestershire then had the better of the rest of the half. However, they failed to turn this into points, missing a couple of penalties and a drop goal attempt. This pattern continued after the break, when Don Meadows lost the ball as he was about to go over the line, but the breakthrough came when he started a movement which ended with Baynham going over on the right wing. Gloucestershire kept up the pressure and a punt ahead saw an exciting chase between Francis Edwards and Marsh, the Devon man just winning the touch-down with a desperate leap. At the death, a scrum on their line drew Devon offside, and Grahame Parker gratefully kicked the winning goal.

Grahame Parker, who kicked the winning goal against Devon [Gloucester Rugby]

Gloucestershire 7 Kent 5
30th January 1937

THIS MATCH WAS Gloucestershire's thirteenth appearance in a County Championship semi-final, their previous record being eleven wins and one loss. It was an icy day with sleet falling onto a muddy pitch,

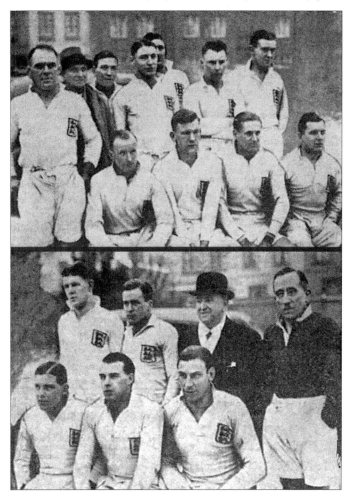

The Gloucestershire semi-final team against Kent: Upper group, back row from left: A D Carpenter, H Owens-Britton (President), C Harris, F G Edwards, J G A'Bear, A Wilcox, D Cummins; front row: P W Redwood, C R Murphy, R E Hook, R R Morris (captain); Lower group: back row: T G N Baynham, E L Phillips, R A Roberts (Secretary), C H Stewart (Referee); front row: W H Woodward, G W Parker, J D Haskins [Journal]

but despite these unpleasant conditions, 6,000 of the Kingsholm faithful turned out, paying £470 on the gate. Kent boasted international talent from far afield, including Vivian Jenkins, the Welsh full-back, as well as Charles Dick and Bill Young, both Scottish internationals.

Gloucestershire: G W Parker (Gloucester); T G Baynham (Bristol), E L Phillips, F G Edwards, R E Hook (Gloucester); R R Morris, P Redwood (Bristol); C Harris, A Carpenter (Gloucester), A Wilcox (Lydney), J G A'Bear (Gloucester), D Cummins, W H Woodward, J P Haskins, C R Murphy (Bristol)

Kent: V G J Jenkins (London Welsh); J A Macdonald, R C A Brandram (captain, Blackheath), R C S Dick (Guy's Hospital), W P Barton (Blackheath); F J Reynolds (Old Cranleighans), N C M Greenhalgh (Wasps); M H A Martin (Blackheath), R A Cooper (Old Brightonians), W M Inglis (R E Chatham), D G Gordon (London Scottish), N A Bromage (Old Dunstonians), P G Hobbs (Richmond), R L France (R E Chatham), W B Young (Harlequins)

Referee: Mr C H Stewart (Cheshire)

Gloucestershire won by a try and a dropped goal to a goal in rather dubious circumstances. There was nothing wrong with Brandram's early try for Kent, nor with Bob Hook's winning try, when he followed up a kick, gathered the ball in his stride and forced his way over. But inbetween these scores, Ronnie Morris's dropped goal was met with incredulity. It clearly went wide of the posts, both sides lined up for a 25 drop-out, and even the most one-eyed home supporter conceded that it had been missed. The only person on the ground who took a different view was the referee who went to the half-way line to restart the game and, despite Morris telling him that he had missed, he stuck to his guns and insisted on awarding the goal. This was possibly the worst ever refereeing decision at Kingsholm, but criticism of it by the ground's partisan supporters, normally so hard on visiting officials, was noticeably muted, the general reaction being a mixture of disbelief and amusement. Kent earned plenty of credit for sportingly accepting the decision.

Gloucestershire went on to beat East Midlands 5-0 in the final at Bristol; Ronnie Morris was again the key figure, wandering over the line in a semi-concussed state to score the winning try. It was certainly a campaign to remember for him, if only he could.

Gloucestershire 4 Somerset 0
23rd October 1937

HEAVY RAIN THE previous day, and a storm an hour before kick-off, led the covered accommodation at Kingsholm to be full to bursting, but the terraces to be rather sparsely populated for this first Championship match of the season for the title holders.

Gloucestershire: G W Parker (Gloucester); T H B Burrough (Clifton), F G Edwards (Birkenhead Park and Gloucester), E L Phillips (Gloucester), T G Baynham ; R R Morris (captain), P Redwood; A Jones (Bristol), A Carpenter, T Price, R Morris (Gloucester), D Cummins, G M Harrison, J Haskins, C Murphy (Bristol)

Somerset: R A Gerrard (Bath); S W Collett (Weston-super-Mare), F W McRae (St Mary's Hospital), G A White (Weston-super-Mare), W R Claridge (Bristol); F S Thornbury (Weston-super-Mare), T R Harris (Bath); F W Williams (Somerset Police), G Taylor (Police Union), H S Murley (Richmond), R E Price (Weston-super-Mare), K Foss (Bath), G Maunder (Somerset Police), W F Gay (Bath), Lieut J Watkins (Royal Navy)

Referee: Mr J B Whittaker (Lancashire)

Gloucestershire went close early on, but firstly Baynham was pulled down short of the line and secondly Burrough lost the ball in the corner after a clever kick by Morris. The home side continued to launch wave after wave of attacking moves, but frustration mounted as they all broke down, and both McCrae and Parker missed penalty shots. It was fast and furious up front, with Gloucester having the upper hand in the scrums and Somerset more lively in the loose. Parker and Gerrard missed further penalty attempts, before Somerset fashioned a couple of good chances, but Claridge lost the ball with the line at his mercy and Parker made a wonderful save when faced with the Somerset forwards dribbling the ball at him. So, half-time arrived with no score.

Gloucestershire started the second half strongly and had several good chances, and finally achieved the breakthrough. Edwards made a dashing break, Redwood passed on to Morris, and the captain dropped a lovely goal without breaking stride, the ball striking the inside of the post and falling just over the cross bar. There was plenty of cut and thrust for the rest of the game, but the defences held firm and the players started to tire from the hectic pace. The lead never looked comfortable. Gloucestershire came closest to a further score in the final minutes, but both Haskins and Morris came up short.

Gloucestershire 3 Devon 13
30th December 1937

THERE WAS A triple tie in the South West group, and this was the first play-off to resolve the issue. J H Bown, who had been playing at centre or on the wing for Gloucester, was brought into the Gloucestershire side at stand-off, where he replaced Ronnie Morris, captain of the previous season's Championship side. "Kit" Tanner took over as captain, playing alongside his fellow clergyman, Bill Phillips, but even with this pairing, there was no divine intervention for the home team. The crowd was estimated at 5,000.

Gloucestershire: G W Parker (Blackheath and Gloucester); C C Tanner (captain), E L Phillips (Gloucester), F G Edwards (Birkenhead Park and Gloucester), R Pearce; P Redwood (Bristol), J H Bown; T Price, A D Carpenter (Gloucester), A Jones (Bristol), R Morris (Gloucester), D Cummins, C R Murphy, J D Haskins (Bristol), Dr Shapiro (Cheltenham)

Devon: C Clive (Barnstaple); M Hurden (Plymouth Albion), R S Llewellyn (Oxford University), W E R Warne (Plymouth Albion), D Bond (Torquay Athletic); R J P Madge (Exeter), J P Merchant (Torquay); Lieut I Aylen (Devonport Services), W Sanders (Plymouth Albion), R Gove (Torquay Athletic), W G M Jones (Plyouth Albion), Lieut N L Evans (Devonport Services), A A Brown (St Luke's College), W White (Torquay), Lieut Arenge-Jones (Gloucester Regt)

Referee: Mr B C Gadney (London)

Bown was successful in kicking for position and Gloucestershire enjoyed long periods of pressure, but could not achieve a breakthrough. A poor match was error-strewn and scoreless until just before half-time, when Bown, who had looked the most dangerous player up to then, had his pass intercepted by Llewellyn. He shot off, kicked past Parker, sent the ball over the line, and followed up to win the chase to touch down for the opening try; Warne converted. The home side pressed again and Tanner came close to scoring twice, but the Devon defence held out. On the balance of play Gloucestershire should have been ahead, but they turned round 0-5 down at half-time.

In the second half, Devon started to play with "great dash", Hurden made a splendid run, but a knock-on saved Gloucestershire, and both Bond and Hurden on opposite wings came close. Tanner eventually cleared with a huge kick, Devon were penalised for off-side in front of their posts, and Parker kicked the goal to reduce the lead. Gloucestershire attacked hard, but Devon tackled well to thwart any further scoring by the home side, and came away for Warne to kick a penalty. They sealed their win at the death with a try by Brown, converted by Warne.

Gloucestershire 3 Somerset 11
31st December 1938

FOR THE SECOND season in succession, Gloucestershire went out of the Championship with a defeat in a South West group replay at Kingsholm. A crowd estimated at 6,000-7,000 attended along with two England selectors. Unable to dislodge Harold Boughton at full-back for Gloucester, Grahame Parker was now playing all his club rugby for Blackheath but retained the faith of the County selectors.

Gloucestershire: G W Parker (Blackheath); J H Hunter (Cheltenham), W A M Baker (Newport), J C Brooks (Kendal), F G Edwards (Leicester); R R Morris (Bristol), E J Parfitt (Gloucester); T Price, A D Carpenter (Gloucester), G A Reid (Bristol), R Morris, J G A'Bear (Gloucester), C R Murphy, P Haskins, D C Cummins (Bristol)

Somerset: R A Gerrard; A V Rogers (Bath), E A Thomas (Somerset Police), G A White, S W Collett (Weston-super-Mare); T R Harris, N Halse (Bath); S H Justin (Bristol), R Davies, F W Williams (Somerset Police), R E Price (Weston-super-Mare), L J Sargeant (Bristol), G M Fursland (Bridgwater), J K Watkins (Royal Navy), F C Goddard (Taunton)

Referee: Mr E Haslemere (Rugby)

Most of the first half was played in Somerset territory, but they scored first, against the run of play, with a penalty kicked by Gerrard. The Somerset defence held firm, and Gloucestershire's only reward for multiple attacks was an equalising penalty by Parker from in front of the posts.

In the second half, Gloucestershire had early chances, which they squandered. This encouraged Somerset to expand their game, and the best three-quarter move of the game resulted in a try by Collett. Gloucestershire then seemed to lose heart and Somerset capitalised with a try scored by Thomas and converted by Gerrard. So, Somerset deservedly won a tight match in which their defence had been the dominant factor in deciding the outcome.

Army Cup Match

Welch Regiment 15 Scottish Borderers 9
20th January 1938

KINGSHOLM WAS CHOSEN as a neutral ground when the 1st Battalion the Welch Regiment, based in Belfast, and the King's Own Scottish Borderers, stationed in Portsmouth, were drawn together in the fourth round of the Army Cup. The match was played on early closing day in Gloucester and prices of admission were Grandstand 1s, Worcester Street 6d and Dean's Walk 3d. The match attracted a crowd of around 1,000.

Welch Regiment: Pte I Owen; 2nd Lt L H Mackie, Pte J Delaney, Lt B T V Cowey (captain), Cpl D Carney; Sgt H Ibbitson, L Cpl H R Coleman; Cpl S Lett, Sgt C R Owen, Pte N Pennell, Pte P Cowell, Pte C Pass, Pte L Roberts, L Cpl C W Hopkins, Pte W E Buss

Scottish Borderers: Capt F M V Tredegar; Lt F H Anderson, 2nd Lt C A Wade, 2nd Lt C G Sheriff, Lt J L Stewart; Pte Nicholl, Pte Gordon; Pte Buchanan, Sgt Miller, Cpl Grieves, L Cpl Minto, Cpl Forbes, Pte Connor, Pte Wilson, Pte Scott

Referee: Mr J H Holder (Gloucester)

The Welch took an early lead when Ibbitson slipped through the defence for a try, which the Welch captain and former Welsh international, Cowey, failed to convert. Forbes soon replied with a try for the Scots. The Welch backs looked more clever and speedy, but the Scottish pack had the upper hand forward. Penalty goals kicked by Minto and Mackie levelled the scores at 6-6 at half-time.

The first ten minutes of the second half were contested in Welch territory, and Minto regained the lead for the Borderers with another penalty goal. However, the Welch backs put together a beautiful passing movement which took play to the Borderers line, and Mackie again brought the scores level with a good try, which went unconverted. The Welch remained on top, and tries by Cowey and Delaney sealed the victory for them.

World War Two Internationals

RED CROSS INTERNATIONAL

APPROVAL FOR HOME and away matches between England and Wales was granted in the first year of the war to raise funds for the Red Cross and to boost public morale. With so many players away on military duties and therefore unavailable for selection, these games were not regarded as full internationals and caps were not awarded. England won the first encounter in Cardiff and it was originally intended that the return would be played in Leicester, but this fell through and the match was switched to Kingsholm. All arrangements for the match were placed in the hands of the Gloucester Club.

The English team: back row: Engineer Commander S F Cooper (Secretary, Rugby Union), C Newton-Thompson, J T W Berry, J K Watkins, R Willsher, F G Edwards, G Gilthorpe, J Haig-Smith (linesman); seated: E J Unwin, J Heaton, P Cranmer, T A Kemp (captain), T F Huskisson, R E Prescott, D E Teden; in front: R H Guest, J Ellis [Journal]

England 17 Wales 3
13th April 1940

TWO MINUTES' SILENCE was held before the match in memory of Prince Obolensky (Rosslyn Park and England). He had played for England in the game at Cardiff and was selected to play in this match, but had been killed a few days prior to the match when his Spitfire crashed on landing. His place was taken by Dickie Guest. The match raised funds not only for the Red Cross but also for the Services Recreational Equipment Fund.

The Welsh team [Journal]

England: P Cranmer (Moseley); E J Unwin (Rosslyn Park), F G Edwards (Gloucester), J Heaton (Waterloo), R H Guest (Liverpool University); T A Kemp (captain, St Mary's Hospital), J Ellis (Wakefield); D E Teden (Richmond), C G Gilthorpe (Coventry), R E Prescott (Harlequins), T F Huskisson (Old Merchant Taylors), R Willsher (Bedford), J K Watkins (United Sevices), C Newton-Thompson (Cambridge University), J T W Berry (Leicester)

Wales: Howard Davies (Swansea); C Matthews (Bridgend), J Matthews (Bridgend), W Wooller (captain, Cardiff), H O Edwards

The touch judge's flag used for the 1940 International [Gloucester Rugby]

J Heaton touches down under the posts [Journal]

(Leicester); Haydn Tanner (Swansea), R Wade (Newport); W J Travers (Newport), W E N Davies (Cardiff), W J Evans (Pontypool), S Williams (Llanelly), E Kenefick (Aberavon), L Manfield (Cardiff), Rev H C Bowen (Llanelly), Ike Owen (Maesteg)

Referee: Mr A S Bean (Durham)

Wales scored first, when Haydn Tanner probed down the side of a scrum, eluding would-be tacklers and then bamboozling the defence with a long pass out to William "Bunner" Travers. This advantage was soon lost when Wales dropped out from their 25, the ball hit Gilthorpe, who passed it to Robin Prescott, who had a speculative drop at goal which dribbled over the bar. Derek Teden then barged his way through the Welsh defence for a try which Jack Heaton converted, so that England led 9-3 at half-time.

In the second half the crowd thought that Wilf Wooller, the Welsh captain, had scored with a marvellous run down the left touch-line, but play was called back for an earlier forward pass. England finished the match the stronger, scoring two further tries to seal a decisive victory. Heaton picked up in midfield, swerved past Davies, touched down under the posts and converted his own try. Then Tommy Kemp, who had been a constant danger, ran the ball before passing to Francis Edwards, the only Gloucester player on the field. To the noisy delight of the crowd, Edwards cut through and put Unwin over with a dash to the right-hand corner.

SERVICES INTERNATIONALS

LATER IN THE war, from 1942 to 1945, Services internationals between England and Wales were played each season, home and away, at Kingsholm and Swansea. As with the Red Cross internationals, these

The English team: back row: Capt Haigh Smith, Tom Voyce, E Williams, Hodgson, Mycock, Evans, Simmonds, Reynolds, Maj Sloan, Mr F Mansell (referee); seated: Newton-Thompson, Parker, Prescott, Col J Hartley, Walker, Huskisson, Longland, Gilthorpe; in front: Kenyon, Ellis [Journal]

The Welsh team: back row: Capt Giles, Edwards, Law, Price, Regan, Payne, Foster; seated: Sullivan, H Davies, Manfield, Risman, G Williams, Wendy Davies, S Williams; in front: Billy Davies, Tanner [Journal]

below: The programme for the 1942 international [Gloucestershire Archives]

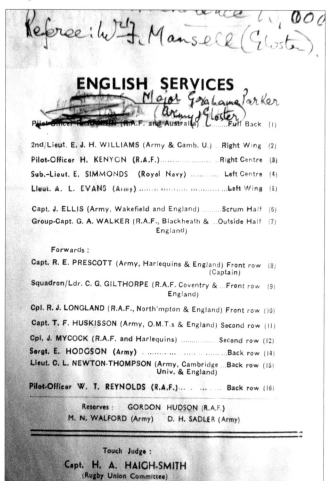

[Gloucestershire Archives]

England pressing near the Welsh line in the 1942 international with the Shed on the left [Journal]

too were not classed as full internationals and caps were not awarded. However, the pariah status of professional Rugby League players in amateur Rugby Union circles was set aside, the selectors being free to choose representatives from both codes, and they did.

England 3 Wales 9
28th March 1942

DURING THE EARLY stages, the England forwards dominated, but they tired as the match wore on; the Welsh backs proved more skilful, and their wing forwards caused England a multitude of problems. Wales opened the scoring with a 40-yard penalty by Risman, before Williams on the England wing showed a fine turn of speed in breaking away and passing inside to Kenyon, who kicked ahead, and Reynolds won the race to score a try in the corner. Wales frittered away other scoring chances by over-elaborating their passing, and half time arrived at 3-3.

Soon after the resumption, Simmonds crossed the Welsh line, but dropped the ball as he attempted to touch down, and that was England's last scoring opportunity. Unconverted tries by Edwards and Foster settled the match in Wales' favour.

England 7 Wales 34
20th March 1943

ENGLISH PREPARATIONS WERE disrupted by the late withdrawal of four of their first choice backs, and their replacement caused a wholesale reorganisation of the back division.

England: Lt R T Campbell (United Services); Sgt Instructor R L Francis (Dewsbury RL), A/C J Laurenson (Wigan RL & Wales RL), L/C C Ward (Bradford Northern RL), Major E T Unwin (Rosslyn Park & England); Capt M M Walford (Oxford University), Sub-Lt B L Cunningham (United Services); Cpl R J Longland (Northampton & England), Flt Lt J B McMaster (Bedford), Capt R E Prescott (captain, Harlequins & England), Cpl J Mycock (Harlequins & England), Surgeon-Lt R L Hall (St Barts), Cpl E H Sadler (Castleford English Rugby Union & Rugby League), Capt D L K Milman (Bedford & England), Cpl A G Hudson (Gloucester)

Wales: Pte A A Davies (Cardiff & Wales); Cpl S Williams (Aberavon & Wales), A/C B Williams (Cardiff), L/Cpl T F Sullivan (Swansea & Wales), Cpl A Edwards (Salford RL & Wales); Sgt W T H Davies (Swansea & Wales), O/Cadet H Tanner (captain, Swansea & Wales); Sec-Lt V J Law (Newport & Wales), Cpl R J Flowers (Pontypool &

The England scrum half, Ellis, gets the ball away from a scrum during the 1942 international [Journal]

Wales), Sgt W G Jones (Aberaman), Cpl R E Price (Weston-super-Mare & Wales), Cpl L Thomas (Llanelly), L/Bom Rees Williams (Swansea), Pte W E Tamplin (Pontypool & Welsh Trials), Sgt Instructor T Foster (Bradford Northern & Wales RL)

Referee: Mr S H Budd (Bristol)

The England team: back row: Capt H A Haigh Smith (touch judge), Cunningham, Ward, Campbell, Hall, McMaster, Hudson, Sadler, Walford, Mr Stanley Budd (referee); front row: Milman, Longland, Prescott, Mycock, Unwin; in front: Francis, Laurenson [Journal]

The Wales team: back row: Capt Ivor Williams (touch judge), Law, Price, Foster, Tamplin, Rees Williams, Thomas, Jones, Flowers; front row: A A Davies, S Williams, Edwards, Tanner, Sullivan, W T H Davies, B Williams [Journal]

Cunningham, the England scrum half, chasing the ball in 1943 [Journal]

Up against a reorganised opposition, the Welsh backs, led by Hayden Tanner, were brilliant. The first try came when Price broke through and Bledwyn Williams side-stepped man after man on his way to the line; Tamplin converted. England fought back with a drop goal by Unwin, but they suffered multiple injuries during the game, and both Ward and Mycock had to leave the field. Wales put a depleted England to the sword in the second half, with two tries each from Tamplin, Sid Williams and Bledwyn Williams. Francis scored England's only try.

England 20 Wales 8
8th April 1944

UNFORTUNATELY GORDON HUDSON, a Gloucester favourite, was unable to play for the England side, but was replaced by another local player in Lieut P N Walker (Army, Oxford University and Gloucester). Wales lost I Owen from their original selection and he was replaced by Flt Lieut A M Rees (RAF and Cambridge University).

England started well and were three points up in as many minutes as a result of a penalty goal kicked by Ward from half-way, and he extended the lead with a second. Coleman scored a try to reduce the arrears, but Parsons, the England scrum half, went over for England's first try. Just

The English team: back row: Capt Haigh Smith (touch judge), Ward, Stott, Walker, Dancer, Gilbert, Doherty, Hastings, Weighill; front row: Lawrenson, Francis, Longland, Prescott, Hollis, Mycock, Parsons [Journal]

The Welsh team: back row: Mr Stanley Budd (referee), Foster, Tanner, Jones, Coleman, Travers, Rees, Rees Williams, Law, Lieut Risman, Capt V J Jenkins (touch Judge); front row: Sullivan, Idwal Davies, S Williams, W Davies, A Davies, Tamplin, Knowles [Journal]

England on the attack, Laurenson with the ball in 1943 [Journal]

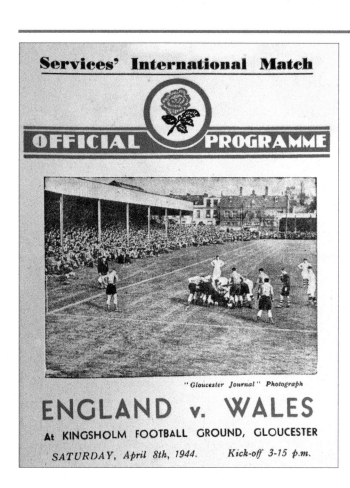

Services' International Match

OFFICIAL PROGRAMME

"Gloucester Journal" Photograph

ENGLAND v. WALES

At KINGSHOLM FOOTBALL GROUND, GLOUCESTER

SATURDAY, April 8th, 1944.   Kick-off 3-15 p.m.

The Welsh fullback, A Davies, is tackled by Gilbert, with Longland running up in support [Journal]

Francis handing off Sullivan; behind Sullivan is Idwal Davies; the other England players are Jackson and Stott [Journal]

IN AID OF THE ROYAL NAVY, ARMY and ROYAL AIR FORCE CHARITIES

ENGLAND (White Jerseys, White Shorts, Blue and White Stockings)	Referee: Mr. STANLEY BUDD (Bristol)		WALES (Red Jerseys, Blue Shorts, Red Stockings)
15 L/Cpl. E. WARD (Army and Bradford Northern)	**Full Backs**		15 Pte. A. A. DAVIES ... (Army and Newport)
	Three-quarters:		
11 Sgt.-Instr. R. L. FRANCIS... (Army and Dewsbury)	L. Wing	R. Wing	11 Cpl. S. WILLIAMS ... (Army and Aberavon)
12 Cfn. J. STOTT ... (Army and St. Helens)	L. Centre	R. Centre	12 F/O IDWAL DAVIES ... (R.A.F. and Swansea)
13 LAC J. LAWRENSON ... (R.A.F. and Wigan)	R. Centre	L. Centre	13 Sergt. T. SULLIVAN ... (Army and Swansea)
14 Lieut. G. HOLLIS .. (Royal Navy and Sale)	R. Wing	L. Wing	14 L/Cpl. J. C. KNOWLES (Army and Newport)
	Half-Backs:		
10 Lieut. P. R. HASTINGS ... ... (Army)	Stand-off	Stand-off	10 Sgt. W. H. T. DAVIES, Capt. (R.A.F. and Bradford)
9 S/Ldr. J. PARSONS ... (R.A.F. and Leicester)	Scrum	Scrum	9 2/Lieut. H. TANNER ... (Army and Swansea)
8 Capt. R. E. PRESCOTT, Captain (Army & Harlequins)			8 Lieut. V. J. LAW ... (Army and Newport)
7 Cpl. R. J. LONGLAND (R.A.F. and Northampton)			7 Sergt. W. H. TRAVERS (Army and Newport)
6 Sergt. G. T. DANCER (R.A.F. and Bedford)			6 Sergt. W. G. JONES... (Army and Newport)
5 Cpl. J. MYCOCK ... (R.A.F. and Harlequins)	**Forwards:**		5 Gunner R. G. COLEMAN (Army and Newport)
4 Schoolmaster J. B. DOHERTY (Royal Navy and Sale)			4 Gunner REES WILLIAMS (Army and Swansea)
3 Cpl. A. G. HUDSON ... (R.A.F. and Gloucester)			3 Sergt.-Instr. T. FOSTER (Army & Bradford Northern)
2 F/Lt. R. G. H. WEIGHILL (R.A.F. and Waterloo)			2 2/Lieut. W. E. TAMPLIN (Army and Pontypool)
1 Major F. W. GILBERT ... (Army and Coventry)			1 Sergt. I. OWEN ... (R.A.F. and Aberavon)
CAPT. H. A. HAIGH-SMITH	Touch Judges		CAPT. V. J. JENKINS

ROYAL AIR FORCE TECHNICAL TRAINING COMMAND BAND By kind permission of the Air Officer Commanding-in-Chief

before the interval, Willie Davies slipped through the defence for a clever try which Tamplin converted, and England were only 9-8 ahead at half-time. The game had been played at a tremendous pace up to this point.

Wales pressed for much of the second half, but the English defence held firm, and the pace started to drop. In the last ten minutes, Francis scored a brilliant try from the left wing, and the English forwards staged a remarkable recovery, Doherty and Weighill scoring two tries on the end of forward rushes which overwhelmed a tiring Welsh side.

Evans with the ball, supported by Travers [Journal]

England 9 Wales 24
7th April 1945

ENGLAND: Lt M T A Ackerman (South African Air Force); Cpl A E Johnston (Warrington & Army), Sgt M P Goddard (New Zealand Air Force), L/Cpl E Ward (Bradford Northern & Army), Lt G Hollis (captain, Sale & RN); A/B E Ruston (RN), Sqn Ldr J Parsons (Wasps & RAF); Cpl R J Longland (Northampton & RAF), Wg Cdr C G Gilthorpe (Wasps & RAF), Cpl P Plumpton (Downside School & RAF), Capt F P Dunkeley (Harlequins & Army), LAC R Peel (Bedford & RAF), Cpl A G Hudson (Gloucester & RAF), Flt Lt R G H Weighill (Waterloo & RAF), Sgt E Bedford (Hull Kingston Rovers & RAF)

The English team: back row: Ackerman, Plumpton, Hudson, Peel, Ward, Bedford, Weighill, Parsons; front row: Goddard, Dunkeley, Longland, Hollis, Gilthorpe, Johnston, Ruston [Journal]

The Welsh team: back row: Bowes, Owens, E Evans, Thomas, Tamplin, Travers; front row: Cliff Evans, Trott, Williams, Risman, Phillips, Edwards, Watkins; in front: Tanner, Davies [Journal]

Wales: CSMI F Trott (Penarth & Army); F/O Cliff Evans (Neath & RAF), F/O B L Williams (Cardiff & RAF), Lt A J Risman (Salford & Army), Sgt A Edwards (Salford & RAF); Sgt W H T Davies (captain, Bradford Northern & RAF), Capt H Tanner (Swansea & Army); Bbr E Evans (Llanelly & Army), Gnr W H Travers (Newport & Army), P/O A

Goddard about to hand off a Welsh forward [Journal]

D S Bowes (Cardiff & RN), BSM H Thomas (Neath & Army), Cpl D Phillips (Swansea & Army), Sgt I Owens (Aberavon & RAF), F/Sgt E V Watkins (Cardiff & RAF), Lt W E Tamplin (Pontypool & Army)

Referee: Mr R A Beattie (Scotland)

The game was won in the first half, when Wales demonstrated the value of team work. England had talented individuals, but Wales were superior in their organisation as a team. Alan Edwards scored a try after ten minutes, Haydn Tanner soon added a dropped goal, Risman kicked a penalty, and both Owens and Tanner ran in tries, before England eventually responded with a penalty kicked by Ward. Wales turned round with a 16-3 lead.

England made a better fist of it in the second half, and were rewarded when Goddard intercepted and put Hollis in for a try, but Edwards caught Ackerman in possession and scored his second try, which Risman converted, before Ward finished the scoring with another England penalty.

Other Representative Matches during the 1940s

MATCHES BETWEEN THE Gloucester Club and Services teams were played during the first half of the Second World War – details are given on the www.gloucesterrugbyheritage.org.uk website. Kingsholm also hosted a few matches between Services representative teams in the latter years of the war and immediately afterwards. This included a visit by Australia, which had been postponed from 1939 to 1947.

Army 14 RAF 30
30th October 1943

THIS MATCH WAS played in aid of RAF and Army charities and the sides were composed largely of wartime internationals. It was reported to be the most enjoyable game seen at Kingsholm since the outbreak of war. With 'thrusters' like Laurenson, Walters and Bruce, and 'flyers' such as Francis and Remlinger, there was plenty of talent on show.

Gloucester players representing their Services in this match – from left: Lt P N Walker, Cpl A G Hudson and Capt T G H Jackson [Journal]

Army: Sgt A A Davies (Cardiff & Wales); Sgt-Instr R L Francis (England), Cadet L F Oakley (Bedford), Maj C R Bruce, Capt T G H Jackson (Scotland); Lt H J C Rees, Lt H Tanner (Wales); Capt R E Prescott (captain, England), Cpl R Flowers, Sgt W T Jones (Wales), Lt P N Walker (Oxford University & Gloucester), Gunner Rees Williams (Wales), Capt G D Shaw (Scotland), Lt W E Tamplin (Wales), Capt R G Firbank (East Midlands)

The RAF team: back row: Flt Lt A D Matthews (touch judge), Sgt J Owen, Cpl A G Hudson, Sgt H Walters, Cpl J Mycock, Sqn Ldr J E I Grey, Flt Sgt J H Dustin; middle row: Cpl R J Longland, A M Rees, Flt Lt H B Toft, Sgt W H T Davies, Cpl A Edwards, Flt Sgt H Watkins, Flt Lt J Parsons; in front: L A C J Laurenson, Sgt J J Remlinger [Journal]

RAF: Sqn Ldr J E I Grey (Bedford); Cpl Alan Edwards (Salford RL & Wales), LAC J Laurenson (Wigan RL & England), Sgt H Walters (Swansea), Sgt J J Remlinger (Wasps); Sgt W T H Davies (Bradford RL & Wales), Flt Lt J Parsons (Wasps & England); Cpl R J Longland (Northampton & England), Flt Lt H B Toft (Waterloo & England), Flt Sgt J H Dustin (RNZAF), Cpl A M Rees (London Welsh), Cpl J Mycock (Harlequins, Sale & England), Flt Sgt H Watkins (Wigan RL & Wales), Cpl A G Hudson (Gloucester & England), Sgt J Owen (Aberavon & Wales)

Referee: Mr Frank Mansell (Gloucester)

The Army team: Back row: Capt R G Firbank, Capt T G H Jackson, Lt W E Tamplin, Gunner Rees Willliams, Lt P N Walker, Cadet L F Oakley; middle row: Cpl R Flowers, Lt H Tanner, Sgt A A Davies, Capt R E Prescott, Maj C R Bruce, Capt G D Shaw, Sgt W T Jones; in front: Sgt-Inst R L Francis, Lt H J C Rees [Journal]

The RAF deserved to win, but the score perhaps flattered their superiority. Although the Army were outscrummaged, their backs operated like a well-oiled machine in the first half, running rings round the RAF defence and they deservedly turned round with a two-point advantage at half-time. Only heroic defence by Walters and Davies prevented the margin being greater.

Action during the game [Journal]

It was a different story in the second half, when the RAF backs came into their own and turned the tables on their opponents. There were some fine individual performances, most notably by Remlinger, a Frenchman, who showed an amazing turn of speed which more than made up for his diminutive size. However, most of the RAF scoring resulted from their backs hunting in pairs and overwhelming the Army defence.

Walters made an opening for Edwards to score, Toft cut through to set up a try by Watkins, before Walters helped Remlinger to get over the line and then scored one himself immediately afterwards. Davies cleared the way for Laurenson to score, and a solo effort by Remlinger rounded off a very fine performance. This spell decided the outcome of the match, but the Army fought back towards the end of the game, with Oakley cutting through and putting Jackson in for a try, but Toft charged down Tamplin's kick at goal.

Royal Air Force 6 National Civil Defence Services 10
10th February 1945

Tickets available in advance were sold out, and the match was watched by a crowd numbering 6-7,000. Before play started they were entertained by the Air Training Corps Band.

It was the flashy but erratic RAF team which had the star players, enjoyed an advantage in speed, and contributed all the inspirational moments in the game. But they just could not shake off the steady, solid slogging of the Civil Defence players, who were slower, but marked well, defended stoutly and took their chances when they came.

E Watkins of the RAF is tackled near the line [Journal]

Fyfe scored a try when he made the only break by a centre in the whole game, and the bustling Civil Defence forwards gained the upper hand to put Wheatley over for their second try, both being converted by Hall. Geddes replied with two penalties for the RAF, one from the touchline, and hit the post with another from the halfway line.

Only in the last few minutes did the RAF manage to exert real pressure, by which time they were down to 14 men, Remlinger having suffered a broken wrist. They were awarded an easy late penalty, but time was up so they ran it in an attempt to win the game. They failed again to breach the defence, and so the tortoises ended up beating the hares.

Combined Services 0 New Zealand Army XV 31
12th January 1946

This fixture attracted the biggest crowd at Kingsholm for many years. The Combined Services team bristled with Welsh internationals and included Johnny Thornton, Gloucester's most recent international, at wing forward. The Club took 15% of the gate for local charities, which amounted to £340 14s 0d.

The Combined Services team: back row: P H Davies, D B Vaughan, H P Hughes, J Thornton, J R C Matthews, R H Lloyd Davies, Mr I David (referee); front row: L Williams, J Anderson, B L Williams, C G Gilthorpe, L Manfield, D Phillips, W G Jones; in front: K H S Wilson, L Constance [Journal]

[Gloucestershire Archives]

COMBINED SERVICES
VERSUS
NEW ZEALAND
KIWIS

KICK OFF 2·30 p.m.

[Gloucester Rugby]

IN AID OF SERVICES' CHARITIES

COMBINED SERVICES	NEW ZEALAND (Kiwis)
Colours—White Jerseys, White Shorts	Colours—All Black

Full Back			Full Back	
15	L.A.C. R. H. LLOYD DAVIES (R.A.F.)		1	H. E. COOK
Three-quarters			**Three-quarters**	
14	F/Sergt. P. H. DAVIES (R.A.F.) *Right Wing*		2	J. R. SHERRATT *Left Wing*
13	P/O B. L. WILLIAMS (R.A.F.) *Right Centre*		3	J. B. SMITH *Centre*
12	Petty Officer L. WILLIAMS (Royal Navy) *Left Centre*		4	E. G. BOGGS *Right Wing*
11	Pte. J. ANDERSON (Army) *Left Wing*		**Five-eighths**	
Half Backs			5	I. PROCTOR
10	Lieut. L. CONSTANCE (R.N.V.R.) *Stand-Off*		6	F. R. ALLEN
9	Major K. H. S. WILSON (Army) *Scrum Half*		**Scrum Half**	
Forwards			7	C. K. SAXTON (Captain)
8	A/B G. M. BEVAN (Royal Navy)		**Forwards**	
7	Wing Commander C. G. GILTHORPE (R.A.F.)		8	N. THORNTON
6	W/Sergt. W. G. JONES (Army)		9	G. BOND
5	Corpl. D. PHILLIPS (Army)		10	F. N. HAIGH
4	Surg.-Lt. (D) J. R. C. MATTHEWS (R.N.V.R.)		11	P. RHIND
3	Instr.-Lt. D. B. VAUGHAN (Royal Navy)	Referee :	12	K. D. ARNOLD
2	Sqdn.-Ldr. L. MANFIELD (R.A.F.)	Mr. IVOR DAVID	13	S. YOUNG
1	Corpl. J. THORNTON (R.A.F.)	(Wales)	14	S. W. WOOLLEY
			15	A. W. BLAKE

BAND OF THE 181 (City of Gloucester) A.T.C. SQUADRON (by kind permission of the Commanding Officer)

The New Zealand Army team: back row: J G Simpson, S W Wooley, E G Boggs, J R Sherratt, A W Blake, G Bond, K D Arnold, Mr I David (referee); front row: F N Haigh, N Thornton, C K Saxton, P Rhind, F R Allen, J B Smith; in front: H E Cook, L Proctor [Journal]

Referee: Mr I David (Wales)

The early stages of the game were strewn with errors, and an injured Haigh had to leave the field. The Kiwis opened the scoring with a grand try from half-way, when Sherratt was given the ball by Allen and beat three would-be tacklers with terrific acceleration, to run round behind the posts. Haigh returned, but Constance had to go off with a broken collar bone, Thornton was put onto the wing, and the consequent lack of weight in the Services pack gave the Kiwis the upper hand. As half-time approached, Allen sold a dummy, cut through and put Simpson clear for the second try, and a Services fumble let Proctor in for another, to give the Kiwis a lead of 18-0 at the interval.

The teamwork of the visitors, who had been playing together for four months, showed in their backing up of the player with the ball,

and in their rapid handling skills. Combined Services had few attacking opportunities, but their defence was often heroic, and the Citizen was keen to point out that 'it was Gloucester's Johnny Thornton who showed them how to tackle. He crashed down Boggs or Smith time and again, and his defensive play was the best on the field.'

An application for the New Zealand Army XV to return to Kingsholm on 16th February to play against Gloucestershire & Somerset was declined, as the Gloucester committee gave precedence to the Club fixture against Bath scheduled on that date. The match was played at Bristol instead.

Australia Late but Welcome Visitors
Gloucestershire & Somerset 8, Australia 30
20th September 1947

THE AUSTRALIANS WERE due to tour in 1939, and had actually arrived in the UK, but war broke out, and the visit had to be postponed for eight years. The only survivor from the original tour party was the captain, Bill McLean. Ticket prices at Kingsholm ranged from 2s to 10s, and the tourists were welcomed enthusiastically by a crowd of 15,000, who were kept in good order by the sixteen policemen hired for the occasion. The referee, Mr T N Pearce, had another job as captain of Essex County Cricket Club.

The home pack gained the upper hand in the early stages of the match, but Walter missed with three penalty attempts, and some quick passing by the visitors put Arthur Tonkin free with only the full-back to beat. A beautiful swerve saw him over for the first try, which Clem

P H Davies running with the ball for Combined Services [Journal]

RUGBY FOOTBALL

THE AUSTRALIANS
visit
Kingsholm, Gloucester
SATURDAY, SEPT 20

(Kick Off 3.30) against a
COMBINED SOMERET AND
GLOUCESTERSHIRE TEAM

Admission : 2/- Deans Walk, 3/-
Worcester Street, 4/- Enclosure
in front of the stand, 5/- Ring
Seats, 7.6 stand seats. Tickets
sold by Mr. A. H. Hudson,
Sports Depot, Northgate Street,
Gloucester.

R. A. Roberts (Hon. Sec.).

[Citizen]

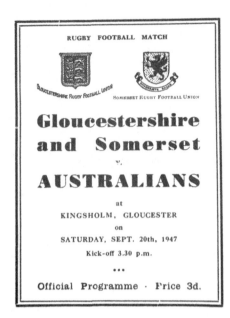

RUGBY FOOTBALL MATCH

Gloucestershire and Somerset
v.
AUSTRALIANS

at
KINGSHOLM, GLOUCESTER
on
SATURDAY, SEPT. 20th, 1947
Kick-off 3.30 p.m.

• • •

Official Programme · Price 3d.

[Gloucester Rugby]

Teams			
GLOUCESTERSHIRE and SOMERSET XV Colour : White		**AUSTRALIAN XV** Colour : Dark Green	
1. S. T. J. Walter *Gloucestershire*	Backs	C. J. Windsor	2
2. F. Discombe *Somerset*	Threeqrs. R.W. L.W.	A. E. J. Tonkin	4
3. T. Hicks *Somerset*	R.C. I.C.	T. Allan	6
4. S. H. Davies *Gloucestershire*	L.C. R.C.	M. L. Howell	7
5. G. Green *Gloucestershire*	L.W. R.W.	J. W. T. MacBride	8
6. I. Lumsden *Somerset* (Captain)	Five-Eighth Fly Half	E. G. Broad	12
7. D. Roberts *Somerset*	Scrum Half	C. T. Burke	13
8. T. Price *Gloucestershire*	Forwards	E. H. Davis	30
9. M. Howell *Somerset*		W. L. Dawson	26
10. L. J. Griffin *Somerset*		R. E McMaster	28
11. A. Meredith *Gloucestershire*		N. Shehadie	24
12. W. J. Jenkins *Somerset*		G. M. Cooke	18
14. J. Thornton *Gloucestershire*		K. C. Winning	23
15. C. Price *Somerset*		C. J. Windon (Captain)	20
16. G. Hudson *Gloucestershire*		W. M. McLean	15

Referee : Mr. T. N. Pearce (Chelmsford)
Linesmen : Mr. T. MILLINGTON (Glos. R.F.U.) and Mr. J. WALKER
Saturday, Oct. 4th. GLOUCESTERSHIRE v. DORSET & WILTS at Kingsholm

Windsor converted. Walter finally managed to
land a penalty to peg the score back, but Australia
then cut loose and scored further tries through Col
Windon and Graham 'Kiwi' Cooke. Both were
converted by Bob McMaster, who added a penalty
before half-time, so that the Counties found
themselves adrift 3-18.

The one-way traffic continued after the interval, with a penalty
from the touch-line by McMaster, and a try from McLean, before the home

*The Gloucestershire and Somerset team: back row: T Millington (touch judge),
Jenkins, Discombe, C Price, Thornton, T Price, Hudson, R A Roberts (secretary);
front row: Davies, Meredith, Griffin, Lumsden, Walter, Howell, Hicks; in front:
Roberts, Green [Mark Hoskins]*

Macbride eludes Johnny Thornton [Journal]

side fought back. Tom Price and Meredith made ground before Griffin
snapped up the ball as it went loose on the 25 and raced into the corner
for a try, which was converted by Walter. McMaster replied with another

*The Australian team: back row: Broad, Shehadie, Howell, Macbride, Dawson,
Winning; front row: Windon, Cooke, McLean, Allen, McMaster, Davis, Tonkin;
in front: Burke, Windsor [Journal]*

Jenkins dives on the ball for Gloucestershire and Somerset [Journal]

try for the Australians. Towards the end of the game the Counties were down to 13 men, with Steve Davies and Roberts off the field injured, and Trevor Allen took advantage to score a final try to round off a comfortable Australian victory.

Mr Outridge was asked to provide tea after the match, quoting £5 for 55 plain teas, and £7 10s for meat teas. The Club went for the expensive option, which was thought appropriate for a special occasion such as this. The result of this profligacy was a dispute with the County Union. The tea was reported to be excellent, but the County objected to the size of the bill. There had also been a breakdown in communications and the Australians had not understood that tea was provided, although there had been no shortage of volunteers to eat what they missed. The Club responded by complaining about the lack of publicity and advertising of the match by the County, which had detracted from the match takings (of which the Club received 15%). The County Union subsequently refused to order teas for their matches at Kingsholm, but the Club did not want Kingsholm to get a bad name with visiting teams, and went ahead and provided them at their own expense.

England Trials

Probables 13, Possibles 6
17th December 1949

ALTHOUGH THE SUN shone at Kingsholm, a biting and strong wind made conditions difficult for this second England trial of the season. Tom Price was the only local player on show, but the crowd still numbered about 10,000. Unfortunately Bill Hook, the Gloucester full back was unavailable, and the locals were not much impressed by the two alternatives for his position.

PROGRAMMES · THREEPENCE EACH

RUGBY FOOTBALL UNION

International Trial - Probables v. Possibles

Saturday, 17th December, 1949.   Kingsholm, Gloucester
Kick-off 2-15 p.m.

PROBABLES (Whites)		POSSIBLES (Blues)	
	Full Back	*Full Back*	
15	M. B. Hofmeyr Oxford University	R. Uren Waterloo	15
	Three-quarters	*Three-quarters*	
14	V. R. Tindall L.W.	J. A. Gregory R.W.	11
	New Brighton	Bristol	
13	B. Boobyer L.C.	T. B. Norman R.C.	12
	Oxford University	United Services	
12	L. B. Cannell R.C	P. B. Reeve L.C.	13
	Oxford University	Old Novocastrians & The Army	
11	L. F. L. Oakley R.W.	J. P. Hyde L.W.	14
	Bedford	Northampton	
	Stand-off Half	*Stand-off Half*	
10	I. Preece Coventry (Captain)	R. H. Haynes Bedford	9
	Scrum Half	*Scrum Half*	
9	G. Rimmer Waterloo	W. K. T. Moore Leicester	10
	Forwards	*Forwards*	
8	J. McG. Kendall-Carpenter Oxford University	T. W. Price Cheltenham	8
7	E. Evans Sale	J. H. Steeds Saracens	7
6	W. A. Holmes Nuneaton	J. L. Baume Northern & The Army	6
5	J. M. Todd Penrith	H. A. Jones Barnstaple	5
4	J. R. C. Matthews Harlequins	S. J. Adkins Coventry	4
3	H. D. Small Oxford University	D. F. White Northampton	3
2	D. B. Vaughan Headingley	R. C. Hawkes Northampton	2
1	J. J. Cain Waterloo	M. R. Steele-Bodger Edinburgh Univ. (Captain)	1

Referee: Mr. H. R. ROSE (Kent)

[Gloucestershire Archives]

Both sides came close to scoring before good handling amongst the Probables backs was rounded off by Ivor Preece tearing up outside his left wing to nip in at the corner. The Possibles struck back with two tries in quick succession, the first scored by Hawkes in a loose forward rush, and the second by Hyde after some clever work by Haynes.

The Probables pack started to turn the screw after half-time, and their dominance was rewarded when Gordon Rimmer made a break from a scrum before passing to Preece, who dodged over for a try near the posts. Murray Hofmeyr's kick squeezed inside the post to put the Probables ahead. Rimmer added to his laurels by sneaking a try on the blind side, which Hofmeyr converted, and Dick Uren nearly managed another, but was held up over the line. Nevertheless the seven point winning margin was regarded as flattering by most critics.

Probables 6 Possibles 6
22nd December 1962

[Gloucester Rugby]

An incident in the 1962 trial [Citizen]

A GREASY BALL AND a muddy pitch combined to make this a day on which the backs found it difficult to shine, but the Possibles pack soon gained the upper hand, and kept their side on the front foot for much

TEAMS

PROBABLES Colour : White			POSSIBLES Colour : Blue	
*J. G. WILLCOX (Capt.) Oxford University	15	Full Backs	*D. RUTHERFORD Percy Park	15
*P. B. JACKSON Coventry	14	Three-Qtrs. Right Wing	†J. M. RANSON Rosslyn Park	14
D. J. J. ALLANSON Rosslyn Park	13	Right Centre	*M. S. PHILLIPS Fylde	13
*M. P. WESTON Durham City	12	Left Centre	C. G. GIBSON United Services, Portsmouth	12
*J. ROBERTS Sale	11	Left Wing	*J. M. DEE Hartlepool Rovers	11
*J. P. HORROCKS-TAYLOR Leicester	10	Half-Backs Stand-off	*R. A. W. SHARP (Capt.) Wasps	10
†T. C. WINTLE St. Mary's Hospital	9	Scrum-Half	S. J. S. CLARKE Cambridge University	9
*P. E. JUDD Coventry	1	Forwards	†D. F. B. WRENCH Harlequins	1
*H. O. GODWIN Coventry	2		†J. D. THORNE Bristol	2
†C. R. JOHNS Redruth	3		B. A. DOVEY Rosslyn Park	3
*T. A. PARGETTER Coventry	4		†J. E. OWEN Coventry	4
†A. M. DAVIS Torquay Athletic	5		D. E. J. WATT Bristol	5
*D. P. ROGERS Bedford	7		†P. E. McGOVAN Redruth	7
†D. G. PERRY Bedford	8		V. R. MARRIOTT Harlequins	8
*B. J. WIGHTMAN Coventry	6		†D. C. MANLEY Exeter	6

* International † Previous Trial

Referee : A. C. LUFF (Notts, Lincs. & Derby)
Touch Judges :
S. H. JOHNSON (Bristol Society of Referees)   B. WELLS (Gloucester Society)

[Gloucester Rugby]

of the game. The long-legged Richard Sharp took the ball to the right, stopped dead, swivelled gracefully, and dropped a lovely left-footed goal to open the scoring. Just before half-time, John Wilcox hooked an easy penalty wide, but some of the defenders had moved towards him as he ran up, and the kick was retaken to level the scores.

For most of the second half, Sharp ran the show, and repeatedly showed what a great player he was. Don Rutherford regained the lead with a well-taken penalty, but late in the game the Probables revived and Brian Wightman scored from a Possibles heel on their line. The England selectors met in the Bell Hotel in Gloucester after the game and promoted the half-backs and five of the Possibles pack to the England side for the final trial at Twickenham a fortnight later.

South & South West 6 Midlands 18
7th April 1975

ENGLAND UNDER 23 REPRESENTATIVE GAME

SOUTH & SOUTH-WEST
v
MIDLANDS

at

KINGSHOLM, GLOUCESTER

on

Monday, 7th April, 1975

KICK-OFF: 7.30

Price: 5p.

[Gloucestershire Archives]

MIDLANDS	SOUTH AND SOUTH-WEST
Full Back	Full Back
15. W. H. HARE (Nottingham)	15. A. J. HIGNELL (Cambridge University)
Three Quarters	Three Quarters
14. S. MAISEY (Coventry)	14. M. J. TRIGGS (Aberavon)
13. J. G. CUBITT (Northampton)	13. D. SORRELL (Bristol)
12. J. BILLAM (Nottingham)	12. R. R. MOGG (Gloucester)
11. T. BARNWELL (Coventry)	11. S. DIX (Gloucester)
Half Backs	Half Backs
10. N. PRESTON (Nottingham)	10. C. R. WOODWARD (Harlequins)
9. M. LAMPKOWSKI (Headingly)	9. R. HARDING (Cambridge University)
Forwards	Forwards
1. D. ROBINSON (Coventry)	1. H. DICKS (Bristol)
2. J. A. RAPHAEL (Capt.) (Northampton)	2. C. K. JOHNS (Penryn)
3. P. TONGUE (Birmingham)	3. B. REDCO (St. Luke's College)
4. R. FIELD (Walsall)	4. S. B. BOYLE (Gloucester)
5. N. JOYCE (Leicester)	5. G. LOVELL (Plymouth Albion)
6. N. A. MALIK (Rugby)	6. N. TURNER (Bristol)
8. D. NUTT (Moseley)	8. G. R. CORIN (St. Ives)
7. R. HESFORD (Wasps)	7. M. J. RAFTER (Capt.) (St. Luke's College)
REPLACEMENTS:	REPLACEMENTS:
J. R. GILL (Mount St. Mary's School)	P. CARTER (Northampton)
S. D. McMEEKING (Nottingham)	S. GOVETTE (Durham University)
D. W. McKENZIE (Oxford University)	R. CORRIEA (Gloucester)
J. N. J. COX (Moseley)	
S. BROWN (Coventry)	

Referee: N. P. JONES (Gloucestershire Society)

Richard Mogg, Stuart Dix and Steve Boyle, the Gloucester representatives in the Under-23 trial [Gloucester Rugby]

THE CITIZEN REPORTED this England Under-23 trial as an evening game played in 'the sort of April weather that would have made Al Jolson croon with ecstasy…like the prophet of old the England selectors must have looked this way and that, but seen nothing, with few exceptions, that could have encouraged them in future team-building'. The only change from the programme was A P Whittle (Weston-super-Mare) replacing Redco at prop for the South and South West.

One of the few players to earn some credit was 'Dusty' Hare, who came into the line to set up the first try, and then put over the touchline conversion. Alastair Hignell replied with a penalty, but Mike Lampkowski broke through two tackles from a scrum and fed Preston who scored mid-way out; Hare converted. Richard Mogg made a couple of promising runs, and Hignell kicked a second penalty as the home side came out firing for the second half, but it was only token resistance, and Preston whistled past a bemused defence to score his second try; Hare again converted.

England 11 South 3
13th December 1975

THE QUALITY OF this trial was unimpressive. The Citizen recorded that: 'dropped passes were as plentiful as lights on a Christmas tree, even acknowledging the freezing hands, and the forward exchanges were untidy.' Although there was local interest in Mike Burton (a late replacement for Fran Cotton) and John Fidler, there was dissatisfaction on the terraces at the omission of Peter Butler, who had been winning games a-plenty for Club and County with his phenomenal goal kicking.

England: A Hignell (Bristol and Cambridge University); P Squires (Harrogate), A Maxwell (Headingley), B Corless, D Duckham

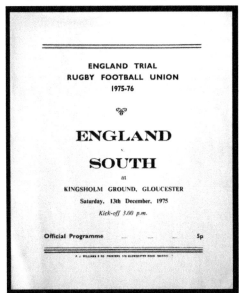

[Gloucestershire Archives]

(Coventry); M Cooper (Moseley), S Smith (Sale); B G Nelmes (Cardiff), P Wheeler (Leicester), M A Burton (Gloucester), W Beaumont (Fylde), R Wilkinson (Bedford), M Keyworth (Swansea), A Neary (captain, Broughton Park), P Dixon (Gosforth)

South: B Richards (Wasps); K C Plummer (Bristol), C Kent (Oxford University), D Cooke (Harlequins), D Wyatt; N Bennett (Bedford), R Harding (Bristol); C Bailward (Bedford), J V Pullin (captain, Bristol), B Adams (Wasps), N Mantell (Rosslyn Park), J H Fidler (Gloucester), P J Handy (St Ives), R Mordell, A Ripley (Rosslyn Park)

Referee: Mr R Newell (Yorkshire)

Mike Burton and John Fidler, the Gloucester representatives in the 1975 trial [Gloucester Rugby]

England took an early lead with a dropped goal from Martin Cooper, and would have added to it, but Alastair Hignell missed a couple of penalty shots. The South equalised with a dropped goal of their own from Bennett, who then tried another but it was charged down by Peter Dixon. Cooper made a break to put Andy Maxwell in for a try, but Hignell missed the conversion and another penalty attempt. The margin was 7-3 at half-time.

One notable moment came when Bill Beaumont grabbed the ball, only to be picked up bodily by Andy Ripley, who dumped him unceremoniously to the ground whilst stripping the ball off him. Your author, viewing events from the Shed, turned to his chums and confidently asserted 'nobody does that to an international second row – that Beaumont will never play for England'. Since he went on to captain England to a Grand Slam and to become a national treasure, never mind boss of rugby throughout the universe, I realise now the error of my ways in failing to give due credit to the unique talent of that very special player and athlete, Andy Ripley.

Alan Old replaced the injured Richards for the second half, which turned into an uninspiring and scrappy affair. An undistinguished game finally ended with Duckham scoring in the corner, but Hignell missed the conversion. His poor kicking this day merely confirmed to the Kingsholm crowd that their Gloucester favourite would have been a much better selection, and they let everyone know it by chanting 'Butler, Butler, Butler' with every Hignell miss.

Cooper (on left) and Maxwell combine to set up the first try [Citizen]

Universities Rugby

English Universities 3 Welsh Universities 5
2nd March 1949

THE TEAMS BELOW are as originally selected, and local interest centred on Howard Terrington, whose club side was Gloucester Old Boys (he would go on to make 87 appearances for Gloucester). However, three late changes disrupted the English back division, although local interest increased because one of the replacements was D Gladwin of Gloucester (the others are not recorded).

English Universities: T H Whittaker (Manchester); K Jones (Loughborough), W Saunders (Manchester), H L Terrington (Loughborough), G T C Clarke (Hull); A Unsworth, A G Milligan (Liverpool); C R Jacobs (Nottingham), C M Meredith (Leeds), P Duffield (Birmingham), G Coates (Bristol), W Mabbott (Loughborough), E B Evans, J Jackson, P M Rhodes (Manchester)

Welsh Universities: K Williams (Swansea); W D Smith (Aberystwyth), L Davies (captain, Swansea), R Wade (Medicals), A G Stevens; J L Brace (Aberystwyth), R Sutton; K Trotman (Swansea), K Jones (Cardiff), T Griffiths (Swansea), H Williams, I Williams, V Morris (Cardiff), P Stone, C Wittingham (Aberystwyth)

England had the upper hand amongst the forwards, but the Welsh three-quarters were more threatening. There was no score in the first half, but soon after the break R Wade cut through and W D Smith scored; Len Davies converted. Whittaker replied with a penalty for the home side, and the English had several opportunities to win the game in the closing stages, but the closest they came was when Whittaker hit the post with another penalty kick.

English Universities 14 Welsh Universities 3
3rd December 1953

ENGLISH UNIVERSITIES: M Gavins; K R Smith, C Jackson, K Bevan, M Staines; P C Delight, R I Shuttleworth; B Ash, R Ellis, R L Walker, S Holmes (captain), D Eaton, P Goodwill, P J Taylor, D Preston

Welsh Universities: G Evans; L P Gravenor, J M Griffiths, C Gilbertson, A Hughes; T Williams, B Price; E Jones, A David, G Thorburn, B Gulley, P Rowlands, J L Hughes, G Jenkins, B Padfield

Referee: Mr Brian Gray (Ireland)

England looked the better team throughout the game, but Wales opened the scoring when Gavins was left with two men to tackle, and Gravenor dashed over in the corner for an unconverted try. England soon drew level with a 45-yard penalty by Gavins, but although the English then pressed hard, the score remained 3-3 at half-time. It was only in the last quarter that marked English superiority was converted into points. Delight, the most dangerous attacking player, ran in two tries and Staines one, with a Gavins conversion completing the scoring.

Western Clubs 6 South African Universities 6
7th February 1957

THE TOURING SOUTH African Universities were popularly known as the Sables. They tucked into a substantial lunch of roast beef and Yorkshire pudding at the Fleece Hotel before the game (well, they were students). Pouring rain all day produced a mud bath and kept the attendance down to about 3,000. The home side was selected from clubs in Gloucestershire, Somerset, Devon and Cornwall.

Western Clubs: I Sheen (Gloucester); R F Blackmore (Barnstaple), J Blake (Bristol), H Stevens (Redruth), R Dash (Bristol); B E Jones (St Luke's College, Exeter), G Lovell (Bristol); C R Johns (Redruth), C Thomas (Gloucester), F J Williams, R C Hawkes (Bristol), R L Ellis (Plymouth Albion), V Roberts (captain, Penryn), A Macdonald (Bristol), B Sparks (St Luke's and Neath)

South African Universities: B D Pfaff; S P Wood, C C Young, P M Searle, W L Taylor; M C Van Zyl, M Smith; C G P Van Zyl, J I L Wessels, K G Kemp, W P Roux, S W Van Der Colf, N U De Lange, C J De Wilzem, J J Steenkamp

Referee: Mr F A Hyde (Gloucestershire)

The conditions made constructive rugby and place kicking decidedly tricky, but the Western Clubs drew first blood when a nicely directed punt towards the corner found right wing, Blackmore, well placed to pick up, dart a few yards, and dive over for the opening try. Stevens added a penalty, but W L Taylor replied with a try for the South Africans, and they salvaged a draw ten minutes from no-side when Pfaff dropped the ball out, kicked ahead, and was given the benefit of the doubt when there was disagreement as to whether he had touched the ball down before Stevens kicked it clear. Overall a draw was considered a fair result in a bruising encounter, which the Citizen summarised as follows:

> For the first time in their tour the combined South African Universities have savoured the strength of a good, solid, tearaway West Country pack. Kindly provided for them by Western Clubs in a Kingsholm mud battle, this new experience will surely leave an indelible mark on the rugby memories of these stalwart Sables.

Western Clubs contest a lineout against the South Africans [Citizen]

Cambridge University 32 RAF 8
27th February 1963

THIS MATCH WAS due to be played at Cambridge, but frost made Grange Road unplayable and Kingsholm was stated to be 'the only club ground within 120 miles of Cambridge fit for play'. RAF personnel from Innsworth were recruited to remove the protective covering of straw immediately before the match and replace it after the game. The RAF fielded a strong team, including a British Lion in Flying Officer J Browne and Gloucester's prop forward, Tug Wilson, a corporal at RAF Innsworth, who had just won his first cap for England against France at Twickenham the previous Saturday. The Cambridge team also boasted an international in Drake-Lee.

RAF: F/O G A Joha; Fl/Lt F F Leate, F/O J Keepe, F/O J Brown, Cpl I Parsons; F/O R H Palin, Cpl M M Diamond; P/O M J D Stear, F/Lt D Diblase, Cpl K Wilson, Cpl R Glazsher, F/O S K Mulligan, F/O A Wright. F/O L H Jenkins (captain), F/Lt B E Morgan

Cambridge University: G C Pritchard; G A Martin, D W A Rosser, G P Francom, W M Bussey; P D Briggs, B Williams; N J Drake-Lee, M Aylwin, J E Thompson, M McMorris, C M Wiggins, A R Pender, T W Boyd, J R H Greenwood (captain)

Thompson opened the scoring with a try for the students, but Keeper soon responded for the RAF, Leate converted, and it looked during the first half as though the RAF could contain the more exuberant university side. Leate and Pritchard exchanged penalties, and half-time arrived with the RAF two points ahead. However, in the second half, Pender and Greenwood were a continual threat, exploiting every weakness in the RAF defence, so that Cambridge scored six tries, including two each for Pender and Martin, with four of them converted to run up 26 unanswered points.

Mike Dineen reported in the Citizen that Cambridge brought 'a fine feeling that almost anything could be achieved providing you had on your side youth, enterprise and cheek. Not for a long time has the Kingsholm fancy had such an opportunity of watching intelligent young men realising opportunities which the crowd could see and even surprising them with reserves of ingenuity which resulted in a resounding defeat for the slower and apparently less fit men of the RAF.'

Gloucester 0 French Universities 17
29th March 1966

IT WAS 54 years after the visit of Racing Club de France before another French team was seen at Kingsholm. The French Universities crossed the Channel to play a warm-up game against Gloucester before their annual match against British Universities (which they won 9-0 a few days later). Their side contained the great Pierre Villepreux at full-back, and a couple of other future internationals.

Gloucester: C Wheatman; J Groves, J A Bayliss, D B W Ainge, P D Meadows; J T Hopson, M H Booth (captain); J C Milner, M J Nicholls, C N Teague, R G Long, A Brinn, G G White, D W Owen, R Smith

French Universities: P Villepreux (captain); R Vialar, J Tarayre, J Puig, J Crampagne; G Savin, G Capdepuy; H Puiz, R Guiter, M Semon, P Dehez, P Biboulet, E Ologaray, P Ramouneda, J Menain

Referee: Mr M H Titcomb (Bristol)

Gloucester may have been below par as a result of suffering a 6-26 defeat at the hands of Newport the previous evening, but nevertheless the Citizen was much impressed with the quality of the French performance:

Those who have taken numerous French lessons in their youth, unless they were particularly dedicated, will hardly admit to being enamoured by the subject; but it took on a vastly different meaning at Kingsholm, where the Combined French Universities played superb rugby to overwhelm a weary Gloucester. For the students gave a lesson, full of beauty and fascination, in the arts of constructive rugby that completely humbled Gloucester but sent spectators home in a glow of ecstasy.

The French superiority was based on an exceptional pack, but their backs ran with an electrifying rhythm and purpose, and Villepreux showed why he would develop into a world-class player with a fine display of prodigious touch kicking and an uncanny sense of positioning.

It was surprising that there was only one score in the first half, an unconverted try by Crampagne from a swift, crisp handling move. Early in the second half, pressure on the Gloucester line brought a try for Savin, when he charged down a kick by Terry Hopson and had only to fall on the ball over the line; he converted his own try. Villepreux ended any lingering Gloucester hopes with two magnificent penalty goals. And the French universities finished with flair and style, indulging in an amazing bout of passing that ended with Ramouneda crossing virtually unopposed for an unconverted try – ooh la la!

English Students 17 French Students 16
15th March 1988

A STRONG FRENCH SIDE, which included five players who had won caps for France B, failed to attract more than a few hundred spectators, but those who did come were rewarded with a hard fought and close game.

England: M E Appleson (Leeds Poly); S T Hackney (Loughborough Univ & West Hartlepool), A J Buzza (Loughborough Univ), P Hopley (St Thomas Hospital), A Underwood (Leicester Univ); M G Strett (Liverpool Poly), M E Hancock (Cambridge Univ); V E Ubogu (Oxford Univ), B W Gilchrist (Cambridge Univ), A R Mullins (City Univ & Harlequins), T Swann (Liverpool Univ), S T O'Leary (St Mary's Hospital & Wasps), S R Kelly (captain, Cambridge Univ), S Holmes (Univ of East Anglia), S Wright (Lanchester Poly); Replacements: C Laity (South Glamorgan Inst), R H S B Moon (Poly of Wales), J S Locke (UWIST), A S Challis (Nottingham Univ), J P Green (South Glamorgan Inst)

France: P Barthelemy (Uereps, Nice); J F Impinna (Uereps, Paris 5) C H Coeurveille (Un P Sabateir, Toulouse), G Cassagne (Uereps, Lyon), P Hontas (Uereps, Bordeaux); T Lacroix (Un Bordeaux), G Accoceberry (Pharm, Bordeaux 2); S Graou (Essige, Toulouse), R Tremoulet (Un P Sabatier, Toulouse), S Canut (Pharm, Montpellier), B Fabre (Sup De Co, Pau), P Reguengo (Uereps, Paris), X Blond (Uereps, Paris), J M Lhermet (INSA, Lyon), O Roumat (LYC G Eiffel, Bordeaux); Replacements: S Ougier (Un P Sabatier, Toulouse), J M Pain (Uereps, Bordeaux), P Ladouce (Uereps, Paris), G Fayard (IUT Le Creusot), T Astruc (Uereps, Montpellier), F Vanhems (Un Bayonne)

Referee: Mr G Davies (Wales)

England enjoyed the majority of possession through their dominant pack, but their backs failed to make the most of the generous stream of ball coming their way. Despite tries from Tony Underwood and Holmes and two penalties from Appleson, England were still 12-16 behind close to the end of the match. At the last gasp, the Cornishman, Alan Buzza, had the final and decisive word, slicing through to score the try, which, with Appleson's conversion, completed a narrow but deserved victory for England.

Schools Rugby

AFTER THE WAR, schools rugby resumed at Kingsholm with an England trial, in which Gloucester were well represented.

West 11 East 0
23rd February 1946

The four local boys chosen to start for the West; from left: Smith (Marling), Byrne (Marling), Goscombe (Central) and Morris (Hatherley) [Journal]

Embling (Kingsholm) and Baker (Marling), who were brought on at half-time [Journal]

West: Neale (Bristol); Varker (Redruth), Challis, Hoskins, Percival (Bristol); Smith (Gloucester), Stiff (Bristol); Morris, Byrne, Goscombe (Gloucester), Vingoe (Newlyn), Bigwood (Bristol), Bryant (Weston-super-Mare), Stevens (St Ives), Evans (Bristol). Replacements brought on at half-time: Baker (Gloucester), Roach (Cornwall), Embling (Gloucester), James (Bristol), Gwennap (Penzance)

East: Harris; Johnson (Coventry), Williamson (Durham), Clarke (captain, Coventry), Bell (Carlisle) or Duffield (Coventry);

Astfalck (Coventry), Grove (Hinkley); Sewell (Carlisle), Lane (Leicester), Atherton, Auton (Northumberland), Gardner, Marston (Leicester), Minor (Coventry) or Joiner (Durham), Wilson (Northumberland)

Referee: Mr G Court

A lineout during the England Schools trial [Journal]

THE STANDARD OF this match got the thumbs-down in the press, with much fumbling amongst the backs, and victory for the West was put down to the dogged work of their pack in the loose, which contained an all-Gloucester front row in Morris, Goscombe and Embling. When the England side to face Wales at Cardiff was selected that evening, it included Smith and Byrne (Marling), Morris (Hatherley) and Goscombe (Central), with Embling (Kingsholm) as a reserve.

Gloucestershire, Somerset & Oxfordshire 12
Devon & Cornwall 0
7th February 1948

THERE WERE FOUR Gloucester representatives in the home side – Smith and Webley (Crypt), Tomlins (Central) and Joshua (Kingsholm) – and Harris (Wycliffe) was captain. The Mayor of Gloucester, Councillor B C Meehan, kicked off this West of England Schoolboys trial.

A smart break by scrum-half, Coles, almost lead to an early try by Griffiths for the home side, but they did not get ahead until Youngs set his backs loose and Harris raced over. Almost immediately Griffiths made a determined run and stretched the lead with the second try. It looked as though Tomlins had scored a third on the stroke of half-time, but it was called back for a forward pass.

Devon and Cornwall came out strongly on the resumption and the home line was under sustained pressure, but they just could not get over it. The match continued to be keenly contested, but eventually Griffiths

Gloucestershire, Somerset and Oxfordshire on the attack [Journal]

The five Gloucestershire representatives in the trial [Citizen]

<table>
<tr><td colspan="3">ENGLISH PUBLIC AND SECONDARY SCHOOLS</td><td></td><td colspan="3">FRENCH SCHOOLS RUGBY UNION</td></tr>
<tr><td colspan="3">COLOURS - WHITE</td><td></td><td colspan="3">COLOURS - BLUE</td></tr>
</table>

1.	G. M. ELLIOTT	Wanstead H.S.	Full Back	H. ARTIGA	Hendaye	1.
2.	R. W. MARTIN	Barnstaple G.S.	Right Wing	G. GANITROT	Beziers	2.
3.	J. E. WOODWARD	High Wycombe G.S. (Capt.)	Right Centre	D. MORELLI	Chateaurenard	3.
4.	F. J. HORNE	Barnstaple G.S.	Left Centre	J. TRESARRIEU	Pau	4.
5.	P. K. GOVETT	Launceston College	Left Wing	L. ROGE	Narbonne	5.
6.	R. C. FULLBROOK	Reading S.	Outside Half	P. CLAVIERES	Paris	6.
7.	D. I. HAMILTON	Leighton Park	Inside Half	G. D'ARRIPE	Toulouse	7.
8.	A. S. MACNAIR	Newbury G.S.	Forwards	L. DULON	Bordeaux	8.
9.	M. U. HUGHES	St. Ignatius College		J. MADELRIEUX	Aurillac	9.
10.	W. A. THOMAS	Leominster G.S.		G. DELAPELLEGERIE	Perieueux	10.
11.	M. J. WEBB	Colston's Bristol		G. ROUGARIES	Perpignan	11.
12.	I. ZAIDMAN	Tottenham G.S.		C. KUSTERLE	Toulon	12.
13.	C. M. SITCH	King Edward's, Birmingham		S. LECHAT	Limoges	13.
14.	M. J. CUTTER	Wanstead H.S.		R. VENTAJOU	Beziers	14.
15.	M. J. JORDAN	Cheltenham G.S.		J. DARRIGAU	Dax	15.

Referee :
Mr. D. D. EVANS

Touch Judges :
I. J. NICHOLAS, Northamptonshire, M. VANNIER, France

Musical Selections by CINDERFORD TOWN SILVER PRIZE BAND

[Gloucester Rugby]

scored his second try, and before the end Webley put the icing on the cake with a fine try to seal a convincing win.

As a result of this trial, Smith and Webley (Gloucester) and Walton (Cheltenham) were selected to play for the West against the East in the final England trial, with Knight (Gloucester) as a reserve.

England 3 France 9 (Under-18)
30th April 1949

D'Arripe scores a try for the French at the Deans Walk end [Journal]

FRANCE STARTED AS hot favourites, having beaten Wales, who had in turn thrashed England. The French pack looked formidably large and England failed to get their hands on the ball for the first ten minutes, but defended stoutly. However, it was no surprise when the French took the lead, their front row dribbling over for a try from a scrum, but England equalised before half-time with a penalty. After the break, England won more ball and their backs started to make openings, but France took their chances better, and two unconverted tries saw them leave Kingsholm with a deserved win.

England 3 Wales 37 (Over-15)
22nd April 1950

THE EVENING BEFORE the match both teams attended a film show at the Plaza, on the morning of the match the Mayor hosted a reception and lunch at the New Inn, and after the match there was dinner at the Cadena Café. The crowd was estimated at 10,000, and included a host of Welsh supporters.

England: G B Richards; G R Benkert, R Leslie, G A Long (captain), J Watson; J Thompson, D T Voyce; H L Mitchell, B J Lane, K J Kingham, M Smedley, P M Kingston, A J Herbert, B K Hinton, V S J Harding

Wales: D James (Pontypridd GS); J Huins (Neath GS), R Sheppard (Newport HS), H Richards (Gowerton CS), G Griffiths (Porth CS); P Davies (Pontypridd GS), D O Brace (Gowerton GS); R Vokes (Newport HS), C Smith (Neath TC), C Hopkins (Llanelly CS), R Robbins (captain, Pontypridd GS), O J Hughes (Gowerton GS), E Cooke (Whitchurch GS),

The Gloucestershire representatives in the England side; from left: D T Voyce (Lydney), D J Lane (Sir Thomas Rich's), B J Hinton (Cheltenham), G B Richards (Bristol), A J Herbert (Marling) and H L Mitchell (Wycliffe) [Journal]

Sir Thomas Rich's School was heavily represented in the 1954 trial with four players shown in front from left – L Swift, B Price, M Booth and T Hancocks – and three of the four officials in the back row from left – Mr J Peart (Bristol, Area Hon Sec and Trustee of the ESRU), Mr A Harris (Hon Sec of Gloucester & District Schools RU and Asst Hon Sec ESRU 15-Group), Mr W J Veale (Headmaster, Sir Thomas Rich's) and Mr S E Langston (Hon Sec and Vice-President of ESRU) [Citizen]

K J Davey (Monmouth S), J Edwards (Neath TC)

Wales kicked off and England were hard pressed to keep them out for the first few minutes, but it was the home side which came closest to scoring first. However, a penalty kick went wide and a try was just prevented. Wales soon went onto the attack again and Huins scored two tries on the right wing. The Welsh added two more before half-time, when they led 14-0. The second half was played almost entirely in English territory with the Welsh pack dominating possession and Wales ran in five more tries, before Long kicked a penalty for England, which served only to prevent a whitewash.

England 3 Wales 6 (Under-15)
31st March 1951

ALL THE PLAYERS were accommodated in private houses as the guests of Gloucester rugby supporters. The guest of honour at the match was Air Marshal Sir Basil Embrey, Air Officer Commander-in-Chief, Fighter Command, who declared that his earliest memory was the roar of the crowd at Kingsholm, because as a small boy, he had lived only half a mile from the ground. The crowd was estimated at more than 10,000.

England: D Hillsden; KP Hiscocks, J Croker, K Poole, J Baugh (captain); WH Parker, A Sewell; C Thompson, L Crighton, W Hudson, G Putt, RC Lamey, J Edgar, H Hodson, J Collins

Wales: J Hughes, R Jones, I James, P Sexton, A Rees, D Parry, C Davies, B Davies, B Popham, H Williams (captain), D Thomas, K Griffiths, G Bowen, D Rowlands, R James

Wales won by two tries to one, despite finishing the game with only 13 players, having had to play a forward short for most of the match, and losing their scrum-half for the last few minutes. A try by the Wales right wing, C Davies, was the only score of the first half. They increased their lead with another after the interval by wing forward, G Bowen. England replied with a try by their captain and left wing, John Baugh.

Probables 0 Possibles 3
20th March 1954

THIS WAS THE final England schools trial (15 group) of the season.
Probables: A Bridges (Coventry); W Pearson, J Lucas (Cumberland), R Clews (Coventry), H Bolland (Sutton Coldfield); A Biddle (captain, Rugby), M Booth (Gloucester); C Wood, R Bedson, A Jarvis (Stafford), B Beason (Leicester), M Caradus (Westmoreland), B Bretell (Birmingham), M Wood (Coventry), A Rowe (Cumberland)
Possibles: R Perkins (Devon); D Stevens (Middlesex), B Price,

T Hancock (captain, Gloucester), R Reasons (Somerset); L Swift (Gloucester), L Hallam (Leicester); M Price (Gloucester), K Hyde (Lydney), J Goodyer (Oxford), J Turton (Devon), T Stevens (Coventry), A Rooney, R Robson (Cumberland), B Short (Kent)

Reserves: M Chamberlain (Lydney), A Phillips (London), K Buckle (Oxford), D Jones (Staffordshire)

B Price getting away with the ball [Citizen]

The selectors made multiple changes in the sides as an undistinguished match progressed. As a result of this trial the England team was selected to play against Wales on 17th April and showed nine changes from the side which started for the Probables in the trial. Of the Gloucester boys, only B Price (Sir Thomas Rich's) was selected for England, being one of those who earned promotion from the Possibles as a result of his fine performance in the trial. T Hancock and M Booth (Sir Thomas Rich's) and K Hyde (Lydney GS) were among the five reserves. L Swift (Sir Thomas Rich's) was the unluckiest – he was judged to have played very well until having to leave the field injured, and the selectors sought news from the Gloucester Royal Infirmary before announcing the England team, but the message came that he had fractured his arm and would not be fit in time to play.

England Schools 6 Wales Schools 5
21st April 1956

ALTHOUGH THE MATCH was defined as Over-15, most of the players selected were aged 18, and Wade had already played at a senior level for Leicester and Leicestershire. Hordes of Welsh supporters descended on Kingsholm, and brought the attendance up to an estimated 8,000. They were treated to a pulsating game of rugby.

The England team from left: back row: Dr P F Cooper (referee), G M Edmondson, F H Brown, J Salisbury, I W Linnell, B L Spencer, M R Wade, M A Ware, B Robson, Mr H Edwards (touch judge); front row: A G Johnson, B F G Johnson, J R C Young, Mr F P Wesencraft (Chairman, English Schools RFU Over-15 Group), A B W Risman, F Drewett, J S Barrett, B Bacon [Journal]

The Mayor of Gloucester, Ald E J Langdon, and the City High Sheriff, Mr J F Curtis, meet the England team [Journal]

England: B D Bacon (Newbury GS, Berks); J R C Young (Bishop Vesey's GS, Warwicks), J S Barrett (Beckenham GS, Kent), M R Wade (Wyggeston GS, Leics), M A Ware (Bec School, Surrey); A B W Risman (captain, Cockermouth GS, Cumberland), F Drewett (Windsor GS, Berks); I W Linnell (King Edward VI School, Birmingham), A G Johnson (Northampton GS, Northants), G M Edmondson (Wigton Nelson Thomlinson School, Cumberland), B F Johnson (Northampton GS, Northants), B L Spencer (Raynes Park GS, Surrey), F H Brown (St Joseph's School, Stoke, Staffs), B Robson (Wigton Nelson Thomlinson School, Cumberland), J Salisbury (Workington GS, Cumberland)

Wales: I Jones (Llanelly GS); C Phillips, R Thomas (Neath GS), D Johnson (HMS Conway, Anglesey), B Skirrow (Cardiff HS); A Rees (Glan Afan GS), H F Merrick (Cathays HS, Cardiff); D Walkey (captain, Bassaleg GS), D Jones (Mountain Ash GS), M Thomas (Tonyrefail GS),

B Harrison (Grove Park GS, Wrexham), J Davies (Cowbridge GS), W T Williams (Carmarthen GS), M Pemberton (Newport HS), L Davies (Garw GS)

Referee: Dr Peter Cooper

England get the ball away to their backs [Journal]

England suffered an early setback, being reduced to 13 men within ten minutes of the start, but their heavier pack worked hard to make up for the loss. The England backs looked extremely dangerous throughout the game, and it was a tribute to the Welsh defence that it withstood almost continuous pressure without conceding a single try. The English points came from two penalties by Risman. Walkley scored the only try of the game for Wales when he won a race for a long cross kick and crashed over the line; Jones converted.

English Boys Clubs 6 Welsh Boys Clubs 0
22nd April 1961

MANY DIGNITARIES WERE present for this match, organised by the National Association of Boys Clubs, a civic reception was held beforehand and the Gloucester Club hosted a meal afterwards. To accommodate it on the Saturday afternoon, Gloucester played their match against Stroud the previous evening. Although labelled as boys, the average age was approaching 18 and most of those selected had already played senior rugby.

England: M Sloggett (Penryn YC, Cornwall); R Wallace (Henbury BC, Bristol), D C Brooks (Whaddon & College BC, Cheltenham), J A Bayliss (Parry Hall YC, Gloucester), D G Evans (Bowburn BC, Co Durham); D Hinds (Ancoats LC, Manchester), J Spalding (Archdeacon YC, Gloucester); P Simmons (Penryn YC, Cornwall), G Brown (Redruth YC, Cornwall), T Clarkson (Bedford BC), D Lodge (captain, Loughton Old Boys BC, Essex), F Moyes (Winfrith Apprentices Association, Dorset), P Lane, N Sysum (Parry Hall YC, Gloucester), D Phillips (Sefton Park YC, Bristol)

Wales: L Lewis (Treorchy BC); C Smart (Neath YMCA), J Bailey (Neath YMCA), J Roberts (Cross Keys BC), P Sanderson (Treorchy BC), R Thomas, R Evans (Neath YMCA), T Coates (Bettws BC), J Derrick (Neath YMCA), D Huish (Treorchy BC), I Barnard (Richard Thomas & Baldwin), M Hicks (Cross Keys BC), D Wassal (Risca BC), C Dyer (captain, Neath YMCA), G Nicholls (Risca BC)

The first half was a mess, neither side able to cope with the slippery ball. But after 50 minutes, the Cheltenham centre, Dave Brooks, delighted spectators by rounding off a three-quarter movement by selling three dummies, which left the Welsh defence sprawling in the mud. Shortly afterwards, another sparkling passage of play, inspired by John Bayliss, gave Terry Clarkson the opening for England's second try.

A Welsh player loses possession when tackled by Evans [Citizen]

THIS NATIONAL ASSOCIATION of Boys Clubs international featured Mike Burton playing at No 8 for England, with his best friend at school in the centre, Roy Morris, son of the legendary 'Digger' Morris of Gloucester.

A great try by centre P Dennis of Neath, converted by J Morgan, gave Wales a lead which they then sat on, much to the displeasure of many in the crowd. However, the tactic worked well and R Davies of Neath, described as 'a little too fiery', made a barging run to set up Wales' second try by prop D Whitlock. A strike against the head by Shearing enabled scrum-half J Pike of Bristol to pluck the ball from the back row and dart over for England's solitary try. Prop forward Reg Pearce converted.

England Schools 15 Scotland Schools 3 (19 group) 10th April 1968

MATCHES AT THIS age group had started twenty years previously, and England had played regularly against Wales and France, but a 3-3 draw at Murrayfield the previous season had been the first fixture against Scotland, and this was Scotland's first trip south of the border. The match drew a crowd of 8,000, which witnessed some sparkling rugby. With a 7:15 kick-off, the second half was played under floodlights.

England had a highly-drilled pack, which excelled at rucking, and they took the lead when Lerwill made a break, Lavery chipped the ball through, and Allen followed up to score the try. In trying to prevent this score, the Scotland captain, Doug Neave, suffered torn leg ligaments and had to withdraw from the fray, which reinforced the England dominance up front. The Scotland defence performed heroically, but shortly before half-time another break by Lerwill put Littlechild into the corner. Bell converted both these tries. Scotland started the second half brightly and were rewarded with a dropped goal by Calder, but in the closing stages

English Boys Clubs 5 Welsh Boys Clubs 8 27th April 1963

ENGLISH BOYS' CLUBS XV v. BOYS' CLUBS OF WALES XV

KINGSHOLM, GLOUCESTER
SATURDAY, 27th APRIL, 1963

	ENGLAND				WALES	
	Colour: WHITE Jerseys, BLUE shorts				*Colour: RED Jerseys, WHITE Shorts*	
1.	J. FULLER	Bath, Somerset	*Full Back*	1.	G. MORGAN	Neath
2.	D. CARMACK	Bristol	*Right Wing*	2.	C. EVANS	Treorchy
3.	R. MORRIS	Gloucester	*Right Centre*	3.	P. DENNIS	Neath
4.	V. BENNETT	Cornwall	*Left Centre*	4.	B. PRICE	Neath
5.	T. AGAMBAR	London	*Left Wing*	5.	P. NOBLE	Averavon
6.	P. JONES	Bath, Somerset	*Outside Half*	6.	B. O'FLYNN	Averavon
7.	J. PIKE	Bristol	*Scrum Half*	7.	A. EDWARDS (Capt.)	Aberavon
8.	J. VERRAN	Bristol	*Prop*	8.	J. EDWARDS	Treorchy
9.	R. SHEARING	Berkshire	*Hooker*	9.	N. REES	Neath
10.	R. PEARCE	Surrey	*Prop*	10.	D. WHITLOCK	Aberavon
11.	M. HURST (Capt.)	Warwickshire	*2nd Row*	11.	R. MORGAN	Treorchy
12.	C. KNEEBONE	Cornwall	*2nd Row*	12.	R. DAVIES	Neath
13.	R. HAINES	Gloucester	*Wing Forward*	13.	P. MOYLE	Bargoed Y.M.C.A.
14.	M. BURTON	Gloucester	*Lock*	14.	L. HUNT	Aberavon
15.	C. ELLIOTT	Cheltenham	*Wing Forward*	15.	P. DYER	Neath

Reserves:	G. WHITEHEAD	Gloucester	*Reserves:*	R. LEWIS	Aberavon
	C. PHILLIPS	Cheltenham		B. THOMAS	Treorchy
				V. THOMAS	Bettws.
				B. DAVIES	Llandarcy

[John Hudson]

English Schools' Rugby Football Union (19 Group)		**Scottish Schools' Rugby Union** (19 Group)
Full Back		**Full Back**
15 R. H. BELL (Hampton G.S. & Middlesex)		15 H. M. BURNETT (George Herriot's School)
Threequarters		**Threequarters**
14 E. J. LITTLECHILD (Arnold School, Blackpool & Lancs.)	RIGHT WING	14 L. G. DICK (Morrison's Academy)
13 P. JOHNSON (St. Brendan's College & Somerset)	RIGHT CENTRE	13 D. E. D. NEAVE (Capt.) (Watson's College)
12 M. HEPPLE (Dame Allan's Boys School & Northumberland)	LEFT CENTRE	12 J. GOODALL (Hillhead High School)
11 P. J. LAVERY (N.Glos Technical College & Glos.)	LEFT WING	11 M. SHARP (Dollar Academy)
Half Backs		**Half Backs**
10 S. J. TRIGG (Normanton G.S. & Yorks.)	OUTSIDE HALF	10 D. CALDER (Royal High School)
9 A. T. D. LERWILL (Millfield & Surrey)	SCRUM HALF	9 J. REID (Royal High School)
Forwards		**Forwards**
1 J. JOANNOU (Capt.) (Christ's Col., Finchley & Middlesex)		1 D. B. BAVISTER (Fetter College)
2 R. J. KENDALL (Dulwich College & Surrey)		2 B. RUTHERFORD (Galashiels Academy)
3 W. A. RUSSELL (Exeter Tech. College & Devon)		3 M. WATTERS (Watson's College)
4 R. M. UTTLEY (Blackpool G.S. & Lancs.)		4 K. McKINNON (Royal High School)
5 A. TURTON (Cheltenham G.S. & Glos.).		5 K. DODDS (Galashiels Academy)
6 N. J. ALLEN (Bradford G.S. & Yorks.)		6 J. D. LAIDLAW (Merchinton Castle School)
8 A. T. HOLLINS (Okehampton G.S. & Devon)		8 D. WADDELL (Hutcheson's Grammar School)
7 S. KING (Chiswick G.S. & Middlesex)		7 J. Y. MACKINLAY (Loretto)

a punt ahead by Hepple was swiftly chased by Littlechild, who beat the cover for the touch-down; Bell again converted.

England 13 Scotland 5 (Under-19)
1st April 1970

THE CROWD OF 7,000 at Kingsholm was boosted by the inclusion as England full-back of Mike Redding, who played fly-half for his club, Gloucester All Blues, and full-back for his school, Sir Thomas Rich's. They were enthralled by a sparkling game played under floodlights on a chilly evening. Snow resumed falling soon after the start, but both teams showed a real determination to play handling rugby.

England: M A Redding; D G Casswell, D G Gullick, G Richards, C J Fuller; J P Horton, D A Hill; A J Cutter, C J Russell, D L G Owen (captain), R J Field, J Pigott, M D Miller, S A Johnson, J M Reardon

Scotland: T M Barr; I Brydon, A R Irvine, J G B Williamson, D Fullerton; J C O Vaughan, J Henderson; R G Christie, W T Ramsay, R G Calder, R Dickson, C Galbraith, I J R Mears, D G Leslie, D O Provan

Referee: Mr G Walters (Wales)

When a Scotland attack broke down, Gullick started a counter-attack which resulted in the first try for England, scored wide out by Casswell. In the dying seconds of the first half, Provan led a Scottish forward rush, and scored beside the posts; Irvine's conversion gave Scotland the lead. Midway through the second half, Horton side-stepped his way through from a scrum to score a try, which Richards converted to put England ahead 8-5. England piled on the pressure with the wind at their backs, and Field eventually crashed over beside the posts to settle the issue, Richards converting with the last kick of the match.

England 16 Wales 0 (Under-19)
29th March 1972

A CROWD OF 10,000 found much to applaud in a methodical and skilful performance by an England side which recorded only its second win in seven encounters at this level against the Welsh.

England: D W N Caplan; C W Lambert, K R Poskitt, S G Jackson, R C Barnwell; P J Ubee, R G Bell; R E L Oliphant, A P Whittle, N S P Enevoldson, T C Cheeseman, N D Mantell, D Morgan, G B Sparks, J V

[John Hudson]

Panter

Wales: C Griffiths; J Harris, C Jenkins, J Walters, W Williams; D Richards, A Lewis; P Bradley, P Rees, C John, R Hughes, R Thomas, S Warlow, J Rees, G Jones

Referee: Mr M Titcomb (England)

An accomplished England side were methodical and skilful in dominating the game, yet their three tries were all of an opportunist nature, although this only emphasised their ability to capitalise upon the chances afforded them. After ten minutes, an attempted penalty by Caplan struck an upright, but the England hooker, Whittle, collected the rebound and charged over; Caplan converted.

Lambert, the burly English winger, pounced on a wild Welsh pass in his own 25 and raced almost the length of the field to outstrip the opposition and score wide out. He then made another interception near halfway, and again left the opposition with little to do except stand and admire as he raced round behind the posts; Caplan converted.

England 9 Wales 15 (19 Group)
6th April 1974

AN ESTIMATED CROWD of 5,000 turned up to watch this international, and basked in the bright sunshine bathing Kingsholm.

England: D Johnson (captain, Gosforth & Northumberland); M K Zoller (Millfield & Surrey), A J Crust (Chislehurst & Sidcup & Kent), P N Harper (Sedburgh & Yorkshire), J G Cubbit (Northampton & Northants); C S Ralston (Workington & Cumberland & Westmoreland), D J Cullen (De la Salle & Lancashire); N W E Weaver (Cranbrook & Yorkshire & Kent), J D Robinson (Thorne & Yorkshire), P G Woodhead (Bradford & Yorkshire), J P Thornton (Hull & Yorkshire), I A Lutter (Wellingborough & Northants), S R Callum (Harlow & Eastern Counties), J P Sydall (De la Salle & Lancashire), N C B Turner (St Brendan's & Gloucestershire)

Wales: A W Ellis (Dwr-y-Felin, Neath); D W Thomas (St Martin's, Caerphilly), M Murphy (St Illtyd's, Cardiff), J L Schropper (Penlan, Swansea), J A Walters (Maesydderwen, Ystradgynlais); W G Davies (Gwendraeth, Llanelli), A D Lewis (captain, St Martin's, Caerphilly); W Williams (Queen Elizabeth, Carmarthen), H I Davies (Tonyrefail), I Heidman (Stanwell, Penarth), R A Jones (Whitland), A E Davies (Llanelli),

- 126 -

R K Williams (Cwmtawe, Pontardawe), D T L Sanders (Howardian, Cardiff), C F Bartlett (St Illtyd's, Cardiff)

Referee: Mr D W G Grey (Scotland)

England started with a brisk breeze at their backs, and within a quarter of an hour had taken a 9-0 lead. Charles Ralston kicked one penalty before hitting a post with a second attempt. He then hit a post from a drop goal, but the ball rebounded to winger Mark Zoller who barged his way over under the uprights; Ralston converted. Wales responded strongly, but England held them out until half-time, despite Zoller being stretchered off with a dislocated shoulder. Wales had the upper hand after the change of ends, and Walters, a thrustful and clever runner on the wing scored two tries, the second winning the game in the final minutes. The game as a whole disappointed, and was marred by repeated if brief bouts of fisticuffs.

Commemorative platter [Gloucester Rugby]

England 3 Wales 0 (19 Group)
13th April 1976

OF PARTICULAR INTEREST to local supporters was the inclusion in the Welsh side of Phil Pritchard, the Wycliffe College skipper who had joined Gloucester a month previously and had already impressed in his few games with the United.

England: W M Rose (Loughborough and Leicestershire); P Clarke (Marple Hall and Cheshire), A N Laycock (St Michaels and Yorkshire), M Burke (Cowley and Lancashire), R D Stephenson (Arnold and Lancashire); S J Fisher (Rossall and Lancashire), I G Peck (Bedford and Bedfordshire); S P Wilkes (Bishop Vesey and Warwickshire), P J Melra (West Park and Lancashire), M F Mottram (Bablake and Warwickshire), P J Jackson (Stockport and Cheshire), K J Davies (Wallingford and Oxfordshire), S R Tipping (Ilkley and Yorkshire), T J Allchurch (captain, Abbey and Worcestershire), N C Geavans (Wolverhampton and Staffordshire)

Wales: G Davies (Preseli); P Pritchard (Wycliffe), H Rees (Maesydderwen), S Grabham (Brynteg), N Matthews (Brynmawr); G Evans (Maesteg), A Billinghurst (St Martins, Caerphilly); R Davies (captain, Cwmtawe), S Davies (Cwmtawe), J Edwards (Carmarthen), K

Edwards (West Mon), E Lewis (Greenhill, Tenby), M Davies (West Mon), G Roberts (Gowerton), D Rees (Glanafon, Aberavon)

Referee: Mr P Beatty (Ireland)

The match was keenly contested and played at pace under the Kingsholm floodlights. Two superb defences dominated in wet conditions, with first half drizzle developing into driving rain. The result was decided by a solitary penalty goal kicked by Marcus Rose during a first half which England dominated. They also came closest to scoring a try when Stephenson was hurled into the corner flag. The most threatening move of the match was constructed by Fisher and Burke with Rose making the extra man, but even this failed to penetrate the Welsh defence. Wales came back in the second half but ended up ruing three missed penalty attempts.

England 37 Ireland 7 (19 Group)
6th April 1977

IRELAND'S FIRST VISIT to Kingsholm attracted a crowd of about 6,000. England came into this game full of confidence with a talented side, unchanged from their 26-0 victory over Wales four days previously, and boasting a record of only one defeat in their previous 24 games.

England: I R Metcalfe (King Edward's, Birmingham); A H Swift (Hutton, Preston), M Burke (Cowley, St Helens), R D Stephenson (Arnold, Blackpool), C R Pitts (King Edward VI, Retford); G H Davies (King Edward VI, Stourbridge), N G Young (Greshham, Holt); G B Marsh (Queen Elizabeth's, Barnet), T J Melia (West Park, St Helens), N A Stothard (Hymer's, Hull), I J Ford (Millfield), I Furlong (Sir Leo Schultz, Hull), T J Allchurch (captain, Abbey High, Redditch), S Gregory (King Edward VI, Nuneaton), R J Stevenson (Cheadle Hulme)

Ireland: H P McNeil (Blackrock); K Hooks (Bangor), JJ Duggan (Rockwell), T R J Shiels (Rainey), R H C Millar (Regent House); D M Dean (St Mary's), P R Macdonnel (St Mary's); P E Connor, J F Hartnett (Blackrock), I W Johnston (Methodist, Belfast), B W McCall (Armagh Royal), D G Lenihan (Christian Brothers, Cork), P M Matthews (Regent House), K D O'Loane (Rainey), M E MacWhyte (Castleknock)

England made a shaky start, and were only narrowly ahead, 11-7, at half time, thanks to two tries from Clive Pitts and a penalty by Mick Burke. Mark MacWhyte with a try and Hugo McNeil with a penalty replied for Ireland.

In the second half, England's powerful pack took control and the backs were able to show their flair, orchestrated by Huw Davies at fly-half. His safe handling, penetrating bursts and good tactical kicking marked him as a future star. England ran in a further five tries, with Pitts completing a hat-trick on the left wing, Tony Swift scoring two from the opposite wing, and Nick Youngs and David Stephenson adding one each. Ian Metclfe landed three conversions to round off a convincing victory.

South West Schools 12 Australia Schools 28
(19 Group)
7th December 1977

THE AUSTRALIAN PARTY included the three Ella brothers, whilst the South West selection included Steve Baker at scrum-half and Mark Calver at prop from Sir Thomas Rich's, Gloucester, and amongst the backs were Richard Tyler and Richard Osborn from Cheltenham Grammar. The persistent rain falling on Kingsholm may have seemed rather foreign to the young Australians, but they did not let it dampen their flair and fine handling skills, and they ran the ball at every opportunity, their advantage in weight ensuring a steady supply of ball.

The South West took an early lead with a penalty kicked by their

Glen Ella receiving the ball from a ruck [Citizen]

SOUTH WEST SCHOOLS	AUSTRALIA
Green and White	Gold
15. M. SCHIEFLER (St. Brendans)	15. G. ELLA
14. N. A. G. THOMSON (Plymouth College)	14. M. WILLIAMS
13. P. McLEOD (Taunton)	13. M. O'CONNOR
12. R. OSBORN (Cheltenham Grammar School)	12. W. LEWIS
11. R. TYLER (Cheltenham Grammar School)	11. M. HAWKER
10. A. J. KIFT (Exeter College)	10. T. MELROSE
9. S. J. BAKER (Sir Thomas Rich's)	9. D. VAUGHAN
1. M. CALVER (Sir Thomas Rich's)	1. J. MATHESON
2. N. MURPHY (Falmouth School)	2. T. RYAN
3. M. H. PICCIRILLO (Plymouth College)	3. R. LESLIE
4. D. SKUSE (Bristol Cathedral School)	4. G. GAVALAS
5. S. J. KINCH (Exeter College)	5. W. MELROSE
6. D. A. VICKERY (Capt.) (Exeter College)	6. A. McLEAN
8. A. DUN (Bristol Grammar School)	8. G. BAILEY
7. C. WATTS (Lawrence Weston School)	7. C. ROCHE
Replacements:	Replacements:
A Q PECK (Truro) (16)	(16) M. ILETT
D. P. JONES (Plymouth Coll) (17)	(17) M. EGAN
G. HEALE (Humphrey Davey) (18)	(18) S. NIGHTINGALE
J. LLEWELLY-ROBERTS (Devon) (19)	(19) T. D'ARCY
M. LANE (St. Brendans) (20)	(20) P. TUCK
A. W. BROOKS (Plymouth Coll) (21)	(21) M. ELLA

Referee: D. M. MARTIN (Cornwall Society)

winger Neil Thomson, but Australia soon ran in the first of their six tries, three in each half. Fly-half Tony Melrose took a reverse pass from winger Max Williams to cut through the defence, and before half-time, Williams romped away to score another wide out, and then Glen Ella came into the line to join in two scissors moves, which left him clear for the third.

In the second half, Ella gave an inside pass for Mike Hawker to score, Glenn Bailey went over from a line-out, and another superb try for Williams followed a clever break and dummy by scrum-half Vaughan. The South West were only able to respond with three more penalty goals by Thomson.

England 16 Scotland 3 (19 Group) 4th April 1978

ENGLAND: M E Drane (Loughborough); D M Trick (Bryanston), J Pedley (Rossall), B Barley (Normanton), C R Pitts (King Edward VI, Retford); M D Schiefler (St. Brendan's), N G Youngs (captain, Gresham's); G B Marsh (Queen Elizabeth, Barnet), B H Kenny (Sherborne), P Faulkner (Blackpool Collegiate), R W B Smart (Newcastle), J A Taylor (Henry Mellish), R J Pearson (Oundle), I Taylor (Cowley), J G Merison (Radley)

Scotland: R B Nelson; G McCutcheon (Hutchesons), G C S Gordon (Trinity, Glenalmond), G M Hastings (George Watson's), D A Smellie (Strathallan); N J Marshall (Morrisons), G R T Baird; J A Turnbull (Merchiston Castle); J K Murdoch (Belmont), W M Anderson (Fettes), G R Marshall (Currie High), K Goudie, M R Ferguson (Stewarts-Melville), A J S Morton (Ayr), N T Roberts (Trinity, Glenalmond)

England started at a furious pace, and after only two minutes prop Geoff Marsh hurtled over the line from a line-out. Hastings replied with a penalty, but England added two more tries before half-time. Youngs put Barley in from a five-yard scrum, and then made the scoring pass for Jon Taylor to barge over.

With a comfortable lead, England's flair vanished and their previously crisp and adventurous passing became slipshod in the second half, which seemed destined to remain pointless until Martin Drane came up from fullback to dive over at the corner flag in the final minutes. Unfortunately this match was marred by two serious injuries in the second half. The England No 8, Ian Taylor, suffered a fractured jaw and was carted off to hospital, where the Scotland prop, Alan Turnbull, later joined him with a broken ankle.

Post-War County Matches

AFTER THE WAR, there was no County Championship in 1945-46, but County fixtures resumed at Kingsholm with a friendly match against Somerset.

Gloucestershire 8 Somerset 3
8th December 1945

THE FIXTURE ATTRACTED a good deal of criticism as being an irrelevant game between two unrepresentative teams. County officials were praised for their enthusiasm, but lambasted for denuding clubs of their players when they were struggling to get teams together to play first class rugby. Many players were not yet back from military service, and Bristol had to be exempted from supplying any players in order to meet their club commitments. The crowd of 2,500 demonstrated the lack of public interest, and they found little to cheer in a dull game.

Gloucestershire: S T J Walter (Cheltenham); L Hammond (Bristol Aero Club), J Taylor (Gloucester), W A Handley, G D Hobson (Cheltenham); W E Jones (Gloucester), G Cullimore (Stroud); T Price, J Hopson (Gloucester), F Cherrington (Cheltenham), R Morris (Gloucester), D Moran (Cheltenham), W J Mills, T Rose, J A Endacott (Stroud)

Somersetshire: E Coleman; S W Collett (Weston), H Corbett (Bristol), L J Mead (Malvern), G H Edwards; J Bailey (Bath), D L Roberts (Somerset Police); H Stone (Watchet), R Davies (Somerset Police), A Holley (Weston), A French (Taunton Services), A Beazley (Bath), D Steer (Somerset Police), J K Watkins (RN)

Referee: Mr F Mansell (Gloucester)

The Gloucestershire team: back row: J Taylor, L Hammond, G Cullimore, W J Mills, F Cherrington, T Rose, R Morris, D Moran; front row: W E Jones, J Hopson, T Price (captain), S T J Walter, J A Endacott, W A Handley, G D Hobson [Journal]

Action from the Somerset game [Journal]

Tom Price leads Gloucestershire out against Somerset [Journal]

Gloucestershire started badly, and soon conceded a try in the corner by Edwards, but gradually came back into the game, largely through the efforts of Willie Jones at stand-off, although 'it was generally on his own initiative. If he had found a pass coming in front of him, instead of high behind his head or bouncing over the ground, he might have been able to give much-needed help to his centres'.

Somerset let several further scoring chances slip, before Handley snapped up a loose ball, broke through, and slipped a smart pass to Hammond for a try by the posts, which Walter converted to give Gloucestershire the lead on the stroke of half-time. Rose scored an unconverted try late in the game to seal the win.

Gloucestershire 6 Somerset 3
9th November 1946

THIS WAS GLOUCESTERSHIRE'S first County Championship match at Kingsholm after the war. They had started their campaign by drawing 3-3 in a poor match with Devon at Exeter.

Gloucestershire: H Gribble (Stroud); T G Jackson (London Scottish), C Bowell (Bristol), W A Handley, C D Hobson (Cheltenham); S C S Farmer (Aldershot Services and Gloucester), Haydn Tanner (Swansea); G A Gibbs, F C Hill (Bristol), T Day, R Morris (Gloucester), A Meredith (Bristol), G Hudson (Gloucester), S Betterton (Stroud), J Thornton (Gloucester)

The Gloucestershire team [Journal]

Somerset: G C Barrett (Bridgwater); R T Moule (Weston-super-Mare), T Walters (Yeovil), T Hicks (Bath), G Hollis (Bristol); I Lumsden, H V Bland (Bath); L J Griffin (Bristol), R Davies (Somerset Police), G R Speke (Bath), W H Gorman (Taunton), F Locke (Wellington), D Steer (Somerset Police), L H White, A Rheinhold (Yeovil)

Referee: Mr H Delo (Coventry)

Gloucestershire on the charge against Somerset [Journal]

COUNTY RUGBY FOOTBALL
AT KINGSHOLM, GLOUCESTER
SATURDAY, MARCH 1st 1947
GLOUCESTERSHIRE
v.
MIDDLESEX
KICK-OFF 3-15 P.M.

PRICES OF ADMISSION:
Stand Seats (Centre) 7/6; Wings 5/-; Inside Rails 4/-;
Enclosure (Standing Only) 3/-.
Dean's Walk 1/-; Worcester Street 2/- (including ALL Tax)
THERE WILL NOT BE A CAR PARK ON THE GROUND.
Ticket Holders enter by Usual Car Park Doors, except Ringside
Ticket Holders who enter by Door Opposite White Hart Hotel.
Please Take Your Seats by 3-0 p.m.
TICKETS purchased from A. HUDSON, Northgate St., Gloucester.

Poster advertising the rearranged match against Middlesex [Gloucestershire Archives]

Gloucestershire showed only marginal improvement in this match. Their pack won a steady stream of possession, which was just as regularly wasted by their backs. Each side kicked a penalty, and it was left to a forward to determine the outcome. Johnny Thornton of Gloucester charged down a kick right on the Somerset line, and fell on the ball to score the only try.

Gloucestershire went on to beat Cornwall 15-3 at Bristol, which left them as winners of the South West group, and put them into a semi-final against Middlesex. This was due to be played away, but after two postponements because of frost at Twickenham and Richmond, Middlesex agreed to switch the match to Kingsholm.

Gloucestershire 24 Middlesex 17
1st March 1947

THERE WAS A severe frost overnight before the match at Kingsholm, but its effects were ameliorated by a covering of straw on the pitch, and the sun came out for the 15,000 spectators packed in to watch these teams contest their fourth semi-final, Gloucestershire having won the previous three.

TEAMS

GLOUCESTERSHIRE Colours : White, with County Crest		MIDDLESEX Colours : Narrow Blue and White Stripes	
	Backs		
1 H. GRIBBLE Stroud		T. C. MARR St. Thomas' Hospital	1
	Three-qtrs. R.W. L.W.		
2 G. E. GREEN Bristol		C. D. McIVER Harlequins	5
	R.C. L.C.		
3 S. H. DAVIES Gloucester		J. A. DAVIES Harlequins	4
	L.C. R.C.		
4 K. DANIELL Gloucester		M. J. DALY (Capt.) Harlequins	3
	L.W. R.W.		
5 S. DANGERFIELD Gloucester		G. H. McNEIL Old Millhillians	2
	Stand-off		
6 W. E. JONES Gloucester		N. M. HALL St. Mary's Hospital	6
	Scrum Half		
7 E. J. PARFITT Lydney		H. de LACY Harlequins	7
	Forwards		
8 T. DAY Gloucester		J. H. STEEDS Middlesex Hospital	8
9 F. C. HILL Bristol		R. W. SAMPSON London Scottish	9
10 G. A. GIBBS Bristol		F. P. DUNKLEY Harlequins	10
11 A. MEREDITH Bristol		D. C. SHIELDS Rosslyn Park	11
12 R. MORRIS (Capt) Gloucester		J. R. MATTHEWS Harlequins	12
14 J. THORNTON Gloucester		A. VENNIKER St. Mary's Hospital	13
15 S. BETTERTON Stroud		D. W. MALCOLM Wasps	14
16 A. G. HUDSON Gloucester		K. S. WRIGHTON Old Millhillians	15

Referee : Mr. R. F. BARRADELL (Leicester)
Linesmen : Mr. T. MILLINGTON and Mr. K. H. CHAPMAN

The teams listed in the match programme [Gloucestershire Archives]

The Gloucestershire team: back row: Parfitt, Millington, Gribble, Gibbs, Thornton, Mr Barradell (referee); Day, Hudson, Betterton, Sam Alder (baggage man); front row: Meredith, Hill, Dangerfield, Jones, Morris, Daniell, Davies, Green, Tom Barrow (President) [Journal]

The Middlesex team: back row: Matthews, McNeil, de Lacy, Shields, Venniker, Marr, McIver, Wrightson; front row: Malcolm, Sampson, Hall, Daly, Davies, Dunkley, Steeds [Journal]

Middlesex went ahead when Willie Jones was caught in possession, and Daly scored under the posts, but Jones soon atoned with a penalty and a trademark dropped goal from his uncannily accurate left foot. Middlesex regained the lead with a try by Davies, who sold two dummies and twisted over beside the posts, and Hall extended the lead with a dropped goal. But as the game wore on the Gloucestershire forwards started to gain the upper hand and created the perfect position for another Jones drop goal. Everyone expected him to slot it over, but Parfitt never gave him the ball and instead dashed straight through to score under the posts whilst all eyes were still focussed on Jones. The conversion reduced the Middlesex lead at half-time to 14-12.

The game swung to and fro at the start of the second half, but eventually the home pack got Jones within range, and thunderous applause greeted his second dropped goal as it soared between the posts. Middlesex were now defending desperately, and gave away a penalty, which Jones kicked, before converting Parfitt's second try. Venniker scored a late runaway try for Middlesex, but it was too little too late.

Gloucestershire's reward was to travel to Blundellsands for the final against a powerful Lancashire side, packed with internationals. Lancashire had won all their games by substantial margins, and were clear favourites. Against all the odds, that wonderful left foot of Willie Jones dropped two goals to secure a draw, 8-8. This was only one of many occasions on which the result of a match was determined by the masterly drop kicks of Willie Jones. His prolific scoring by this method is reputed to be the principal reason why the authorities reduced the points scored for a dropped goal from 4 to 3. But not yet, and Lancashire had to travel to Kingsholm for the replay.

Gloucestershire 3 Lancashire 14
26th April 1947

[Gloucestershire Archives]

Action from the Middlesex game [Journal]

The crowd in front, and on top, of the gymnasium [Journal]

ALMOST 19,000 PACKED into Kingsholm, many of them making sure of their place two and a half hours before kick-off. The crowd was almost three times as large as that which had viewed the first game at Blundellsands, and there was widespread confidence that Gloucestershire would prevail on their own patch.

Gloucestershire: H Gribble (Stroud); G E Green (Bristol), S H Davies, K Daniell (Gloucester), W H M Baker (Newport); W E Jones (Gloucester), E J Parfitt (Lydney); G A Gibbs (Bristol), R C Hill (Bristol), T Day, R R Morris (Gloucester), A Meredith (Bristol), G Hudson (Gloucester), S Betterton (Stroud), J Thornton (Gloucester)

Lancashire: J Bradburn (Wigan Old Boys); R H Guest, J Heaton (Waterloo), A C Shuker (Broughton Park), C B Holmes (Manchester); W B

'Digger' Morris is presented with a lucky mascot [Journal]

Cartmel, G Rimmer (Waterloo); R Logan (Sale), T N Reynolds (Fylde), E Evans, J Mycock (Sale), S V Perry (Waterloo), P M Rhodes (Manchester), H F Luya, J J Cain (Waterloo)

The Gloucestershire team: back row: Gadney (referee), Thornton, Gibbs, Gribble, Meredith, Betterton, Barrow (President), Hudson; front row: Green, Daniell, Hill, Morris, Jones, Parfitt, Davies, Day, Baker [Journal]

The Lancashire team: back row: H Fry (linesman), Reynolds, Rhodes, Cain, Luya, Logan, Evans, Whittaker (Secretary); front row: Mycock, Guest, Cartmell, Perry, Heaton, Holmes, Rimmer, Shuker, Bradburn [Journal]

Referee: Mr Cyril Gadney (England)

The home pack started well, but was matched when the Lancashire forwards had warmed up, and a penalty for off-side allowed Heaton to put Lancashire ahead. Lancashire steadily won more possession, particularly from the lineouts, and their three-quarters looked dangerous on several occasions before Shuker swerved inwards and split the Gloucestershire defence wide open to score by the posts; Heaton converted for an 8-0 lead

Willie Jones kicks for touch with the Worcester Street stand behind him [Journal]

at half-time.

The second half was largely a story of Lancashire pressure and Gloucestershire defence, but the home team broke out occasionally, and Jones missed with one penalty before he was successful when Lancashire were caught off-side at a scrum and presented him with a second opportunity. An interception by Cartmel led to a try for Holmes, but Heaton's conversion was charged down. Luya completed the scoring with a try from close in. Lancashire's class had finally told, and there was no disputing their right to the title.

Gloucestershire 26 Dorset & Wiltshire 13
4th October 1947

GLOUCESTERSHIRE CHOSE KINGSHOLM to open their next campaign against the newcomers to the South West group.

Gloucestershire: S T J Walter (Blackheath); G E Green (Bristol), K Daniell (Gloucester), J C Morgans (Lydney), S Dangerfield (Gloucester); J V Smith (Stroud), E J Parfitt (Lydney); T Price, H J Meadows (Gloucester), G A Gibbs, A Meredith (Bristol), T Day (Gloucester), H H Mills (Stroud), D J Pratten (Bristol), G Hudson (Gloucester)

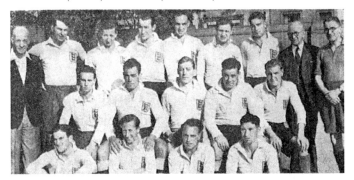

The Gloucestershire team against Dorset & Wilts: back row: T Millington (touch judge), A Meredith, H Mills, G Hudson, H Meadows, T Day, G Pratten, R A Roberts (secretary), F Draycott (referee); middle row: K Daniell, T Price, G Gibbs (captain), J Walter, F Dangerfield; front row: J V Smith, G Green, J Morgans, E Parfitt [Journal]

Dorset & Wilts: G E S Woodhouse (Blandford); D A Lee (HMS Royal Arthur), L G Mitchell (Burderop College), F P Slann (US Portland), R M Redgrave (Bovington); R G Abbott, L Griffin (Bournemouth); F D Carpenter (Worth Maltravers), J James (RAF Hullavington), H Gaston (Salisbury), B Eveleigh (captain, Bovington), A G Watt (Shaftesbury), H J Hale (Dorchester), N Cameron (RAF Old Sarum), W J Waterman (Bournemouth)

The Dorset & Wilts team [Journal]

Referee: Mr F Draycott (Warwick)

Gloucestershire enjoyed a comfortable win by four goals and two tries to two goals and a penalty. Their pack commanded up front, and their backs made a multitude of breaks despite the loss of J V Smith after twenty-five minutes, Ken Daniell moving up to stand-off in his place. Even though this meant taking a man out of the pack, the home side continued to rule the roost up front. Tries from Mills, Green and Dangerfield set up a 15-5 lead at half-time, and Morgans, Hudson and Day added three more in the second half.

Gloucestershire followed this with nail-biting away wins, 10-9 against Somerset at Taunton, and 6-5 against Cornwall at Falmouth, before clinching the group with a 9-6 win over Devon at Bristol, but defeat

Gloucestershire on the attack with the Worcester Street stand in the background [Journal]

10-14 at the hands of Eastern Counties at Bristol in the semi-final ended their involvement. However, it presented an opportunity for Rowe Gabb to become the first referee from the Gloucester and District Referees Society to take charge of a County Championship final as he oversaw Lancashire beating Eastern Counties 5-0 at Cambridge to secure the title.

Gloucestershire started their 1948-49 season with an away win against Dorset & Wiltshire, before meeting more traditional rivals at Kingsholm.

Gloucestershire 9 Cornwall 8
23rd October 1948

A CROWD OF 10,000, including two England selectors, turned out for Cornwall's first visit to Kingsholm since the war.

Teams			
GLOUCESTERSHIRE Colour : White		**CORNWALL** Colours : Black with Amber rings	
1. W. Hook Gloucester	Full Back	J. Collins Camborne	A
2. G. E. Green Bristol	Three-qtrs. R.W. L.W.	M. Terry Bath & Penzance - Newlyn	B
3. R. H. Wood Bristol	R.C. L.C.	R. D. Kennedy Camborne School of Mines	C
4. K. N. Daniell Gloucester	L.C. R.C.	E. K. Scott Redruth (Captain)	D
5. S. F. Dangerfield Gloucester	L.W. R.W.	Les. Williams Cardiff	E
6. W. E. Jones Gloucester	Half Backs Fly Half	H. Richards Rosslyn Park and Penzance - Newlyn	F
7. D. D. Evans Gloucester	Scrum Half	V. Taylor Penzance - Newlyn	G
8. T. Day Gloucester		T. Bidgood Redruth	H
9. F. C. Hill Bristol	Hooker	L. Semmens Plymouth Albion	I
10. T. Price Cheltenham		I. Richards Penryn	J
11. J. Watkins Gloucester	Forwards	J. George Falmouth	K
12. J. S. Jones Cheltenham		J. Lawry Falmouth	L
13. D. G. Pratten Bristol		V. G. Roberts Penryn	M
14. R. N. V. Muller Bristol		D. Hurrell Camborne School of Mines	N
15. A. G. Hudson Gloucester (Captain)		W. A. Phillips Redruth	O

Referee : Mr. A. H. Harvey (Leicestershire)

Touch Judges : Mr. E. JEFFERIES (Gloucestershire)   Mr. H. HAM (Cornwall)

[Gloucestershire Archives]

Cornwall looked very strong at first, their pack pushing Gloucestershire off the ball, but once Willie Jones got into action with some long range kicking, Gloucestershire were soon attacking and he opened the scoring with his second penalty attempt. Cornwall replied immediately with a loose rush on the left, their forwards sweeping Hook aside, and Les Williams tore into the middle of it all like a bolt from the blue to score a try under a heap of players. Phillips converted easily. But Gloucestershire were just as quick in replying, when Daniell found a chance to slip through the defence and swerved nicely round the full back to score an unconverted try. 'Trouble brewed up when Jones claimed a mark and Les Williams tackled him. The referee did not allow the mark and amid the crowd's booing Cornwall swept on, the players shaping up to each other in fighting manner.' The incident passed however and half-time arrived at 6-5.

After the break, Cornwall continued to have more chances and Gloucestershire were constantly defending, and in due course Cornwall got the try which had seemed bound to come from an interception by Richards, which Terry touched down. However, quick following up by Dangerfield enabled the Gloucestershire winger to score what proved to be the winning try.

This contributed to Gloucestershire progressing to a semi-final against Middlesex at Twickenham, where the pack was completely outplayed, but a 3-3 draw was secured, somewhat fortunately, thanks to a Bill Hook penalty. Middlesex were brought back to Kingsholm for the replay.

Gloucestershire 10 Middlesex 0
19th February 1949

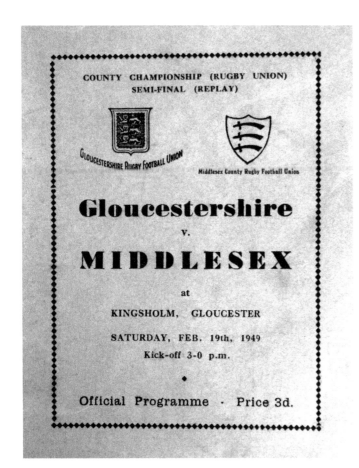

[Gloucestershire Archives]

Teams

GLOUCESTERSHIRE Colour : White, with County Crest		MIDDLESEX Colours : Blue and White, Blue Shorts	
1. W. G. Hook Gloucester	Full Back	G. Williams London Welsh	1
2. J. A. Gregory Blackheath	Three-qrs. R.W. L.W.	G. Sullivan St. Mary's Hospital	5
3. J. V. Smith Stroud	R.C. L.C.	B. Boobbyer Rosslyn Park	4
4. G. M. Ednie Cheltenham	L.C. R.C.	D. C. Parker Blackheath	3
5. S. F. Dangerfield Gloucester	L.W. R.W.	C. McIver Middlesex Hospital	2
6. J. E. D. Wilcox Clifton	Half Backs Fly Half	G. W. Spiers Old Haberdashers	6
7. I. Pearce Cheltenham	Scrum Half	H. de Lacy Moseley and Ireland	7
8. T. W. Price Cheltenham		H. H. Campbell London Scottish	8
9. C. M. Meredith Bristol		J. H. Steeds Middlesex Hospital	9
10. J. Watkins Gloucester		A. Q. Bell Old Paulines	10
11. R. Redman Bristol	Forwards	J. R. C. Matthews Harlequins	11
12. R. Hodge Gloucester		D. C. Shields Middlesex Hospital	12
13. G. A. Hudson Gloucester (Captain)		R. D. Gill Oxford University	13
14. D. G. Pratten Bristol		D. J. O'Brien London Irish (Captain)	14
15. C. Dunn Gloucester		A. B. Curtis London Irish	15

Referee : Mr. A. S. Bean (Durham)

Touch Judge : Les. Webber (Glos. Referees' Society).

The Gloucestershire team: back row: Webber (touch judge), Ednie, Hill, Pratten, Redman, Hodge, Watkins, Wilcox, Pearce, Bean (referee); front row: Smith, Gregory, Hook, Hudson, Dangerfield, Dunn, Price [Journal]

ON A FINE day, a near-capacity crowd packed out Kingsholm. Gloucestershire made an exciting start, threatening to score in the first minute, but a foot in touch brought them back. When Middlesex were awarded a penalty, Sullivan took so long over his kick that he was barracked loudly by the crowd, and he then missed. The referee objected to the barracking, ordered Sullivan to take the kick again, and consequently suffered a few comments about his own competence and paternity. Another woeful effort sent the Shed into paroxysms of laughter and derisory comment. Long touch-finders from Bill Hook gave the home side some attacking positions, and from one of these, Wilcox shot through a gap and fed Ednie, who swerved past three defenders to score by the posts for an easy conversion by Hook.

Steeds, the Middlesex hooker, being tackled by Tom Price; on the right are Charlie Dunn and Fred Hill [Journal]

Middlesex pressed hard at the start of the second half, but they were kept at bay by fierce tackling, until Hook put a long kick into touch inside the Middlesex 25. Directly from the lineout Gordon Hudson battled his way over the line for a try which Hook again converted.

Gloucestershire were through to another final, but again had to make the long journey north to Blundellsands, where Lancashire won 9-3.

Gloucestershire 3 Devon 3
26th November 1949

THE ATTENDANCE OF 8,000 at kick-off, which increased to 10,000 later, was judged to be poor for a County match at this time.

Gloucestershire: S T J Walter (Cheltenham); J A Gregory (Bristol), J C Morgans (Lydney), R Sutton (Gloucester), M Fletcher (Lydney); J E D Wilcox (Clifton), I Pearce; T Price (Cheltenham), F Hill, G Gibbs (Bristol), F Steinhobel (Cheltenham), J Watkins, C Dunn, R Hodge, G Hudson (captain, Gloucester)

Devon: T E Irish (Plymouth Albion); S G Brown (Exeter), I Murrin (Newton Abbot), H Edwards (St. Luke's College and Neath), K Maddocks (St. Luke's College); A Kift (Newton Abbot), M G Andrews (Brixham), W Towell (Torquay Athletic), E Blackmore (Torquay Athletic), W F Bristowe,

Charlie Dunn, man-of-the-match for Gloucestershire [Gloucester Rugby]

G R D'A Hosking, A Meredith (Devonport Services), L Davies (Exeter), H A Jones (Barnstaple), D H Rees (University College, Exeter)

Referee: Mr A S Bean (Durham)

Gloucestershire had the better of the opening exchanges, but Walter missed a golden chance with a shot at a penalty goal from 35 yards out in front of the goal. So it was Devon who opened the scoring when Brown put in a short diagonal punt which Walter was slow in getting across to, and Brown coming up at great speed flung himself over right in the corner; Irish missed narrowly with the conversion.

Devon were getting a bit too keen and incurred four penalties in succession for being offside. Walter gained plenty of ground in his kicks for Glo'ster but missed badly with two shots at goal. However, Gloucestershire's best piece of work came with quick passing out to Fletcher, who was flung into touch at the flag.

So it was 0-3 at half-time. In the second half, the home side had the better of it territorially, but Devon enjoyed more possession. Dunn in particular was playing a great game for Gloucestershire, which led to Morgans bursting through at full speed with a short pass, but, following a long consultation between the referee and the players, it was determined that he had knocked on as he received the ball. Devon struggled tenaciously to hold on to their slender lead and Tom Price only just missed a penalty goal from the touchline.

At last Gloucestershire began to get the ball, and there was some beautiful running by Gregory, Fletcher and Morgans, who were spurred on to even greater efforts when Tom Price levelled the score with a grand penalty goal. Gloucestershire followed this up with a terrific burst in which Gregory was the star performer, but they just could not score, although Gibbs and Steinhobel were stopped within inches of the line. A brilliant run the length of the field by Walter, Morgans, Hudson and Fletcher, in which the Lydney man touched down, was stopped by the referee who ruled a forward pass and was heartily booed, not for the first time during the game.

Gloucestershire 8 Glamorgan 0
9th March 1950

GLOUCESTERSHIRE PUT OUT what was regarded as an experimental team, but several young players were judged to have acquitted themselves well, in particular Gibbs, Rees, Hughes and Sutton.

Gloucestershire: N Gibbs (Bristol); J Taylor (Bristol University), R Sutton (Gloucester), K Rees (Lydney), D Golledge (Bristol); D Hughes (Lydney), I Pearce; T Price (Cheltenham), D Woodward (Bristol), R Parry (Gloucester), F Steinhobel (Cheltenham), S Betterton (Lydney), B Dainty (Stroud), G Hudson (Gloucester), C Price (Lydney)

Glamorgan: V Evans (Neath); T Singleton (Glamorgan Wanderers), G Llewellyn (Bridgend), T Watkins, R Ley (Maesteg); A Thomas (Swansea), N Pallott (Glamorgan Wanderers); L Llewellyn (Briton Ferry), J Kelleher (Neath), T Farmer (Bridgend), M Williams (Aberavon), H Mayled (Maesteg), G David (Glamorgan Wanderers), E Jones (Neath)

Much of the game was tame, uninspired and sometimes scrappy, and for most of it Gloucestershire held a lead of a penalty goal kicked by Woodward.

Then Golledge snapped up the ball in the loose near the touch line and slipped away with Hudson and Pearce in close support. Golledge drew the defence well and Hudson took a perfect pass to run on strongly and score under the posts. It was a fine piece of opportunism and after Woodward had made the easy conversion, there was new life in the

Gloucestershire side. Encouraged by Tom Price flinging a long ball out to the backs in his own 25, Gloucestershire threw the ball about with the greatest confidence after this, and the closing stages brought some most attractive football, but no further scoring.

Gloucestershire 5 Somerset 3
28th October 1950

IN 1950-51, GLOUCESTERSHIRE saw off Dorset & Wilts 23-0 at Cheltenham, before bringing Somerset to Kingsholm. A crowd estimated at 10,000 gathered in fine weather.

Gloucestershire: W G Hook (Gloucester); J A Gregory (Bristol), R Sutton (Gloucester), J C Morgans, J Taylor; D Hughes (Lydney), L W Pearce; T W Price (captain, Cheltenham), F C Hill, E C McCall (Bristol), F Steinhobel (Cheltenham), P D Young (Clifton), B C Dainty (Stroud), A G Hudson (Gloucester), D G Pratten (Bristol)

The Gloucestershire Team v. Somerset 28th October 1950

Somerset: G C Barrett (Weston-super-Mare); G H Addenbrooke (Bath), J R Griffin, R T Moule (Bristol), J Sainsbury (Weston-super-Mare); M D Corbett (Bristol), B A Tuttlett (Clifton); H Bastable (Bridgwater), D Coles (Weston-super-Mare), J A Scott, E G Hopton (Bristol), I Macey (Wellington), A Lewis (Bath), A.M Balm, D Gunson (Bristol)

Referee: Mr B H L Ewin (Notts)

Somerset suffered an early blow when Scott was carried off with a rib injury within three minutes of the kick-off, but they made inroads into Gloucestershire territory and took the lead after eight minutes with a Barrett penalty from 45 yards. In reply Hook was only just short with a penalty goal attempt from inside his own half before missing with three easier opportunities.

The first real thrill came when Gloucestershire half-backs, Pearce and Hughes, set their three-quarters in motion, and there was a roar from the crowd when Gregory outpaced three Somerset defenders, but he went into touch about 15 yards short of the line. Not long before half-time outside half Hughes featured in a brilliant break which took play inside the Somerset half. He punted ahead, but Taylor and Morgans could not quite get the touchdown. Subsequently Taylor dropped

Action from the Somerset game [Journal]

on the ball when it was carried over the Somerset line but a try was disallowed, it being judged that the ball had been knocked forward.

Hook missed another penalty to leave Somerset in the lead at half-time. Somerset resumed in fine style with passing movements which stretched the Gloucestershire defence to the limit. Hook missed his seventh penalty attempt, but:

the Somerset line was now subjected to severe pressure. Gregory, after a fast clever run, cross kicked and Taylor almost got over in the corner after a fine threequarter movement in which Morgans was prominent. But Gloucestershire got their score following the subsequent lineout. Tom Price forced his way over for a try which Hook converted with a fine kick from a very wide angle.

Despite his generally poor kicking in this match, Bill Hook was the only Gloucester player in the County side which next travelled to Exeter and won 9-5, the first time that the County had selected so few from the City Club. Gordon Hudson returned for the 19-3 success over Berkshire at Reading. He then scored a try, and Bill Hook a penalty, to see Gloucestershire home 6-5 against Cornwall at Bristol. This secured a home semi-final at Kingsholm against East Midlands, who were regarded as formidable opponents and clear favourites.

Gloucestershire 3 East Midlands 3
3rd February 1951

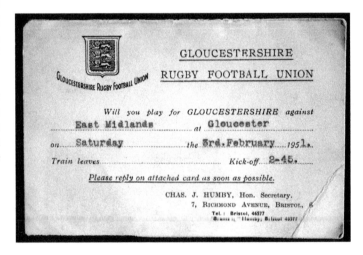

The invitation to play in the match against East Midlands which was sent to Gordon Hudson [John Hudson]

EIGHT FULL INTERNATIONALS, three wartime internationals and several trialists took part in this match, which attracted the attention of two England selectors. East Midlands, with five of the full internationals, were a strong side, which had lost to Cheshire in the final the previous season; there was a late change from the teams listed in the programme, E J O'Mullane (Northampton) replacing F M Fletcher (Bedford) at scrum-half.

Only ten minutes into the game, Gloucestershire heeled from a loose scrum, and J V Smith landed a lovely drop goal from thirty yards out. Soon after, Bill Hook was only just short with a penalty attempt from near the half-way line. But East Midlands started to rally as half-time approached, and were rewarded with a try by John Hyde in the corner.

The game was played at great pace, with no quarter given by either side. The Gloucestershire pack gained a territorial advantage for much of the game, despite their taller and heavier opponents getting the

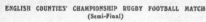

ENGLISH COUNTIES' CHAMPIONSHIP RUGBY FOOTBALL MATCH
(Semi-Final)

GLOUCESTERSHIRE RUGBY FOOTBALL UNION

GLOUCESTERSHIRE
v.
EAST MIDLANDS

at the

KINGSHOLM GROUND, GLOUCESTER
SATURDAY, FEBRUARY 3rd, 1951
Kick-off 2-45 p.m.

Official Programme - - Price 3d.

OUR VISITORS

We welcome East Midlands as our visitors at Kingsholm to-day. The County Championship has been won by East Midlands once, in 1934. On that occasion they defeated Gloucestershire by 10 points to nothing.
At Bristol in 1937 Gloucestershire beat East Midlands by 5 points to nothing in the Final.
Last season East Midlands accounted for Devon in the Semi-Final at Northampton but went down to Cheshire in the Final.

[Gloucestershire Archives]

Teams

Gloucestershire Colour: White, with Crest		East Midlands Colours: Emerald Green, White Shorts	
1	W. G. Hook Gloucester	Full-Backs	H. W. Rose Bedford	1
2	J. A. Gregory Bristol	Three-Qts. Right Wing	D. McNally Northampton	5
3	J. V. Smith Stroud	Right Centre	L. F. L. Oakley Bedford	4
4	R. Sutton Gloucester	Left Centre	A. C. Towell Bedford	3
5	J. E. Taylor Lydney	Left Wing	J. P. Hyde Northampton	2
6	D. Hughes Lydney	Half-Backs Stand-off	R. H. Haynes Bedford	6
7	I. W. Pearce Cheltenham	Scrum Half	F. M. Fletcher Bedford	7
8	T. W. Price Cheltenham (Captain)	Forwards	C. R. Jacobs Northampton	8
9	F. C. H. Hill Bath		T. Smith Northampton	9
10	E. McCall Bristol		J. H. Whiting Northampton	10
11	F. Steinhobel Cheltenham		W. R. Hamp Northampton	11
12	P. D. Young Clifton		J. F. Bance Bedford	12
13	D. G. Pratten Bristol		G. Jenkins Bedford	13
14	A. G. Hudson Gloucester		R. C. Hawkes Northampton	14
15	B. C. Dainty Stroud		D. F. White Northampton (Captain)	15

Referee : Mr. T. E. Priest (Surrey)

Touch Judge : Mr. R. R. Morris (Gloucestershire)

The Gloucestershire team: from left, back row: R Morris (linesman), D G Pratten, B C Dainty, E McCall, F C H Hill, P D Young, G Hudson, J A Gregory, J Purcell (baggage man), T Millington (President), T E Priest (referee); front row: R Sutton, W Hook, I W Pearce, T Price, J E Taylor, D Hughes, F Steinhobel, J V Smith [Journal]

R Sutton, J V Smith, D Hughes and J E Taylor of Gloucestershire start an attack against East Midlands [Journal]

better of line-outs and scrums. They pressed hard as the game wore on, but a narrow miss by Hook with another long-range penalty was the closest they came to scoring. Overall East Midlands had proved the better side, with their backs looking the more likely to score. It took a determined defence to hold them at bay.

The teams met again for the replay at Northampton, where East Midlands won 6-0.

Gloucestershire 6 Dorset & Wilts 0
8th December 1951

GLOUCESTERSHIRE MADE A late positional change to their team, switching round Howard Terrington and David Hughes. Heavy rain driving across the ground made kicking goals near to impossible, and this kept the scoring down.

Gloucestershire: P D Sullivan; J E Gregory, B Rowsell, D Hughes, J E Taylor; H Terrington, V Davies; J Woodward, J Howell, R Farmiloe, A McDonald, R N Muller, D G Pratten (captain), R Hodge, A G Hudson

Dorset & Wilts: C T Bowen; M Lillington, L S A Hodgins, K Roberts, E Lane; Glyn Johns, M Bampton; J Sear, J C Chadwick, F Prideux, G Wakeham, R M Macfarlane, T Lewis, R Proctor (captain), N Sampson

Referee: Mr H Delo

It was the Gloucestershire forwards who made most of the early inroads, and they set up Gregory and Rowsell to put Taylor over in the corner for the first score. Just before half-time, a fine kick by Gregory took play up to the Dorset & Wilts line, and the Gloucestershire captain, Pratten, forced his way over for the second try. The home team continued to have most of the play in the second half, but failed to add to their lead.

Gloucestershire 3 Cornwall 8
8th November 1952

HAVING LOST THEIR first two matches, Gloucestershire had only the wooden spoon to play for.

Gloucestershire: S T J Walter (Cheltenham); J A Gregory, Glyn Davies (Bristol), D Hughes (captain, Lydney), J E Taylor; W B Cartmell, V Davies; G W Hastings (Gloucester), R MacEwen (Clifton), J Woodward (Bristol), H G Wells (Gloucester), K Penn (Lydney and London Welsh), C Price (Lydney), R Hodge, D Ibbotson (Gloucester)

Cornwall: J Collins (Camborne); M Terry, M Jenkins, J M Williams (Penzance and Newlyn), H Stevens; H Oliver (St. Ives), T Thomas; T Bidgood (Redruth), F Sampson (Hoyle), G Bailey (St. Ives), K Vivian (Camborne), J Jenkin (Penzance and Newlyn), V G Roberts (captain, Penryn), J McG Kendall-Carpenter (Penzance and Newlyn), A Bone (St. Ives)

Referee: Dr B S Mills (Northumberland)

Until half-time Gloucestershire looked to have an outside chance of snatching their first County championship win of the season. At that stage they were leading by a prodigious penalty goal kicked by full-back Walter, but Gloucestershire saw little of the ball in the second half, when Cornwall cranked up their game and swept to a deserved victory.

That Cornwall did not build up a substantial lead was due to some dour, backs-to-the-wall, defensive work, and some inspired play by the Gloucestershire wing forwards, Dennis Ibbotson and Cliff Price. Both played well but Ibbotson was outstanding – time and again he saved his side with his deadly tackling.

Dennis Ibbotson, man-of-the-match in a losing cause against Cornwall in 1952 and try scorer against Devon in 1953 [Gloucester Rugby]

Gloucestershire 8 Devon 0
7th November 1953

A STRONG WIND BLOWING across Kingsholm and a greasy ball did not offer the prospect of an open game, and so it proved.

Gloucestershire: T U Wells; J A Gregory, B J Broad (Bristol), J Taylor (Gloucester), C G Woodruff (Cheltenham); Glyn Davies (Bristol), I W Pearce (Cheltenham); G Hastings (Gloucester), G Carpenter (Lydney), R A M Whyte (Clifton), A Macdonald (Bristol), P D Young (Dublin Wanderers), P Ford, R Hodge, D Ibbotson (Gloucester)

Devon: C T Bowen (Newton Abbot); J L Stark (Exeter), P M Luffman (Plymouth Albion), D Glyn John, G Griffiths (St. Luke's College);

R G Grace (Exeter), R Meadows (Devonport Services); E Woodgate (Paignton), G H Shapland (Barnstaple), W Woodgate (Paignton), E Carter (Devonport Services), I Zaidman (St. Luke's College), G Ridd (Barnstaple), Bryn Meredith, M Joseph (St. Luke's College).

The Citizen declared that this was 'a game which seldom reached the standard expected of a county match'. It soon settled into a slog between two powerful packs, with Devon having the upper hand in the first half, but the Gloucestershire eight finishing the game more strongly. The outstanding players on both sides were the wing forwards, Peter Ford and Dennis Ibbotson for Gloucestershire and Ridd and Joseph for Devon, and it was their play which subdued the opposing back divisions.

There was no score at half-time. After the interval Roger Whyte gave Gloucestershire the lead with a very fine penalty goal and the home county's other points came when Hodge took advantage of a cross-kick to send Ibbotson over for a try, which Whyte converted. However, the consensus of opinion was that Devon had done enough to earn a draw and Gloucestershire were fortunate to gain the win.

Gloucestershire 9 Hertfordshire 8
25th February 1954

THIS QUARTER-FINAL OF the County Championship was a special day for Brian Collett, playing prop for Hertfordshire on the Kingsholm ground where his father, J C Collett, and his uncle, D Crichton Miller, had both played for Gloucester between the wars.

Gloucestershire: T S Halls; J E Taylor, M J P Baker (Gloucester), A Barter (Cardiff), C G Woodruff (Cheltenham); G Davies (captain, Bristol), I T W Pearce (Cheltenham); G Hastings (Gloucester), G Carpenter (Lydney), R A M Whyte (Harlequins), P D Young (Dublin Wanderers), A Macdonald (Bristol), P Ford, R C Hodge, D Ibbotson (Gloucester)

Hertfordshire: C E Holroyd (West Herts); D J Skipper (Oxford University), L Clough (Letchworth), S Waterfall (Harpenden), R Winchester (Hendon); S J MacDermott (London Irish), G N Peters (Richmond); W R Grimsdell (Harlequins), M Jory (captain, Harlequins), J B G Collett (Old Stortfordians), R W D Marques (Harlequins), W Hodges (Old Hertfordians), L Webb (Bedford), J Smith, J D Haslett (Saracens)

Referee: Mr. J. H. Darville (Middlesex)'

Mike Baker kicked off the scoring with an early penalty from close range for Gloucestershire, but Hertfordshire soon responded in similar fashion. The first try came from a scrum close to the Hertfordshire line, when Illtyd Pearce scooted round on the blind side to put the home side ahead before half-time.

The second half was played in increasing gloom, but Hertfordshire upped the pace, charged down a kick by Glyn Jones, and scored a try, from which the conversion put them ahead for the first time, a lead they deserved. But Gloucestershire retaliated fiercely, Davies broke away, and passed the ball to Roger Whyte just over the half-way line; he raced towards the corner with two men inside him, but instead of passing to them, he cut inside himself and went over to score the winning try.

Gloucestershire 8 Somerset 8
13th November 1954

A CROWD OF 7,000 was somewhat smaller than usual for a County match at this time, but Gloucestershire had already lost to Cornwall and were not expected to progress further in the Championship. Late changes to the programme were B Dainty (Stroud) replacing P Ford for Gloucestershire, and D Williams and C Webber (both Bridgwater) replacing R Standing and J W Collard for Somerset.

	Gloucestershire		Somerset	
	Colour: White, with Crest		Colours: Black, White, Crimson	
1	T. U. Wells Bristol	Full-Backs	R. Challis Bristol	A
2	R. Sutton Gloucester	Three-Qts. Right Wing	H. Davies R.A.F. Locking and W-S-Mare	B
3	J. E. Taylor Leicester	Right Centre	J. Blake R.A.F. Locking and Bristol	C
4	D. W. Holman Richmond	Left Centre	R. Standing Bristol	D
5	B. J. Broad Bristol	Left Wing	K. C. Smith Bristol	E
6	D. S. Jones Gloucester	Half-Backs Stand-off	H. J. C. Brown Yeovil and Northampton	F
7	T. Base Bristol	Scrum Half	B. A. Tuttiett Clifton (Captain)	H
8	A. D. Townsend Cheltenham	Forwards	D. M. Davies Somerset Police	I
9	C. C. Thomas Gloucester		D. Coles Weston-Super-Mare	J
10	G. W. Hastings Gloucester		H. R. Bastable Bridgwater	K
11	G. Cripps Bristol		R. C. Hawkes Bristol	L
12	P. D. Young Dublin Wanderers (Capt.)		E. G. Hopton Bath	M
13	P. Ford Gloucester		J. W. Collard R.A.F. Locking and W-S-Mare	T
14	D. A. Howarth Cheltenham		A. M. Bain Bristol	U
15	D. G. Ibbotson Gloucester		J. G. Telling Taunton	X

Referee : Mr. T. E. Priest (Surrey)

Touch Judge : Mr. E. J. Parfitt (Gloucestershire)

[Gloucestershire Archives]

This was not the usual derby match between these two teams in that it had many thrilling moments and a high standard of rugby was maintained throughout. It appeared at first that the home county would run all over their opponents and Gloucestershire opened the scoring when Holman swerved through a gap near Somerset's 25 and Roy Sutton also handled before second-row forward Gordon Cripps forced his way over for a try. Cripps also added the goal points and a little later scored a penalty goal. At this stage nobody would have imagined that this would be the extent of Gloucestershire's scoring. But the Somerset pack started to exert its authority and although the Gloucestershire backs continued to see more of the ball, the Somerset defence was generally too good for them.

Before half-time Webber took advantage of a short punt by Tuttiett to dive over for a Somerset try which Bain converted and in the second half Bain levelled the scores with a grand penalty goal from near the touchline.

Gloucestershire 14 The Rest 8
26th September 1956

MULTIPLE CHANGES IN the team selections right up to kick-off disrupted this trial, which was concluded to have raised more questions than it answered. However, one player to stand out was D W Jones who:

looked a fly-half of class. He has that nimble poise, balance and speed off the mark that can transmit quick thought into action. Once he

gathered over his own line, evading a bunch of marauding forwards, raced round them, pivoted abruptly and kicked neatly to touch.

The Gloucestershire scorers were Cripps, who dashed in for a try following a bludgeoning run by Don Solomon, and Blair who scored the final try; Cripps kicked a conversion and a penalty; and Sheen a penalty. For The Rest, Troote was up to gather Thomas's cross kick and plunge over for a try; and L Watts kicked over Sheen's head and ran half the length of the field to dribble over for a great try, which Holder converted.

Gloucestershire 17 Cornwall 8
27th October 1956

THE TOTAL OF nine Bristol players in the Gloucestershire side was a record for that club.

Gloucestershire: I Sheen (Gloucester); M G Ellery, T Wynne Jones (Bristol), G Powell (Ebbw Vale), R Blair; D W Jones (Gloucester), E Blackman (Bristol); G Hastings (Gloucester), J Thorne, J Hellings, D Neate, A Macdonald (captain), J Bull (Bristol), B Green (Gloucester), T E. Base (Bristol)

Cornwall : A Stevens (Redruth); N Sharp (Camborne School of Mines), R Hosen (Penryn and Northampton), G Luke (Penzance and Newlyn and St Luke's College), E McLoughlin (Redruth); J Thomas, P J B Mitchell (Penzance and Newlyn); C R Johns (Redruth), R Carter (Camborne), J Jenkin, A Williams (Penzance and Newlyn), G Harris (Camborne), J Bowden (Hayle), P Williams (Truro), V G Roberts (captain, Penzance and Newlyn and Harlequins)

There was a surprised tone to the Citizen reporting of this match:

Eight points down after a quarter of an hour's play and careering headlong (so most people thought) towards another ignominious beating, the home county suddenly took a grip on themselves and stopped the rot. There followed a bitter and remorseless fight back! Slowly at first, but with ever increasing fury it gathered momentum. The surging Cornish tide, which at first had threatened to overwhelm Gloucestershire, was checked and thrown back. Finally came a grandstand finish — a finish which gave the home county's supporters more to cheer about than in any game for three years as Gloucestershire steadily piled up the points. With a bewildered Cornwall rocked almost to a standstill, there was no possible shadow of doubt about Gloucestershire's mastery in the closing stages.

Cornwall's try was converted by Hosen, who also landed a fine penalty goal. Gloucestershire opened their own account with a push-over try credited to Macdonald. Powell got the second try with a great individual run from nearly half way; and a clever wheel, during a forward attack, ended in Brian Green crossing for the third. The home county's other points came from an opportunistic 35 yards drop goal by David Jones; and a penalty goal and a conversion by Powell.

Gloucestershire 8 Devon 6
26th October 1957

THIS WAS THE first game in which Alan Holder and Mickey Booth were paired at half-back for Gloucestershire. The wet greasy conditions militated against open back play, but 'the fierce, unyielding struggle, contested in the most heart-warming traditions of tough, rugged West County Rugby, never lacked excitement.'

Late replacements in the Devon team were R Beer (Barnstaple) for G Williams and S Foster (Torquay Athletic) for F A Prosser.

The Citizen reported that:

Alan Holder [Gloucester Rugby]

Mickey Booth [Gloucester Rugby]

Teams

Gloucestershire Colour: White, with Crest		Devon Colours: Green and White	
1	I. Sheen Gloucester	Full-Backs	C. G. Bowen Newton Abbot
2	C. G. Woodruff Harlequins	Three-Qts. Right Wing	M. W. Blackmore 5 Barnstaple
3	K. M. Walter Cheltenham	Right Centre	W. J. Glastonbury 4 Plymouth Albion
4	A. Barter Cardiff	Left Centre	G. Williams 3 Weston-S-Mare
5	T. W Jones Bristol	Left Wing	K. Maddocks 2 Plymouth Albion
6	A. Holder Gloucester	Half-Backs Stand-off	B. E. Jones 1 Pontypool
7	M. Booth Gloucester	Scrum Half	D. B. Rees 7 Neath
8	G. Hastings Gloucester	Forwards	G. E. R. Ridd 8 Torquay Athletic (Captain)
9	J. Thorne Bristol		B. R. Homer 9 Exeter
10	J. Herbert Gloucester		L. Jenkins 10 St. Luke's College
11	A. Macdonald Bristol (Captain)		R. L. Ellis 11 Plymouth Albion
12	B. J. Green Gloucester		T. C. Jones 12 R.N.E. College
13	P. Ford Gloucester		F. A. Prosser 13 Devonport Services
14	G. Cripps Bristol		D. C. Manley 14 Exeter
15	T. E. Base Bristol		B. Sparks 15 Torquay Athletic

Referee : Mr. J. R. Searle (East Midlands)

Touch Judges : Mr. S. H. Davies. Mr. W. G. Avery (Devon Referee Society)

[Gloucestershire Archives]

drive the ball to Devon's line. Gordon Cripps made no mistake with the conversion from a fairly easy position.

So, the Citizen was able to exult:

That bolt-from-the-blue, last-minute try becomes a fascinating habit at Kingsholm! A week ago it cost Gloucester a victory. But on Saturday it sent County supporters delirious with joy and excitement. Just when all seemed lost, with the shutters going up sadly for another year, there were Gloucestershire gloriously back in the championship fight again. A seemingly inevitable and undeserved defeat had been miraculously averted. And, instead of a Gloucestershire reverse, the reigning champions, Devon were themselves forced to swallow the bitter pill reserved for fallen conquerors. It was a memorable, splendid performance on Gloucestershire's part. That bulldog determination never to give up; to keep on battling while the remotest possible chance existed of saving the game, brought a just and satisfying reward.

Gloucestershire 23 The Rest 11
22nd September 1958

THE TEAMS WERE confronted by a rain-soaked Kingsholm for this county trial, but overcame the conditions with plenty of enterprising play. Dave Phelps and Mickey Booth stood out as a class act at half-back, Cyril Thomas had the better of the hooking duel, Bert Macdonald and Gareth Payne showed up well in the lineouts, and the length of Ian Sheen's touch kicking was impressive.

The lion's share of the work fell on the two iron-hard powerful packs. They went at it hammer-and-tongs. And slowly, remorselessly that slashing, battering, superb Gloucestershire eight began to master the Devon forwards in the loose. Inspiringly led by Bristol's Bert Macdonald; forceful raiders with the ball at their feet and magnificently together as a pack, they blasted Devon more and more on the defensive. Peter Ford, George Hastings, John Herbert and Brian Green — the four Gloucester men in the home County's grand match-winning pack — all pulled their weight lustily. Ford, in particular, was a charging live-wire, here, there and everywhere and seemingly always on the ball.

For Devon, Glastonbury kicked two penalty goals, whilst Gloucestershire chalked up a very nice drop goal landed by Holder. The last quarter found the visiting county desperately hard-pressed for most of the time, and it was not until the last minute that wing forward Terry Base got the all-important try after Gloucestershire had used their feet to

Gloucestershire: I Sheen (Gloucester); M G Ellery (Bristol), A Holder (Gloucester), J Radford, T Wynn-Jones (Bristol); D Phelps, M Booth; M Burford, C Thomas, J Herbert (Gloucester), A E Macdonald (captain, Bristol), G Payne (Stroud), P Ford (Gloucester), G Cripps, T E Base (Bristol)

The Rest: G Hale (Stroud); R Smith, J Hart (Gloucester), J Taylor (Cheltenham), F Way (Bristol); D W Jones (Cheltenham), T Wintle (Lydney); A Townsend (Cheltenham), J Fowke, R Fowke (Stroud), D W Neate (Bristol), B J Green (captain, Gloucester), R Porter (Cheltenham), B Dovey (Lydney), D Ibbotson (Gloucester)

Referee: Mr R A Gabb (Gloucester)

Mike Ellery and Phelps combined to break through and set up John Herbert for the opening try, and Ellery scored the second himself showing great pace to outstrip the opposition. Further tries were scored for Gloucestershire by Gordon Cripps, Peter Ford and Terry Base. Cripps converted four of his side's five tries. Frank Way and John Taylor both produced fine individual runs in scoring tries for The Rest, and Bob Smith got their third; Hale kicked one conversion.

Gloucestershire 6 Somerset 13
25th October 1958

THE COUNTY STARTED their Championship campaign with a good 11-3 win over Devon at Exeter and there was cautious optimism for their chances against Somerset at Kingsholm, but their last victory over this old foe was five years previously and they had a reputation as Gloucestershire's bogey team.

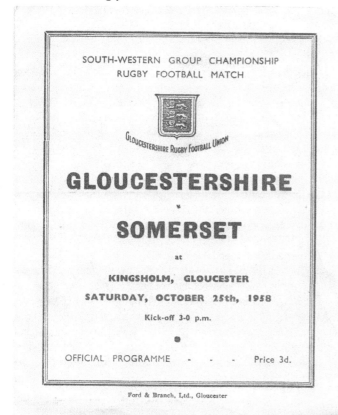

SOUTH-WESTERN GROUP CHAMPIONSHIP
RUGBY FOOTBALL MATCH

GLOUCESTERSHIRE RUGBY FOOTBALL UNION

GLOUCESTERSHIRE
v
SOMERSET

at

KINGSHOLM, GLOUCESTER

SATURDAY, OCTOBER 25th, 1958

Kick-off 3-0 p.m.

OFFICIAL PROGRAMME - - - Price 3d.

Ford & Branch, Ltd., Gloucester

[Gloucestershire Archives]

The match proved to be one of missed opportunities and was settled by the place kickers. The chief culprit in the matter of the missed penalties was the Gloucestershire captain and Bristol back row forward, Gordon Cripps. After several Cripps failures, the Kingsholm crowd were

Teams

	Gloucestershire Colour ; White, with Crest		Somerset Colours : Black, White, Crimson	
1	I. W. Sheen Gloucester	Full-Backs	G. Hopkins Weston-super-Mare	A
2	M. G. Ellery Bristol	Three-Qts. Right Wing	H. J. Dolman Bath	B
3	K. M. Walter Cheltenham	Right Centre	H. J. C. Brown St. Luke's College	C
4	J. Radford Bristol	Left Centre	G. Williams Weston-super-Mare	D
5	F. Way Bristol	Left Wing	T R. J. Leonard Camb. Univ., Harlequins	E
6	D. Phelps Gloucester	Half-Backs Stand-off	J. Blake Bristol (Captain)	F
7	M. Booth Gloucester	Scrum Half	G. Drewett Bath	G
8	*G. W. Hastings Gloucester	Forwards	T F. J. Williams Bristol	H
9	T J. D. Thorne Bristol		P. J. Hill Bath	I
10	R. Fowke Stroud		*D. St. G. Hazell Bristol	J
11	B. J. Green Gloucester		D. C. Wooding Weston-super-Mare	K
12	T D. W. Neate Bristol		*J. D. Currie Oxford Univ., Harlequins	L
13	R. Porter Cheltenham		M. J. Jordan Taunton	M
14	T G. Cripps Bristol (Captain)		D. Hodge Bridgwater	N
15	T. E. Base Bristol		K. Palmer Bristol	O

* INTERNATIONAL   T TRIAL

Referee : Mr. D. A. Brown (Northumberland)
Touch Judges : J. V SMITH (Gloucestershire)   F. W. WILLIAMS (Somerset)

calling for George Hastings to take the kicks, and he was at last given the ball. His very first shot, a 45 yarder, came hearteningly close. But there were still no points. And it was left to Cripps, kicking again in the second half, to land Gloucestershire's only penalty goal, which was a good one from wide out. The best Gloucestershire three-quarter was right wing Mike Ellery, who showed up well at times both in attack and defence, and a good effort on his part led to Cripps getting Gloucestershire's only try.

Both back divisions became handicapped during the game through injuries. Centres John Brown of Somerset, and John Radford of Gloucestershire, turned into little more than passengers, and each county found it necessary to pull a forward out of the pack for duty in the respective threequarter lines. Somerset, helped by the home county's mistakes, made the better use of their chances, and in doing so ensured victory. They had the more reliable kicker on the day in Gordon Drewett, who scored seven points from two conversions and a penalty.

Despite this setback, victory 8-6 over Cornwall at Bristol set up a replay against Somerset to decide the group. Gloucestershire triumphed this time, 12-6 at Weston-super-Mare. Dorset & Wilts were beaten 18-0 at Cheltenham in the quarter-final, which meant a journey all the way up to Hartlepool to face Durham in the semi-final. A 0-0 draw there in a sea of mud brought the teams back to Kingsholm for the replay.

Gloucestershire 8 Durham 6
14th March 1959

[Gloucestershire Archives]

THE DEMAND FOR tickets was so great that additional ringside seats were provided inside the railings around the playing area, and some 9,000 spectators were gripped by a nerve-wracking match.

Gloucestershire had their dogged defence and their captain, Gordon Cripps, who did all their scoring, to thank for their somewhat fortunate victory. Cripps kicked two magnificent goals – a penalty from nearly 60 yards, and a touchline conversion of his own try. This came when Alan Holder charged down a drop goal attempt by Weston and chased away with the ball at his feet; centre John Radford carried on, and Cripps gained possession near the line to score. With their pack dominant throughout the game, Durham scored a try in each half, by Moffitt and Collard, but they failed with all their kicks at goal, and ultimately this undermined their

efforts. They mounted a determined assault on the Gloucestershire line for the last few minutes, and were awarded a penalty in injury time, but that kick failed too, and the match had slipped from their grasp.

Mickey Booth gets the ball away against Durham [Citizen]

Gloucestershire were through to the final for the first time for ten years, against the reigning champions, Warwickshire, who retained their title with a 14-9 victory at Bristol.

Gloucestershire 22 Cornwall 0
22nd October 1960

THIS WAS THE opening match in the County Championship campaign played in dismal weather, but the Kingsholm turf withstood a solid downpour with little damage.

Gloucestershire: R Hillier (Stroud); M Ellery, L Watts, D Weeks, P Mills; J Blake, B Redwood (Bristol); J Fowke, C Thomas, A Townsend (Gloucester), D Neate, D Watt, T Base (Bristol), J.Young (Clifton), P Ford (captain, Gloucester)

Cornwall: H Stevens (Redruth); J Cobner (Penryn), R J Moyle (Launceston), G Luke (Penzance-Newlyn), D Thomas (Penryn); J Thomas, P Mitchell (Penzance-Newlyn); A Nicholls (Falmouth), K Abraham, C R Johns (Redruth), A Williams (Penzance-Newlyn), B R Loveday (Launceston), P McGovan (Redruth), T A Thomas (Falmouth), D C Mills (Harlequins)

Referee: Mr R J Todd (Hampshire)

Gloucestershire got off to a flying start. Within three minutes Thomas won the ball in a lineout and the home pack brought the crowd to its feet with a fine foot-rush which resulted in Jack Fowke diving over for the first try of the afternoon, but Redwood missed the conversion. A couple of Cornish attacks were thwarted by fine clearances by Hillier and after half an hour Watts kicked a penalty to increase the Gloucestershire lead. Cornwall soon had a chance to retaliate but Loveday sliced his effort wide.

With half-time looming, L. D. Watts, the Bristol centre, gave Gloucestershire supporters their thrill of the game so far. Weekes had shouldered through a collection of Cornish forwards. He lost possession but Watts came in with a kick-ahead which he pursued like a rocket. But he was just too late, Cornwall's Moyle touched it down.

So, it was 6-0 at half-time. In the second half, Blake missed narrowly with a dropped goal attempt, before Redwood received the ball from a scrum fifteen yards out and jinked his way over the line for a try, which Watts converted with a kick which hit the post.

As if that was not good enough Redwood then reverse passed to Blake who took everyone but himself by surprise. With mouths open, the 29 other players watched him dash over. Watts failed with the conversion kick.

Jack Fowke, who scored the first try against Cornwall [Gloucester Rugby]

Gloucestershire 25 Monmouthshire 20
5th October 1961

THERE WAS MUCH local interest in seeing how a young Mike Nicholls would make out at county level. He passed the test well.

Gloucestershire: J Crouch (Cheltenham); M G Ellery (Bristol), J Bayliss (Gloucester), J Blake (captain, Bristol), C Lewis (RAF Innsworth); T Hopson, M Booth; A Townsend, M. Nicholls (Gloucester), J New, D E J Watt (Bristol), R Long, P Ford (Gloucester), D W Neate, T E Base (Bristol)

Monmouthshire: T Carpenter (Ebbw Vale); S Watkins (Cross Keys), M Price (captain, Pontypool), R Knott (Ebbw Vale), D R Pulsford (Pontypool); G Legge (Cross Keys), R Evans (Pontypool); L Dimmick (Ebbw Vale), D Jones (Newbridge), M Hurn, A T Davies (Abertillery), R Manwaring (Cross Keys), A Pask (Abertillery), D Nash (Ebbw Vale), H J Morgan (Abertillery)

Referee : Mr H King (Gloucestershire)

Booth kicked Gloucestershire into the lead with a penalty after only two minutes, but Monmouthshire soon struck back with some inventive play which resulted in a try for Pask, converted by Knott. Lewis regained the lead when he lunged over in the corner. Crouch's conversion fell short, but he was soon in the action again, tackling Pulsford to prevent a try.

Shortly before half-time, the Gloucestershire threes went close and Blake was upended on the Monmouthshire line. He had the presence

of mind, however, to pass to Base who leant over for a try which was converted by Booth who also added a further three points with a penalty to give a half-time score of 17-5 in Gloucestershire's favour.

Gloucestershire extended their lead when Ford picked up the ball in the loose and Neate scored the try, but it was soon reduced again when Pask scored his second try and Knott converted.

Gloucestershire's captain, J Blake, soon put matters right, however, when he took the ball from Neate after Booth had booted it across the field and touched down for a try which Booth converted. In the final stages, Monmouthshire reduced the arrears again when Watkins crossed and Knott added the extra points to put Monmouthshire only five points below Gloucestershire.

Gloucestershire 16 Devon 3
28th October 1961

THERE WERE SEVERAL new faces in the Devon side, which had reached the final of the County Championship in the previous season, but then lost five players to Rugby League.

Gloucestershire: R Hillier (Gloucester); M Ellery, L Watts (Bristol), J Bayliss, P Meadows (Gloucester); J Blake (captain, Bristol), M Booth (Gloucester); J New (Bristol), M Nicholls, A Townsend, R Long (Gloucester), D Watt (Bristol), P Ford (Gloucester), D Neate (Bristol), T Base (Bristol)

Devon: M Caunter; P S Lewis (Torquay Athletic), B Carless (Exeter), M A Pearey (Devonport Services), P Thorning (Richmond); M P Arscott (Rosslyn Park), K A Hopper (Exeter); M Tait (Plymouth Albion), M J Smith (Crediton), R Smerdon (Plymouth Albion and St. Luke's), N Southern (Plymouth Albion), M Davies (Torquay), P J Brown, D C Manley (captain, Exeter), M Woodward (Plymouth Albion)

Referee: Mr J M L Mock

The Citizen neatly summarised a disappointing match:

The might of two counties may have met at Kingsholm, but the overall standard of play did not suggest it on Saturday. The tempo was enthusiastic but considering the array of talent available for our entertainment the moments of magic were only thinly, almost grudgingly woven into a rather threadbare tapestry. It was a somewhat breathless game for all concerned, but my guess is that the most breathless man on the field was the referee, what with all that running and all that blowing.

Gloucestershire made an uncertain start, but settled down once winger Mike Ellery had scored the first try, which Mickey Booth converted. Laurie Watts booted a penalty from long distance and Bowen replied in kind for Devon to make the score 8-3 at half-time. The home pack settled the game in the second half. At a defensive scrum on their own line, Devon heeled the ball, only for Base, the Gloucestershire wing forward, to beat the Devon scrum half to the ball, picking it up and plonking it over the line without having to take a forward step. Then right at the end of the game, Nicholls hooked a ball back for Gloucestershire, and Base and Neate both handled before Peter Ford gave the scoring pass to Dave Watt; Laurie Watts converted.

Having warmed up with an 11-9 win over Monmouthshire at Newport, Gloucestershire opened their 1962-63 Championship campaign against Somerset at Kingsholm.

Gloucestershire 11 Somerset 3
27th October 1962

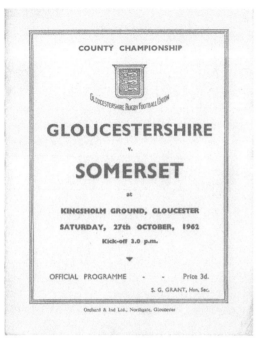

[Gloucestershire Archives]

The Gloucestershire team: back row: E Calver (touch judge), K Cottle (Treasurer), Wright, Townsend, Neate, Watts, Watt, Dovey, Hampton, Long, Pitt, D Walter (committee), G Wright (committee); front row: Hopson, Booth, Ford, E J Parfitt (President), Thorne, Smith, Bayliss [Journal]

A TROUNCING OF NEWPORT in a Club game the previous Saturday encouraged the Gloucestershire selectors to include eight Gloucester players, with debuts for Ron Pitt and Dick Smith.

Referee: Mr R A Crowe (Eastern Counties)

A good team effort was enhanced by an outstanding performance by the irrepressible Mickey Booth, which left 'memories always of Booth's tireless cheek, his sharp-witted kicks placed just where he and the pack needed them to be placed'. The highlight of the first half was a wonder try by Terry Hopson, who 'selling dummies to right and left wove his way over for a centrally placed try which Booth had no difficulty in converting.'

In the second half, Booth himself scored, first 'he foxed the Cidermen's pack with a dummy dive pass', and then 'darted round the outside of the closely-locked ruck'. The match was rounded off with a fine try by Hampton 'after an edge-of-the-precipice run along the touchline'.

TEAMS

	GLOUCESTERSHIRE Colour : White		SOMERSET Colours : Red, Black and White	
1	G. WRIGHT Cheltenham	Full Back	G. HUNT Saracens	A
2	J. HAMPTON Lydney	Three-Qtrs. Right Wing	R. V. BRIDGEMAN Bristol	B
3	J. BAYLISS Gloucester	Right Centre	M. J. LEWIS Bristol	C
4	R. PITT Gloucester	Left Centre	R. G. COLLARD Bridgwater	D
5	L. D. WATTS Bristol	Left Wing	J. LEWIS Bridgwater	E
6	T. HOPSON Gloucester	Half-Backs Stand-off	G. WILLIAMS Weston-s-Mare	F
7	M. BOOTH Gloucester	Scrum-Half	R. T. ROBINSON Taunton	G
8	A. TOWNSEND Gloucester	Forwards	R. V. GROVE Bristol	H
9	J. D. THORNE Bristol		P. J. HILL Bath	I
10	B. T. H. DOVEY Rosslyn Park		D. St. G. HAZELL Bristol	J
11	D. E. J. WATT Bristol		J. D. CURRIE Bristol	K
12	R. LONG Gloucester		J. WATSON St. Mary's Hosp.	L
13	P. FORD (Capt.) Gloucester		C. T. MOATE Bridgwater	M
14	D. W. NEATE Bristol		G. REDMOND Weston-S-Mare	N
15	D. SMITH Gloucester		L. DAVIES Bristol	O

Referee : Mr. R. A. B. CROWE (Eastern Counties)
Touch Judges :
Mr. E. CALVER (G.R.U. Gloucester Society)   Mr. K. C. SMITH (Somerset R.U.)

Dave Watt wins a line-out against Somerset [Citizen]

Mickey Booth releases his backs under pressure from a couple of Somerset players; other Gloucestershire players, from left, are Allen Townsend, Dave Watt, Roy Long and Peter Ford [Citizen]

Defeat 0-11 by Cornwall at Bristol, was followed by victory 14-0 against Devon at Torquay, which left the group tied between three counties. The first replay was against Cornwall at Redruth, which did not augur well for Gloucestershire's prospects, but they brought off a shock 10-3 win, and Devon travelled to Kingsholm for the second replay.

Gloucestershire 12 Devon 8
16th February 1963

THE SOUTH WEST group was renowned for tough, close encounters, with penalties often proving decisive, and a muddy Kingsholm, following a thaw, promised more of the same. So, the six tries scored in this match, all by backs, came as a pleasant surprise, although the conditions foiled the kickers. It was described as 'one of the most enthusiastic and sporting matches (in spite of some upper cuts, hooks and crosses!)'.

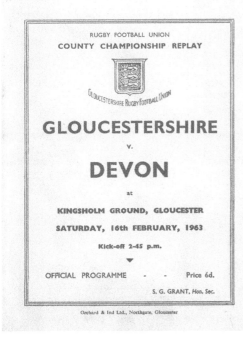

[Gloucestershire Archives]

TEAMS

DEVON Colours : Green and White		GLOUCESTERSHIRE Colour : Red
1 M. CAUNTER Torquay	Full Backs	1 P. J. COLSTON Bristol
2 P. THORNING Richmond	Three-Qtrs. Right Wing	2 J. HAMPTON Lydney
3 J. UZZELL St. Luke's College	Right Centre	3 J. BAYLISS Gloucester
4 M. J. BEER Taunton	Left Centre	4 L. D. WATTS Bristol
5 P. S. LEWIS Torquay Ath. & St. Luke's Col.	Left Wing	5 M. COLLINS Bristol
6 M. P. ARSCOTT Rosslyn Park	Half-Backs Stand-off	6 J. N. BLAKE Bristol
7 E. B. CARLESS Exeter	Scrum-Half	7 T. C. WINTLE Lydney and St. Mary's Hospital
8 M. TAIT Plymouth Albion	Forwards	8 K. WILSON Gloucester
9. P. T. L. SCOTT Britannia, R.N.C.		9 J. D. THORNE Bristol
10 R. SMERDON Plymouth Alb. & St. Luke's Col.		10 B. A. DOVEY Lydney and Rosslyn Park
11 R. SOUTHERN Plymouth Albion		11 D. E. J. WATT Bristol
12 M. DAVIS Torquay Ath. & St. Luke's Col.		12 B. A. HUDSON Gloucester
13 P. J. BROWN Exeter		13 P. FORD (Capt.) Gloucester
14 T. W. HEMPTON Exeter and St. Luke's College		14 D. W. NEATE Bristol
15 D. C. MANLEY (Capt.) Exeter		15 D. SMITH Gloucester

Referee : H. KEENAN (Durham)
Touch Judges :
C. GRIFFIN (D.R.R.S.) F. KING (G.R.F.U.)

Colston scoring the second try for Gloucestershire [Journal]

Gloucestershire were well anchored by the England front row of 'Tug' Wilson, John Thorne and Bev Dovey, and dominated the scrums, although they were outdone in the line-outs. John Hampton ran in the first try when he scooped up the rebound from an attempted drop goal by John Blake which bounced back off one of the uprights. A second try scored by Peter Colston built a 6-0 lead at half-time.

Trevor Wintle gets another Gloucestershire move under way against Devon
[Journal]

A fine try by Thorning on the resumption put fresh heart into Devon. As the game became spicier, Mike Collins restored the Gloucestershire lead, only for Lewis to hack the ball the length of the field and outstrip the home defence. John Hampton's second try settled the issue as regards winning both the match and the group.

The subsequent quarter-final against Oxfordshire at Bristol was won at a canter, 42-8. Given home advantage for the semi-final, Gloucestershire again chose Kingsholm.

Gloucestershire 3 Warwickshire 11
30 March 1963

JUST UNDER 11,000 were packed into Kingsholm like sardines. Warwickshire presented a considerable challenge, having been Champion County in four of the previous five seasons. Their twelve Coventry players formed a well-knit team. Gloucester's sporting bishop, the Rt Rev Basil Guy, was in the stand along with the Mayors of Gloucester and Cheltenham, as pockets of Gloucestershire

[Gloucestershire Archives]

TEAMS

WARWICKSHIRE Colour: White		GLOUCESTERSHIRE Colour: Red
15 D. R. COOK Coventry	Full Backs	1 P. J. COLSTON Bristol
14 *D. B. JACKSON (Capt). Coventry	Three-Qtrs. Right Wing	2 J. HAMPTON Lydney
13 A. E. DAVIES Coventry	Right Centre	3 J. BAYLISS Gloucester
12 C. WHEATLEY Coventry	Left Centre	4 L. D. WATTS Bristol
11 J. R. MELVILLE Coventry	Left Wing	5 M. COLLINS Bristol
10 R. J. FRAME Coventry	Half-Backs Stand-off	6 J. N. BLAKE Bristol
9 G. H. COLE Coventry	Scrum-Half	7 T. C. WINTLE Lydney and St. Mary's Hospital
1 M. R. McLEAN Coventry	Forwards	8 *K. WILSON Gloucester
2 *H. O. GODWIN Coventry		9 *J. D. THORNE Bristol
3 *P. H. JUDD Coventry		10 *B. A. DOVEY Lydney and Rosslyn Park
4 *J. E. OWEN Coventry		11 D. E. J. WATT Bristol
5 *T. A. PARGETTER Coventry		12 B. A. HUDSON Gloucester
6 S. J. PURDY Rugby		13 P. FORD (Capt.) Gloucester
8 C. M. PAYNE Harlequins	* International	14 D. W. NEATE Bristol
7 *P. D. G. ROBBINS Coventry		15 D. SMITH Gloucester

Referee : M. F. TURNER (Surrey)
Touch Judges :
H. PATEMAN (W.S.O.R.)   H. NELMES (G.R.F.U.)

The Gloucestershire team: back row: D Pegler (reserve), S Wright (committee), Colston, Hampton, Wilson, Watt, Hudson, Neate, Watts, Dovey, G Wright (reserve), D Walter (committee), H Nelmes (touch judge); front row: K Cottle (committee), Collins, Thorne, Smith, Ford, E J Parfitt (President), Blake, Bayliss, Wintle, S Grant (committee) [Journal]

supporters yelled the county's battle-cry, 'Timber'. They were treated to a thunderous match, rough and rugged, with each side hustling the other into errors.

The Warwickshire pack decided the match. They were described in the Citizen with a mixture of respect and envy as 'the most disciplined bunch of muscle-bound toughs Kingsholm has seen since the professional-minded and socially-thick Springboks gave us a lesson in how to win matches and not friends two seasons ago'. They stuffed the ball up their jerseys for most of the game, and when they did let it out, their scrum half, Cole, worked the touch-lines very effectively with repeated overhead kicks. Melville scored a try in the first half, but John Hampton replied with a try scored from his own half, starting with an interception and marked by a glorious long run, the crowd living every stride and bellowing their encouragement. This was the truly memorable moment of the match, but Warwickshire soon re-established their grip on the game, and a Davies try, and Cole conversion and dropped goal, settled the issue in their favour.

Melville scores the first try for Warwickshire [Journal]

Gloucester 14 County President's XV 14
2nd May 1963

THIS MATCH WAS tacked on to the end of the season in order to raise money for various charities.

Gloucester: R Hillier; R Timms, R Pitt, G Mace, A Osman; T Hopson, M Booth; F Fowke, K Taylor, A Townsend, A Davis, B Hudson, P Ford, D Owen, G White.

County President's XV: P Colston; J Hampton, A Wright, M Collins, R Bassett; T Nicholls, C Kimmins; K Wilson, J Pullin, M Peglar, J Currie, D Neate, A Murphy, D Rollitt, A Weaver

Referee: Mr H King (Gloucestershire)

The Citizen headline read 'Sparkling Rugby in Kingsholm Thriller' and went on to declare that 'no one could cavil at the free-throwing, fast running brand of rugger served up at Kingsholm last night. It was just the sort of stuff likely to warm a rugger man's heart during those long, empty summer months!' The County President's XV opened the scoring with a nonchalant try by Weaver, which Nicholls converted, and increased it with a splendid try by Bassett. Terry Hopson reduced the arrears with a try near the posts which Russell Hillier converted, and shortly afterwards he drop kicked a penalty goal.

Peter Ford, as usual, seemed to be everywhere at once, and set a fine example for the Red and Whites, as Gloucester were commonly referred to in this era, who took the lead early in the second half when Hillier kicked a penalty. Wright levelled the scores with an unconverted try, and the County President's XV snatched the lead for the second time when Collins scored an unconverted try, but a tremendous, bull-dozing run by Gary White, Gloucester's mobile wing-forward, ended in an equalising try a few minutes before no side. It was thought appropriate that Hillier's conversion failed, leaving the match as an honourable draw.

Gloucestershire 16 Monmouthshire 0
3rd October 1963

THE 1963-64 COUNTY season kicked off with this friendly against Monmouthshire. The sides appeared strong on paper, but, despite a comfortable win for Gloucestershire, the standard of play from both teams was derided as being well below that expected at County level.

Gloucestershire: A Holder (Gloucester); J Hampton (Rosslyn Park), J Taylor (Gloucester), L D Watts, M Collins; J N Blake (Bristol), J Morris (Lydney); A Townsend, M. Wetson (Gloucester), B A Dovey (Rosslyn Park), B A Hudson (Gloucester), D W Neate (Bristol), P Ford (captain, Gloucester), D Rollitt (Bristol University), R Smith (Gloucester)

Monmouthshire: D T Jones (Newbridge); F E Coles (Pontypool), D T Hardacre (Cross Keys), M C Cooper (Pontypool), M Williams; W Hunt, R Evans (Ebbw Vale); C Cobley (Pontypool), B Wilkins (Abertillery), L Dimmick, G J Bishop (Pontypool), R Gladwin (Abertillery), A Hughes, D Hughes (Newbridge), M Treanor (Ebbw Vale)

Referee: Mr A L Cornish (Bristol)

Gloucestershire took the lead approximately half way through the first half when they won the ball at a scrum inside the Monmouth 25 and passed it out to the three-quarters via Morris and Blake. After they had lost possession, John Hampton got a hand to the loose ball and Dave Rollitt, who had sprinted right across field, took a neat pass to touch down in the corner. His try went unconverted, and at half-time the score remained at 3-0.

Not long after the re-start, the Gloucestershire forwards pressed hard before the ball was passed out to Hampton, who rushed down the touch-line to score a try in the corner. Laurie Watts converted with a splendid kick and shortly afterwards he added another three points when he landed an equally accurate penalty. 'Then, in the last two minutes, wing three-quarter, Mike Collins, scored the best try of the match when he dashed forward in a 40 yards sprint, passing at least half a dozen Monmouthshire players before touching down almost under the posts.' Watts converted to complete the scoring.

In the County Championship, the South West Group ended as usual in a tie, and, with Gloucestershire awarded home advantage, Kingsholm was chosen for the play-off match.

Gloucestershire 3 Somerset 0
14th December 1963

THIS MATCH ATTRACTED BBC television and radio coverage, and a crowd of 6,000. Two things were found worthy of special note; first was the splendid playing surface, and second was Peter Ford's 'neat line in short shorts instead of his usual long bags'.

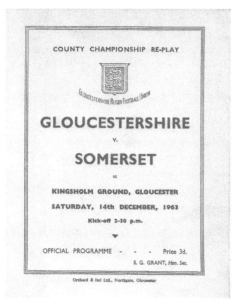

[Gloucestershire Archives]

TEAMS

SOMERSET Colours: Crimson, White and Black		GLOUCESTERSHIRE Colours: Red	
A	C. D. N. HARVEY Bath	**Full Backs**	P. J. COLSTON Bristol	1
B	J. V. COLES Bristol	**Three-Qtrs.** **Right Wing**	J. HAMPTON Rosslyn Park	2
C	C. W. McFADYEAN Bristol	**Right Centre**	J. BAYLISS Gloucester	3
D	R. G. COLLARD Bridgwater	**Left Centre**	D. J. WEEKS Bristol	4
E	J. LEWIS Bridgwater	**Left Wing**	M. COLLINS Bristol	5
F	J. K. THOMAS Taunton	**Half-Backs** **Stand-off**	T. HOPSON Gloucester	6
G	J. AMOR Bristol	**Scrum-Half**	M. BOOTH Gloucester	7
H	*D. St. G. HAZELL Bristol	**Forwards**	*B. A. DOVEY Rosslyn Park and Lydney	8
I	P. J. HILL Bath		*J. D. THORNE Bristol	9
J	R. J. GROVE Bristol		M. J. PEGLER Bristol	10
K	*J. D. CURRIE Bristol		B. A. HUDSON Gloucester	11
L	D. L. HODGE Bridgwater		D. W. NEATE Bristol	12
M	L. DAVIES Bristol		P. FORD (Capt.) Gloucester	13
N	G. REDMOND Bristol		D. ROLLITT Bristol University	14
O	G. G. WHITE Gloucester		R. SMITH Gloucester	15

* International

Referee : J. G. SAUNDERS (*Lancs.*)

Touch Judges

T. A. B. MAHONEY (Somerset R.U.)   R. DAVIS (GRU. Gloucester Refs. Society)

Gloucestershire were handicapped early on when a leg injury sustained by John Bayliss made him a passenger for the rest of the match. But it was a typical derby game, hard fought, scrappy, and with packs and defences dominating. The difference was reported to be 'Mickey Booth at scrum-half playing to Peter Ford at wing forward. These two have an understanding which is rare in rugby and even more rare between a half-back and a wing forward.' It was a piece of Peter Ford opportunism which led to the only score in the match; Mike Collins sliced a penalty kick, Ford caught it, and started a handling move which ended with Dave Rollitt going over in the corner.

Two Gloucester back row forwards, Ford and White, scramble for the ball, but playing on opposite sides for Gloucestershire and Somerset respectively [Journal]

Dorset & Wilts were brushed aside 26-0 in the quarter-final, but Gloucestershire stumbled at the semi-final stage again, going down 9-19 to Lancashire at Bristol.

Gloucestershire 21 Cornwall 6
28th November 1964

BOTH SIDES HAD to make eleventh hour changes to their selections, Cornwall losing their lustiest forward, 'Bonzo' Johns, and Gloucestershire losing their little general, Mickey Booth. The attendance at 9,000 was the largest at Kingsholm for several seasons.

Gloucestershire: D Rutherford (Gloucester); J M Hampton (Rosslyn Park), J A Bayliss (Gloucester), D J Weeks, M R Collins; R Wallace (Bristol), J Morris (Lydney); B A G Hudson (Gloucester), J D Thorne (Bristol), B A Dovey (Rosslyn Park), D E J Watt, D W Neate (Bristol), P J Ford (captain, Gloucester), D M Rollitt (Loughborough College), R Smith (Gloucester)

Cornwall: R Hosen (Northampton); K Plummer (Penryn), J Glover (Bristol), T Mungles, I Jose (Hayle); R A W Sharp (captain, Bristol), J Michell (Penzance Newlyn); A N Other, R Harris (Plymouth Albion), C B Stevens (Penzance Newlyn), C Kneebone (Penryn), A Williams (Penzance Newlyn), P E McGovan (Redruth), R S Grazsher (Plymouth Albion), A C Thomas (Northampton)

Don Rutherford, who kicked nine points against Cornwall [Don Rutherford]

Referee: Mr M H R King (Surrey)

Cornwall came close to an early lead when Richard Sharp missed with a drop goal attempt. Winger Collins then gained possession for Gloucestershire and made a brilliant outside break which outwitted three Cornish defenders in a run of 25 yards, before passing inside to Weeks who crossed for a try. Rutherford converted, and was involved again half an hour into the match when Ford, Rollitt and Collins led a footrush upfield, which forced a scrum close to the Cornwall line. Thorne heeled to Morris, who passed out to Wallace, who slipped the ball to Rutherford, who dropped a goal from 15 yards. 8-0 at half-time.

After the interval Plummer scored an unconverted try for Cornwall. Then Peter Ford scored a try from a footrush led by Morris, who was later instrumental in setting up another try. He executed a reverse pass to send Bayliss away on a fine run, and he passed on to Hampton who scored under the posts. Rutherford converted both. Tries by Jose for Cornwall and Hampton with his second for Gloucestershire completed the scoring.

With this victory, Gloucestershire were straight into the quarter-final as group winners, without any need for the usual replays, and it was staged at Kingsholm.

Gloucestershire 3 Oxfordshire 6
9th January 1965

GLOUCESTERSHIRE STARTED THE game as overwhelming favourites, but put in an utterly lack-lustre performance. Oxfordshire won on merit, and thus became the first South group side to win through to the semi-final of the County Championship.

Defences dominated in the first half, but Oxfordshire had the better of the exchanges, and they deservedly registered the only points when Hurst charged down a kick and scored a try by the corner flag. Gloucestershire were reduced to long range efforts, but penalty and drop goal attempts by Rutherford just fell short. A try by Hampton after the interval, when he side-stepped along the wing beating several defenders

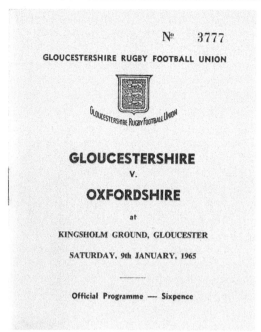

[Gloucestershire Archives]

Nº 3777

GLOUCESTERSHIRE RUGBY FOOTBALL UNION

GLOUCESTERSHIRE

v.

OXFORDSHIRE

at

KINGSHOLM GROUND, GLOUCESTER

SATURDAY, 9th JANUARY, 1965

Official Programme — Sixpence

GLOUCESTERSHIRE			OXFORDSHIRE	
(Red Jerseys)			(White Jerseys)	
(1) *D. RUTHERFORD (Gloucester)		Full Backs	I. B. MOFFATT (St. Lukes Coll., Exeter)	15
(2) J. HAMPTON (Lydney & Rosslyn Park)		Right - Wings - Left	D. S. KILGOUR (Oxford)	11
(3) R. WALLACE (Bristol)		Right - Centres - Left	R. J. HAZELDINE (Moseley)	12
(4) D. J. WEEKS (Bristol)		Left - Centres - Right	*G. WINDSOR-LEWIS (Capt., Oxford)	13
(5) M. R. COLLINS (Bristol)		Left - Wings - Right	*A. C. B. HURST (Wasps)	14
(6) T. HOPSON (Gloucester)		Stand-Off Halfs	L. EVANS (Oxford)	10
(7) M. H. BOOTH (Gloucester)		Scrum Halfs	M. S. PALMER (Lichfield)	9
(8) B. A. HUDSON (Gloucester)		Forwards	R. J. HANCE (Oxford)	1
(9) *J. D. THORNE (Bristol)			G. WEBB (Oxford)	2
(10) *B. A. DOVEY (Lydney & Rosslyn Park)			C. FAIRBROTHER (Banbury)	3
(11) D. E. J. WATT (Bristol)			M. J. PARSONS (Oxford)	4
(12) D. W. NEATE (Bristol)			P. T. ROBERTS (Northampton)	5
(13) *P. FORD (Capt., Gloucester)			D. W. G. BARRETT (Oxford)	6
(14) D. M. ROLLITT			S. K. MULLIGAN	8
(Loughborough College & Bristol)			(London Irish & R.A.F.)	
(15) R. SMITH (Gloucester)			P. W. SUTCLIFFE (Oxford)	7

*Internationals

Touch Judge:	Referee:	Touch Judge:
B. EDWARDS	D. J. F. FORD (Middlesex)	A. TUCKER
(G.R.U. Gloucester Referees' Society)		(Oxford Society of Referees)

Kick-of 2.30 p.m.

Mickey Booth waiting for his forwards to cough up the ball [Journal]

and taking the last two over with him, levelled the scores, but a drop goal by Moffatt five minutes from the end won the match.

Gloucestershire 3 Monmouthshire 16
30th September 1965

DON RUTHERFORD WAS given the captaincy of Gloucestershire for the first time in this friendly fixture, following the retirement of Peter Ford.

Gloucestershire: D Rutherford (captain, Gloucester); J Hampton (Rosslyn Park), P R Hillard (Bristol), J Bayliss (Gloucester), M R Collins; R Wallace (Bristol), J Morris (Lydney); B A Dovey (Bristol), M J Nicholls, J Mace (Gloucester), D E J Watt (Bristol), R G Long, R Smith (Gloucester), D M Rollitt, T E Base (Bristol)

Monmouthshire: Barry Edwards (Ebbw Vale); J Worwood (Newbridge), G H Britton (Newport), A Lewis (Ebbw Vale), L J Hewer (Newbridge); G Musto (Cross Keys), J Palmer (Newbridge); D Williams (Ebbw Vale), A G Talbot (Cross Keys), W R Shipp (Newbridge), W J Morris (Newport), J S Jarrett (Pontypool), D Morgan (Newbridge), J Evans (Newport), K Poole (Newport)

Referee: M H Titcomb (Bristol)

The Citizen's correspondent was deeply unimpressed:

Inept Gloucestershire suffer thrashing – Gloucestershire's was the worst performance by a County team I have ever seen. Almost without exception the home players handled like nervous electricians and there was an all-round lack of cohesion from front to back. Monmouth, by no means a spectacularly good side, were made to look very fine indeed by comparison with the All White, all fumbling home team at Kingsholm last night.

Gloucestershire took an early lead when Hampton made a splendid tackle, recovered the ball, and Terry Base went in for a try. Thereafter it was nearly all Monmouthshire. By half-time they were in the lead with a try and a drop goal by Musto and a conversion and penalty kicked by Edwards. In the second half, Poole nipped in to steal the ball for a try, and towards the end the only threatening attack by the home side ended when Monmouthshire ran the ball from their own line back into the home 25.

Gloucestershire 0 Devon 0
27th November 1965

DEVON CAME INTO this match in some disarray, having lost to Cornwall and Somerset, and put out a team showing 12 changes. Gloucestershire having won against both those counties needed only a draw to be sure of winning the group for the fourth season in succession.

Gloucestershire: D Rutherford (captain, Gloucester); J Hampton (Rosslyn Park), J Bayliss (Gloucester), P R Hillard, M Collins (Bristol); T Hopson, M Booth; J Fowke (Gloucester), J Pullin, B Dovey, D Watt (Bristol), A Brinn (Gloucester), B Capaldi (Cheltenham), D Rollitt (Bristol), R Smith (Gloucester)

Devon: S Morris (Newton Abbot); D Ottley (St Lukes), K Appleyard (Newton Abbot), M Bamsey (Exmouth), B Brown (Devonport Services); A Crighton (Barnstaple), C McCue (Newton Abbot); J Highton (Devonport Services), T Scott (Rosslyn Park), N Southern (Plymouth Albion), A Davis (Devonport Services), P Larter (Northampton), B Lee (Harlequins), J Perryman (Newton Abbot), C Cross (captain, Plymouth Albion)

Referee: Mr A E R Cotterill (Staffs)

An enthusiastic if unfancied Devon side harried the home side early, missed an opportunity to go ahead with a penalty, and seemed sure to score a pushover try just before the interval, only to infringe and allow Rutherford to kick clear. However, Gloucestershire had been playing into

a low sun and a strong wind in the first half, so were fancied to dominate after the break, but most of the pressure continued to come from Devon with 'lusty and even lustier play in the loose'. When play did move into the Devon half, they were penalised, but Rutherford's kick came back off the post. Then 'from a set scrum in front of the Devon posts, Booth did his dummy run from the back of the scrum, leaving the ball in the back row, and, of course, Devon fell for it, giving Rutherford a golden opportunity to score 3 points. He missed by a coat of paint.' The game descended into a 'period of incredible tedium' and a disgusted Citizen reporter summarised the game as one at which 'there were at least 7,000 dissatisfied customers at Kingsholm who watched this pointless draw. Neither side looked like scoring and Gloucestershire, with a great deal more talent at their disposal, seemed content to play a defensive game even when they were in the Devon half.'

Gloucester 24 Gloucestershire B 12
15th September 1966

GLOUCESTER: D B W Ainge; N J Foice, R G Pitt, K R Morris, J Groves; G Mace, J Spalding; C N Teague, M J Nicholls, J L Fowke, R G Long, A Brinn, G G White (captain), S W Owen, R Smith

Gloucestershire 'B': R J Hillier (Stroud); J Morse (Cinderford), W Morris (Lydney), D Brook (Cheltenham), B Pollard; T Byrne (Stroud), J F Morris (captain, Lydney); P Tapsell, D A Protherough (Cheltenham), B Parker (Lydney), A Colwyn (Cheltenham), M Wallington (Clifton), P McCarthy (Stroud), B Capaldi (Cheltenham), K Starr (Rosslyn Park)

Referee: Mr C T W Allen (Bristol).

Gloucestershire 'B' proved to be a real handful in the first half and, although Gloucester scored first with a try by Roy Long, converted by David Ainge, it was no more than their just dues that they held a narrow interval lead thanks to a try from Morse sandwiched between two penalties by Hillier. He kicked a third to stretch the lead early in the second half.

'It was at that point that Gloucester, like a tensed spring, suddenly uncoiled,' as their greater fitness started to tell. Ainge kicked three penalties and Hillier one. Gary White had gone off to hospital with a suspected broken wrist and it surprised everyone when:

Almost unobtrusively White – he had dislocated a finger – returned to the game and astonished everyone by taking a pass from Pitt and scoring a try in the corner, Ainge converting with a superb kick. There was no hint of fatuous complacency about Gloucester now as Morris and Dick Smith combined to send over Foice – and again Ainge added the extra points. That intensive training again paid dividends as Gloucester eventually asserted their authority over a County 'B' team that proved exceptionally lively and full of ideas.

Gloucestershire 3 Somerset 6
26th November 1966

DAVID TYLER WAS originally named as a reserve for Gloucestershire in this match, but received a better offer from Somerset when invited to start for them as a replacement for the winger they had originally selected, John Beer, who dropped out through injury.

Gloucestershire: R Wallace (Bristol); J Groves, R G Pitt (Gloucester), P R Hilliard (Bristol), N J Foice; D B W Ainge (Gloucester), J F Morris (Lydney); B Nelmes, J Pullin (Bristol), J L Fowke, A Brinn, R G Long (Gloucester), B Capaldi (Cheltenham), J Jarrett (Pontypool), R Smith (Gloucester)

Somerset: T Dolman (Bath); D Hazzard (Weston-super-Mare),

C F McFadyean (Moseley), C E Frankcom (Bedford), D Tyler (Bristol); B Perry (Bristol), J M Galley (Bath); R M Grove (Leicester), B Collins (Bath), A J Rogers (Bristol), A Watson (St Marys Hospital), R J Orledge (Bath), B Vickery (Somerset Police), P Hawkins (Bridgwater), D A Phillips (St Lukes)

Referee: Mr TB Kearns (Ireland)

David Ainge missed with an early penalty attempt for Gloucestershire, and then sliced a kick, which turned out well when Nick Foice grabbed it and burst down the right hand touchline; he bundled over the Somerset fullback, but this delayed him sufficiently to be caught short of the line. Hawkins missed a simple penalty for Somerset, before Ainge successfully kicked one from 40 yards, but then missed another. Just before half-time, Dick Smith made a scintillating run, beating several defenders and racing deep into the Somerset 25, but his pass was dropped, so it remained 3-0 at the interval.

Gloucestershire pressure early in the second half forced Somerset to concede a penalty, but Ainge missed. Nelmes then made a barging run looking 'like a miniature tank', but it was Somerset who had the next chance to score, only for Hawkins to miss with another penalty kick. Somerset then brought the crowd to its feet with the most sparkling handling move of the match, and McFadyean raced through to dive over for a try midway out. The conversion was missed, so the scores remained level, but Somerset were now on top. Dick Smith sold two dummies to outstrip the defence and run the ball clear, but no score resulted and Ainge had to leave the field with an injured hand. Wallace moved to outside-half and was soon caught off-side in front of his own posts. McFadyean duly kicked the penalty to win the game.

Gloucestershire 16 Somerset 3
17th February 1968

IN 1967-68 THE South West group was yet again tied, and 7,500 turned up at Kingsholm to watch the replay. Both captains were Gloucester players – Don Rutherford, the current Club captain, for Gloucestershire, and Gary White, his immediate predecessor, for Somerset. The pitch at Kingsholm was in reasonable shape despite hosting two games in the previous three days.

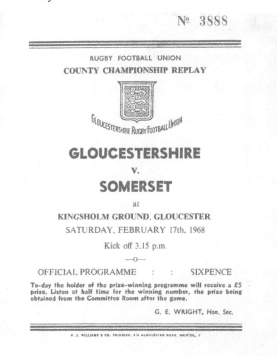

TEAMS

GLOUCESTERSHIRE Colours: White		SOMERSET Colours: Red, Black and White
15. †D. RUTHERFORD Gloucester	Full Backs	15. R. JONES Somerset and Bath Police
14. P. R. HILLARD Bristol	Three-Qtrs. Right Wing	14. J. V. COLES Bristol
13. P. M. KNIGHT Bristol	Right Centre	13. G. HAND Loughborough Colleges
12. R. G. PITT Gloucester	Left Centre	12. †C. W. McFADYEAN Moseley
11. M. R. COLLINS Bristol	Left Wing	11. *I. DUCKWORTH Bath
10. R. L. REDWOOD Cheltenham	Half Backs Stand-off	10. V. WILLIAMS Bath
9. *M. H. BOOTH Gloucester	Scrum-Half	9. R. T. ROBINSON Somerset and Bath Police
3. †B. A. DOVEY (Capt.) Bristol	Forwards	1. *R. V. GROVE, Leicester
2. †J. V. PULLIN Bristol		2. A. RAINES Weston-super-Mare
1. A. J. ROGERS Bristol		3. P. PARFITT Bath
4. B. G. NELMES Bristol		4. R. ORLEDGE Bath
5. †D. E. J. WATT Bristol		5. J. MATTHEWS Taunton
6. †D. M. ROLLITT Bristol		6. R. JENKINS Bristol
8. R. C. HANNAFORD Gloucester		8. †D. GAY Bath
7. *B. CAPALDI Cheltenham		7. G. C. WHITE Gloucester

† International   * Trialist

Referee:
A. E. R. COTTERILL
(Staffordshire Society)

Touch Judge:
N. JONES
(Gloucester Society)

Touch Judge:
R. A. M. WHITE

[Gloucester Rugby Heritage]

The Gloucestershire team: back row: D E J Watt, R C Hannaford, D M Rollitt, B Capaldi, B J Nelmes, R G Pitt; seated: D Rutherford, M R Collins, A J Rogers, B A Dovey (captain), H G Smith (president), J V Pullin, P R Hillard, P M Knight; in front: M H Booth, R L Redwood. The Gloucestershire officials: D Ritchie-Williams, K J Cottle (treasurer), G E Wright (secretary), N A Jackson (reserve), E Roberts, S T Day, E J Cumming, W R Ryland, G Cullimore, J V Smith, E R Dash, C J Humby, C H Sibery, D J Walter (match secretary), J E Taylor, S G Grant (vice-president) {Journal]

Gloucestershire spurned several chances in the first half, and Somerset opened the scoring with a try in the corner by Ian Duckworth. The home supporters began to worry when Don Rutherford missed with a penalty and a drop goal, and Mickey Booth with two drop goal attempts. However, they were amused when Booth gave a fine pass to the

Somerset touch judge, Mr R A White, running the line in the disguise of a Gloucestershire player. He may have only been living up to his name by wearing a white sweater, but it matched the colour of the Gloucestershire team jerseys. He was persuaded to change into a maroon jersey after this incident, and Gloucestershire fortunes then changed as well. Mike Collins scored an equalising try on the stroke of half-time, Rutherford converted, and the course of the game was altered.

Don Rutherford kicks for touch [Citizen]

Mickey Booth about to be tackled by Gary White [Citizen]

Gloucestershire stormed into the attack after the break. When Booth kicked a high up-and-under, it was fumbled, and, as Peter Knight attempted to pounce on the ball over the line, he was held back. The referee awarded a penalty try, which Rutherford converted. The home side then played some magnificent rugby, which was rounded off by tries in the corner for Bob Redwood and Knight, both set up by Booth.

The outstanding players on the day were Booth and Hannaford. The Citizen summarised the match by declaring that:

> The brilliant Booth and powerful pack subdued Somerset – it has been said in authoritative circles that the Gloucestershire pack is never better nor happier than when Mickey Booth is behind them – he gave an impeccable service to his new partner, Bob Redwood; making clever solo bursts, one of 40 yards; and testing the opposition with the astute up-and-under, perfectly executed. Gloucestershire had a crushing ascendancy in the back row, where Charlie Hannaford, restored to his normal position as the centre-piece, portrayed the violent reserves of his artistry with a compelling performance that made his Somerset counterpart, David Gay, England's current No 8, appear as a poor performer indeed.

This win put Gloucestershire into a quarter-final against Oxfordshire, which was won 18-3 at Oxford, but the semi-final was lost 6-11 to Warwickshire at Coventry.

Gloucestershire 9 Cornwall 15
9th November 1968

THE ATTENDANCE WAS estimated as 8,500.

Gloucestershire: D B W Ainge (Bristol); P Lavery (London Irish), P Tate (Cheltenham), J A Bayliss (Gloucester), M R Collins; J R Gabitass (Bristol), M H Booth (Gloucester); B G Nelmes (Bristol), D East (Gloucester), B A Dovey (captain, Bristol), J S Jarrett (Gloucester), D E J Watt (Bristol), B Capaldi (Cheltenham), D M Rollitt (Bristol), R Smith (Gloucester)

Cornwall: C Bate (captain, Penryn); K Plummer (Bristol), G Jones (HMS Collingwood), V Parkin (Bristol), D H Prout (Northampton); T Palmer (Gloucester), D Chapman (Hayle); C B Stevens (Penzance-Newlyn), R F S Harris (Penryn), C R Johns (Redruth), B Ninnis (St Ives), C Kneebone (Penryn), R George (Redruth), R Hosken (Harlequins), C R McKeown (Penryn)

Referee : Mr F D Parker (Manchester)

This proved to be the expected stern duel and scoring in the first half was limited to penalty goals, Cornwall taking an interval lead with three successful kicks by Bate against Gloucestershire's two from Ainge. Gloucestershire went straight to the attack on the resumption, but their efforts broke down and the game was into the last quarter before Ainge equalised with a third penalty. And so it remained until a tremendous finish saw Bate kick two more penalties to secure victory.

International Invitation Teams

Gloucester 6 International XV 12
18th April 1961

THE PROCEEDS OF this match went towards the construction of changing rooms at the Memorial Ground off Tuffley Avenue, Gloucester. Mickie Steele-Bodger and Tom Voyce organised what was described as 'a star-spangled team – the might of England and Wales past, present and future – captained by the Player of the Year, Phil Horrocks-Taylor'. The attendance was 4,000, and there was a warm welcome back to Kingsholm for George Hastings.

Gloucester: R Hillier; J King, J Taylor, P Hole, R Timms; A Holder, G Mace; A Townsend, K Taylor, J Fowke, A Brinn, B Hudson, P Ford (captain), H Symonds, T Davies

International XV: A Priday (Cardiff & Wales); P L Rees (Newport & Wales), R Leslie (Scotland), W Patterson (Sale & England), J Hyde (Northampton & England); J P Horrocks-Taylor (Leicester & England), B Templeman (Penarth); P T Wright (Blackheath & England), M T Wetson (Wasps), G Hastings (Gloucester & England), C R Jacobs (Northampton), J D Currie (Harlequins, Northern & England), H J Morgan (Abertillery & Wales), G Davidge (Newport & Wales), B Price (Newport & Wales)

Referee: Mr A Thomas (Gloucestershire)

All the scoring in the first half was by the International XV. Mike Dineen of the Citizen described the only try as: 'a forward handling movement which made the International pack appear as threes, resulted in Newport's P L Rees crossing for a try in the first five minutes'. Subsequently 'a fine kick by that classical full-back, Priday, gave the distinguished visitors their six-point half-time lead'.

There was a wonderful revival by Gloucester in the second half. Garry Mace, who played a blinder for the home team, was tackled but managed to slip a pass to Jeremy Taylor, who passed on to Jim King on the right wing; Jim found a gap and went over for a try. Alan Holder and Mace both missed with drop goal attempts before Brian Hudson just failed to get over for a try. But the pressure told and King squeezed over for his second try to level the scores.

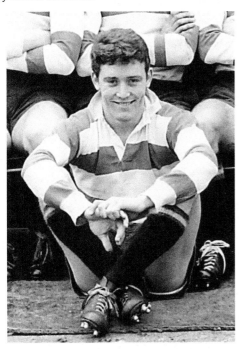

Garry Mace [Gloucester Rugby]

Then came the winning score. Phil Horrocks-Taylor secured possession in the middle of the field and strode diagonally towards the left wing, drawing the Gloucester defence and attracting them away from Patterson, who took advantage to score. Mike Dineen was much impressed: 'it was as surely Horrocks-Taylor's try as Major Gargarin is the first cosmonaut. And his drop goal in the 35th minute had the same inevitability. Richard Sharp? – he's got nothing on this boy. And never will have.' Provocative stuff, which still elicits differing views more than fifty years on, but all credit to Horrocks-Taylor on this particular day.

Club Centenary Match
Gloucester 24 International XV 14
3rd October 1973

GLOUCESTER RUGBY FOOTBALL CLUB

GLOUCESTER

v

INTERNATIONAL XV

on WEDNESDAY 3rd OCTOBER, 1973

KICK-OFF 7 p.m.   Ground 40p

[Gloucestershire Archives]

RUGBY at Kingsholm

SPECIAL CENTENARY ATTRACTION

GLOUCESTER v.

INTERNATIONAL XV

(Raised by D. W. Rutherford)
(ALL PAY)

WEDNESDAY, OCTOBER 3rd :: K.O. 7 p.m.

Tickets now available at Hudson & Co., Sports Outfitters, Northgate Street, and at Kingsholm.

Wing Stand 75p, Ground 40p, OAP & Scholars 20p

Any unsold tickets will be available on the night of the match at Kingsholm.

[Citizen]

THIS MATCH WAS organised to celebrate the centenary of the Gloucester Club, which played its first match on 10th October 1873. Originally it had been hoped that the Barbarians would provide the opposition, but when this fell through, Don Rutherford, former captain of Gloucester and by this time Technical Director of the Rugby Union, stepped in and organised an International XV. His side was bristling with star players and is arguably the strongest ever to play at Kingsholm. Some 9,000 spectators were there to see them perform, and preferably be humbled.

Gloucester: P E Butler; R J Clewes, T Palmer, R Jardine, R Etheridge; R L Redwood, J H Spalding; M A Burton, M J Nicholls (captain), K Richardson, P J Winnell, J H Fidler, J A Watkins, D B W Owen, J H Haines

INTERNATIONAL XV

Players originally selected for this evening's match

(Pen Pictures by John Reason, *Sunday Telegraph* Rugby Correspondent)

P. VILLEPREUX

PIERRE VILLEPREUX (Toulouse and France)
Full-back. Aged 30. 5 ft. 11 in., 12 st. 7 lb. The French have produced a succession of great full-backs for their international team and Pierre Villepreux has been one of their very best. A gifted counter-attacker, he loves to play the running game and sets up his wingers possibly better than any other full-back of recent years. He can also kick goals from vast distances with his instep, a method which he modestly describes as "illegitimate". Twenty-eight caps.

J. P. A. G. JANION (Richmond and England)
Wing or centre. Aged 27. 6 ft. 1 in., 15 st. Jeremy Janion has had a busy year. He toured South Africa with London Counties in May and then took the place of the injured David Cooke on England's tour of Fiji and New Zealand. He did not play in the international but had a fine game for England the year before when they toured South Africa and beat the Springboks at Ellis Park. His success against "Joggie" Jansen that day had an important bearing on the result. Nine caps.

JOHN DAWES (London Welsh and Wales)
Centre. Aged 33. 5 ft. 10 in., 12 st. 12 lb. If the British Lions ever have a better captain than "Syd" Dawes, they will be lucky, and if wing-threequarters ever have a more selfless centre to set them up and send them on their way they will be even luckier. The loud "Hear, hears" which have just echoed round Kingsholm were uttered by Gerald Davies and David Duckham. Twenty-five caps.

JO MASO (Narbonne and France)
Fly-half. Aged 28. 5 ft. 11 in., 12 st. 7 lb. Jo Maso played so brilliantly in Sir William Ramsay's Rest of the World team two years ago that hard-bitten characters like Colin Meads and Frik du Preez could not understand why he was not a permanent fixture in the French team. Judging by the noise they make when he runs on the field, the French public has always thought the same. A brilliantly gifted attacking player, and the man who made the one-handed reverse pass behind the back fashion it is in France today. It switches direction well, too. Eighteen caps.

DAVID DUCKHAM (Coventry and England)
Wing. Aged 27. 6 ft. 1 in., 14 st. 7 lb. David Duckham is another world class player like Gerald Davies, who moved from the centre to the wing and who is so talented that it is hard to be sure which is his best position. He combines power and elusiveness in a way which is rare in such a big man and as he showed when playing for the Barbarians against the All Blacks, is a master of broken field running in counter-attack. Twenty-five caps.

J. S. DAWES

J. MASO

D. J. DUCKHAM

J.-L. BEROT (Toulouse and France)
Fly-half. Aged 26. 5 ft. 9 in., 12 st. 5 lb. Jean-Louis Berot began his international career as a scrum-half and had won at least three caps before a referee thought he ought to show him how to put the ball into the scrum. Berot promptly retired to fly-half where he has played ever since. As lively off the field as he is on it, he rivals Mike Davis as a pop singer (which is saying something) and he is an even better mimic of Louis Armstrong! Plays a spectacular set of drums, too. Seventeen caps.

J.-L. BEROT

STEVE SMITH (Sale and England)
Scrum-half. Aged 22. 5 ft. 10 in., 13 st. 4 lb. Steve Smith was flown out to South Africa as a replacement when Lionel Weston was injured in England's overwhelming win against Griqualand West. He did as much as anyone to help N.W. Counties beat the All Blacks last season and finished the season strongly in the England team. Curiously, he lost his place to Jan Webster on England's short tour of New Zealand last month, but that was probably due as much to England's choice of spoiling tactics as anything. Three caps.

SANDY CARMICHAEL (West of Scotland and Scotland)
Tight head prop. Aged 29. 6 ft. 2 in., 15 st. 7 lb. Sandy Carmichael has played for Scotland in every match since 1967 and as he showed when playing for the Barbarians against the All Blacks earlier this year, he did not lose his place. A knowledgeable scrummager and an excellent forward in a lineout peel, he is one of the two best tight-heads in the game. Thirty caps.

JEFF YOUNG (London Welsh and Wales)
Hooker. Aged 30. 5 ft. 10 in., 15 st. 6 lb. Jeff Young has played for Wales regularly since 1968 and is the strongest and probably the best scrummaging hooker in the game. His powerful frame has cemented together some Welsh tight forward units which, to say the least, have had some elements of doubt about them in recent years. He toured South Africa with the British Lions in 1968 and was preferred to John Pullin the the first test. Twenty-three caps.

S. J. SMITH

IAN McLAUCHLAN (Jordanhill and Scotland)
Loose head prop. Aged 31. 5 ft. 9 in., 14 st. 6 lb. Ian McLauchlan made his name overnight when he took over from the injured Ray McLoughlin in the 1971 British Lions team and scored the only try of the test against the All Blacks. He combines technical skill with a persistence in the loose which makes it hard to understand why he had to wait so long to establish himself in the top rank of the world's props. Now captain of Scotland, and not short of a word or two, he played for his country against England this year when he had a broken leg. Eighteen caps.

I. McLAUCHLAN

J. YOUNG

A. B. CARMICHAEL

C. SPANGHERO (Narbonne and France)
Lock. Aged 25. 6 ft. 5 in., 15 st. 7 lb. Claude Spanghero comes from a famous French Rugby family and many people think he is the most talented of all the brothers. He is a wonderful natural athlete and runner, and if you ever have the good fortune to shake him by the hand, do not worry. Your hand will eventually re-emerge from his huge grasp, though your fingers may be a bit numb! Twelve caps.

C. SPANGHERO

C. W. RALSTON (Richmond and England)
Lock. Aged 29. 6 ft. 6 in., 16 st. 7 lb. Chris Ralston emerged successfully from being the underdog on two England tours, to Japan and to South Africa, and has now established himself as one of the best locks in the game. He has just returned from England's tour to New Zealand, where the drubbing he gave Sam Strahan had much to do with England's victory in the international. Thirteen caps.

N. A. MacEWAN (Gala and Scotland)
Flanker. Aged 31. 5 ft. 9 in., 13 st. 4 lb. Nairn MacEwan did not start his international career until he was 29 but since then has won 14 caps in succession. He has taken part in several notable Scottish victories and is one of those Scotsmen who achieved the unique distinction of appearing in Scotland teams which beat England twice in eight days. Scotsmen regard this as some small recompense for Culloden. Nairn MacEwan is no Goliath, but he is a terrier on the loose ball.

C. W. RALSTON

A. NEARY (Broughton Park and Lancashire)
Flanker. Born 25.11.48 in Manchester. 6 ft. 1 in., 14 st. 6 lb. Anthony Neary was educated at De La Salle College, Salford, and at Liverpool University, where he took a degree in law. He played for England Schools at both Rugby and basketball and represented both the U.A.U. and British Universities. He is another of the forwards who has had a lot of experience with Lancashire and he played for North-West Counties against the 1969-70 Springboks, against the Fijians and against the All Blacks. He toured Japan and the Far East with England and he was also on England's successful tour of South Africa.

BENOIT DAUGA (Mont de Marsan and France)
No. 8. Aged 31. 6 ft. 5 in., 16 st. 5 lb. Benoit Dauga is the greatest forward France has produced and with 50 caps, has won more than any of his countrymen. His ball skill has always been remarkable and the sense of adventure with which he has played the game has made him respected and admired among Rugby players as one of the world's elite.

N. A. MacEWAN

A. NEARY

B. DAUGA

1873   1973

CENTENARY MATCH

GLOUCESTER R.F.C.

VERSUS

AN
INTERNATIONAL XV

WEDNESDAY, 3rd OCTOBER
1973 - Kick-off 7.0 p.m.

KINGSHOLM - GLOUCESTER

671

Official Programme 10p   Lucky Number

Profiles of the International XV players in the match programme, and programme cover [Gloucestershire Archives]

International XV: P Villepreux (Toulouse & France); J P A G Janion (Richmond & Eastern Counties), J S Dawes (captain, London Welsh & Wales), J Maso (Narbonne & France), D J Duckham (Coventry & England); J-L Berot (Toulouse & France), S J Smith (Sale & England); I McLauchlan (Jordan Hill & Scotland), J Young (London Welsh & Wales), A B Carmichael (West of Scotland & Scotland), B Dauga (Mont de Marsan & France), C W Ralston (Richmond & England), N A MacEwan (Gala & Scotland), M Billiere (France), A Neary (Broughton Park & England)

Referee: Mr R F Johnson (England)

Gloucester made their intentions clear from the start when an up and under from Bob Redwood led to Mike Burton crashing over, only to be pulled back for a minor infringement, and then Bob Clewes suffered a similar fate when he crossed the line. So it was the International XV who registered the first points on the scoreboard when Jeremy Janion was put clear, side-stepped around Butler, and scorched 75 yards to score a try which Pierre Villepreux converted. Gloucester struck back when the ball came to Bob Redwood on the blind side of a ruck. Ron Etheridge, Richard Jardine and Burton carried it on and John Haines picked it up when it came loose and dashed through a gap to score from ten yards out. Gloucester now had the bit between their teeth and forced their opponents into errors. The pack drove through with the ball at their feet, Keith Richardson fielded his own hack ahead and, as Villepreux came in to tackle, shouldered him out of the way and went over for a try, which Butler converted.

Sandy Carmichael gets hands on the ball in a lineout with John Fidler behind [Citizen]

line, but the referee took no heed of their advice (or their various other suggestions) and awarded the try.

The second half featured David Duckham, his sweeping runs and flowing blond locks captivating the crowd. It seemed certain that he would score on more than one occasion, but stupendous tackles by Haines, Palmer and Dave Owen denied him. Gloucester extended the margin when numerous players including Bob Clewes, Butler and John Fidler, who each handled twice, took part in a movement before Etheridge put Redwood over in the corner. But the International XV started to get the upper hand in the scrums and pushed Gloucester off the ball and three of their players combined to put Steve Smith in at the corner. They continued to press near the home line, but heroic defence in which Mike Nicholls and John Spalding were prominent, kept them at bay.

With three minutes to go and still only four points between the teams, Watkins charged down a kick to launch a final Gloucester attack. Burton and Owen both went for the line but were repelled, so Spalding spun the ball wide, where Etheridge was brought down agonisingly close by Janion, but Richard Jardine was on hand to pick up the ball and score.

Sandy Carmichael and John Watkins compete for possession [Citizen]

When Villepreux put in a mighty kick but failed to find touch in the Gloucester 25, Butler fielded and started an attack which Etheridge and Tom Palmer kept moving. When the winger beat his man with a dummy, Butler was clear along the touchline to score in the corner. The International XV responded with a try following a dazzling display of passing; the crowd were vociferously adamant that there had been a forward pass and that Janion had put a foot in touch on his way to the

Commemorative plate signed by the Gloucester players [Fred Reed]

Butler converted and Gloucester had a famous win.

Whilst allowance had to be made for the fact that the International XV was a scratch side, enormous credit was due to Gloucester for rising so magnificently to the occasion, and at the time many judged this to be the team's finest ever performance. Mike Nicholls, a man of action rather than words, was moved to comment 'I'm really chuffed. All the players played wonderful rugby.' Gordon Hudson, Club Chairman, said 'Ten man rugby? They played like 30 men tonight'. At the centenary dinner three days later, Don Rutherford was presented with a silver tray in recognition of his efforts in raising the team.

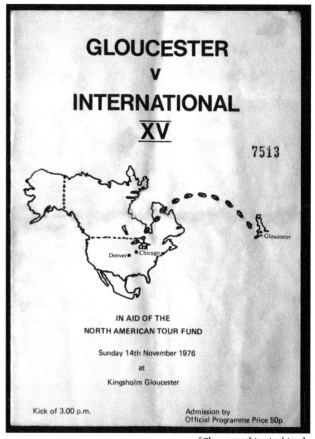

[Gloucestershire Archives]

Gloucester 38 International XV 38
14th November 1976

THIS MATCH WAS organised to raise funds for the Club's first overseas tour to the USA in May/June 1977. Despite the foggy conditions, some 8-10,000 spectators turned out to see their local heroes take on an International XV which had been organised by the Gloucester players themselves. The thickening fog in the second half reduced the players to shadowy shapes, but failed to dampen the spirits of players and spectators alike. The players and spectators were exchanging greetings and wise-cracks throughout, and 'the crowd regularly roared its admiration of the speed and sidestep of Gerald Davies, the tremendous pass and explosive thrust of Gareth Edwards, and the power running of Roy Bergiers'.

The changes from the teams listed in the programme were so numerous as to defy the record keeping of the scribes at the game, but Gerald Davies and Roy Bergiers were both late replacements, Tony Neary

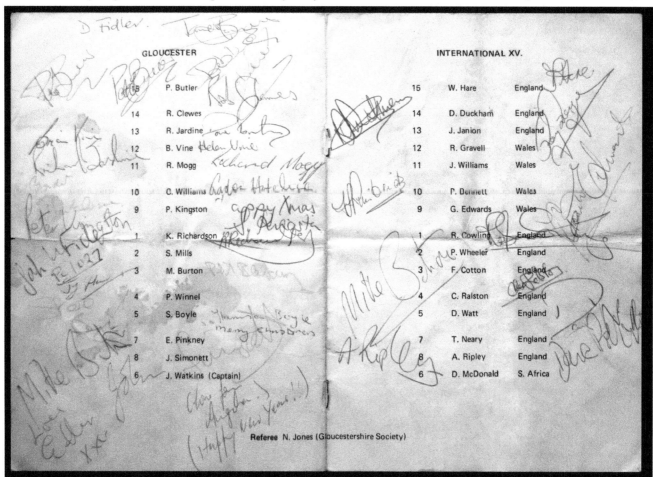

[Gloucestershire Archives]

- 156 -

Player profiles of the International XV in the match programme [Gloucestershire Archives]

was fog bound but replaced by Dave Rollitt. Jeremy Janion was injured and replaced by John Bayliss, and in the front row, John Pullin replaced Peter Wheeler, and Mike Burton replaced Fran Cotton. During the game, Andy Ripley was injured and replaced by Dick Smith, and David Duckham gave way for Tom Palmer on the left wing.

However, a good time was had by all, and Gloucester put up a stirring performance, matching their illustrious opponents throughout. Most notable were the fine tussle between Richard Mogg and Gerald Davies, Peter Kingston doing well against Gareth Edwards, and outstanding performances by Eddie Pinkney, Ron Etheridge, Fred Reed, Steve Boyle and skipper John Watkins.

The score was 24-20 to Gloucester at half-time, but they were 14 points adrift mid-way through the second half, before a flurry of tries levelled the scores, which the referee thought an appropriate point at which to blow the final whistle.

Try scorers for the International XV were Gerald Davies (3), Dick Smith, Dugald McDonald, Gareth Edwards, John Bayliss and Dave Sorrell, with Dusty Hare, McDonald and Davies each landing a conversion. The Gloucester tries were scored by Bob Clewes (3), Eddie Pinkney (2), Steve Boyle, Fred Reed and Richard Mogg, with conversions by Gordon Hutchison, Dave Pointon and Boyle.

County Centenary Match
Gloucestershire 33 President's XV 24
27th September 1978

A CROWD OF 10,000 turned out to see this match to celebrate the centenary of the Gloucestershire RFU, English Rugby's most successful county with 13 Championships to their credit. They might have

expected to see an exhibition game, but it proved to be a keenly contested affair with high class defence as well as skilful running. Gloucestershire outscored their illustrious opponents by six tries to five, and Peter Butler's kicking added to the points difference. A star-studded President's XV was pulled together by Mike Burton, captained by Willie John McBride, and wore green jerseys with the Gloucestershire emblem. This was Dave Rollitt's last game for the County – he had already moved to London, changed clubs from Bristol to Richmond, and the following week made his first appearance for Middlesex.

Gloucestershire players arriving for the centenary game – from left: John Simonett, Steve Boyle Mike Curran, Steve Mills – and on the right, Eric Stephens, a member of the County executive [Citizen]

Gloucestershire: P E Butler (Gloucester and England); R J Clewes (Gloucester), P Johnson (Clifton), R Jardine (Gloucester and England B), R R Mogg (Gloucester, England U-23 and England B); C G Williams

(Gloucester and England), P Kingston (Gloucester and England); M A Curran, S G F Mills (Gloucester), A Sheppard (Bristol), N Pomphrey (Bristol and England B), S B Boyle (Gloucester, England U-23 and England B), M J Rafter (Bristol and England, captain), J H Haines (Gloucester), D M Rollitt (Richmond and England); Replacements: A J Hignell (Bristol and England), J F Simonett (Gloucester)

The Gloucestershire team [Citizen]

Willie John McBride leads out the President's XV [Citizen]

County President's XV: R W Hare (Leicester and England); J J Williams (Llanelli and Wales), L Dick (Gloucester and Scotland), S P Fenwick (Bridgend and Wales), P Williams (Gloucester); A G B Old (Sheffield and England), B Williams (Newport and Wales); C Smart (Newport and England U-23), P J Wheeler (Leicester and England), J Dixon (Abertillery), C W Ralston (Richmond and England), W J McBride (Ballymena and Ireland, captain), G J Adey (Leicester and England), R J Mordell (Rosslyn Park and England), A G Ripley (Rosslyn Park and England); Replacements: R Smith, S J W Baker (Gloucester)

Referee: Mr R F Johnson (London)

After only four minutes, the President's team opened the scoring when Brynmor Williams weaved his way through and sent Peter Wheeler over for a try near the posts. They lost Gary Adey to injury, replaced by Dick Smith, before the County struck back. A deliberate knock-on allowed Peter Butler to slot a penalty, and then Peter Kingston broke on the blind side to put Nigel Pomphrey in for a try, which Butler converted. A minute before the break, Mike Rafter went over for another, Butler converting, but there was still time for Brynmor Williams to score his second to reduce the deficit to 13-8 at half-time.

Gary Adey making a break for the President's XV, with Chris Ralston and Colin Smart in support, and Dave Rollitt of Gloucestershire behind [Citizen]

Early in the second half, Peter Kingston made ground by selling some brilliant dummies, before passing to Chris Williams. Kingston was on hand to take the return pass and show the opposition a clean pair of heels for a splendid try, which the ever dependable Butler converted. Brynmor Williams and Lewis Dick were the principle architects in the next move by the President's XV, which resulted in a try for Alan Old to score and convert. Steve Boyle, who had been doing a splendid job of marking McBride in the line-outs, now charged down an attempted clearance kick by J J Williams and followed up to score, and Richard Mogg picked up a loose pass and scorched in for another, converted by Butler. A try by Richard Jardine rounded off a splendid performance by Gloucestershire, but a late rally by the President's XV was rewarded with tries for Lewis Dick and Steve Fenwick, one of which was converted by Old. They made the final score more respectable but in no way diminished the triumph for Gloucestershire.

Willie John McBride commented after the game: 'all credit to Gloucestershire for a fine display. We were a scratch side and they were well-drilled, so perhaps the result was inevitable. But I enjoyed every minute. I was impressed by the crowd. We never see such large crowds at matches in Ireland.'

The Irish Wolfhounds

THE IRISH WOLFHOUNDS were originally formed in 1955 and played their first match the following year, captained by Jean Prat. They had many similarities to the Barbarians, but were set up to promote rugby in provincial parts of Ireland. One England player who appeared for the Wolfhounds in a vigorous game against Munster suggested that menus rather than programmes should have been printed for the match after he heard one of the Munster locks saying to his partner 'have you tried the scrum half, he's delicious'. The Wolfhounds went on their first tour in 1957, including in their party Tony O'Reilly, Phil Horrocks-Taylor and Phil Davis. Their first foray into England was to play against Harlequins in 1959 and they subsequently visited Kingsholm on four occasions.

Gloucester 14 Irish Wolfhounds 18
22nd September 1965

AROUND 5,000 SPECTATORS were present to see a match which the Citizen headlined as 'Sparkling Rugby in Kingsholm Thriller'. Peter Ford, never one to leave his boots at home, come out of retirement to play and had lost none of his presence with 'tentacles grabbing at all and sundry'.

Gloucester: D Rutherford; N Foice, J Bayliss, R Morris, A Osman; T Hopson, M Booth (captain); J Fowke, M Nicholls, J Mace, A Brinn, R Long, P Ford, D Owen, R Smith

Wolfhounds: T Price; A Duggan, A Boniface, G Boniface, D Senior; R Doran, A Twomey; S McHale, N Gake, R Waldron, B Dauga, D Heywood, M Doyle, R Arneil, N Murphy

Referee: D G Walters (Wales)

Gloucester were deemed unlucky to come out on the wrong side. Mike Dineen reported in the Citizen that 'if Terry Hopson had had a foot to spare when he went for the line in a determined run; if the injured Don Rutherford had got a foot more left on the penalty which hit the crossbar; if, if, if'. Booth and Hopson worked the touch lines very effectively to allow the Gloucester pack to keep their side in the game. Hopson had one of his magical days, captured by Dineen as 'Hopson had got the devil in

Terry Hopson [Gloucester Rugby]

him and whether the Gloucester fly-half was touch-kicking a gigantic length or cutting through the opposition, tackling or making the most of a loose ball, he was out on his own.' He contributed to the scoring with a try and a drop goal; the other Gloucester points came from Don Rutherford with a conversion and two penalties, despite having pulled a muscle early in the game.

For the Wolfhounds, Gale, Doyle and Senior scored tries, with Terry Price converting all three and adding a penalty. Dineen also gave a wonderful description of Mickey Booth's typically influential role in the match:

> The greatest thrill must have been the sight of Booth making a superb break early on in the match, turning on an alarming speed and outwitting the opposition with a dummy. He tried it all; the foxy run from the back of the scrum without the ball, and the imitation long pass out to the centres, but nothing he did measured up to these gimmicks like the pure, almost instinctive run, the side-step and the advance into Wolfhounds territory.

Gloucester 16 Irish Wolfhounds 8
22nd September 1966

DESPITE HAVING TO make ten changes from the side originally selected, the Wolfhounds still put out a strong team, including five internationals.

Gloucester: D B W Ainge; N J Foice, K R Morris, R G Pitt, J Groves; G Mace, J Spalding; J L Fowke, M J Nicholls, C N Teague, R G Long, A Brinn, G G White (captain), D W Owen, R Smith

Wolfhounds: A Hickie (University College, Dublin); E Coleman (Terenure), A Duggan (Lansdowne), C Lawson (Wanderers), R Hall (Paris University Club); T J Brophy (Liverpool), B Sherry (Terenure); T O'Shea (Cardiff), M M Walker (Leicester), S McHale (Lansdowne), M G Culliton, J McGowan (Wanderers), J J Rupert (Tyrosse), S Monigal (Clontarf), G Gill (University College, Dublin)

Referee: Mr D G Walters (Gowerton)

Mike Dineen summarised the match in the Citizen as follows:

> There is nothing second-rate nor superficial about the pack on which Gloucester prides itself – there never has been of course. And the fortitude, skill and lasting qualities of their robust forwards laid the foundations of this magnificent victory. So many of the Wolfhounds hopes rested on the mercurial Tom Brophy, but the former England player for most of the game had no more freedom than a stuffed duck in a drainpipe; Dick Smith, almost with the air of a Victorian schoolmaster, saw to that. And when the remarkable open-side wing forward was not dealing with matters of immediate importance in defence he contrived to spearhead Gloucester's attacks with a controlled smooth violence that radiated from a centre of balance and sense of positioning that made his phenomenal running appear simple to the uninitiated onlooker. Smith is a wiry figure of Mephistophilean power on the field.

The highlight of the match came when 'a superb run by Dick Smith, which began in his own half and left defenders strewn in his meteoric path, ended near the Wolfhound's line as he passed to Ron Pitt, who crossed midway out'. Gloucester scored further tries through Gary White and Smith, with David Ainge contributing two conversions, before

Dick Smith [Gloucester Rugby]

a clever cross-kick by Garry Mace was fielded by John Groves to go over for their final try. Gloucester had the game won by the time the Wolfhounds staged a late revival, scoring tries through Lawson and Duggan, with Hickie converting one of them.

Gloucester 16 Irish Wolfhounds 6
16th September 1969

THE WOLFHOUNDS BOASTED eight internationals in their line-up.

Gloucester: E J F Stephens; R J Clewes, T Palmer, J A Bayliss, J Dix; J T Hopson, J H Spalding; J Fowke, M J Nicholls, R Cowling, A Brinn, J S Jarrett, G G White, P Hayward, R Smith (captain)

Wolfhounds: R Moakes (Nottingham); J Tydings (Young Munster & Ireland), J P Lux (Bayonne & France), K Flynn (Wanderers & Ireland), K J Fielding (Loughborough Colleges & England); R Beese (Cross Keys), J Quirk (Black Rock & Ireland); V Perrins (Newport), J V Pullin (Bristol & England), D Williams (captain, Ebbw Vale & Wales), S Geary (Newport), A Esteze (Beziers), G Prothero (Bridgend), D Heywood (London Irish), T Doyle (Terenure & Ireland)

Referee: Mr K Pattinson (North Midlands)

The game was settled by the forward battle and it was the Gloucester back row which held the key to victory. However, it was the Wolfhounds who took the lead when Moakes kicked a penalty which bounced over via the crossbar; Eric Stephens soon replied for Gloucester and then Moakes kicked a second. Gary White then led a glorious foot rush and found Phil Hayward in support to go over for a try which Stephens converted. This put Gloucester ahead for the first time, but it was only in the last few minutes of the match that they put the result beyond doubt. Stephens kicked another penalty before the match ended with a glorious finale. Hayward broke from a scrum, took a short pass from John Spalding and beat four opponents before passing to Dick Smith, who touched down under the posts. Stephens converted with the last kick of the match.

Gloucester 6 Irish Wolfhounds 3
18th September 1973

THE WEATHER PLAYED a large part in this match, the treacherous conditions at Kingsholm being completely unsuitable for a handling game.

Gloucester: P Butler; R J Clewes, R E White, T Palmer, R Etheridge; R L Redwood, J H Spalding; R F Cowling, M J Nicholls (captain), K Richardson, A Brinn, J H Fidler, D B W Owen, J S Jarrett, J H Haines

Wolfhounds: A H Ensor (Wanderers & Ireland); V Becker, T Gleeson (Lansdowne), R Finn (University College, Dublin), J Brady (Wanderers); M Quinn (Lansdowne & Ireland), J Molony (captain, St Marys & Ireland); P O'Callaghan (Dolphin & Ireland), P Whelan (Bohemian), I McLaughlan (West of Scotland & Scotland), E Campbell (O Wesley & Ireland), S Dearing (Garryowen), T Norton (O Belvedere), C Scaife (Wanderers)

Referee: Mr D Monger (Warwickshire)

In the first five minutes the players discovered that 'the ball slipped out of their hands like a bar of soap on a Friday bath night'. This played into the hands of Gloucester's greatest asset, their pack, and when the ball came out as far as John Spalding and Bob Redwood, they kicked it high in the air for their forwards to chase. In the second half their use of the strong wind made this tactic even more effective. The tackling of Dave Owen and Tom Palmer was an example to the rest of the team, and the Wolfhounds were completely stifled. Peter Butler kicked a penalty in each half and Mick Quinn replied with one three minutes from the end. This report may be short but you may rest assured that it contains everything of note in the match.

Peter 'The Boot' Butler prevails again [Gloucester Rugby]

The Bosuns

THE BOSUNS WERE an invitation XV founded in 1964 by Simon Nicolls (Rosslyn Park and Royal Navy). The majority of their matches were in aid of the Star Centre for Youth, and they came to play at Kingsholm in three successive seasons.

Gloucester 34 Bosuns 8
6th November 1967

THIS SPECIAL MATCH was played on a Monday evening to mark the official opening of the new floodlights at Kingsholm. The Bosuns put out a strong side containing five internationals alongside triallists and county players.

Gloucester: D Rutherford; N J Foice, R G Pitt, J A Bayliss, J Groves; J T Hopson, M H Booth; J L Fowke, M J Nicholls, M A Burton, A Brinn, J S Jarrett, G G White, D W Owen, R Smith

Bosuns: B B Wright (New Brighton); P C Sibley (Bath), P J Burnett (London Scottish), D J J Allanson (Rosslyn Park), M R Collins (Bristol); I D Wright (St Luke's College), D T Stevens; A L Horton (Blackheath), I A Hart (New Brighton), D L Powell (Northampton), P A Eastwood (United Services, Portsmouth), D E J Watt (Bristol), P J Bell (Blackheath), J Barton (Coventry), D Phillips (St Luke's College & Bristol)

Referee: Mr A M Lees (Manchester)

The Bosuns may have been very gifted players individually, but they were a scratch side, and from the start they were reduced to near impotence by a Gloucester team which went straight on the attack and was energetic, muscular and organised. They were led from the back by Don Rutherford, giving his usual cultured performance at full-back. Mickey Booth and Terry Hopson were in complete harmony and showed their mastery at half-back, whilst John Bayliss and Ron Pitt exuded a bristling threat in the centre. Dick Smith, Gary White, Alan Brinn and Dave Owen gained control in the loose, Jim Jarrett ruled the line-outs, and Mike Burton and Jack Fowke dominated their opponents in the set scrums. Booth scored the first try, scuttling round the blind side of a scrum, and the whole back division then handled to send Foice in next to the posts; Rutherford converted both. Sibley struck back with a try for the Bosuns, but a Booth dropped goal established a 13-3 lead at half-time.

Booth opened the second half account with a beautifully judged punt for Hopson to gather and score; Rutherford converted. But the crowd had to wait for the last 15 minutes to see an explosion of action.

John Bayliss [Gloucester Rugby]

Gary White scored, kicking through from a lineout, John Groves got over from a tapped penalty, John Bayliss made the line from a brisk passing move, and Booth scored his second try following a clever run by Jarrett; Rutherford converted two of them and sandwiched inbetween was a try for the Bosuns, which was perhaps the best of the night. Burnett rounded off a lavish passing move involving backs and forwards; Hart converted.

Gloucester 30 Bosuns 8
16th October 1968

Gloucester: E Stephens; J Clewes, D Brooks, J Bayliss, J Groves; T Palmer, J Spalding; M Burton, P Kocerhan, C N Teague, J S Jarrett, A Brinn, J Haines, K Richardson, M Neal

Bosuns: I Moffatt (Northampton); J Novak (Guys Hospital & Harlequins), V Dobbs (Saracens), H Waller (Richmond), P Sibley (Bath); C Hogg (Harlequins), N Cosh (Blackheath); J O'Shea (Cardiff & Wales), G Millar (Harlequins), R Challis (London Scottish), A Else (Bedford), J Heggadon (Saracens), J Powell (captain), A Mortimer (Wasps), P Hayward (Blackheath)

Referee: Mr K Hutton (Gloucestershire)

Unsurprisingly the Bosuns again suffered from the lack of cohesion typical of an invitation side, and were confronted by a rock-hard Gloucester defence and the boot of Eric Stephens, who landed 3 penalties and 3 conversions. Stephens started the scoring with a penalty before Richardson grabbed a try after Haines had apparently knocked on a kick ahead by Groves. Stephens converted and Palmer dropped a goal before half-time arrived at 11-0.

Eric Stephens [Gloucester Rugby]

Stephens again started the half with a penalty, before Clewes made a break, passed on to Brooks, and Neal was outside to score the try, which Stephens converted. The Bosuns then grabbed all of their points in the space of ten minutes. Dobbs intercepted a kick ahead by Palmer and ran through from the 25 to get the first try, which Moffatt converted beautifully. This was soon followed by a superb try by Novak, who avoided Groves and Stephens in running three-quarters of the length of the pitch to score. Gloucester rounded off the scoring with two more tries – John Bayliss flew over by the posts after Spalding had sold a dummy to make the opening; Stephens converted: and Mike Burton snatched up a loose ball and plummeted over just before the final whistle.

Gloucester 3 Bosuns 16
15th October 1969

GLOUCESTER WERE SEVERELY weakened by the omission of county players and some other regulars being rested ahead of important matches coming up in the next three days, and Wheatman was brought in at full-back at the last minute. Although 1,500 spectators turned up and the Star Centre benefited, it was to be the last visit to Kingsholm by the Bosuns. Whilst the match was in progress the referee lost his watch, but Arthur Orr found the silver timepiece lying on the grass, checked it was still ticking and returned it to its owner.

Gloucester: C Wheatman; J Dix, D O Brooks, K R Morris, J Horner; T Palmer, M H Booth (captain); J L Fowke, F Reed, M A Burton, N A Jackson, J A Jarrett, M J Bayliss, M J Potter, J Haines

Bosuns: J Uzzell (Cardiff & Wales); R Wyatt (St Lukes College), A Orr, M Smith (London Scottish), R Elliott (Bath); C Hogg (captain, Harlequins), A Cleaver (Cheltenham); P Parfitt (Bath), G Patterson, H Bryce (London Scottish), D Pope (New Brighton), J C Gibbons (Harlequins), J Powell (Wasps), R Smith (Plymouth), N Cullimore (London Scottish)

Referee: Mr N P Jones (Gloucestershire)

The Bosuns play revolved around their Harlequins New Zealander, Campbell Hogg, who proved dangerous whenever he was allowed an opportunity. The Bosuns struck first after five minutes when they broke from their own 25, Mike Smith worked the ball outside to Wyatt, who cross-kicked to under Gloucester's posts, where Hogg caught the ball, only to slip up short of the line, but he threw the ball back to John Powell, who roared over by the corner flag. Uzzell missed with the conversion but kicked a second attempt and Mike Smith and Tom Palmer swapped penalties before half-time came at 11-3.

Five minutes into the second half:

Bosuns finished their scoring spree with one of the most bewildering displays seen at Kingsholm for a long time. They started from their own in-goal, ran to the Gloucester line and for fully two minutes they sent the ball winging backwards and forwards across the front of the posts until Neil Cullimore decided to call a halt to the handling practice. With Gloucester mesmerised, he nipped over to score. Uzzell promptly converted the gift.

The rest of the game was largely devoted to Gloucester pressing and pressing but they just could not convert it into points. John Horner shook off Wyatt and Smith with deceptive ease on a beautiful run, but failed to get over, and Palmer missed with dropped goal and penalty kicks.

Police Matches

British Police 10 Royal Air Force 17
15th January 1953

[Gloucestershire Archives]

THE BRITISH POLICE team included former Gloucester captain, Jack Watkins, and two Welsh internationals in Dai Davies and W E Tamplin. The Mayor of Gloucester, Alderman Matthews, kicked off.

[Gloucestershire Archives]

The RAF had the better of the early exchanges and were rewarded when Channer broke away inside his own half and Beatson handled beautifully before Rowlands hurtled over to score in the corner. Channer missed the conversion, but was successful with an excellent drop goal to extend the RAF lead to 6-0 at half time.

In the second half the powerful Police pack gained the upper hand and starved the dangerous RAF backs of ball. Tamplin was the outstanding player and converted both of the Police tries, scored by himself and Smith. However, Channer dropped a second goal and converted a try by Len Shelley to secure a hard earned victory for the airmen.

After the game a dinner was hosted by the Police Athletic Association at the Midland and Royal Hotel, attended by the players and many senior Police, RAF and GRFC officials, who proposed toasts and gave speeches aplenty.

Gloucester 26 British Police 3
20th September 1972

Gloucester: P Butler; R Jardine, J Bayliss (captain), T Palmer, J Dix; R Redwood, G Mace; P Blakeway, M Nicholls, R Cowling, J Fidler, J Jarrett, D Owen, J Watkins, R Smith

British Police: G Protheroe (Swansea); A Cotterell, K Jones (Staffs Police), D Robinson (Fylde), T Stephenson; R Evans (South Wales Police), A Lewis (Abertillery and South Wales Police), A Davies, A Jenkins (South Wales Police), G Howls (captain, Ebbw Vale and South Wales Police), T Diaper (South Wales Police), T Darnell (Coventry), J F Herniman (Gloucester), S Skibicki (Stafford)

Referee: Lt Col C Tyler (London)

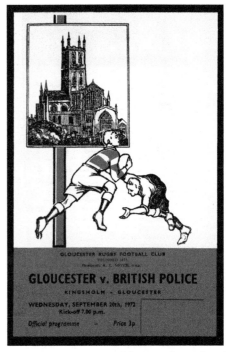

[Gloucestershire Archives]

THE POLICE ON the field kept the home team penned in their own half for the first quarter. Their tough pack included Gloucester's Jerry Herniman who regularly trod the beat at Kingsholm. In the last quarter, passing and handling errors crept in, and Gloucester then ran away with the game. John Watkins thrived in this environment, and his spectacular foraging for loose ball led to him having a hand in all four of Gloucester's tries. Dick Smith and Peter Butler were the other stars.

Watkins scored the first try, going straight over from a line-out, and Tom Palmer added a second. In the final minute of normal time, from a tap penalty, Smith juggled the ball twice as he broke away, but retained possession (the law had only recently been changed to allow this), and passed on to Watkins who put Robin Cowling in beside the posts. In extra time the same sequence was followed again from another tap penalty, but this time the final pass went to John Bayliss to complete the scoring.

Jerry Herniman [Gloucester Rugby]

John Watkins [Gloucester Rugby]

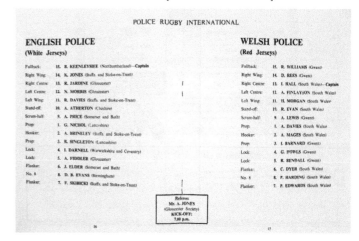

Gloucester 18 British Police 12
14th November 1973

English Police 12 Welsh Police 16
31st January 1973

THE WELSH SIDE included former British Lion, Alan Lewis, and was led by another former international, Ian Hall. The English side included Richard Jardine and John Fidler of Gloucester and Winston Morris from Lydney; There were some late replacements which were not recorded.

The English Police threw away possible victory, despite displaying greater power in the pack and a more adventurous three-quarter line than their counterparts from the valleys. They slid behind 0-9, before scoring their only try when Atherton burst away from a ruck and passed inside to John Fidler, who made good ground before setting up David Bowen-Evans, who passed to Ian Darnell, who lobbed the ball out to Richard Jardine to score. At one point the score closed to 12-13 with a conversion and two penalties from Terence Richardson, but further chances were missed later in the game, and the Welsh ran out winners thanks to tries from Ron Evans and Terry Diaper (a late replacement), and a conversion and two penalties by Williams. In some respects England were pleased with their performance against a strong side, seven of whom had 'appeared for East Glamorgan in the roughhouse with the All Blacks earlier in the season'. Following this game, both Fidler and Jardine were selected for the British Police in their annual fixture with the French Police.

GLOUCESTER
(Red and White)

FULL BACK
15 P. BUTLER (c)

THREEQUARTERS
14 R. J. CLEWES (c)   r.w.
13 J. A. BAYLISS (c)   r.c.
12 R. WHITE (c)   l.c.
11 R. ETHERIDGE (c)   l.w.

HALF BACKS
10 T. PALMER (c)   o.h.
9 J. SPALDING (c)   s.h.

FORWARDS
1 K. RICHARDSON (c)
2 M. NICHOLLS (c) (Capt.)
3 R. COWLING (c)
4 A. BRINN (i) (c)
5 J. FIDLER (c)
6 D. OWEN (c)
8 J. JARRETT (c)
7 J. HAINES (c)

BRITISH POLICE

FULL BACK
15 R. WILLIAMS

THREEQUARTERS
14 A. FINLAYSON   r.w.
13 A. BLACK   r.c.
12 I. HALL (i)   l.c.
11 H. MORGAN   l.w.

HALF BACKS
10 R. EVANS (i)   o.h.
9 A. LEWIS (i)   s.h.

FORWARDS
1 A. DAVIES
2 D. YOUNG
3 M. KNILL
4 R. BENDALL
5 G. HOWLS
6 A. MOORE
8 R. BETHEL
7 C. DYER

REFEREE :
Mr. T. KAVANAGH (Warwickshire Society)

[Gloucestershire Archives]

GLOUCESTER MANAGED ONLY one try scored by Bob Clewes, converted by Peter Butler, but four penalties by Butler saw them home.

England Police 6 Wales Police 15
15th January 1975

POLICE RUGBY
INTERNATIONAL

ENGLAND
(WHITE JERSEYS)

Ⓥ

WALES
(RED JERSEYS)

at
KINGSHOLM
GLOUCESTER
Kick-off 7.00pm

WEDNESDAY 15th JANUARY 1975

5p   5p

[Gloucestershire Archives]

THE ENGLAND SIDE included Richard Jardine and John Fidler of Gloucester.

England: I Burrell (Met Police and London Scottish); S Tiddy (Met Police and Middlesex), R Jardine (Gloucester and Gloucestershire), M Gray (Met Police), A Corlett (Merseyside Police); R Kirton, S Wilson (West Midlands Police); A Trotter (Kent Police), A Brindley (Staffs Police and Staffs), B Greaves (West Mercia Police, Moseley and North Midlands), J Fidler (Gloucester and Gloucestershire), I Darnell (captain,

West Midlands Police, Coventry and Warwickshire), D White, A Moore (Met Police), P Lovell (Devon and Cornwall Police and England Under-19)

Wales: M Pengilly (South Wales Police); D Rees (Gwent Police), A Finlayson (South Wales Police and Wales), H Morgan, N Tottel (South Wales Police); R Evans (South Wales Police and Wales), G Evans; G Thomas, D Young (South Wales Police), G Howls (captain, Gwent Police and Ebbw Vale), I Barnard (Gwent Police and Newport), C Jones, C Dyer, P Edwards, G Bale (South Wales Police)

Referee: W J Fowler (Gloucester)

Richard Jardine (left) and John Fidler (right) [Gloucester Rugby]

The Welsh police deserved their victory because of the extra flair they showed in moving a greasy ball, Half-time saw the Welsh 9-3 ahead, all penalties, but the English police team fought hard, even though they were reduced to 13 fit men for most of the second half. Another penalty reduced the arrears to 9-6, but three minutes from the end Phil Edwards scored the only try of the match to settle the issue.

Gloucester 31 British Police 6
8th October 1975

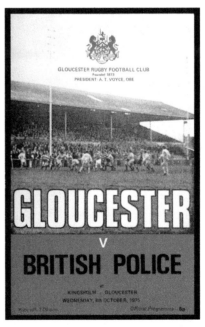

GLOUCESTER RUGBY FOOTBALL CLUB
Founded 1873
PRESIDENT: A. T. VOYCE, OBE

GLOUCESTER
V
BRITISH POLICE

at
KINGSHOLM : GLOUCESTER
WEDNESDAY, 8th OCTOBER, 1975
Kick-off 7.00 p.m.   Official Programme 5p

[Gloucestershire Archives]

THIS WAS A match memorable chiefly for Paul Williams, who spent half the game in the medical room having stitches in a gashed ear,

[Gloucestershire Archives]

[Gloucestershire Archives]

but he played a blinder when he was on the field and scored two tries. In his absence Eddie Pinkney moved out to the wing, but the combination of John Watkins and Dick Smith, who had been called out of semi-retirement to play, still made for a very effective back row.

Peter Butler made a break, exploited by Dix and Jardine to put Williams over for the first try, which Butler converted from the touchline and followed up with two penalties. Williams pounced on a handling error to kick through and win the chase but sacrificed his ear in scoring. Butler kicked another impressive conversion, but then impeded Tiddy who had kicked the ball past him and the referee awarded a penalty try, which Pengilley converted. Pengilley failed with several penalty opportunities, hitting the post with one, and Butler showed him how it should be done with his third successful effort.

Williams then returned with his head swathed in bandages and immediately embarked on a sparkling run. He found Butler and Watkins in support and they sent Dick Smith over behind the posts; Butler converted. Within a minute Gloucester had scored again, Pinkney making a great run with Watkins at his elbow to release the twinkle-toed Dix to dive over in the corner; astonishingly Butler's conversion just sailed wide.

Gloucester 68 British Police 15
4th October 1989

THIS MATCH WAS played to mark the 150th anniversary of the Gloucestershire Constabulary. The Police side were without their England and Lions stars, Dean Richards, Wade Dooley and Paul Ackford,

and were no match for a Gloucester team which treated the crowd to an entertaining but one-sided display of free-flowing rugby.

Gloucester: T Smith; Morgan, Mogg, Caskie, Breeze; Hamlin, Gardiner; Preedy, Dunn, Pascall, Scrivens, Etheridge, Gadd, I Smith, Clark. Replacement: Cummins

British Police: Hogg; Hanavan, Morris, Sataro, Evans; Davies,

The British Police team [Ron Etheridge]

Lee; Wilson, Weaver, McCoy, Matthews, Brierley, Phillips, Williams, West. Replacement: Williams

Referee: A Spreadbury (Somerset)

Tim Smith, Ian Smith and John Gadd were prominent in bursting through to create acres of space for their three-quarters, and fourteen tries resulted, scored by Morgan (3), Etheridge (2), Mogg (2), Gadd (2), Dunn, Breeze, Gardiner, I Smith, and T Smith. Hogg, Hanavan and Phillips responded with tries for the police.

Southern Hemisphere Visitors

Western Counties 0 South Africa 42
10th December 1960

A CAPACITY CROWD WATCHED the Springboks completely outclass a combined Gloucestershire and Somerset side, despite the visitors playing the second half one short after their full-back was injured. The locals lamented that the only Gloucester player selected for the Counties was their captain, Peter Ford. The Springboks named 17 players in the programme, but had sorted out their selection by kick-off, with van Niekerk, Roux and Uys not playing, and H J van Zyl (Transvaal) coming in on the wing.

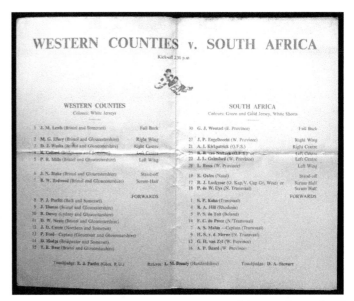

[Gloucestershire Archives]

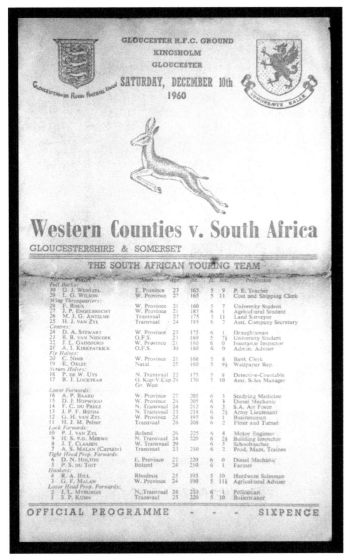

[Gloucestershire Archives]

Jannie Engelbrecht opened the scoring with a try in the corner, and the South Africans scored three more from Attie Baard (2) and Hennie van Zyl before half time. The second was a brilliant effort, the defence torn apart with a scissors movement, sharp passing and blistering pace.

Western Counties threatened at the start of the second half, but Gainsford snapped up a loose ball and ran half the length of the field to score by the posts. When a reverse pass from Avril Malan put Frik du Preez over for the sixth try, the Counties' defence fell apart, and du Preez, Engelbrecht, Gainsford and Keith Oxlee helped themselves to further

Bob Redwood about to pass with Peter Ford in support [Journal]

tries to complete the rout by 6 goals and 4 tries to nil. Everything about the visitors seemed bigger and better, most of all their scrum half, Dick Lockyear, who passed the ball up to 40 feet, and kicked the conversions.

Southern Counties 0 South Africa 13
28th January 1970

T HIS MATCH WAS originally scheduled to be played at Bournemouth, but was switched to Kingsholm on police advice, because the presence of many anti-apartheid demonstrators was anticipated. They did indeed turn out in force, but Castle Grim proved defensible and the match went ahead with only a few incidents within the ground.

The Southern Counties proved to be much sterner opposition than expected and the game reached half time with no score, but a minute into the second half the Springboks scored an unconverted try. Martin van Rensburg went bulldozing forward, Visagie carried on, and Gert Miller, on the wing, got over.

SOUTHERN COUNTIES
v.
SOUTH AFRICA
at

KINGSHOLM · GLOUCESTER

WEDNESDAY, 28th JANUARY, 1970

Kick off 2.45 p.m.

✻ ✻ ✻

OFFICIAL PROGRAMME : : PRICE 1/-

Orchard & Ind Ltd., Printers, Northgate, Gloucester.

[John Hudson]

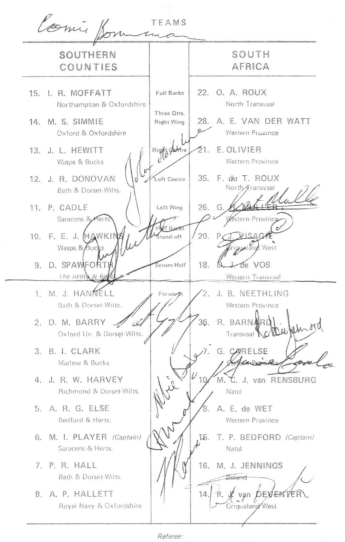

TEAMS

SOUTHERN COUNTIES		SOUTH AFRICA
15. I. R. MOFFATT Northampton & Oxfordshire	Full Backs	22. O. A. ROUX North Transvaal
14. M. S. SIMMIE Oxford & Oxfordshire	Three Qtrs. Right Wing	28. A. E. VAN DER WATT Western Province
13. J. L. HEWITT Wasps & Bucks	Right Centre	21. E. OLIVIER Western Province
12. J. R. DONOVAN Bath & Dorset-Wilts.	Left Centre	35. F. du T. ROUX North Transvaal
11. P. CADLE Saracens & Herts.	Left Wing	26. G. H. MULLER Western Province
10. F. E. J. HAWKINS Wasps & Bucks	Half Backs Stand-off	20. P. J. VISAGIE Griqualand West
9. D. SPAWFORTH The Army & Bucks	Scrum-Half	18. D. J. de VOS Western Transvaal
1. M. J. HANNELL Bath & Dorset-Wilts.	Forwards	2. J. B. NEETHLING Western Province
2. D. M. BARRY Oxford Un. & Dorset-Wilts.		36. R. BARNARD Transvaal
3. B. I. CLARK Marlow & Bucks		7. G. CARELSE
4. J. R. W. HARVEY Richmond & Dorset-Wilts.		10. M. C. J. van RENSBURG Natal
5. A. R. G. ELSE Bedford & Herts.		8. A. E. de WET Western Province
6. M. I. PLAYER *(Captain)* Saracens & Herts.		15. T. P. BEDFORD *(Captain)* Natal
7. P. R. HALL Bath & Dorset Wilts.		16. M. J. JENNINGS Boland
8. A. P. HALLETT Royal Navy & Oxfordshire		14. R. J. van DEVENTER Griqualand West

Referee:

Mr W. K. M. JONES

[John Hudson]

There was little further excitement until Southern Counties mishandled close to their line nine minutes from time, which let de Voss pick up and nip over by the posts; van Rensburg converted. Six minutes later a penalty 60 yards out saw the huge Gawie Carelse just lack the distance, but right at the end, the Springboks scored again to make the score more comfortable, when prop, 'Tiny' Neathling, grounded close to the posts for van Rensburg to convert easily.

Western Counties 25 Fiji 13
10th October 1970

THIS MATCH WAS played on the very day on which Fiji was granted independence, and the Fijian High Commissioner travelled down to Kingsholm to celebrate the occasion. On a damp, grey, drizzly afternoon, it was a sell-out and there were reported to be 20,000 packed into the ground.

[Gloucestershire Archives]

The match, though injury and penalty strewn, was exciting. Dick Smith scored very early on, after the Fijians had thrown long at a line-out near their own line. Western Counties went on to dominate the first half hour, before they were undone by a typical Fijian surge right down the field, with backs and forwards combining at speed. It culminated in a try for prop Jona Qoro who sidestepped four defenders on his way to the line. The conversion brought Fiji level but a penalty by full back Waterman and a dropped goal by Jon Gabitass restored the Counties' lead. Back came the Fijians, and a kick ahead found scrum half Batibasaga who threaded his way through the defence before converting his own try, which made it Western Counties 11 Fiji 10 at half-time.

England hooker John Pullin retired at the interval with a nasty head wound, and was replaced by his Bristol colleague, John White. Early in the second half, a dropped goal by Batibasaga gave the Fijians the lead for the one and only time in the match, the Counties quickly regaining

WESTERN COUNTIES (GLOUCESTERSHIRE and SOMERSET) Colour: Red		FIJI Colours: White with Palm Emblem	
15. J. WATERMAN Somerset	Full Back	15. INOKE BUADROMO QVSOB	Full Back
14. P. KNIGHT Gloucestershire	Threequarters Right Wing	14. RAVUAMA LATILEVU Sigatoka	Threequarter Right Wing
13. M. C. BEESE Somerset	Right Centre	13. KINIVILIAME NALATU Castaways	Right Centre
12. J. BAYLISS Gloucestershire	Left Centre	12. PETAIA VUKULA SPSM	Left Centre
11. M. R. COLLINS Gloucestershire	Left Wing	11. PIO TIKOISUVA St. John/Marist	Left Wing
10. J. R. GABITASS Gloucestershire	Half Backs Out-Half	10. ISIMELI BATIRUSAGA Sigatoka	Half Backs Out-Half
9. J. SPALDING Gloucestershire	Scrum Half	9. SEMESA SIKIVOU Nausori	Scrum Half
	Forwards		Forwards
1. A. J. ROGERS Gloucestershire		1. JOSATEKI SOVAU Soutaka	
2.*J. V. PULLIN Gloucestershire		2. ATONIO RACIKE St. John/Marist	
3. B. G. NELMES Gloucestershire		3. JONA QORO Western Marine	
4.*D. E. J. WATT Gloucestershire		4. APENISA TOKAIRAVAU Forestry	
5.†A. J. BRINN Gloucestershire		5. JOPE NAUCABALAVU (Vice-Captain) QVSOB	
6.*D. M. ROLLITT (Captain) Gloucestershire		6. MALI KURISARU Sigatoka	
8. R. C. HANNAFORD Gloucestershire		8. SELA TOGA (Captain) Soutaka	No 8
7.†R. SMITH Gloucestershire		7. VUNIANI VARO Combined	Back

*International   †Trialist
Substitutes: D. Tyler, M. Lloyd, J. White, B. Burridge
Touch Judge: R. A. Ellis (Gloucester Society of Referees)

Substitutes: Josaia Visei, George Barley, Ilaitia Tuisese, Setareki Tamanivalu
Touch Judge: C. Cole (Somerset Society of Referees)

Referee R. F. Johnson (Kent Society of Referees)
Music by the Band of the Royal Gloucestershire Hussars

[Gloucestershire Archives]

The Western Counties team against Fiji [Citizen]

it when Charlie Hannaford scored from a careless knock back. Radrodo crossed for the Fijians after a brilliant passing move, but the final pass was judged forward, and thereafter the Fijian game became untidy. Jon Gabitass, who played much of the game with a fractured cheekbone, punished them with two penalties and then converted his own try from a blindside break by Dick Smith to finish the scoring.

Unfortunately this match must rank as one of the most violent seen at Kingsholm. The headline in the Citizen read 'Fijians image tarnished in Kingsholm bloodbath'. Their play was politely described as 'over-enthusiastic' and it led to a stream of penalties being awarded against them for foul play, which ruined their few constructive attacks and resulted in 15 minutes of injury time being added on. By the end of the game, the casualty list included: John Spalding, two fractured ribs; Jon Gabitass, a depressed fractured cheekbone; John Pullin, numerous stitches to a variety of head wounds received from head-butts in the scrums; and Tony Rogers, laid out cold by an uppercut which broke his nose.

Western Counties 12 New Zealand 39
28th October 1972

THIS WAS THE first match of the All Blacks tour. With Gloucester and Gloucestershire having fallen to the might of the All Blacks on previous tours, the expansion to Western Counties nominally promised stronger opposition. In reality this was a Gloucestershire side masquerading as Western Counties and contained seven Gloucester

This cartoon was published on the front page of the Citizen on match day with a caption – 'I couldn't help overhearing the advice you were screaming at us in the first half, friend – should us cream puffs really go back to Kiwiland and learn to play rugby?'[Citizen]

players, a selection which ensured that a packed Kingsholm provided vociferous support for the home side.

Western Counties: P Butler (Gloucester); A Morley, P Knight (Bristol), J Bayliss (Gloucester), C Williams; J Gabitass, J Cannon (Bristol); M Burton (Gloucester), J Pullin (Bristol), R Cowling (Gloucester), D Watt (Bristol), A Brinn, R Smith, J Watkins (Gloucester), C Hannaford (Bristol)

New Zealand: J Karam: B Williams, B Robertson, G Batty; M Parkinson, B Burgess, S Going; K Murdoch, R Urlich, J Matheson, H Macdonald, P Whiting, A Scown, I Kirkpatrick, A Sutherland

Referee: Mr D P d'Arcy (Ireland)

OFFICIAL PROGRAMME   FIVE NP

WESTERN COUNTIES
(GLOUCESTERSHIRE & SOMERSET)
v.
NEW ZEALAND

KINGSHOLM GROUND, GLOUCESTER
SATURDAY, OCTOBER 28th, 1972
Kick-off 3.00 p.m.

P. J. WILLIAMS & CO. PRINTERS, 318 GLOUCESTER ROAD, BRISTOL.

[Gloucestershire Archives]

Chris Williams and Dick Smith chase after Mike Parkinson, with Bob Burgess
and Ian Kirkpatrick in support [Journal]

John Cannon dive-passes to get the ball out to the Western Counties backs
[Gloucestershire Archives]

Ian Kirkpatrick about to feed the ball from a lineout, with Ron Urlich and Keith
Murdoch in support [Gloucestershire Archives]

Bryan Williams races in to complete his hat trick [Gloucestershire Archives]

The partisan support produced no miracles. The All Blacks
thoroughly outplayed the home side, and built a 21-0 lead by half-time.
Peter Butler found himself busy at full back, but it took 16 minutes for
Joe Karam to register the first points with a penalty. Five minutes later,
Mike Parkinson dummied his way over for the first try; Bruce Robertson
ran under the posts for the second; and in injury time at the end of the
first half, Parkinson again plunged over for the third; Karam converted
all three.

Early in the second half, Colling scored the All Blacks' fourth to
put them out of reach, but Western Counties responded, and Mike Burton
rumbled and jinked his way over for a try, which was converted by Butler.
Back came the All Blacks, and Bryan Williams was rewarded with a try
after chasing an up-and-under. Butler hit back with two penalties, the
second awarded when Bayliss was viciously kicked in the ribs as he tried
to smother the ball. It was but a temporary halting of the tide, as Williams
rounded off his hat trick with two tries in two minutes to complete a
resounding victory for the visitors.

Lin Colling whips the ball away from a ruck [Gloucestershire Archives]

Gloucester 29 Southern Counties 7
12th December 1972

AN ADDITIONAL FIXTURE was arranged at Kingsholm at the request of Southern Counties in order to give them a warm-up match before their encounter with the All Blacks at Oxford a week later. Gloucester put out a full-strength team since Southern Counties asked to be fully tested, and they were. Arguably just as much as the following week, when New Zealand won 23-6.

[Gloucestershire Archives]

GLOUCESTER		SOUTHERN COUNTIES		
(Red and White)		**FULL BACK**		
FULL BACK		15 S. CRABTREE (C)		
15 P. BUTLER (C)		(Bristol)		
		THREEQUARTERS		
THREEQUARTERS		14 R. ELLIS-JONES (C)	R.W.	
14 R. WHITE (C)	R.W.	(London Welsh)		
13 J. BAYLISS (C) (Capt.)	R.C.	13 R. O. P. JONES (C)	R.C.	
12 R. JARDINE (C)	L.C.	(Oxford)		
11 J. DIX	L.W.	12 I. RAY (C)	L.C.	
		(Oxford)		
HALF BACKS		11 P. CADLE (C)	L.W.	
10 T. PALMER (C)	O.H.	(Saracens)		
9 G. MACE	S.H.	HALF BACKS		
		10 *D. LLEWELLYN (C)	O.H.	
FORWARDS		(London Welsh)		
1 R. COWLING (C)		9 D. SPAWFORTH (C)	S.H.	
2 M. NICHOLLS (C)		(Army)		
3 M. A. BURTON (I) (C)		FORWARDS		
4 A. BRINN (I) (C)		1 M. HANNELL (C)		
5 J. FIDLER		(Bristol)		
6 J. A. WATKINS (I) (C)		2 H. MALINS (C)		
8 E. PINKNEY		(Richmond)		
7 R. SMITH (C)		3 K. RICHARDSON (C)		
		(Gloucester)		
		4 J. S. JARRETT (C)		
		(Gloucester)		
		5 J. S. HARWOOD (C)		
		(Oxford)		
		6 M. MARSHALL (C)		
		(Richmond)		
		7 S. GODFREY (C)		
		(Loughborough College)		
		8 J. VAUGHAN (C) (Capt.)		
		(London Welsh)		

REFEREE :
Mr. J. BURGUM (North Midlands Society)

(I) *International*
(C) *County*
* *Wales 'B'*
International

Gloucester had to play a man short for three-quarters of the game after Bob White was forced to leave the field with a dislocated shoulder following a terrific run to the line. They moved Eddie Pinkney out onto the wing to replace him and then proceeded to run in five tries. Mike Nicholls took five heels against the head whilst conceding none despite being supported by only six other forwards in the set scrums. Pete Butler, who appeared concussed during the second half, John Watkins, John Dix and Tom Palmer were the Gloucester players who caught the eye most frequently.

After missing two penalty shots, Butler landed his third attempt in the 16th minute and four minutes later converted a fine try by Richard Jardine after the break by White which ended in his dislocation. In the 26th minute Garry Mace won the ball at the tail of a line-out, and fed it to Watkins, who scored the second try. Five minutes later, Southern Counties struck back when a fly kick saw the ball go loose. Cadle, the Saracens wing, grub kicked it ahead of Dix, and beat him to the touch down for a try which Llewellyn could not convert. Within three minutes, however, Gloucester struck again. Jardine found a gap and passed to Butler, who drew the cover before handing on to Dix. He jinked inside Barraclough's tackle to score a try, to which Butler added the conversion points.

Counties then enjoyed a period of possession, but were unable to break through the smothering tackles of the home side. Another splendid bout of passing started by Watkins and Pinkney saw the ball fed across the field where Butler and Dix inter-handled before sending Dick Smith in for an exciting try in the corner. Butler converted from the touchline. Three minutes later Llewellyn succeeded with a penalty given after Nicholls had argued with the referee, but missed another nine minutes afterwards when the pack again transgressed. The final score came three minutes before the end, when a rush by Dix and Watkins took play to the visitors' line and from a scrum a scissors move between Mace and Palmer resulted in a try by the posts.

Public School Wanderers 38 Belgrano 20
28th February 1973

THIS WAS THE fourth of eight matches on a tour of the UK by the Argentinian club. They were serious opponents and keen to run the

[Gloucestershire Archives]

Referee : Mr. NICK JONES (Gloucestershire Society)

Public School Wanderers		Belgrano Athletic Club	
FULL BACK		**FULL BACK**	
15 C. D. SAVILLE		1 P. GUILLIGAN or 10 P. STOCKS	
Blackheath & Barbarians			
THREEQUARTERS		**THREEQUARTERS**	
11 C. KENT	WING	2 J. ESCOBAR	
Oxford University			
12 C. S. WARDLOW	CENTRE	3 L. ESTERAS or R. MULLER	
Coventry & England			
13 C. W. W. REA	CENTRE	4 O. TERRANOVA	
London Scottish & Scotland			
14 W. C. C. STEELE	WING	5 P. URDAPILLETA	
Bedford & Scotland			
HALF BACKS		**HALF BACKS**	
10 I. ROBERTSON	OUTSIDE HALF	9 C. MARTINEZ (Capt.)	
London Scottish & Scotland			
9 N. STARMER-SMITH	SCRUM HALF	11 A. GOMEZ	
Harlequins & England			
FORWARDS		**FORWARDS**	
1 R. COWLING		24 L. SEGLIN or 27 G. PHILLPOTS	
Gloucester			
2 M. NICHOLLS		28 O. CARBONE	
Gloucester			
3 G. SHAW		26 A. VOLTAN	
Neath & Wales			
4 J. JARRETT		20 R. BTESCH or 21 A. OTANA	
Gloucester			
5 A. BRINN		or 29 J. DYAN	
Gloucester & England			
6 J. WATKINS		14 E. ELOWSON (No. 8)	
Gloucester & England			
7 D. HUGHES		16 M. ESTERAS	
Newbridge & Wales			
8 J. R. GREENWOOD		17 A. BADANO	
Waterloo & England			

[Gloucestershire Archives]

Action from the game [Citizen]

ball, but were up against a powerful Public School Wanderers side, which included eight internationals. Both teams treated the crowd to a feast of fast and open rugby.

Belgrano exploded out of the blocks and forced PSW to touch down behind their own line. From the resulting scrum, slick passing through several pairs of hands put Urdapilleta over in the corner for a sizzling try in the second minute. PSW struck back immediately, with Chris Rea making a lot of ground before Steele dived over to score. In trying to play a fast open game, Belgrano became too loose, and the more experienced PSW team exploited this weakness to score four more tries before half-time. John Watkins darted over from a ruck, before Kent ran in two and Steele another.

Trailing 4-20, Belgrano began the second half with a try by Seglin, which gave Escobar the opportunity to land the first conversion of the evening. Kent completed his hat trick, before a gallop by Alan Brinn resulted in a try to delight the home crowd. Steele then weaved his way past half a dozen defenders to score the best try of the evening, to which Mike Nicholls added the only PSW conversion. Rea went over for the ninth and last PSW try, but Belgrano kept going, and scored late tries through Martinez and Muller to round off a highly entertaining game.

English Students 9 Argentina 15
10th October 1978

THIS WAS THE second match of the Argentinian tour, and was played on a midweek evening ahead of their game against England the following Saturday. The English Students included eight Under-23 internationals, and plenty of players who would go on to enjoy distinguished careers as full internationals. The tourists' first game had been a very feisty affair, with two players sent off, but this was a more subdued affair, only Clive Woodward having to leave the field as a result of being felled by a high tackle.

English Students: M Rose (Durham University); J Basnett (Wolverhampton Polytechnic), A Harrower (Madeley College), C Woodward (Loughborough University), P Asquith (Westminster Hospital); I Wilkins (St Paul's College, Cheltenham), M Conner (UWIST); S Wilkes (West Midlands College), M Howe, J Doubleday (Royal Agricultural College, Cirencester), P Ackford (Kent University), S Bainbridge (Alsager College), T Allchurch (Durham University), N Jeavons (Wolverhampton Polytechnic), P Polledri (Bristol Polytechnic)

Argentina: E Sanguinetti; M Campo, J Escalante, R Madero, A Capelletti; H Porta (captain), R Landajo; A Cerioni, A Cubelli, H Nicola,

R Pasaglia, A Iachetti, H Silva, G Travaglini, G Paz
    Referee: Mr N R Sansom (Scotland)

The tourists eventually won, but the students made them work hard for it. The difference between the sides proved to be Hugo Porta, the Argentine captain and world-class fly-half, who scored all of his side's points with a try, conversion, and three penalties. Just before the final whistle the crowd had cause to cheer a consolation score for the Students, when Gloucester's Ian Wilkins ran in a sizzling try, taking a pass from Conner on his hip, and racing thirty yards to the line.

South and South West Division 3 Australia 16
22nd December 1981

SOUTH AND SOUTH-WEST VERSUS AUSTRALIA

[Gloucestershire Archives]

THE 1981 AUSTRALIANS arrived at Kingsholm as battle-hardened tourists, expected to play as a well-organised team. The weather for this Tuesday evening fixture was very different from the roasting hot day experienced by previous Australian visitors to Kingsholm in 1908. Indeed the kick-off was brought forward because the Arctic conditions threatened to make the pitch ever less playable as the game wore on. By the end of the match the surface was frozen rock hard.

Table from the image:

South and South West		Australia
White Jerseys, Black Shorts, Maroon Stockings		Gold Jerseys and Green Shorts
15 C. RALSTON, Bath and Somerset	Full Back	15 P. McLEAN, Queensland
14 * A. SWIFT, Swansea	Wing	14 P. GRIGG, Queensland
13 R. PELLOW, Wasps and Cornwall	Centre	13 G. ELLA, New South Wales
12 J. CARR, Bristol and Gloucestershire	Centre	12 M. O'CONNOR, Queensland
11 R. MOGG, Gloucester and Gloucestershire	Wing	11 M. MARTIN, New South Wales
10 * J. HORTON, Bath and Somerset	Stand-off half	10 M. ELLA, New South Wales
9 R. HARDING, Bristol and Gloucestershire	Scrum-half	9 A. PARKER, Queensland
1 M. PREEDY, Gloucester and Gloucestershire	Prop	1 A. D'ARCY, Queensland
2 * S. MILLS, Gloucester	Hooker	2 C. CARBERRY, Queensland
3 * P. BLAKEWAY Captain, Gloucester & Gloucestershire	Prop	3 D. CURRAN, New South Wales
4 P. STIFF, Bristol and Somerset	Lock	4 D. HALL, Queensland
5 N. POMPHREY, Bristol and Gloucestershire	Lock	5 S. WILLIAMS, New South Wales
6 M. TEAGUE, Gloucester	Flanker	6 C. ROCHE, Queensland
7 * M. RAFTER, Bristol and Gloucestershire	Flanker	7 P. LUCAS, New South Wales
8 * R. HESFORD, Bristol and Gloucestershire	No.8	8 M. LOANE Captain, Queensland
Replacements:		Replacements:
16 * A. MORLEY, Bristol and Gloucestershire		16 J. MEADOWS, Victoria
17 D. SORRELL, Bristol		17 M. MATHERS, New South Wales
18 S. BAKER, Gloucester		18 G. CORNELSEN, New South Wales
19 * A. SHEPPARD, Bristol and Gloucestershire		19 P. COX, New South Wales
20 K. BOGIRA, Bristol and Gloucestershire		20 M. COX, New South Wales
21 S. JONES, Bath and Somerset		21 G. ELLA, New South Wales

* International

Referee
K.C. PARFITT
(Port Talbot)

Touch Judge: W. JONES (Ammanford)   Touch Judge: A.W. BEVAN (Brynammon)

As soon as play was underway, the crowd had plenty to keep them warm, as the S&SW, with Phil Blakeway to the fore, tore into the Aussies, shoving them back in the scrums and piling on the pressure. Indeed the all-Gloucester front row was doing so well in the scrums that it provoked an Australian fist to come through and break Blakeway's nose. A couple of penalties were missed, before John Horton dropped a goal to put the home

Bob Hesford leading a drive with Mike Teague and Mike Rafter in support [Citizen]

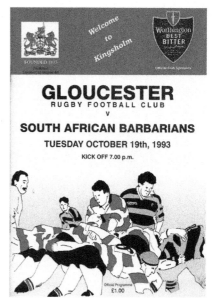

Bob Hesford with the ball, Mike Rafter at his back, and Peter Stiff and Malcolm Preedy in support [Citizen]

side ahead, and only resolute Australian defence prevented any further score before half-time.

At this point, Blakeway had to be replaced by Austin Sheppard (Bristol), because his eyesight was being affected by his broken nose. His absence turned the game in Australia's favour. Although Mike Teague and Bob Hesford continued to have storming games, the dominance in the scrum was lost, and the Australians were quick to capitalise on some dreadful defensive errors to score three tries through Mark Ella, Martin and Lucas, and thus win comfortably.

By the end of the game there were plenty of walking wounded, bruised by the ground as much as the opposition. The injury to Blakeway kept him out of the England side against the tourists the following Saturday, when Australia registered one of the victories in the Grand Slam they went on to achieve on this tour.

Gloucester 11 South African Barbarians 15 19th October 1993

A CROWD OF MORE than 3,000 turned out for this match. The SA Barbarians included four internationals in their side – Adrian Garvey (Zimbabwe), Johan Barnard and Eden Meyer (Namibia) and Thinus Linee (South Africa), who was one of the first black players to represent his country.

GLOUCESTER
RUGBY FOOTBALL CLUB
v
SOUTH AFRICAN BARBARIANS
TUESDAY OCTOBER 19th, 1993
KICK OFF 7.00 p.m.

Gloucester: M Roberts; P Holford, D Cummins, I Morgan, C Dee; A Johnson, B Fenley; P Jones, J Hawker, A Deacon, D Sims, R West, B Fowke, I Smith (captain), P Miles; Replacement: A Martin

SA Barbarians: G Lawless; E Meyer, R Muir (captain), M Linee, F Naude; J De Beer, K Putt; J Barnard, D Van Der Walt, A Garvey, R Opperman, L Blom, J Bernard, K Otto, G Combrink

Referee: Mr J Wallis (Somerset)

Gloucester could and perhaps should have won; they played with pace and commitment, but they fell short because they failed to take many of the scoring opportunities which they set up and one conversion and five penalty kicks failed. Dave Sims was outstanding amongst the forwards and Paul Holford was man of the match for his tackling, which saved at least three tries.

Gloucester had the better of the game early on and took the lead with a penalty kicked by Martin Roberts. But he then missed with two further attempts, handed over the kicking duties to Johnson and he missed another. De Beer missed one for the visitors and Blom had a try disallowed for a double movement, before Naude made a lightning break and scored under the posts; De Beer converted. Gloucester fought back and Dave

Sims took the ball in a lineout and forced his way up to the line, but he, Cummins and Fowke were all repelled until Sims got the ball again and battered his way over. Roberts missed the conversion, but Gloucester had their noses ahead 8-7 at half-time.

Damian Cummins on the attack with Paul Holford in support and Edem Mayer, the Namibian international, chasing back [Citizen]

Johnson extended this lead with a penalty. The SA Barbarians then ran a penalty from one side of the pitch to the other and Naude scored in the corner. A point behind, Gloucester threw everything at the visitors for the last 15 minutes, but Johnson missed two more penalties, one hitting the post, before De Beer kicked one at the death to seal the win for the SA Barbarians.

England Emerging Players 19 New Zealand 30
23rd November 1993

THE EMERGING ENGLAND side was coached by Keith Richardson of Gloucester, and included three Gloucester players – Dave Sims, Richard West and Paul Holford – which helped to raise the attendance to 10,500.

[Gloucestershire Archives]

England Emerging Players: P Challinor (Harlequins); P Holford (Gloucester), N Beal Northampton), D Hopley (Wasps), P Hull Bristol); M Catt (Bath), M Dawson (Northampton); C Clark Oxford University), K Dunn (Wasps), J Mallett (Bath), D Sims, R West (Gloucester), C Sheasby (Harlequins), S Ojomoh (Bath), D Ryan (captain, Wasps)

New Zealand: S Howarth; E Clarke (Auckland), M Berry (Wellington), L Stensness (Auckland), E Rush (North Harbour); S Bachop (Otago), J Preston (Wellington); M Allen (Taranaki), N Hewitt (Hawke's Bay), G Purvis (Waikato), B Larsen (North Harbour), R Fromont (Auckland), L Barry (North Harbour), P Henderson (Southland), J Mitchell (captain, Waikato)

Referee: D Mene (France)

Dean Ryan established his captaincy credentials in this match, leading his men to a stirring performance with bellows of encouragement which could be heard all over Kingsholm. His side had two early opportunities to take the lead, but Paul Challinor missed with penalty attempts, and New Zealand built a 10-0 lead through Shane Howarth kicking a penalty and converting a try by Eric Rush. England came back with two Challinor penalties, but Eroni Clarke darted through in the centre for a try which Howarth again converted. Just before half-time, England won a lineout close to the New Zealand line, Kevin Dunn threw the ball to Dave Sims, who drove through, with Dunn and Ryan in support, for a try which made the score 11-17 at the interval.

Matt Dawson passing the ball out, with Richard West in the centre and Dave Sims on the right [Citizen]

The All Blacks in pursuit of Matt Dawson [Citizen]

Challinor kicked a penalty to further reduce the arrears early in the second half, and for a while New Zealand were under pressure. But they fought back, and Howarth scored a try, converted it, and added a penalty, before Stephen Bachop dropped a goal to complete the All Blacks scoring. Emerging England finished strongly, besieging the New Zealand line with a succession of tapped penalties, and were rewarded when Damian Hopley beat five or six would-be tacklers to deliver a scoring pass to Challinor.

England A 20 South Africa A 35
11th December 1996

THIS WAS THE middle of three England A matches played in four days, against Argentina on Tuesday, South Africa on Wednesday and Queensland on Friday. The England A team went into this match unbeaten for the previous 18 months, with Rob Fidler and Chris Catling of Gloucester making their debuts at this level.

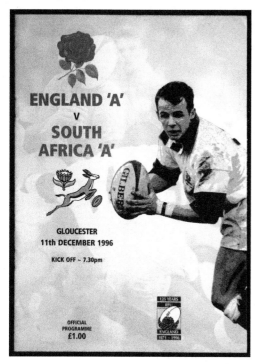

[Gloucestershire Archives]

England A: C Catling; B Johnson, J Baxendell, N Greenstock, S Bromley; M Mapletoft, A Healey; M Volland, S Mitchell, N Webber, D Grewcock, R Fidler, G Allison, R Jenkins, S Ojomoh. Replacement: P Sampson

South Africa A: D du Toit; M Hendricks, J Joubert, E Lubbe, M Goosen; L Koen, G Scholtz; O Le Roux, N Drotske (captain), W Meyer, R Opperman, H Louw, C Krige, P Smit, R Erasmus. Replacement: J Coetzee

Referee: Mr D McHugh (Ireland)

South Africa opened the scoring when Krige was driven over from a line-out, but England struck back when Chris Catling and Mark Mapletoft combined to put Spencer Bromley in for a try. Another Krige try and a couple of penalties by Koen put England behind 7-18 at half-time, but by then the two South African props, Ollie Le Roux and Willie Meyer had been shown yellow cards within two minutes of each other – both for stamping on Danny Grewcock.

This helped England to recover with a penalty from Mapletoft and a try when Austin Healey dummied over from a ruck under the posts, which Mapletoft converted to reduce the arrears to a single point. A further Mapletoft penalty ten minutes from time gave England the lead for the first time in the match at 20-18, but the strength of the South African pack told as England tired. In the last ten minutes, South Africa scored three

tries through Marius Goosen, McNeil Hendricks and finally a pushover credited to Rassie Erasmus.

Jenkins & Fidler in action against South Africa A [Citizen]

Mark Mapletoft launches an England attack [Citizen]

South West Under-21 6
New Zealand Under-21 35
2nd December 1997

FIVE GLOUCESTER PLAYERS – Rob Jewell, Paul Knight, Andy Robinson, Ed Mallett and Andy Hazell – lined up at Kingsholm to face the Haka challenge thrown down by the fledgling All Blacks, who were touring the country at the same time as their senior side. This was a warm-up game for the All Blacks before their encounter with England U-21s three days later, and they were awesome as they ran in six tries.

South West: J Fabian (Exeter); N Horncastle (Wasps), J Ewens, M Tindall (Bath), R Jewell (Gloucester); J Martin (Bristol), P Knight; A Robinson (Gloucester), T Robinson (Bristol University), S Mason (Bristol), W James (Bath), E Mallett (Gloucester), R Baxter (Exeter), A Hazell (Gloucester), S Gumbey (Camberley). Replacements: C Drake (Birmingham University), J Creasey (Reading)

New Zealand: G Donovan; A Holder, H Martine, D Barry, S Moimoi; C Hoare, C Smith; P Taite, J Tubberty, M Watti, M Veale, P

The Baby Blacks perform the Haka [Citizen]

Jon Fabian takes on the All Blacks from full-back [Citizen]

Caughlan, M Wilkins, M Holah, S Broomhall. Replacements: J Roberts, M Wright

The South West made a bright start, deserved their early lead from a Jon Fabian penalty, and nearly extended it when Nick Horncastle intercepted and headed for the corner. He kicked ahead when Charles Hoare threatened to tackle and narrowly lost the chase for a touchdown. This seemed to spur the All Blacks into action, and they responded with a penalty from Hoare to level the scores, followed by three tries in quick succession, with Salesi Moimoi involved in all of them. When a relieving penalty by the South West went straight to Moimoi, he broke several tackles to set up Hoare for a try. From the restart several punishing rolling mauls created the chance for Moimoi to go over in the corner. And then a Moimoi burst almost resulted in a try for Anthony Holder, but the ball was recycled and Daniel Berg crept over on the other side of the field.

The second half followed a similar pattern, with an early penalty by Fabian and a good chance spurned by the South West when Knight made a good break, but his subsequent kick to Jewell out wide was knocked on, before the All Blacks again went up a gear and ran amok with three more tries. Lock Marty Veale drove over for the first, a quick tapped penalty gave Chris Smith the next (the only one converted by Hoare), and nine minutes from time replacement Justin Roberts sped up the left wing and fed Glen Donovan to score. The match almost ended on a high note for the South West, when Mike Tindall made a break and fed Horncastle, but the All Blacks never give up and he was denied by a last ditch tackle by Holder.

Other International Visitors

Gloucester 6 Romanian XV 10
15th September 1956

THE FIRST RUGBY club in Romania was founded in 1912, but the national team won the bronze medal for rugby at the Olympic Games in Paris in 1924 (when few teams competed). This Romanian team was drawn from the three leading clubs in the country, all based in Bucharest – Central Army, Locomotive and Dynamo – and was essentially the Romanian national team. They arrived in Gloucester following a 6-6 draw against Leicester, and were entertained at the Guildhall by the Mayor and Sheriff of Gloucester. The Shed delighted in the sight of Peter Ford armed with a large bunch of flowers to give to the visitors before the kick-off.

George Hastings tackled by Anastase Marinache as he tries to break away from a lineout [Citizen]

pounced to score. Soon after Gloucester again coughed up possession, Krammer broke away on a 50-yard run, and sent wing forward Viorel Moraru racing away for the second try. Alexandru Penciu kicked the conversions, and a late penalty by Holder did no more than reduce the arrears.

Romanian rugby went on to enjoy something of a golden age from the 1960s to the 1980s, when they registered wins over France, Wales and Scotland.

Gloucestershire 62 Japan 10
22nd September 1976

THE GRASS AT the start of the season at Kingsholm was invariably long in the 1970s and was described as lush when the Japanese took

The Romanian team training at Kingsholm [Citizen]

Gloucester: I Sheen; D Perks, A Holder, J M Jenkin, R Blair; D W Jones, B Reade; G W Hastings, C Thomas, A Townsend, D A Jones, B Hudson, P Ford (captain), B Green, D Ibbotson

Romanian XV: A Penciu; J Dobre, C Krammer, R Nanu, A Barbu; R Chiriac, D Ionescu; A Teofilovici, N Soculescu, M Blagescu, A Marinache, V Mladin, V Moraru (captain), E Dumitrescu, I Dorotiu

Referee: Mr R J Todd (Hampshire)

This settled into a very evenly contested game. The visitors proved to be superbly fit, and frequently looked dangerous because of their speed and very rapid following up. But they were denied much possession because Cyril Thomas ensured that Gloucester had the lion's share of the ball in the tight. Indeed the Gloucester pack had the upper hand, with Ford, Hastings and Jones to the fore, but their backs offered little threat. When Romania had the ball they tended to kick it away, although long and accurate kicking did pen Gloucester back. There was no score at half-time.

Soon after the restart Alan Holder put Gloucester ahead with a dropped goal, and with ten minutes to go the Kingsholm crowd were looking forward to a hard-earned victory. But then disaster struck, and two shock tries in quick succession, both converted, snatched the win for the visitors. First, Romania pounced on a Gloucester error to tear into the Gloucester 25, where Sheen briefly checked them, but the ball went loose and Barbu

RUGBY FOOTBALL UNION

GLOUCESTERSHIRE RUGBY FOOTBALL UNION

GLOUCESTERSHIRE
COUNTY CHAMPIONS 1975/76

V

JAPAN

AT

KINGSHOLM, GLOUCESTER

ON WEDNESDAY, SEPTEMBER 22nd, 1976

Kick-Off: 7.00 p.m.

[Gloucestershire Archives]

the field in front of a crowd of 10,000. Gloucestershire were weakened by injuries, but could still field eight present and future internationals including British Lions Mike Burton and Steve Boyle, and the Kingsholm faithful appreciated the selection of eleven Gloucester players. The only change from the programme was Bob Clewes coming in on the wing in place of Morley. Japan fielded ten of the side which had played against Wales in Japan the previous year.

The Japanese touring party [Gloucestershire Archives]

GLOUCESTERSHIRE White		JAPAN Cherry and White
15. D. P. Sorrell *(Bristol)*	*Full Back*	15. Nobuyuki Ueyama
14. A. J. G. Morley *(Bristol)* †	*Right Wing*	14. Masaru Fujiwara
13. B. J. Vine *(Gloucester)*	*Right Centre*	13. Shigetaka Mori
12. R. Jardine *(Gloucester)*	*Left Centre*	12. Masao Yoshida
11. R. R. Mogg *(Gloucester)*	*Left Wing*	11. Ken Aruga
10. C. G. Williams *(Gloucester)* †	*Outside Half*	10. Yuji Matsuo
9. P. Kingston *(Gloucester)* †	*Scrum Half*	9. Akio Ueda
1. G. A. F. Sargent *(Gloucester)*	*Prop*	1. Tsukasa Takata (Capt.)
2. S. G. F. Mills *(Gloucester)*	*Hooker*	2. Manabu Sasada
3. M. A. Burton *(Gloucester)* †	*Prop*	3. Masayuki Miyauchi
4. S. B. Boyle *(Gloucester)*	*Lock*	4. Toshio Terai
5. R. A. Powell *(Llanelli)*	*Lock*	5. Naoshi Kumagai
6. J. A. Watkins (Capt.) *(Gloucester)* †	*Blind Side*	6. Keiichi Toyoyama
8. A. J. Troughton *(Bristol)*	*No. 8*	8. Ichiro Kobayashi
7. P. Polledri *(Bristol)*	*Open Side*	7. Hideo Akama

Replacements:
F. C. Reed *(Gloucester)*
A Sheppard *(Bristol)*
E. A. Pinkney *(Gloucester)*   † = International
R. M. Harding *(Bristol)*
R. J. Clewes *(Gloucester)*
R. Etheridge *(Gloucester)*

Replacements:
Toshiaki Yasui
Tsuyoshi Hatakeyama
Yoshiaki Izawa
Ryozo Imazato
Shigekazu Hoshino
Nobufumi Tanaka

Referee: D. L. HEAD (London Society)

Touch Judges: W. J. Fowler (Gloucester Society); R. F. Brown (Bristol Society)

[Gloucestershire Archives]

the line from 45 yards out. Troughton and Sorrell set up rucks leading to try number three, Richard Jardine bursting through to the posts. Another Burton stampede, aided by Sargent, cleared the path for Troughton to score the fourth. Then Brian Vine went over for a fifth try, and, Sorrell having kicked all five goals, Gloucestershire were 30 points up. Now came the first Japanese score, which brought the house down. Yoshida made a glorious break in the centre and after that there was no catching the flying

Alvin Troughton breaks away from a scrum against Japan, with John Watkins and Steve Boyle in support [Citizen]

The tour programme [Gloucestershire Archives]

Memento presented to GRFC by Japan [Gloucester Rugby]

Mike Burton got the game off to a storming start when he burst through from lineout possession won by Troughton, and his fellow Gloucester prop, Gordon Sargent, backed him up to score. The home side went further ahead when David Sorrell came up from full back to make space for a brilliant side-stepping run by Richard Mogg that took him to

Aruga. There was still time though for Chris Williams to create another hole in midfield and for Burton to send in hooker Steve Mills to make the half-time score 34-6.

Japan staged a courageous recovery in the third quarter, swarming into the rucks and playing with great elan. A tapped penalty and a perfectly judged kick from Mori led to a try from Fujiwara that set the crowd alight. Gloucestershire looked sluggish at this stage, but the picture was to change dramatically. In the final fifteen minutes the alien conditions only three days after arriving at Heathrow, and the power of the Gloucester forwards in the loose, took their toll and the floodgates opened. As the Japanese tired, the Gloucestershire pack, who were running like threequarters by the end, took charge, and set up a brace of tries for both Mogg and Jardine, and another for Williams.

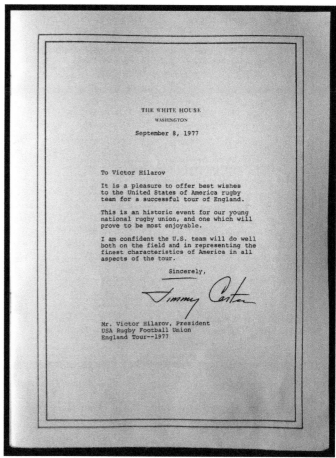

Tom Voyce and John Watkins with a Japanese official [Gloucestershire Archives]

Civil Service 6 USA 15
28th September 1977

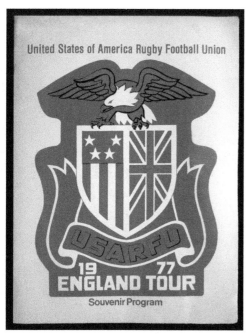

FOR A BRIEF period early in the 20th century, as a result of American Football becoming too violent, rugby prospered in the USA and particularly in California. American Football soon came back as the

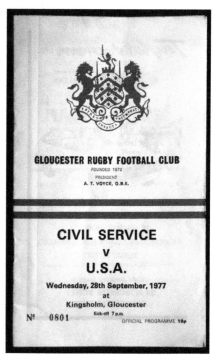

[Gloucestershire Archives]

[Gloucestershire Archives]

CIVIL SERVICE R.F.U.	UNITED STATES R.F.U.
White	
Full Back	**Full Back**
15. P. Hatfield, O. Modernians	15. D. Jablonski
Three Quarters	**Three Quarters**
14. C. Wilding, Fylde	14. R. Duncanson
13. M. Triggs, Bridgend	13. M. Halliday
12. P. Maney, Headingley	12. G. Schneeweiss
11. W. McNicholl, Boroughmuir	11. M. Liscovitz
Half Backs	**Half Backs**
10. M. Gosling, Cardiff	10. S. Gray
9. M. Weir, Fylde	9. S. Kelso
Forwards	**Forwards**
1. W. Dickinson, Richmond	1. E. Parthmore
2. M. Davidson, Blaydon	2. J. Lopez
3. H. Hopkins, Swansea	3. R. Ederle
4. D. Drew, Penzance	4. G. Kellerher
5. J. Piggott, Liverpool	5. C. Sweeney (Capt.)
6. J. Kempin, Leicester	6. J. Lombard
8. L. Connor, Waterloo	8. W. Frawmann
7. H. Jenkins, Llanelli	7. B. Haley
Replacements	**Replacements**
R. Westlake S. Kenny	16. T. Scott 19. B. Andrews
A. Bates M. Chalk	17. R. Bordley 20. G. Brackett
P. McCarthy K. Short	18. M. Ording 21. M. Conroy
Referee: R. C. Quittenton (Sussex Society)	
† International § Under 23 International * County	

[Gloucestershire Archives]

national sport, but not before the USA had won gold medals for rugby at the 1920 Olympics in Antwerp and the 1924 Olympics in Paris, where they

A lineout with Civil Service in white [Citizen]

defeated France 17-3 on their home turf. The game then effectively died in the USA and as an Olympic sport.

A revival came in the 1970s, with the USARFU founded in 1975. In 1977 The US Eagles set off on their first overseas tour. The highlight was to be a match against England at Twickenham, but this was preceded by five warm-up games, the first against the Civil Service at Kingsholm, where 7,000 turned out for this ground-breaking fixture, believed to be the largest attendance at any USA match up to this time. Entrance to the ground cost 50p, and the charge for the wing stands was 75p.

The Civil Service took to the field with a heavy pack, which caused problems for the Eagles in scrum and line-out throughout the game. The consequent lack of possession rather hampered the ability of the Americans to utilise their clear advantage in pace, although their occasional use of the long torpedo pass, more reminiscent of American Football, added to the entertainment. Civil Service gained an early lead with a penalty by Gosling, but two in reply by Jablonski put the USA ahead at half-time.

When a penalty was reversed in the second half, the Eagles went further ahead, but another Gosling penalty closed the gap. Civil Service were ruing four missed shots at goal, and conceded the clinching try in injury time at the end of the game. The star of the show was Halliday, who had learned his rugby growing up in South Africa, but now hailed from Iowa. He scored with a brilliant individual effort, swerving and weaving his way through the middle of the defence, ignoring an overlap outside him, but making it over the line. Jablonski, his Californian team mate, kicked the conversion.

Gloucestershire 21 Zimbabwe 12
1st October 1980

THE STANDS WERE sold out at Kingsholm for the visit of Zimbabwe, and gate receipts amounted to £2,680-20. The visitors were strengthened for this match by the arrival of John de Wet, an Olympic judo competitor, at prop, and Ray Mordt, the South African winger who

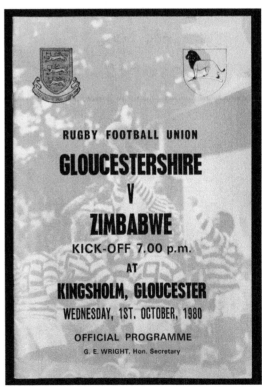

RUGBY FOOTBALL UNION
GLOUCESTERSHIRE
V
ZIMBABWE
KICK-OFF 7.00 p.m.
AT
KINGSHOLM, GLOUCESTER
WEDNESDAY, 1ST. OCTOBER, 1980
OFFICIAL PROGRAMME
G. E. WRIGHT, Hon. Secretary

[Gloucestershire Archives]

Gloucester v. Zimbabwe

GLOUCESTER White	Referee: R. Quittenton	ZIMBABWE Green and White
15	P. E. Butler *(Gloucester)*	FULL BACK	J. Peltzer	15
14	R. R. Mogg *(Gloucester)*	RIGHT WING	R. Mordt	14
13	C. J. Williams *(Bristol)*	CENTRE	R. Smith	13
12	A. Thomas *(Bristol)*	CENTRE	N. Mellett	12
11	A. J. G. Morley *(Bristol)*	LEFT WING	D. Delport	11
10	D. P. Sorrel *(Bristol)*	STAND OFF	F. Inocco	10
9	R. M. Harding *(Bristol)*	SCRUM HALF	I. Buchanan *(Capt.)*	9
1	G. A. F. Sargent *(Gloucester)*	PROP	J. de Wet	1
2	S. F. Mills *(Gloucester)*	HOOKER	C. Rogers	2
3	A. Sheppard *(Bristol)*	PROP	R. Halsted	3
4	N. Pomphrey *(Bristol)*	LOCK	M. Martin	4
5	J. H. Fidler *(Gloucester)*	LOCK	S. Barton	5
6	M. Rafter *(Capt.)* *(Bristol)*	FLANKER	K. Eveleigh	6
7	P. Wood *(Gloucester)*	FLANKER	K. Schlachter	7
8	R. Hesford *(Bristol)*	No. 8	N. Jenkinson	8

Replacements:
P. Howell *(Gloucester)*
K. Bogira *(Bristol)*
P. Cue *(Bristol)*
P. Kingston *(Gloucester)*
M. Preedy *(Gloucester)*
S. Gorvett *(Bristol)*

Replacements:
R. Gibbison
K. Delport
G. Mordt
L. Lachenicht
I. Marais
J. Locke

Touch Judges:
M. J. Morgan *(Bristol Referees' Society)*   A. M. J. Fisher *(Gloucester Referees' Society)*

[Gloucestershire Archives]

had played in all four tests against the British Lions that summer. The only change from the programme was Peter Kingston starting at scrum-half for Gloucestershire in place of Harding.

The Citizen match report bore the headline 'No Sanctions on The Boot', which referred not only to the political situation in Zimbabwe, but also to the stream of penalties awarded as a result of repeated transgressions for off-side, which allowed Peter Butler to capitalise. He kicked goals from four of them, and added a drop goal and a conversion for

Zimbabwe's replacement scrum half, Robert Delport gets the ball away from a ruck [Citizen]

a personal tally of 17 points. It was a hard game up front, and considered to be a good test of the home pack ahead of their County Championship opener against Cornwall.

Zimbabwe started with huge enthusiasm and at high speed, Mellett scored a brilliant try, and Inocco kicked the conversion and two penalties, but they tired as the match wore on and Gloucestershire lasted the pace better. The home side's try came from a break by Alan Morley, well supported by his back row as the ball went from Mike Rafter to Paul Wood to Bob Hesford, who scored. Perhaps the best tribute to the boot of Peter Butler came from some national press correspondents who came and saw and wrote that the value of a penalty should be reduced to two points.

South West Colts 22 Spain Colts 0 31st December 1980

THE SPANISH COLTS had finished third in the European Colts championship the previous season. The South West treated this as a warm-up before an England trial.

South West: M Blackmore (Tiverton); C Garcia (Bristol), N Stear (St Austell), T Bick (Berry Hill), M Stevens (Redruth); D Dagenhart (Bodmin), C Stanley (Walcot OB); A Harris, R Sprankling (Bridgwater & Albion), J Tearce (St Ives), R Durrant (Penzance & Newlyn), A Cooke (Hale), G Williams (St Ives), K Squires (Barnstaple), J Hall (Oldfield OB). Replacements: D Cooper (Redruth), K Plummer (Bristol), M Priest (Bideford), S Hucker (Bristol), R Foote (Stroud), A Stanley (Gordon League)

Spanish team not known

The Spanish Colts captain, Sergio Longney, presents the Spanish pennant to City Sheriff, Mike Pullon [Citizen]

Spain competed well in the first quarter, but faded badly and spent most of the second half deep in their own territory. They showed flair running the ball, and strength in the front row, taking three strikes against the head, but too often their skills let them down. South West led 10-0 at half-time, thanks to a try by Geoff Williams and two dropped goals, from Colin Stanley and Terry Bick, who was one of the game's outstanding players, showing pace and penetration whenever he had the ball. Two tries by John Hall and Alan Cooke in the second half, both converted by David Dagenhart, ensured a comfortable victory.

England Colts 33, Wales Youth 9
16th April 1983

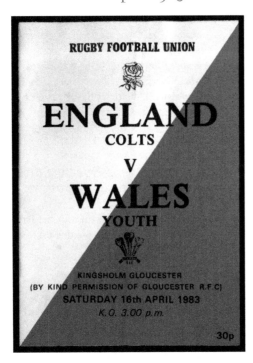

[Gloucestershire Archives]

[Gloucestershire Archives]

THIS WAS THE first Colts international to be staged at Kingsholm. England went into it on the back of a triumphant three-match tour of Italy. Brockworth's Chris Howard was included in the England side at the last minute, a car accident the evening before the game ruling Peter Moss out. Howard played on the wing, Whitworth moving to full-back.

Wales took the lead just before half-time with a fine solo try from Ben Childs, who ended up scoring all of his side's points, adding the conversion and a penalty. But England proved much the stronger in the second half, with Nigel Redman leading the way up front with a dominant performance in the line-outs. Exciting running with plentiful ball led to six tries for England, scored by Alston, Elkington, Shillingford, Packman, Whitworth and Walters. Chris Howard seized his chance, not only playing a full part in a stirring performance by the English backs, but also kicking two conversions and a penalty.

Action from the game, with England wing, Frank Packman, outnumbered as the Welsh go on the attack [Citizen]

South & South West 15 Romania 3
1st January 1985

THE MUDDY CONDITIONS at Kingsholm on a Tuesday evening helped to level the gulf in ability between the teams, and the final score failed to reflect the one-sided nature of the match. Although the referee earned a lot of credit for doing his best to allow play to flow, the game was not much of a spectacle for the 7,000 spectators, from whom £9,667-00 was taken on the gates.

[Gloucestershire Archives]

John Orwin dominated the front of the line-out, and Romania could not cope with his power in the rucks and mauls, nor with the commitment of Mike Teague and the magic of David Trick. Romania scored first through a penalty, but went behind just before the interval

SOUTH & SOUTH WEST DIVISION (Colours: White)		Position	ROMANIA (Colours: Yellow and Blue)	
15	C. MARTIN (Bath)	Full Backs	15	S. PODARESCU (Dinamo Bucuresti)
		Threequarters Right - Wing - Left		
14	D. TRICK (Bath)		14	M. TOADER (Steaua Bucuresti)
13	J. PALMER (Capt.) (Bath)	Right - Centre - Left	13	A. LUNGU (Dinamo Bucuresti)
12	A. REES (Bath)	Left - Centre - Right	12	V. DAVID (Steaua Bucuresti)
11	A. SWIFT (Swansea)	Left - Wing - Right	11	M. ALDEA (Dinamo Bucuresti)
		Half - Backs Stand Off		
10	S. BARNES (Bristol)		10	D. ALEXANDRU (Steaua Bucuresti)
9	R. HARDING (Bristol)	Scrum	9	M. PARASCHIV (Capt.) (Dinamo Bucuresti)
		Forwards Prop		
1	G. CHILCOTT (Bath)		1	G. LEONTE (Steaua Bucuresti)
2	K. BOGIRA (Bristol)	Hooker	2	V. ILCA (Grivita Rosie Buc.)
3	A. SHEPPARD (Bristol)	Prop	3	E. MELNICIUC (Bitlinta Baia Mare)
4	J. ORWIN (Gloucester)	Lock	4	I. CONSTANTIN (Reava Bucuresti)
5	N. REDMAN (Bath)	Lock	5	G. CARAGEA (Dinamo Bucuresti)
6	M. TEAGUE (Gloucester)	Blind Side	6	H. DUMITRAS (C.S.M. Suceava)
7	R. SPURRELL (Bath)	Open Side	7	O. MORARU (Grivita Rosie Buc.)
8	R. HESFORD (Bristol)	No. 8	8	S. CONSTANTIN (Ferul Constanta)

Replacements:
16 S. HALLIDAY (Bath)
17 R. HILL (Bath)
18 S. HOGG (Bristol)
19 P. BLAKEWAY (Gloucester)
20 D. PALMER (Bristol)
21 N. POMPHREY (Bristol)

Replacements:
16 I. BUCAN (Dinamo Bucuresti)
17 E. GRIGORE (Ferul Constanta)
18 S. DUMITRU (Ferul Constanta)
19 A. RADULESCU (Steaua Bucuresti)
20 T. COMAN (Steaua Bucuresti)
21 M. MARGHESCU (Dinamo Bucuresti)

Touch Judge: GUS THOMPSON (Glos. Soc.)   Touch Judge: GARTH CROMWELL (Glos. Soc.)

Referee: ANDRE PEY TAVIN (France)

[Gloucestershire Archives]

Mike Teague drives forward with John Orwin following up [Citizen]

Gareth Chilcott goes in against the Romanians [Citizen]

when Trick score a try on the end of a flowing move, and Stuart Barnes converted.

The second half was one-way traffic, but it was midway through the half before Barnes eventually slotted a penalty at his fifth attempt.

The final score came from a burst of speed by Trick, which allowed him to slip the ball for Chris Martin to race over. Barnes again converted, but overall was judged to have had a poor game, and this may have reduced the number of caps he went on to earn for England. Immediately after the match the national selectors announced their team for the international against Romania at Twickenham the following Saturday, and gave a first cap to Rob Andrew, who seized his chance and subsequently got the nod ahead of Barnes for many a future international.

England B 50 Spain 6
20th January 1991

ENGLAND AT THIS time were coached to play a tight game, and the senior side had just met with success in using such tactics to beat Wales with a rash of penalties. When their second string was faced with a muddy Kingsholm, it astonished many commentators to find them adopting an expansive approach, but it paid off handsomely. The selection of Fidel Castro at hooker caused some amusement amongst the crowd, but he gave no long speeches.

England B: J Lilley (Leicester); I Hunter (Northampton), P De Glanville (Bath), G Thompson (Harlequins), A Adebayo (Bath); D Pears (Harlequins), R Moon (Llanelli); V Ubogu, G Dawe (Bath), G Pearce (captain, Northampton), D Ryan (Wasps), N Redman (Bath), S Dear (Rosslyn Park), N Back (Leicester), B Clarke (Saracens)

Spain: F Puertas (Canoe); D Saenz (Arquitectura), S Torres (Santboiana), J Moreno (Arquitectura), C Garcia (Olympic); M Sanchez (Ciencias Sevilla), J Diaz (Getxo); J Alvarez (captain, El Salvador), F Castro (Getxo), A Altuna (Bayonne), A Malo (Santboiana), F Mendez (Cisneros), J Rodriguez, J Gutierrez (Arquitectura), E Illaregui (Saint Jean de Luz); Replacements: J-A Gonzalez (Valencia), J Candau (El Salvador)

Referee: Mr G Simmonds (Wales)

Rupert Moon extracting the ball from a ruck [Citizen]

A good-sized crowd acknowledged the commitment of a Spanish side which never stopped tackling, and enjoyed a measure of success in the line-out, but overall there was only one team in it. Wherever the ball went, there was Neil Back, winning the ball and adding continuity to movements. At half-time, England B were 18-0 ahead, and this encouraged them to run the ball at every opportunity in the second half during which they scored seven tries. The final tally was four goals, five tries and two penalties to one goal. Adebayo, Rupert Moon and Victor Ubogu scored two tries apiece, and the others came from Dean Ryan, Ian Hunter and a penalty try. Spain had the consolation of Sanchez kicking through and following up to score.

Gloucester 50 Portuguese President's XV 0
2nd April 1994

THE PORTUGAL NATIONAL side in all but name came to Kingsholm to play their first fifteen-a-side game for eleven months, although the previous week they had taken part in the Hong Kong sevens. This match was the start of their warm-up for European and World Cup qualifying matches.

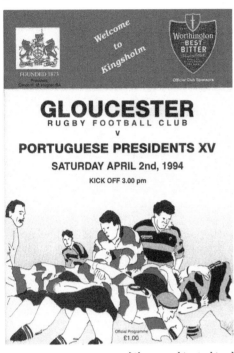

[Gloucestershire Archives]

Gloucester: T Smith; J Perrins, D Caskie, S Morris, A Sharp; D Cummins, B Fenley; T Windo, A Knight, P Jones, S Devereux, P Bell, P Glanville, I Smith (captain), M Nicholls

Portuguese President's XV: J Gomez; T Morais, V Durao, N Mourao, P Murinelo; N Durao (captain), P Fernandes; P Domingos, M Baptiste, E Meledo, A Andredo, A Pezus, A Cunha, P Paizenio, J Pires

Referee: Mr M Bayliss (Gloucester)

The home side made the better start and soon showed their intent to ship plenty of ball out to their backs. They strung enough passes together for Damien Cummins to get close and Pete Glanville, following

Mark Nicholls on the ball as Gloucester drive forward against the Portuguese [Citizen]

up, went over for the first try. A quick penalty by Don Caskie then caught the Portuguese napping and Tim Smith scored. Mark Nicholls was credited with the third from a pushover, which established a 19-0 lead at half-time. The Portuguese had demonstrated that they were keen to run with the ball, but their lack of weight denied them much possession.

Bruce Fenley launches another Gloucester attack watched by Matt Bayliss, the referee, on the left [Citizen]

A fierce hailstorm at the start of the second half contrasted starkly with the weather which the visitors had come from in Hong Kong. They then had to contend with Andy Sharp running in two tries from the left wing and Jerry Perrins running round behind the posts for another. Nuno Durao tried to break the Portuguese duck with a drop goal, but it went wide and Bruce Fenley and Simon Morris completed the haul of eight tries for Gloucester. Tim Smith added five conversions.

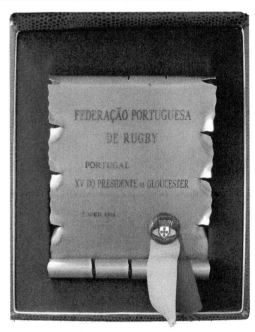

Memorial plaque presented by the Portuguese Federation [Gloucester Rugby]

England A 33 Italy A 9
19th February 1995

ENGLAND TESTED A selection of young players ahead of the Rugby World Cup. The playing surface at Kingsholm, which cut up badly as the game progressed, was very different from that which England would encounter for their next match in Durban. Italy fielded a more experienced side with ten capped players.

[Gloucestershire Archives]

England A: P Hull (Bristol); J Sleightholme (Bath), N Greenstock (Wasps), S Potter (Leicester), H Thorneycroft (Northampton); J Harris (Leicester), S Bates (captain, Wasps); R Hardwick (Coventry), R Cockerill, D Garforth (Leicester), L Dallaglio (Wasps), G Archer (Newcastle Gosforth), S Shaw (Bristol), R Hill, A Diprose (Saracens). Replacements: C Wilkins (Wasps), C C Clark (Bath)

Italy A: J Pertile (Roma); R Crotti (Milan), S Bordon (Rovigo), M Piovene (Padova), F Mazzariol (Treviso); L Troiani (captain, L'Aquila), G Faltiba (Sandona); G Grespan (Treviso), G de Carli (Roma), A Castellina (L'Aquila), M Capuzzoni (Milan), R Cassina (Casela), M Giacheri (Treviso), A Sgorlon (Sandona), D Scaglia (Tarvisum). Replacement: G C Cicino (L'Aquila)

Referee: Mr D Gillet (France)

England won the game in the second quarter when Harvey Thorneycroft, Steve Bates and Jon Sleightholme ran in tries. Richard Hill added another at the start of the second half. The referee then took over, and at times it seemed that he had swallowed his whistle, as he appeared

Lawrence Dallaglio shapes to pass to Stuart Potter as he is tackled by Stefano Bordon [Citizen]

to blow it every time he let out breath. England in particular incurred his displeasure, as the second half penalty count went against them 4-18, but the end result of this penalty extravaganza was that the teams shared six penalty goals equally.

South West 16 Western Samoa 31
9th December 1995

THIS WAS A dress rehearsal for the Samoan team before they played England at Twickenham, and followed their 15-15 draw with Scotland. England players, whether 1st team, A team or age group, were excluded from selection for the South West team. Pete Glanville was delighted with the venue, saying: 'it is always a bonus when these games are played at Kingsholm – it lifts me by 10% every time just to run out onto the ground'.

[Gloucestershire Archives]

South West Division GREEN SHIRTS, GREEN SHORTS			Western Samoa BLUE SHIRTS, WHITE SHORTS	
PAUL HULL (CAPT.) (Bristol)	FULL BACK	15	VELI PATU (Vaiala)	
NICK BEAL (Northampton)	RIGHT WING	14	BRIAN LIMA (Marist)	
ANDY TURNER (Exeter)	CENTRE	13	TOO VAEGA (Te Atatu/Moataa)	
SIMON ENOCH (Pontypridd)	CENTRE	12	KAISA TUIGAMALA (Scopa)	
PAUL HOLFORD (Gloucester)	LEFT WING	11	ALEX TELEA (Ponsonby)	
RICHARD DIX (Harlequins)	FLY HALF	10	DARREN KELLETT (Ponsonby/Marist)	
BRUCE FENLEY (Gloucester)	SCRUM-HALF	9	JOE FILEMU (Wellington)	
TONY WINDO (Gloucester)	PROP	1	MIKE MIKA (Otago University)	
KEVEN DUNN (Wasps)	HOOKER	2	ONEHUNGA MATAUIAU (Moataa)	
DAVE HINKINS (Bristol)	PROP	3	PETER FATIALOFA (Manukau/Marist)	
DAVE SIMS (Gloucester)	LOCK	4	FILIGA LIO FALANIKO (Marist)	
CRAIG YANDELL (Saracens)	LOCK	5	MARK BIRTWHISTLE (Suburbs)	
PETER GLANVILLE (Gloucester)	FLANKER	6	SAM KALETA (Ponsonby)	
JOEL PEARSON (Bristol)	FLANKER	7	SILA VAIFALE (Marist)	
EBEN ROLLITT (Bristol)	No.8	8	PAT LAM (CAPT.) (Auckland/Marist)	

REPLACEMENTS
CHRIS FORTEY (Gloucester)
CHRIS CLARK (Bath)
ROBERT FIDLER (Gloucester)
BEN HYDE (Taunton)
SIMON MARTIN (Bristol)
BEN STAFFORD (Bristol University)

REFEREE
Didier Mene (Fr)

REPLACEMENTS
MATTHEW VAEA (Marist)
ALAN AUFAGAVAIA (Suburbs)
FERETI FERETI (Apia)
GEORGE LATU (Vaimoso)
STEPHEN SMITH (Beaconsfield)
BRENDAN REIDY (Marist/St Pauls)

TOUCH JUDGES
Patrick Thomas (Fr)
Jean-Christophe Gaubor (Fr)

[Gloucestershire Archives]

South West started strongly and, although they missed an early penalty, Craig Yandell caught a lineout ball cleanly and was driven up

Western Samoa face up to the South West with their war dance before the kick-off
[Citizen]

Action from the game, including No 11, Paul Holford [Citizen]

to the goal line, where he peeled off from the maul and wriggled over for a try. Unfortunately for the Samoans, their captain, Pat Lam, suffered a knee injury and had to be replaced, but Darren Kellett got them onto the scoreboard with a penalty. Richard Dix responded with a dropped goal to restore the South West's lead, but it did not last long. Joe Filemu, Sam Kaleta and Kaisa Tuigamala were all involved in a move which put Veli Patu over for the first Samoan try. Dix kicked his second dropped goal, but Too Vaiga set up a try for Mark Birtwhistle, which Kellett converted to establish a 15-11 lead for the visitors at half-time.

South West were soon on the back foot in the second half and although heroic defence saw Glanville turn over a ball to prevent a score, Paul Holford tackle Brian Lima into touch and Beal stop Vaiga and Lima. Kellett did kick two penalties before a Samoan back row move had the ball going via Filemu and Patu to Alan Autagavaia to score. South West were down but not out and Paul Hull made a good break, carried on by Bruce Fenley, who sent a long pass out to Simon Enoch, who raced over for a try. But Samoa had the last word with a try from Telea after a fabulous run by Lima.

The Third and Most Golden Age of Gloucestershire Rugby

DURING THE FIFTEEN seasons, 1969-84, Gloucestershire appeared in eight County Championship finals, including seven in succession, and won four of them. Kingsholm was a particularly happy hunting ground for the County during this era. And yet it all started rather inauspiciously in 1969-70, when the County kicked off with a so-called friendly against Glamorgan at Bridgend. The heavy 14-38 defeat gave little clue as to what was to come. But a narrow 12-9 victory over Cornwall at Redruth in the first County Championship match augured well, and set the County up for the next game at Kingsholm.

Gloucestershire 28 Devon 17
8th November 1969

GLOUCESTERSHIRE: P M Knight (St Luke's College); P R Hillard (Bristol), J A Bayliss (Gloucester), J R Gabitass (Bristol), K R Morris (Gloucester); J T Hopson (Gloucester), J F Morris (Lydney); A J Rogers, J V Pullin, B A Dovey, D E J Watt (Bristol), A Brinn, P Hayward (Gloucester), D M Rollitt (captain, Bristol), R Smith (Gloucester)

Devon: R Codd (St Luke's College); M Maynard (Exeter), B Davies (Plymouth Albion), J Bevan, G Angell; R Whitcombe, A Pearn (St Luke's College); P Baxter (Exeter), S Delve (Torquay Athletic), N Bradford (Exeter), T Harvey (Newton Abbot), R Glazsher (Plymouth Albion), A Cole (captain, Exeter), A Hellins (St Luke's College), D Hughes (Exeter)

Referee: Mr R J Johnson (Kent)

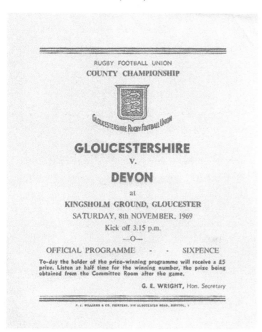

[Gloucester Rugby Heritage]

Terry Hopson opened the scoring for the home side, sprinting down the wing for a try which John Morris converted, but Devon soon struck back, Codd converting a try by Maynard, and Bevan then kicking them into the lead with a drop goal, before a try by Whitcombe extended it further. Although Morris dropped a goal for the home side, Devon exerted most of the pressure and were good value for their 11-8 lead at the interval.

Within a minute of the resumption, Gloucestershire had equalised with a superb try. Hopson and Bayliss brought off a scissors move

to a nicety. Bayliss brushed aside would be tacklers with near contempt before sending Hillard over wide out. Morris then nipped round a scrum, gave a dummy, and shot over near the posts; Hopson dropped a goal from more than 40 yards; and Morris added a couple of penalties. A couple of late scores by Devon merely added a little respectability to the score.

This was followed by a 23-6 success against Somerset at Bridgwater, and a comfortable quarter-final win, 23-3, over Hertfordshire at Croxley Green. A home semi-final beckoned at Kingsholm.

Gloucestershire 9 Lancashire 6
7th February 1970

THIS MATCH-UP BETWEEN old foes drew the largest crowd at Kingsholm for many a year, and they witnessed a tremendous tussle. Lancashire arrived as the title-holders, with twelve successive victories behind them in the County Championship.

*Part of the crowd packed into Kingsholm for the semi-final against Lancashire
[Journal]*

Gloucestershire: P M Knight (Bristol and St Luke's College); J Berry (Cheltenham), J Bayliss (Gloucester), J R Gabitass, M R Collins (Bristol); T Hopson (Gloucester), J Morris (Lydney); A J Rogers, J V Pullin, B A Dovey, D E J Watt (Bristol), A Brinn, P J Hayward (Gloucester), D M Rollitt (captain, Bristol), R Smith (Gloucester)

Lancashire: B J Driscoll (Manchester); A A Richards (Fylde), D Roughly, M A J Glover (Liverpool), C P Hanley; P S Mahon (Waterloo), E W Williams (New Brighton); M J Hindle (Fylde), P W Barratt, R S Jackson (captain, Broughton Park), A R Trickey (Sale), M M Leadbetter, A Neary (Broughton Park), E Lyon (Waterloo), D Seabrook (Orrell)

Referee: Mr D J Ford (Surrey)

Within a minute of the start, the referee called the captains together for the first of several lectures about the violence of the encounter, but there was no easing in the ferocity of the exchanges. Barry O'Driscoll kicked a penalty to give Lancashire the lead after five minutes, but Tony

[Gloucester Rugby Heritage]

Neary was lucky to stay on the pitch after two stern warnings from the referee.

Early in the second half, Gloucestershire equalised when Terry Hopson broke through and passed to John Bayliss who flung the ball out to Peter Knight, and he hurled himself over in the corner. They took the lead with a John Morris penalty. However, O'Driscoll equalised with a second penalty, and it looked as though that might be enough to take Lancashire through as the away team in a drawn match. However, ten minutes from time, Morris kicked another penalty, and Gloucestershire held out, thanks in part to Lancashire choosing to run a penalty even though it was within fairly easy kicking range.

Action during the game against Lancashire [Journal]

Gloucestershire were hot favourites for the final against Staffordshire at Burton-on-Trent, but went down to a shock 9-11 defeat.

Gloucestershire nearly fell at the first hurdle in 1970-71, scraping a 9-8 win against Devon at Torquay, before Somerset were entertained at Kingsholm.

Gloucestershire 14 Somerset 0
14th November 1970

THERE WAS A very poor turnout for this game, which was put down to both the inclement weather and the England game against Fiji

being televised simultaneously.

Gloucestershire: R Etheridge (Gloucester); M R Collins (Bristol), R White (Cheltenham), A Morley (Bristol), P M Knight (St Luke's College); P Simmons (Rosslyn Park), J P Morris (Lydney); B A Nelmes, J V Pullin, A J Rogers, D E J Watt (Bristol), A Brinn (Gloucester), D M Rollitt (captain), R C Hannaford (Bristol), R Smith (Gloucester)

Somerset: J S Waterman (captain, Bath); B Thompson (Bristol); M C Beese (Liverpool D C Tyler (Bristol), C Brown (Weston-super-Mare), S Perry, M C Lloyd (Bath); B A Dovey (Bridgwater and Albion), A Parfitt (Bath), R Farthing (Taunton), R J Orledge, P M E Heindorff (Bath), P Costelloe (Rosslyn Park), R Lye, T Martland (Bath)

Referee: Mr R A Harding (Surrey)

[Gloucester Rugby Heritage]

Gloucestershire were totally dominant throughout the first half, during which Somerset rarely made it out of their own territory, and yet the lead was a mere eight points at half-time. These points were scored when Alan Morley broke away to put Charlie Hannaford in next to the posts; John Morris converted, and White kicked a penalty.

In the second half Somerset may have realised that everything was against them when a Gloucester dog ran onto the pitch and seemed to disturb Farthing as he lined up an easy penalty; the kick went wide. White made no such mistake when he had a penalty chance free of canine interference, and Peter Knight rounded things off with a try in the corner.

Cornwall were subdued 9-3 at Bristol, and the group was won again. The County returned to Bristol for the quarter-final against Dorset & Wilts, which was won 18-3. This meant a long trip north for the semi-final at Gosforth, where a narrow victory over Northumberland was secured 9-6 at the last gasp, John Gabitass scoring the winning try in the last minute of injury time. Gloucestershire were through to their second successive final, but this time it was to be played at Kingsholm.

Gloucestershire 3 Surrey 14
6th March 1971

A CAPACITY CROWD OF 18,000 packed into Kingsholm on a cold and windy day. They had high hopes of success for the home side, despite Surrey's multi-national array of stars. Surrey committee members wearing bowler hats were prominent towards the front of the stand. Although their team had shared the title with Durham four seasons previously, they had never won it outright. Their captain was Bob Hiller, which added to the entertainment, since he had a booming voice to go with his booming boot, and frequently employed it in repartee with the inhabitants of the Shed. B Russell (Richmond) was a late replacement for Kennedy at Hooker for Surrey.

Gloucestershire team & officials before the match [Gloucester Rugby Heritage]

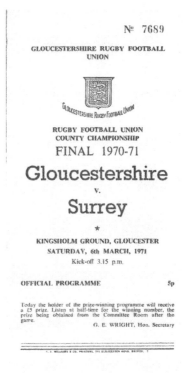

№ 7689

GLOUCESTERSHIRE RUGBY FOOTBALL UNION

RUGBY FOOTBALL UNION
COUNTY CHAMPIONSHIP
FINAL 1970-71

Gloucestershire
v.
Surrey
★
KINGSHOLM GROUND, GLOUCESTER
SATURDAY, 6th MARCH, 1971
Kick-off 3.15 p.m.

OFFICIAL PROGRAMME   5p

Today the holder of the prize-winning programme will receive a £5 prize. Listen at half-time for the winning number, the prize being obtained from the Committee Room after the game.

G. E. WRIGHT, Hon. Secretary

T. J. WILLIAMS & CO. PRINTERS, 314 GLOUCESTER ROAD, BRISTOL, 7

[Gloucestershire Archives]

[Citizen]

GLOUCESTERSHIRE		SURREY	
Colours: White		Colours: Red and White	
15. E. STEPHENS Gloucester	Full-Back	15. *R. HILLER (Captain) Harlequins	Full Back
	Three-quarters		Three-quarters
14. P. KNIGHT Bristol & St. Luke's College	Right Wing	14. R. C. CUNIS Rosslyn Park	Right Wing
13. P. J. Simmons Rosslyn Park	Right Centre	13. C. T. GIBBONS London Welsh	Right Centre
12. †D. DIAMOND Loughborough College	Left Centre	12. *R. H. LLOYD Harlequins	Left Centre
11. M. R. COLLINS Bristol	Left Wing	11. *J. M. NOVAK Harlequins	Left Wing
	Half Backs		Half Backs
10. J. GABITASS Bristol	Stand Off	10. *I. D. WRIGHT Northampton	Stand Off
9. J. SPALDING Gloucester	Scrum Half	9. *N. C. STARMER SMITH Harlequins	Scrum Half
	Forwards		Forwards
1. R. COWLING Gloucester		1. †N. P. HINTON Richmond	
2. *J. V. PULLIN Bristol		2. *K. M. KENNEDY London Irish	
3. B. G. NELMES Bristol		3. *M. G. ROBERTS London Welsh	
4. †A. BRINN Gloucester		4. *A. F. McHARG London Scottish	
5. N. JACKSON Gloucester		5. *T. G. EVANS London Welsh	
6. *C. R. HANNAFORD Bristol		6. A. M. PHILLIPS London Welsh	
8. *D. M. ROLLITT (Captain) Bristol		8. *T. M. DAVIES London Welsh	
7. †R. SMITH Gloucester		7. *J. TAYLOR London Welsh	

*International   †Trialist

Touch Judge: N. Jones (Gloucester Society)   Touch Judge: J. Williamson (London Society)

Referee: R. F. Johnson (Kent)

[Gloucestershire Archives]

Gloucestershire kicked off into the wind, and, on his debut for the County, Eric Stephens nearly made a perfect start for the home side in the second minute, when his penalty kick hit the bar but failed to go over. In the event it was Surrey who opened the scoring when Alastair McHarg, a unique number 8 who popped up in all sorts of unlikely positions around the field, hacked through and scored under the posts for an easy conversion by Bob Hiller. Surrey continued to monopolise possession, and put Wright into position to kick two dropped goals, which built an 11-0 lead at half-time.

Stephens revived the hopes of the Kingsholm crowd with a simple penalty from in front of the posts, but the Surrey pack continued to dominate, and in the closing minutes John Novak shook off two half-hearted tackles and raced over for a try midway out. Hiller's conversion hit the post and stayed out, but by then it mattered not. Gloucestershire now had the unenviable record of losing in their last five County Final appearances.

Bob Hiller kicking with Alistair McHarg and Paddy Hinton [Citizen]

A lineout during the final [Journal]

Gloucestershire 24 Monmouthshire 8
7th October 1971

IN 1971-72, AN early season win at Kingsholm restored confidence after a 12-52 thrashing by Glamorgan at Penygraig. Only sloppy finishing prevented a larger margin of victory. Ron Etheridge was man of the match for his 'sound covering, superb handling, clearances under pressure and occasional sorties in attack'.

Gloucestershire: R Etheridge (Gloucester); D Turley (Lydney), A J Morley, C J Williams, P M Knight; J H Gabitass (Bristol), J A Cannon (Clifton); M A Burton (Gloucester), D N Evans (Bristol), G Sargent (Lydney), J A Fidler (Cheltenham), D E J Watt (captain, Bristol), J A Watkins (Gloucester), D M Rollitt (Bristol), R Smith (Gloucester)

Monmouthshire: B Anthony (Newbridge); R Parry (Ebbw Vale), I Taylor (Pontypool), A Tovey (Ebbw Vale), G Collins (Pontypool); M Grindle (captain), G Turner; G Howls (Ebbw Vale), A Williams (Newbridge), G Price (Pontypool), C Jones (Ebbw Vale), R Bendall (Newbridge), G Evans (Ebbw Vale), C Davies (Newbridge), G Evans (Newport) [This the team as selected and in the programme, but there were unrecorded changes before kick-off, which accounts for Browning scoring two tries even though not on the team sheet]

Referee: Mr W J Fowler (Gloucestershire)

The first score was a penalty by Sargent, but Monmouthshire soon equalised with a try from Tony Browning. The home side were ahead again when a quick tap penalty went to Nick Evans, who shrugged off several tackles as he powered over; Sargent added the conversion. The early sequence of scoring was repeated when Sargent kicked a second penalty and Browning scored a second try. Then 'Evans made a brilliant interception but his hack through was fielded by Mike Grindle. From behind his goal the Monmouthshire captain tried to find touch but Peter Knight caught the kick and was over before anyone realised it.' A second try for Knight put his side well ahead and he also had a hand in the final score when he cut inside and, being collared, found Turley on hand to take the scoring pass. It was not a good day for kickers – Sargent managing only three successes from seven attempts, whilst Brian Anthony failed with all but one of his seven shots for Monmouthshire.

When it came to the County Championship, Gloucestershire slipped up in Cornwall, but wins against Devon and Somerset were enough to earn a group play-off against Somerset, which was staged at Kingsholm.

Gloucestershire 24 Somerset 0
8th January 1972

THERE WAS SOME controversy over the team selections because Alan Brinn and Mike Burton of Gloucestershire and Mike Beese of Somerset were stood down from this match ahead of their first England caps the following Saturday. This was normal practice at the time, but it was alleged that the chief England selector actually wanted them to play.

Gloucestershire: E J F Stephens (Gloucester); P M Knight, C J Williams, J R Gabitass, A J Morley (Bristol); R L Redwood (Cheltenham), J A Cannon (Clifton); A J Rogers, J V Pullin (Bristol), R J Cowling (Gloucester), D E J Watt (captain, Bristol), N A Jackson (Gloucester), D M Rollitt, R C Hannaford (Bristol), R Smith (Gloucester)

Somerset: B Thompson (Bath); D Turner (Weston-super-Mare), D G Tyler (Bristol), C Hunt (Weston-super-Mare), M R Collins (Rosslyn Park); G A Phillips, R Harding; N K Carter (Bath), J R White (Bristol), B A Dovey (captain, Bridgwater and Albion), P M B Heindorff (Bath), R J Orledge (Bristol), R Lye, D J Gay (Bath), D A Phillips (Bristol)

Gloucestershire team [Journal]

Referee: Air Commodore G C Lamb (RAF and London)

After only ten minutes, Eric Stephens, the Gloucestershire full-back and goal kicker, had to leave the field with an injury to his mouth. He returned later, but was put out on the wing, and relinquished his goal kicking duties. After Bob Redwood had failed in his stead, Jon Gabitass succeeded with two penalty shots, and Peter Knight finished off a fine three-quarter move by diving over in the corner to give Gloucestershire a 10-0 lead at half-time.

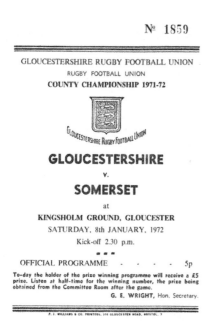

[Gloucestershire Archives]

Early in the second half this lead was extended when Alan Morley crossed for a try which Gabitass converted. Exchanges became somewhat tigerish, the referee's whistle was prominent, and when Dave Watt sought to debate one penalty, another ten yards was conceded. A second try for Morley and another by Charlie Hannaford completed the scoring, but not before Stephens had been helped off the field for a second time, having been battered from all sides by friend and foe alike. In a comedy of errors, Peter Knight blundered in trying to clear, Somerset tried to take advantage, Stephens stopped them with a tackle near the line, the ball went back to Redwood, who cleared hurriedly, and the ball smashed into the back of the head of the unfortunate Stephens.

Gloucestershire went on to beat Berkshire 38-19 at Bristol in the quarter-final, and Middlesex 19-16 at Richmond in the semi-final. They had to travel away again for the final against Warwickshire at Coventry, but they prevailed 11-6, thanks to tries by Alan Morley and Charlie Hannaford. Gloucestershire thus won their first County Championship title since 1937.

Gloucestershire 24 Cornwall 6
21st October 1972

THE FOLLOWING SEASON, Gloucestershire started the defence of their title in some style at Kingsholm, with a side containing eight internationals. Cornwall, led by 'Stack' Stevens tried to disrupt with kick and rush tactics, but never really threatened when faced with a polished performance by the Champions.

Gloucestershire: P Butler; A Morley, J Bayliss, C Williams, P M Knight; J Gabitass, J Cannon; R Cowling, J V Pullin, M Burton, D E J Watt (captain), A Brinn, J Watkins, R C Hannaford, R Smith

Cornwall: P Winnan; K Plummer, F F Johns, J Cocking, S Tiddy; D Yelland, G Thomas; D B Stevens (captain), R Harris, T A Pryor, J Blackburn, D Collins, R Thomas, R Corin, P Hendy

Referee: Mr P E Hughes (Manchester)

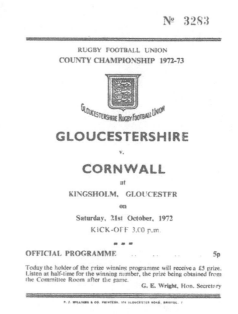

[Gloucestershire Archives]

Cornwall took an early lead from a Winnan penalty, but Gloucestershire struck back when, from 20 yards out, Dick Smith took the ball at the tail of a line-out and sliced through the defence to score beneath the posts. Peter Butler kicked the conversion and then a penalty to establish a 9-6 lead by the time that Gloucestershire turned round and had the wind at their backs.

In the second half, Alan Brinn, John Bayliss and Dick Smith all came close to scoring before Alan Morley finally got over the line; Butler again converted. Winnan responded with a penalty, but it did little to stem the tide. Butler replied in kind and then converted Morley's second try to polish off a good afternoon's work.

An 18-18 draw against Devon at Exeter led to a play-off again being necessary to determine the South West Group winner. This was greeted with some dismay because of the fixture congestion which resulted. A strong body of opinion argued that points scored or points difference should be taken into account to decide the outcome at the group stage. Nevertheless the decider at Kingsholm was well worth the entrance money, and produced a riveting last quarter.

Gloucestershire 22 Devon 19
9th December 1972

Gloucestershire: P E Butler (Gloucester); A J Morley (Bristol), R Jardine, J A Bayliss, J Dix; R L Redwood (Gloucester), J Morris (Lydney); M A Burton (Gloucester), J V Pullin (captain, Bristol), R F Cowling, A Brinn (Gloucester), D E J Watt (Bristol), J A Watkins (Gloucester), D M Rollitt (Gloucester), R Smith (Gloucester)

Devon: R Staddon (captain, Exeter), A Mort (St Luke's), R Friend (Plymouth Albion), A Jeffrey (Exeter), R Warmington; N Bennett (St Luke's), A Pearn (Bristol); P Baxter (Exeter), B Curry (Plymouth), D Pulford (Devonport Services), J Scott, J Baxter, A Cole (Exeter), A Hollins (Bedford), M Rafter (St Luke's)

Referee: Mr N R Sanson (Berkshire)

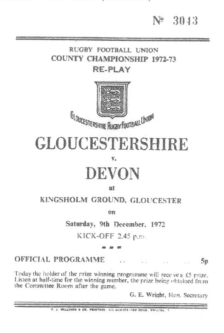

[Gloucestershire Archives]

THE GAME DEVELOPED into a goal kicking duel between Alan Pearn and Peter Butler who were the two leading points scorers in the country at the time. Alan Morley scored two tries in the first half, and with Butler converting one and kicking two penalties, Gloucestershire turned round with an apparently comfortable 16-6 lead.

But two tries in as many minutes from Devon plus a conversion and penalty saw the lead change hands, and Gloucestershire found themselves defending desperately. Penalties came thick and fast in the final quarter, with Butler kicking two out of five, and Pearn missing two. Gloucestershire had salvaged a draw in the final minute of the group game between these teams, and Devon had the opportunity to return the favour in the last minute of this match. But Pearn's kick shaved the outside of the tip of a post to send Gloucestershire into the quarter-finals, and a home tie against Oxfordshire.

Gloucestershire 39 Oxfordshire 12
13th January 1973

UP AGAINST THE reigning champions at Kingsholm, Oxfordshire were labelled as clear underdogs, and the pundits were right. Gloucestershire did not by any means have everything their own way, but they were far too strong for their opponents.

Gloucestershire: P E Butler; A J Morley, J Johnson, R Jardine, P M Knight; R L Redwood, J Morris; R F Cowling, J V Pullin (captain), G Sargent, J Fidler, A Brinn, D M Rollitt, M J Potter, J N Haines

Oxfordshire: P Raybould; R Reynolds, I Ray, R O P Jones (captain), D S Kilgour; R P Tupper, A Baraclough; R A J Lewis, A Jenkins, M R Jones, R A Powell, J S Harwood, R T Davies, R McCarthy, R G A Sankey

Referee: Capt P Lillington

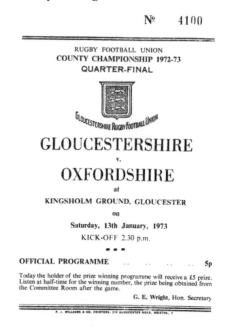

[Gloucestershire Archives]

This was another match in which Peter Butler ruled the roost with his goal kicking, converting all five of his side's tries, and kicking four out of five penalty attempts. The tries were scored by Alan Morley, Gordon Sargent (taking a scissors pass from Johnson to barrel over under the posts), Peter Knight (a solo effort starting on the left touchline and ending with a try out on the right), John Morris and John Pullin. In a dominant forward performance, Alan Brinn, Mick Potter, Dave Rollitt and Gordon Sargent were outstanding.

Gloucestershire went on to have home advantage for the semi-final and final, both being played at the Memorial Ground, Bristol, where they first edged out Eastern Counties 7-6, before falling at the final hurdle to Lancashire 12-17.

Gloucestershire 15 Monmouthshire 9
1st October 1973

THE VISITORS ARRIVED at Kingsholm fresh from a victory over Japan a few days previously, but showed little of that form in this game.

Gloucestershire: T Hamilton; J Berry (Cheltenham), P C Johnson (Clifton), R Jardine (Gloucester), D T Crabbe (Lydney); D Pointon, C Thomas (St Paul's College); B G Nelmes (captain, Cardiff), F C Reed, P J Blakeway, N A Jackson (Gloucester), R Hughes, K Binns (St Paul's College), D B W Owen (Gloucester), F J Russell (Stroud)

Monmouthshire: G Fuller (Newport); R Harris (Abertillery), J Martin (Newbridge), P Evans (Cardiff), A Barwood (Abertillery); M Grindle (Ebbw Vale), M Brickell (Abertillery); J McGreedy (Newbridge),

G Williams (Newport), M Dowling (Newbridge), L Jones (Newport), E Phillips (Newbridge), D Haines (Newport), C James (Tredegar), G Evans (captain, Newport)

Referee: Mr H J Williams (Gloucestershire)

Gloucestershire enjoyed a very good first half, in which their lock, Bob Hughes of St Paul's College and Neath, was the star, playing a part in all three of his side's tries. They took the lead after 15 minutes when the backs made for the right corner flag, Hughes' blonde head appeared in the middle of the action, Frank Russell made a dash for the line and when he was brought down, Kelvin Binns was on hand to go over. Hughes initiated the second, seizing on a loose ball and exchanging passes with Russell, before the ball went via Richard Jardine to David Crabbe, who scorched across the line. In first half injury time, Hughes and Jardine again featured in a move sparked by Johnson which ended in Berry nipping across on the left for the third try. Meanwhile Martin Brickell had kicked a penalty for the visitors, so it was 12-3 at half-time

In the first minute of the second half, Tim Hamilton had to go off after receiving a set of studs in his ear, John Berry moved to fullback and Binns was pulled out of the pack onto the wing. Monmouthshire struck back with two Brickell penalties to narrow the gap, but Pointon, with his seventh goal shot, finally found the target with a penalty to make the result safe.

Gloucestershire 21 Devon 9
20th October 1973

THIS WAS BILLED as the annual clash between the respective kicking talents of Peter Butler and Alan Pearn, and so it proved.

Nº 1021

RUGBY FOOTBALL UNION
COUNTY CHAMPIONSHIP 1973-74

GLOUCESTERSHIRE
v.
DEVON
at
KINGSHOLM GROUND, GLOUCESTER
on
Saturday, 20th October, 1973
KICK-OFF 3.00 p.m.
- - -

OFFICIAL PROGRAMME 5p

Today the holder of the prize winning programme will receive a £5 prize. Listen at half-time for the winning number, the prize being obtained from the Committee Room after the game.
G. E. Wright, Hon. Secretary.

P. J. WILLIAMS & CO. PRINTERS, 114 GLOUCESTER ROAD, BRISTOL, 7

[Gloucestershire Archives]

In the first half, Butler kicked five penalties and Pearn three, although his third provoked a roar of disapproval from the crowd, when he took a short penalty, but kicked it at the referee, who immediately gave another penalty, with Pearn this time choosing to kick at goal. The second half was not much different, Butler winning by two penalties to nil. After they were behind by nine points, Devon were forced to try running the ball, but every attack was snuffed out by a resolute Gloucestershire defence.

TEAMS

GLOUCESTERSHIRE Colours Red		DEVON Colours White with narrow green hoops	
15 P. R. BUTLER GLOUCESTER	Full Backs	15 R. STADDON (Capt.) EXETER	
14 *A. J. MORLEY BRISTOL	Three Qtrs. Right Wing	14 A. MORT ST LUKES COLLEGE	
13 P. JOHNSON CLIFTON	Right Centre	13 G. FABIAN DEVONPORT SERVICES	
12 R. JARDINE GLOUCESTER	Left Centre	12 R. FRIEND PLYMOUTH ALBION	
11 R. ETHERIDGE GLOUCESTER	Left Wing	11 M. SLEMEN ST LUKES COLLEGE	
10 D. POINTON ST PAULS COLLEGE	Half Backs Stand-off	10 G. JONES DEVONPORT SERVICES	
9 C. THOMAS ST PAULS COLLEGE	Scrum-Half	9 A. PEARN BRISTOL	
1 R. J. COWLING GLOUCESTER	Forwards	1 M. BRADFORD EXETER	
2 *J. V. PULLIN (Capt.) BRISTOL		2 D. FUGE PLYMOUTH ALBION	
3 *M. A. BURTON GLOUCESTER		3 P. BAXTER EXETER	
4 *A. BRINN GLOUCESTER		4 J. SCOTT ST LUKES COLLEGE	
5 N. JACKSON GLOUCESTER		5 N. DIMENT EXETER	
6 *J. A. WATKINS GLOUCESTER		6 M. RAFTER ST LUKES COLLEGE	
8 *D. M. ROLLITT BRISTOL		8 C. MILLER DEVONPORT SERVICES	
7 J. HAINES GLOUCESTER		7 M. CONNOLLY DEVONPORT SERVICES	

* Internationals

Touch Judge : N. P. JONES (GLOS. REFEREES SOCIETY)	Referee : N. J. MURPHY (HAMPSHIRE REFEREES SOC)	Touch Judge : N. DOYLES (DEVON REFEREES SOC.)

[Gloucestershire Archives]

The County went on to a magnificent semi-final victory, 27-15, against Warwickshire at Coventry, and then won the final, 22-12 against Lancashire at Blundellsands.

County Champions in 1974 [Gloucester Rugby]

Gloucestershire 18 England Under-23 12
24th April 1974

ENGLAND'S YOUNG PRETENDERS were pitched against the County Champions at Kingsholm on a Wednesday evening. They found it hard going up front, and conceded five strikes against the head in the scrums.

Gloucestershire: P Butler; R Clewes, R Jardine (Gloucester), C Williams, A J Morley (Bristol); D Pointon (St Paul's College), R Harding; A J Rogers, J V Pullin (captain, Bristol), B Nelmes (Cardiff), A Brinn, J Fidler, J Haines, J A Watkins, D Owen (Gloucester)

England Under-23: W H Hare (Nottingham); P J Squires (Harrogate), C P Kent (Oxford University), S Jackson (Upper Clapton), R Wain (Moseley); W N Bennett (Bedford), S J Smith (Sale); R F Locker (Harlequins), J A G D Raphael (captain, Northampton), J Croasdell (Loughborough Colleges), R M Wilkinson (Bedford), N Mantell (Rosslyn Park), G Phillips (Northampton), P Hendy (St Ives), R Hesford (Durham University)

Referee: Capt P Lillington (London & Army)

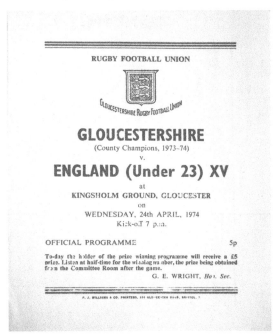

[Gloucestershire Archives]

Gloucestershire were penalised at the first scrum, and Dusty Hare kicked the goal, but Peter Butler soon levelled the scores with a kick in front of the posts, and added two more before half-time to establish a 9-3 lead.

When the second half got underway, Peter Squires gathered the ball from a cross-kick by Bennett to score the first try, and Hare's conversion made it 9-9. Butler put his team ahead with another penalty, before Richard Jardine slipped an inside pass to Alan Morley, who sliced through the middle for a try, converted by Butler. That settled the match, although Hare kicked a final penalty near the end.

Gloucestershire 14 Somerset 3
26th October 1974

IN 1974-75, GLOUCESTERSHIRE again opened their campaign at Kingsholm, but looked far from Champions with a lack-lustre performance.

Gloucestershire: P E Butler (Gloucester); A J Morley (Bristol), J A Bayliss (captain), R Jardine, S Dix; R L Redwood, P Kingston; M A Burton (Gloucester), D V Protheroe, B G Nelmes (Cardiff), J Fidler, A Brinn, J A Watkins (Gloucester), D M Rollitt (Bristol), J H Haines (Gloucester)

Somerset: D G Tyler (Bristol); R Simon (Taunton and St Luke's College), M C Beese (Bath), R Hazzard (Weston-super-Mare), A P J Hicks; J Horton, M Lloyd (Bath); M Fry, J E White (captain, Bristol), J Meddick (Bath), R Orledge (Bristol), J Luff (Cardiff), B Lease (Ebbw Vale), R Lye (Bath), D Phillips (Bristol)

Referee: Mr D M Browning (Midlands)

Somerset started far the better and deserved an early lead from a Hazzard penalty. The only fire from the home side came when they were penalised at a scrum, and 'Meddick was KO'd from what looked suspiciously like a Gloucestershire punch'. Somerset missed with a couple of drop kicks at goal, and a couple of penalty attempts, but Peter Butler took his one opportunity to equalise just before the interval. With the wind and the sun at their backs in the second half, Gloucestershire looked a more dangerous proposition, with John Watkins to the fore, even more prominent than usual with his head swathed in bandages. Butler kicked a penalty from his own half to take the lead, and John Haines and Alan Morley scored tries late in the game to secure the victory.

Brinn supported by Burton against Somerset [Journal]

Gloucestershire went on to win the group, and to beat Hertfordshire 15-12 at Bristol in the quarter-final, before returning to Kingsholm for the semi-final.

Gloucestershire 28 Warwickshire 3
22nd February 1975

WARWICKSHIRE HAD ROMPED through to this stage with four easy victories and a points advantage of 177-29, whilst Gloucestershire had struggled to progress. But they were able to take comfort from the fact that they had triumphed the previous season after similarly inauspicious early results had led up to their win against Warwickshire at Coventry. Chris Williams won his first County cap at outside-half, where he was paired with Peter Kingston, with whom he had played for England Schools, St Paul's College and Lydney. The gate was some 12,000, and they were treated to one of the best performances ever seen from their County side.

Gloucestershire: P E Butler (Gloucester); A J G Morley (Bristol), J A Bayliss (captain), R Jardine, S Dix (Gloucester); C Williams (Headingley), P Kingston (Gloucester); BG Nelmes (Cardiff), V D Protherough (Moseley), M A Burton, A Brinn, J H Fidler, J A Watkins (Gloucester), D M Rollitt (Bristol), J H Haines (Gloucester). Replacements: A J Hignell, K Phelps (Bristol), D T Crabbe, N A Jackson, E A Pinkney (Gloucester).

Warwickshire: P A Rossborough (captain); R E Barnwell, P S Preece, G W Evans, D J Duckham; A R Cowman, C Gifford (Coventry); Tom J Gallaher (Solihull), T John Gallaher, J M Broderick, I R Darnell, D Simpson (Coventry), M Malik, R Piggott, T Cowell (Rugby). Replacements: W J Gittings, P Evans, P Coulthard, J E Barton (Coventry), T Temple (Nuneaton), F Melvin (Rugby).

Referee: Capt P L Lillington (London)

[Gloucestershire Archives]

Richard Jardine makes a tackle and knocks the ball loose, watched by John Bayliss, the Gloucestershire captain[Journal]

Before the match, John Bayliss told his men 'Don't forget, we're not taking any prisoners', and they followed his orders to the letter with a demolition job which astonished even the most fervent of home supporters. Bayliss led from the front and made the first bustling break, Peter Kingston scuttled round the blind side of a scrum, sold a dummy and shot into the corner for the first try. Peter Butler kicked the conversion from the touchline to a roar of acclaim. Two penalties by Butler gave Gloucestershire a 12-0 lead at half-time, and Warwickshire appeared utterly demoralised.

Warwickshire on the attack [Citizen]

There was no let-up in the second half. Kingston pounced on a loose ball and scooted over for his second try. John Watkins looked as though he had picked up a clothes line when he surged over with several opponents being towed along in his wake. Butler converted at his second attempt and rounded things off with another penalty. Warwickshire's gifted backs rarely saw the ball, and they had only a Rossborough penalty to show for their efforts.

The Gloucestershire pack was utterly dominant, with the front row mauling their opponents to distraction in the scrums, John Fidler dominating the line-outs, and the back row causing mayhem in both attack and defence. At half-back, Peter Kingston played a blinder and Chris Williams had a dream debut. John Bayliss and Richard Jardine gave their opposite numbers a torrid afternoon, and Peter Butler had the satisfaction of another polished performance including four penalties and two conversions from the touch-line, success made all the sweeter by the presence of the current England full-back in the Warwickshire ranks. After this magnificent performance, it was no surprise that Gloucestershire chose to return to Kingsholm for the final.

Gloucestershire 13 Eastern Counties 9 22nd March 1975

THIS WAS THE sixth successive appearance by Gloucestershire in the County Championship final, with Alan Brinn playing, and Denis Power coaching, in all of them. For Eastern Counties this was their first visit to Kingsholm, and they were up against the reigning champions, but there was not thought to be much between the sides, with Eastern Counties having looked impressive when seeing off Lancashire in their semi-final. Particular interest was shown in Alan Morley and Jacko Page, who had just won their first international caps for England against Scotland. A huge crowd, conservatively estimated at 15,000, turned up in vile weather, along with all the England selectors, who met the next day to choose the party to tour Australia that summer.

Eastern Counties took the lead with a penalty goal after two minutes, and led for most of the first half. The heavy pitch made life

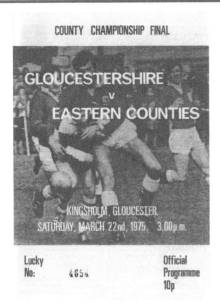

[Gloucestershire Archives]

Burton, Protherough and Fidler are the Gloucestershire players in this action shot against Eastern Counties [Citizen]

GLOUCESTERSHIRE (All Red)			EASTERN COUNTIES (All White)	
15.	P.E. Butler (Gloucester)	Full-back	A.M. Jorden (Bedford, capt.) * +	15.
14.	A.J.G. Morley (Bristol) *	Right wing	D.J.K. McKay (Rosslyn Park)	14.
13.	J.A. Bayliss (Gloucester, capt.)	Centre	J.P.A.G. Janion (Richmond) *	13.
12.	R. Jardine (Gloucester)	Centre	I.R. Vinter (Saracens)	12.
11.	S. Dix (Gloucester)	Left wing	D.M. Wyatt (Bedford)	11.
10.	C.G. Williams (Headingley)	Outside-half	P.L. Byrne (Blackheath)	10.
9.	P. Kingston (Gloucester)	Scrum-half	J.J. Page (Northampton) * +	9.
1.	B.G. Nelmes (Cardiff)	Prop	C.J. Bailward (Bedford)	1.
2.	V.D. Protherough (Moseley)	Hooker	P. d'A. Keith-Roach (Rosslyn Park) +	2.
3.	M.A. Burton (Gloucester) *	Prop	K.B.P. Cairns (Saracens)	3.
4.	A. Brinn (Gloucester) *	Lock	A.K. Rodgers (Rosslyn Park) +	4.
5.	J.H. Fidler (Gloucester)	Lock	N.O. Martin (Harlequins) * +	5.
6.	J.A. Watkins (Gloucester) *	Flanker	A.L. Bucknall (Richmond) * +	6.
8.	D.M. Rollitt (Bristol) *	No. 8	A.T. Hollins (Bedford)	8.
7.	J.H. Haines (Gloucester)	Flanker	S. Callum (Upper Clapton)	7.
	*International		+ Blue	

Replacements:
D. Pointon (St. Paul's College)
D.T. Crabbe (Gloucester)
C. Patterson (Bristol University)
M.J. Nicholls (Gloucester)
N.A. Jackson (Gloucester)
E.A. Pinkney (Gloucester)

Replacements:
D.J. Ling (Ipswich)
T. O'Hanlon (Richmond)
J. Stokoe (Blackheath)
G. Swainson (Blackheath)
P. Holden (Saracens)
B. Carter (Moseley)

Referee: A.A. WELSBY (Manchester Society)

Touch Judge: N.P. JONES (Gloucester Society)   Touch Judge: D.M. ROBINSON (Eastern Counties & London Society)

[Gloucestershire Archives]

The Gloucestershire team against Eastern Counties [Journal]

difficult for everyone and evened up the contest, although the home pack was dominant in the scrums, and big John Fidler ruled the lineout throughout. There were some tetchy moments and a few punches were thrown. But Richard Jardine engineered an opportunity for Alan Brinn, who had been playing in the Gloucester second team for the previous month, to hurtle over for a try on the stroke of half-time. This allowed his side to turn round 4-3 ahead, a useful advantage since they had chosen to play into the wind and rain in the first half.

It was a horrible day for place kicking, and it looked as though this might prove decisive when Peter Butler missed three penalties in the first half and his first three attempts in the second. But Jorden was having an equally torrid time, and Butler eventually came good when it mattered most, putting over a 45-yard effort. Towards the end, the ball squirted out to Barry Nelmes, who looked around for someone to pass to but, failing to find anybody to right or left, ran through an inviting gap straight ahead, and slipped the ball to Stuart Dix who raced in at the corner. Butler kicked a superb conversion from the touchline, the ball glancing over off the bar. Eastern Counties scored a late try through Callum, one of the few forwards not engaged in a bout of fisticuffs at the time. Wyatt, who had taken over the kicking duties from Jorden, put over the conversion, but it was too little too late, and Gloucestershire had retained the Championship title more convincingly than the scoreline might suggest.

Gloucestershire 9 Monmouthshire 4
14th October 1975

GLOUCESTERSHIRE STARTED THEIR 1975-76 season with another of those so-called friendlies against a Welsh county. Stuart

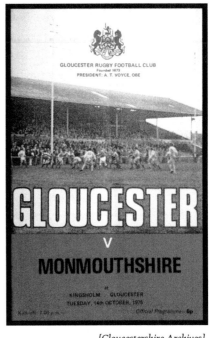

[Gloucestershire Archives]

GLOUCESTERSHIRE	
White	
Full Back	
15. P. Butler	Gloucester
Three Quarters	
14. J. Dix	Gloucester
13. R. Jardine	Gloucester
12. J. Bayliss (Capt.)	Gloucester
11. D. Pointon	Gloucester
Half Backs	
10. C. Williams	Headingly
9. P. Kingston	Gloucester
Forwards	
1. B. Nelmes	Cardiff
2. J. Pullin	Bristol
3. M. Burton	Gloucester
4. R. Powell	Llanelly
5. J. Simonett	St. Paul's Coll.
6. M. Rafter	Bristol
8. D. Rollit	Bristol
7. J. Haines	Gloucester

MONMOUTHSHIRE	
Dark Blue	
Full Back	
15. D. Thomas	Cross Keys
Three Quarters	
14. A. Haines	Cross Keys
13. A. Tovy	Ebbw Vale
12. A. Thomas	Abertillery
11. I. Evans	Ebbw Vale
Half Backs	
10. K. James	Abertillery
9. A. Lewis	Abertillery
Forwards	
1. A. Faulkner	Pontypool
2. R. Windsor	Pontypool
3. C. Price	Pontypool
4. R. Floyd	Pontypool
5. W. Evans	Pontypool
6. T. Cobner (Capt.)	P'pool
8. C. Davies	Newbridge
7. T. Gardner	Ebbw Vale

Referee: N. P. JONES (Gloucestershire Society)

[Gloucestershire Archives]

Dix and John Fidler dropped out injured just before the match and were replaced by Dave Pointon on the wing, even though he was normally playing at stand off for his club, and John Simonett. Despite the preponderance of local players in the County side, the programme cover was a little one-eyed in advertising the game as Gloucester v Monmouthshire. The visitors featured the famed Pontypool front row.

The most notable feature of this match was a sending off. Bobby Windsor, Monmouthshire's international hooker, was severely lectured by the referee after punching John Pullen, his England international opposite number, which followed a similar assault on John Bayliss. Windsor merely conceded a penalty, but these incidents probably contributed to another decision later in the game. Early in the second half, British Lions scrum-half Allan Lewis put his knee into John Haines after the Gloucester flanker had killed a vital loose heel on his own line and Lewis was immediately given his marching orders. He left to a stunned silence around the ground. There was obvious resentment in the Monmouthshire camp at the decision, and one of their officials commented after the game 'we could have accepted it had it been Windsor. But it is not difficult to understand why we are so bitter over the referee's decision'.

Monmouthshire scored the only try of the game in the first half when Gloucestershire won a lineout and immediately moved the ball across their backs, but a bad pass from Richard Jardine to Pointon was picked up by winger Tony Haines who stepped inside Butler to score. In the second half, the home side secured sufficient territory against 14 men to allow Peter Butler to kick three penalties and thereby secure the win, but it was far from convincing as Haines missed four kickable penalty attempts for Monmouthshire in the second half.

Gloucestershire did not return to Kingsholm for the rest of the season, but retained the Championship for a third year in succession, the crowning glory a splendid 24-9 demolition of Middlesex at Richmond in the final. All Gloucestershire's points were scored by Peter Butler, with a try, a conversion and six penalties.

During the summer of 1976, the RFU proposed that Gloucestershire and Oxfordshire should be merged, but this was stoutly resisted by the Gloucester Club amongst others.

In 1976-77, Gloucestershire enjoyed handsome victories over Cornwall at Bristol, 30-0, and Devon at Exeter, 27-15, but the group was decided at Kingsholm.

Gloucestershire 22 Somerset 3
13th November 1976

Gloucestershire: D P Sorrell (Bristol); R Clewes (Gloucester), C J Williams (Bristol), R Jardine, R R Mogg; C G Williams, P Kingston; G A F Sargent, S G F Mills, M A Burton (Gloucester), N Pomphrey (Bristol), S B Boyle, J A Watkins (captain, Gloucester), D M Rollitt, M Rafter (Bristol)

Somerset: D G Tyler (Bristol); P Kent (Bridgwater), C Kent (captain, Rosslyn Park), M C Beese (Bath), R S Carter; R Hazzard (Bristol), F Came (Swansea); M J Fry (Bristol), S Luxmore (Clifton), R R Speed (Bristol), B Jenkins (Bath), A Shorney (Avon & Somerset Police), R Lye (Bath), S J Davies (Bristol), N Turner (Rosslyn Park)

Referee: Mr P Hughes (Lancashire and Manchester)

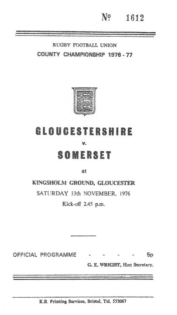

No. 1612

RUGBY FOOTBALL UNION
COUNTY CHAMPIONSHIP 1976 - 77

GLOUCESTERSHIRE
v.
SOMERSET

at
KINGSHOLM GROUND, GLOUCESTER
SATURDAY 13th NOVEMBER, 1976
Kick-off 2.45 p.m.

OFFICIAL PROGRAMME   -   -   -   5p
G. E. WRIGHT, Hon Secretary.

K.B. Printing Services, Bristol. Tel. 553067

[Gloucestershire Archives]

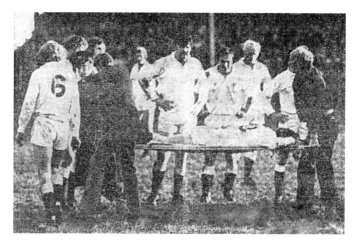

Chris Williams knocked out of the game [Journal]

CHRIS WILLIAMS WAS laid out in a tackle early on, and had to be stretchered off with severe concussion, to be replaced by Ian Wilkins (St Paul's College, Cheltenham), but Somerset restarted with a penalty. David Sorrell then had three penalty shots at goal; the first was successful, and the second hit a post and came out. The third also rebounded off a

Came passes the ball out for Somerset [Citizen]

post, but this time was retrieved by Gloucestershire, and Richard Jardine dashed over unchallenged for a try, which established a 7-0 lead at half-time.

Hazzard reduced the arrears with a penalty, but a drop goal by Wilkins and two penalties by Sorrell built a winning margin, which was enhanced further when Nigel Pomphrey started a move which ended with Richard Mogg dashing over for a try wide out, which Sorrell converted.

Gloucestershire were back at Kingsholm a fortnight later to play their quarter-final.

Gloucestershire 37 Oxfordshire 12
27th November 1976

A TEAM PACKED WITH ten Gloucester players found another, John Orwin, lining up for the opposition.

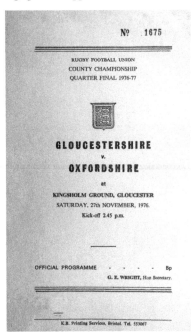

Gloucestershire Colours: Red		Oxfordshire Colours: White
15. *P. E. BUTLER Gloucester	Full Backs	15. M. HODGSON Oxford
14. R. CLEWES Gloucester	Right Wing	14. N. POLLARD Oxford
13. C. J. WILLIAMS Bristol	Right Centre	13. G. HORNER Henley
12. D. P. SORRELL Bristol	Left Centre	12. G. LEWIS London Welsh
11. R. R. MOGG Gloucester	Left Wing	11. E. SANDBACH Oxford
10. *C. G. WILLIAMS Gloucester	Outside Half	10. R. TUPPER Oxford
9. *P. KINGSTON Gloucester	Scrum Half	9. M. GROOM Oxford
1. G. A. F. SARGENT Gloucester	Forwards	1. G. McKENZIE Oxford
2. S. G. F. MILLS Gloucester		2. A. JENKINS Henley
3. *M. A. BURTON Gloucester		3. I. HEYWOOD Northampton
4. N. POMPHREY Bristol		4. J. MAWLE Bedford
5. S. B. BOYLE Gloucester		5. J. ORWIN Gloucester
6. *J. A. WATKINS (Capt.) Gloucester		6. D. OSBORNE Northampton
8. *D. M. ROLLITT Bristol		8. J. TAYLOR Oxford
7. M. RAFTER Bristol	*International	7. D. JACKSON (Capt.) Bedford
Replacements:		Replacements:
16. G. TROTT Stroud		J. WARD Henley
17. R. POWELL Llanelli		N. BLOODWORTH Henley
18. E. PINKNEY Gloucester		K. ALFREDS Henley
19. J. WALTER St. Paul's College		D. PITT Oxford
20. I. WILKINS St. Paul's College		R. KAYS Oxford Old Boys
21. R. HARDING Bristol		I. GALE Henley

Touch Judge: H. J. WILLIAMS Gloucester Referees' Society	Referee: K. A. PATTINSON North Midlands Referees' Society	Touch Judge: D. HOWARD Oxford Referees' Society

[Gloucestershire Archives]

Chris Williams, C J Williams and Bob Clewes. The men of the match were John Watkins, consistently first at the breakdown to rip the ball free, and Peter Kingston, who provided an impeccable service to Chris Williams and a dangerous threat down the blind side.

No. 1675

RUGBY FOOTBALL UNION
COUNTY CHAMPIONSHIP
QUARTER FINAL 1976-77

GLOUCESTERSHIRE
v.
OXFORDSHIRE

at
KINGSHOLM GROUND, GLOUCESTER
SATURDAY, 27th NOVEMBER, 1976.
Kick-off 2.45 p.m.

OFFICIAL PROGRAMME - - - - 5p

G. E. WRIGHT, Hon Secretary.

K.B. Printing Services, Bristol. Tel. 553067

[Gloucestershire Archives]

Peter Kingston sets up Gloucestershire's first try against Oxfordshire [Citizen]

Oxfordshire applied early pressure, but missed a penalty, and the home side started to dominate, only for Sandbach to make an interception and run the length of the field to score by the posts. It proved to be a short-lived advantage. The Citizen reported that 'the visitors would have stood more chance of stopping the Severn Bore than the splendid Gloucestershire pack'. Peter Butler ended with 17 points from two tries, three conversions and a penalty. Other try scorers were Richard Mogg, Nigel Pomphrey,

This win earned Gloucestershire an away trip to play Lancashire at Vale of Lune, where they were undone 15-19, their first defeat in the Championship since March 1973, which had been at the hands of the same opponents.

The RFU implemented a system of fixed dates for County games in 1977, as a result of which the Gloucester Club said that Kingsholm would not be available for County group matches on Saturdays from the

1978-79 season onwards. Bristol lined up alongside Gloucester in trying to minimise disruption of club fixtures, and in proposing that the County matches be played midweek under lights. The Gloucestershire Union insisted that matches should continue to be played on Saturdays, and that was how it stayed, despite Somerset saying they would be happy to play midweek. Meanwhile the first group match of the 1977-78 championship was played at Kingsholm, on a Saturday.

Gloucestershire 20 Devon 6
8th October 1977

IT WENT DOWN well with the Kingsholm faithful that ten Gloucester players were selected for the home side, but the steady drizzle was not appreciated on or off the field.

Gloucestershire: P Butler; R J Clewes, R Jardine (Gloucester), P Johnson (Clifton), R Mogg (Gloucester); D Sorrell (Bristol), P Kingston; P Blakeway, F Reed, M Burton (Gloucester), N Pomphrey (Bristol), J Fidler (Gloucester), M Rafter (captain, Bristol), D Rollitt (Richmond), J Haines (Gloucester)

Devon: G Fabian (Devonport Services); K Butterworth, F Donovan (Torquay Athletic), P Arbourne, J Jenkins (Exeter); L Ware (Plymouth Albion), G Milford; C Mills (Exeter), J Lockyer, B Steer (Plymouth Albion), J Scott (Rosslyn Park), P Ackford (Plymouth Albion), G Warne (Crediton), D Folland (Barnstaple), R Catchpole (Plymouth Albion)

Referee: Mr M J Fisk (Yorkshire)

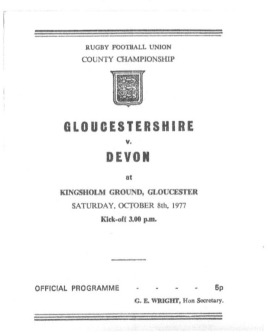

RUGBY FOOTBALL UNION
COUNTY CHAMPIONSHIP

GLOUCESTERSHIRE
v.
DEVON

at

KINGSHOLM GROUND, GLOUCESTER
SATURDAY, OCTOBER 8th, 1977
Kick-off 3.00 p.m.

OFFICIAL PROGRAMME - - - - 5p
G. E. WRIGHT, Hon Secretary.

[Gloucestershire Archives]

'Devon heeled from the first scrum…Ware made a break, but ran into the Gloucestershire pack. The outside half received treatment, but recovered later.' Indeed his penalty was the only score of the first half. But three penalties early in the second half by Peter Butler put the home side ahead, before Dave Rollitt pulled the ball down from a lineout and fed Peter Kingston, who passed out along the line. Richard Jardine dummied and with Rollitt in support Bob Clewes went diving over in the corner. The Gloucestershire pack took over towards the end of the game. Mike Burton crashed over under the posts, and Rollitt capped off the afternoon nicely with a pushover try.

A line-out during the Devon game [Journal]

Dave Rollitt out-numbered by Devon players as he pursues the ball [Citizen]

Having won the South West group, Gloucestershire went on to win their semi-final 19-9 against Kent at Blackheath, but lost the final 7-10 to North Midlands at Moseley.

Gloucestershire 38 Somerset 3
28th October 1978

IN THE 1978-79 group stage, Gloucestershire enjoyed one of their biggest victories at Kingsholm. They started as favourites, and included nine Gloucester players. Fixtures between these neighbouring rivals were not renowned for open and entertaining rugby, but this was a remarkable exception. Gate receipts were £2,398.20.

Gloucestershire: P Butler; R Clewes (Gloucester), A Morley (Bristol), P Johnson (Clifton), R Mogg; C Williams, P Kingston; G

Sargent, S Mills (Gloucester), J Doubleday, N Pomphrey (Bristol), S Boyle, J Watkins (Gloucester), S Gorvett, M Rafter (captain, Bristol)

Somerset: P Pearce (Clifton); P Simmons (Bath), N Hunt (Bristol), C Bird (Bath), D Newman (Bristol); J Palmer, D Murphy (Bath); G Paul (Weston-super-Mare), S Luxmore (Clifton), J Meddick (Bath), A Shorney (Avon and Somerset Police), N Gaymond (Bristol), F Hartley (captain, Exeter), S Davies (Bristol), S Jones (Bath)

Referee: Major P Lillington (Army & London)

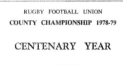

RUGBY FOOTBALL UNION
COUNTY CHAMPIONSHIP 1978-79

CENTENARY YEAR

GLOUCESTERSHIRE
v.
SOMERSET

at

KINGSHOLM GROUND, GLOUCESTER
SATURDAY, 28th OCTOBER, 1978
Kick-off 2.30 p.m.

OFFICIAL PROGRAMME   -   -   -   -   **5p**

G. E. WRIGHT, Hon Secretary.

[Gloucestershire Archives]

Peter Kingston breaks away against Somerset [Citizen]

Steve Gorvett gets a pass away to John Watkins in the Somerset match [Journal]

It was all Somerset from the start and they scored first with a John Palmer drop goal, but within two minutes Gloucestershire had taken the lead, when Peter Kingston broke up the narrow side of a ruck and put Chris Williams in for a try converted by Peter Butler. Then three first-half tries in eight minutes settled the match. A combined handling move by forwards and backs, which ended with Richard Mogg racing through, was the best of the bunch. Gordon Sargent scored another, and Kingston broke from a maul near the Somerset line and turned inside to send Steve Gorvett crashing over. As tempers rose in the scrum, half-time was taken at 20-3.

In the second half, Williams set up an attack which saw Alan Morley running in from thirty yards for an excellent try, matched by an equally excellent conversion by Butler. Mogg almost got over for his second try, but from the resulting ruck, Kingston fed Mike Rafter who strolled over unopposed; Butler converted. And Gloucestershire rounded off the match with some breath-taking passing, which saw John Watkins take the ball on the left wing and send Morley in for the final try just before the end. The ever-reliable Butler added the two points to the acclaim of a delirious crowd which had seen him kick five conversions, most of them from wide out.

The County returned to Kingsholm for their semi-final, which they went into as clear favourites.

Gloucestershire 13 Middlesex 21
9th December 1978

GLOUCESTERSHIRE HAD NOT suffered defeat at Kingsholm since the Surrey game in 1971, and had appeared in eight of the nine previous county finals. Nevertheless a large and highly vocal following failed to prevent the game slipping away from them in the last quarter.

Gloucestershire: P Butler; R Clewes (Gloucester), A Morley (Bristol), B Vine (Lydney), L Dick; I Wilkins, P Kingston; G Sargent, S Mills (Gloucester), J Doubleday, N Pomphrey (Bristol), S Boyle, J Watkins (Gloucester), S Gorvett, M Rafter (captain, Bristol)

Middlesex: C S Ralston (Rosslyn Park); C Lambert (Harlequins), D Croydon (Saracens), R Gordon (London Scottish), T Morrison (London New Zealanders); T Bryan (Northampton), J Montgomery (Metropolitan Police), T Caxton (Harlequins), I Thomas (London Welsh), C McGregor (Saracens), M Hess, C W Ralston (Rosslyn Park), A Alexander (Harlequins), A Ripley, R Mordell (Rosslyn Park)

Referee: Mr P E Hughes (Lancashire & Manchester)

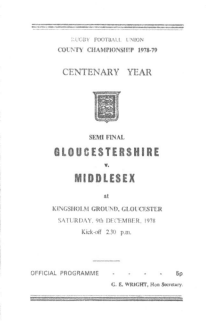

Gloucestershire started slowly, and conceded a try by Lambert and a conversion and penalty by Ralston. Although they rallied towards the end of the first half, they turned round 0-9 down. They kept up the pressure, steadily worked their way back into the game, and three penalties by Peter Butler brought the scores level, but Middlesex struck back with another try by Lambert, converted by Ralston, before Dick scored one for the home side. The missed conversion left Middlesex ahead,

Orwin wins a line-out against Middlesex [Citizen]

and they proved stronger at the death when a good move between Bryan and Gordon split the defence; Gordon touched down behind the posts and Ralston converted to seal a deserved if unexpected win.

The County had a good run in the 1979-80 Championship, but only one of the six games played was at home, and that at Bristol. The campaign ended with defeat in the final, 15-21, against Lancashire at Vale of Lune.

Gloucestershire 18 Somerset 3
8th November 1980

GLOUCESTERSHIRE CAME TO Kingsholm having beaten Cornwall 7-6 at Bristol, and Devon 18-16 at Torquay, so this win at Kingsholm clinched the South West group for the twelfth successive season. Gloucestershire had to make a late change to their side when Phil Blakeway dropped out through injury. Gate receipts were £3,447.20

Gloucestershire: P Butler; R Mogg, P Taylor (Gloucester), J Carr (Bristol University), L Dick Cheltenham); D Sorrell (Bristol), P Kingston; G Sargent (Gloucester), K Bogira, A Sheppard (Bristol), J Fidler, S Boyle (Gloucester), M Rafter (captain), R Hesford (Bristol), P Wood (Gloucester)

Somerset: N Hopkins (Bath); J Lane (Bristol), G Williams (Avon & Somerset Police), C Bird, D Trick; J Palmer, D Murphy; G Chilcott, S Luxmore, J Meddick (Bath), P Stiff (Bristol), A Shorney (Avon & Somerset Police), R Spurrell, G Parsons, R Lye (captain, Bath). Replacements: J Jeffrey (Clifton), E Liddiard (Avon & Somerset Police)

Referee: Mr C J High (Cumbria)

It was the home pack which won the game, and in particular the Gloucester powerhouse of John Fidler and Steve Boyle, ably supported by Paul Wood and Mike Rafter in the back row. Within two minutes of the kick-off, the ever dependable Peter Butler had kicked his first penalty, and he added two more before half-time. Butler and Palmer swapped penalties in the second half, and the result was finally put beyond doubt with the only try of the game – Paul Taylor took the ball in a scissors move and burst through the Somerset defence to score near the posts; Butler converted. The next round was played at Kingsholm only a week later.

Somerset put Carr on the ground but he has support arriving [Journal]

Referee: Mr P J Wakefield (Eastern Counties & London)

The home pack soon started the pulverising process, with John Fidler and Steve Boyle to the fore, but their backs did not make best use of the constant stream of good ball that was provided to them. The only score of the first half came when Paul Taylor broke through and was stopped only a yard short of the line, but flicked the ball to the man-of-the-match, the effervescent Paul Wood, who forced his way over for a try, converted by David Sorrell.

In the second half, Sorrell kicked a penalty and converted a try when Boyle burst over from a tap penalty. The highlight of the match came when Peter Kingston and Sorrell switched play to the blind side to put Richard Mogg away. He threw back his head, scorched past his opposite number on the outside, and beat two covering defenders with deft sidesteps off his left foot to race in at the corner; the crowd roared its approval.

This win set up a semi-final against Warwickshire, which was won 3-0 at Bristol, and so to the final at Kingsholm.

Gloucestershire 19 Buckinghamshire 0
15th November 1980

DESPITE ATROCIOUS CONDITIONS, this quarter-final was won at a canter by a Gloucestershire side who were held in the set scrums, but had the beating of their opponents in all other respects. Peter Butler had to drop out through injury and was replaced by Phil Cue.

Gloucestershire P Cue (Bristol); J Carr (Bristol University), C Williams (Bristol), P Taylor, R Mogg (Gloucester); D Sorrell (Bristol), P Kingston (Gloucester); J Doubleday, K Bogira, A Sheppard (Bristol), S Boyle, J Fidler (Gloucester), M Rafter (captain), R Hesford (Bristol), P Wood (Gloucester). Replacement: P Howell (Gloucester)

Buckinghamshire: P Williams (Aylesbury); P Barcilon (Saracens), T Williams (Aylesbury), P Southcott (Bedford), K Bennett (High Wycombe); S Tansley (Metropolitan Police), J Whitelock (captain, High Wycombe); P Rendall, A Simmons (Wasps), G Pearce (Northampton), M Rose (Borough Road College), J Bonner, G Ball, K Bonner (Wasps), B Hagan (Marlow)

[Gloucestershire Archives]

Gloucestershire 6 Northumberland 15
31st January 1981

ALTHOUGH THIS WAS the final of the County Championship, arguably the biggest game outside international matches at the time, the Gloucester club initially declined to host it, because they had a fixture scheduled at Kingsholm against Bridgend. But eventually the Club game was cancelled, and, on home turf, Gloucestershire were firm favourites to win the title. The fog which had been lingering earlier in the day lifted sufficiently to allow the 10,000 crowd reasonable visibility; £4,244.20 was taken on the gate. Northumberland were enjoying their centenary season, and celebrated it in the best possible way.

All seemed to be going according to plan for the home side as a Peter Butler penalty from wide out put them ahead, but a dropped goal by Johnson brought Northumberland level before the interval.

[Gloucestershire Archives]

Well into the second half a second penalty by Butler restored the home side's lead. Further chances came and went, most notably when a break by Lewis Dick sent the massive Nigel Pomphrey storming towards

THORN COUNTY CHAMPIONSHIP FINAL
GLOUCESTERSHIRE
Colours: White

15	P. E. Butler	Gloucester	Full Back
14	I. Dick X	Cheltenham	Right Wing
13	P. Cue	Bristol	Right Centre
12	P. Taylor	Gloucester	Left Centre
11	R. R. Mogg	Gloucester	Left Wing
10	D. Sorrell	Bristol	Stand Off
9	P. Kingston X	Gloucester	Scrum Half
1	G. A. F. Sargent	Gloucester	Prop
2	K. Bogira	Bristol	Hooker
3	A. Sheppard X	Bristol	Prop
4	N. Pomphrey	Bristol	Lock
5	J. Fidler	Gloucester	Lock
6	M. J. Rafter (Capt.) X	Bristol	Flanker
7	P. Wood	Gloucester	Flanker
8	R. Hesford	Bristol	No. 8

Replacements:
16	J. Carr	Bristol University
17	P. Howell	Gloucester
18	S. Baker	Gloucester
19	K. White	Gloucester
20	P. Blakeway X	Gloucester
21	S. Boyle	Gloucester

Touch Judge:
B. Abrahams East Midlands Referees' Society

Referee:
R. C. Quittenton Sussex London Society

THORN COUNTY CHAMPIONSHIP FINAL
NORTHUMBERLAND
Colours: Green with Red & Amber Hoops

15	R. Patrick	Gosforth	Full Back
14	J. Pollock	Northern	Right Wing
13	I. Tindle	Northern	Right Centre
12	R. W. Breakey	Gosforth	Left Centre
11	J. S. Gustard (Capt.)	Gosforth	Left Wing
10	D. Johnson	Gosforth	Stand Off
9	M. Young X	Gosforth	Scrum Half
1	C. White	Gosforth	Prop
2	R. Cunningham	Gosforth	Hooker
3	J. Bell	Gosforth	Prop
4	T. C. Roberts	Gosforth	Lock
5	S. Bainbridge	Gosforth	Lock
6	I. Richardson	Gosforth	Flanker
7	R. Anderson	Gosforth	Flanker
8	G. Smallwood	Northern	No. 8

Replacements:
16	W. Telford	Alnwick
17	T. Bell	Alnwick
18	I. Pringle	Morpeth
19	I. Ramage	Gosforth
20	P. Holden	Northern
21	C. Dixon	Tynedale

Touch Judge:
D. G. Crossley Bucks Referees' Society

X Indicates International

Les Jones with the ball, Mike Rafter and John Orwin in support [Citizen]

[Gloucestershire Archives]

the line, but Northumberland just managed to keep him out, before Butler came close to extending the lead when his dropped goal attempt shaved the post. With the fog rolling in, the score remained 6-3 and a hard-fought home victory in a fierce and unrelenting contest seemed to be on the cards.

But it was Northumberland who pulled out all the stops in the last few minutes and shocked the home supporters by upping their game and twice cutting through to score tries, both of which were converted. Their pack chased a cross-kick over the line for Terry Roberts to touch down, and Johnson's conversion gave them a 9-6 lead. The final nail in the coffin came only a minute later when Pollock scored in the corner after a strong run by Bainbridge, Johnson converting from a difficult angle.

Kingsholm was stunned, and all that could be heard at the end was a rendition of the 'Blaydon Races' by the small number of 'lads and lasses there, all with smiling faces', who had made the long journey south. Malcolm Young, the Northumberland scrum-half, retired after this game, his teammates unkindly claiming that he was the sole surviving member of the last Northumberland side to win the Championship (in 1898).

Gloucestershire 39 Devon 3
10th October 1981

Rugby Football Union

THORN EMI
COUNTY CHAMPIONSHIP

GLOUCESTERSHIRE
V
DEVON

Saturday 10th October 1981
KINGSHOLM GROUND
Kingsholm Road, Gloucester
KICK OFF 3p.m.

Cost of programme: 20p

[Gloucestershire Archives]

THIS WAS THE opening game of the new County Championship campaign.

Gloucestershire: P Cue; A Morley, J Carr (Bristol), S Parsloe, R Mogg; L Jones (Gloucester), R Harding (Bristol); G Sargent (Gloucester), K Bogira, A Sheppard, N Pomphrey (Bristol), S Boyle, J Orwin (Gloucester), M Rafter (captain), R Hesford (Bristol)

Devon: K Turton (Plymouth Albion); K Butterworth (Torquay Athletic), B Haine (Plymouth Albion), S Donovan (Exeter), P Drewett (Exeter University); S Webb, K Sumner (Exeter); W Davies (Devonport Services), B Priday, T Harris, S Day (captain, Exeter), C Pinnear (Exeter University), G Lovell (Plymouth Albion), G Jones (Torquay Athletic), G Baxter (Plymouth Albion). Replacement: T Woodrow (Exeter)

Referee: Mr F A Howard (Lancashire & Liverpool)

The home side put on a wonderful display of power rugby, with John Orwin, on his debut for the County, Steve Boyle, Bob Hesford and Nigel Pomphrey dominant up front, and Les Jones, also on debut at this level, the star behind the scrum. Devon were back-pedalling from the start, but in the early stages Gloucestershire failed to convert their dominance into points. Their best move involved glorious handling by Jones, Steve

Steve Boyle crashes over for the first of his two tries against Devon [Citizen]

Scrum half, Richard Harding, breaks away for Gloucestershire with John Orwin and John Carr in support [Citizen]

Gloucestershire 16 Lancashire 24
28th November 1981

GLOUCESTERSHIRE CAME INTO this match having lost to Lancashire at the same stage in 1977, and in the 1980 final. Mike Teague, already an England B player, got his first County recognition with a place on the bench. The crowd of 8,000 paid £7,884.30 to see an exciting and dramatic game, in which Lancashire's classy backs and lively forwards proved too good for the home side.

Gloucestershire: P Cue; A Morley, J Carr, P Taylor (Bristol), R Mogg; L Jones (Gloucester), R Harding (Bristol); M Preedy (Gloucester), K Bogira (Bristol), P Blakeway, S Boyle, J Orwin (Gloucester), N Pomphrey, M Rafter (captain), R Hesford (Bristol)

Lancashire: K O'Brien (Broughton Park); J Carleton (Orrell), A Wright, A Bond (Sale), M Slemen (Liverpool); P Williams (Orrell), S Smith (Sale); D Tabern, M Dixon (Fylde), D Southern (Orrell), W Beaumont (Fylde, captain), J Sydell (Waterloo), P Moss (Orrell), R Stevenson (Sale), K Moss (Liverpool)

Referee: Mr R Quittenton (London)

Parsloe, Gordon Sargent, Pomphrey and John Carr, but on the end of it Phil Cue dropped the scoring pass. However, by half-time, tries had come from Boyle and Hesford.

Immediately after the break, Cue made amends by sending Richard Mogg on his way for a magnificent try, which sent the crowd into raptures, but with 15 minutes to go Gloucestershire's lead remained stubbornly stuck at 18-3. Then the power came on, passes were taken, and Devon capitulated as Gloucestershire racked up a further 18 points, with tries from Boyle, Carr, Pomphrey and Alan Morley.

[Gloucestershire Archives]

Mike Rafter congratulates Bob Hesford for scoring a try against Devon [Citizen]

Gloucestershire went on to lose to Somerset but beat Cornwall, which was enough to win the group and set up a quarter-final against Dorset and Wilts, which was won 38-6 at Swindon. And so it was back to Kingsholm for the semi-final.

Alan Morley with Mike Rafter in support against Lancashire [Gloucestershire Archives]

John Orwin holds off Bill Beaumont and feeds the ball to Malcolm Preedy during the Lancashire match [Citizen]

Bob Hesford deflects a lineout ball to Richard Harding [Gloucestershire Archives]

Richard Harding passes the ball out for Gloucestershire [Gloucestershire Archives]

more O'Brien penalties had stretched the deficit to 13 points.

The home pack fought back with some powerful scrummaging, and put Phil Cue into a position to kick two penalties and Richard Harding to grab a gutsy try on the blindside. But the Lancashire backs put the game beyond reach with two tries coming from a scorching run by Slemen and a charge down of a Les Jones kick. Steve Boyle's try, converted by Jones, gave a glimmer of hope, but a fourth penalty by O'Brien rounded off a deserved Lancashire victory.

In 1982-83, Gloucestershire won the County Championship for the fourteenth time, more than any other county, beating Yorkshire 19-7 in the final at Bristol. Although they had three home games during the season, they were all played at Bristol.

In 1883-84, the format of the County Championship changed and Gloucestershire appeared in Division One. After away wins against Surrey, 22-3 at Sunbury, and Northumberland, 19-16 at Gosforth, they returned to Kingsholm for the match which would decide the division.

Gloucestershire 23 Yorkshire 6
12th November 1983

A HEAVY PROGRAMME OF club, divisional and international commitments meant that Gloucestershire went into this game without the benefit of a single training session. The game was advertised as a battle between the Gloucestershire pack and Yorkshire's speedy backs orchestrated by Alan Old.

Gloucestershire: S Hogg; A Morley, R Knibbs (Bristol), R Mogg (Gloucester), J Carr; S Barnes, R Harding (captain, Bristol); M Preedy, S Mills, P Blakeway, J Orwin, J Fidler, J Gadd (Gloucester), W Hone, R Hesford (Bristol)

Yorkshire: D Norton (Headingley); M Harrison, S Townsend (Wakefield), S Burnhill (Roundhay), R Underwood (Leicester); A Old (captain, Sheffield), H Jazyna (Morley); P Huntsman (Headingley), B Coyne (Middlesborough), J Tinker (Harrogate), P Jones (Nottingham), R Walters (Huddersfield), P Buckton (Liverpool), P Winterbottom (Headingley), P Lockyer (Moseley)

Referee: Mr R Parker (North Midlands)

[Gloucestershire Archives]

Gloucestershire chose to kick off into the wind, and were soon chasing the game. Kevin O'Brien kicked an early penalty, and then England and Lions captain, Bill Beaumont took a quick line-out throw from Mike Slemen to stroll through a static defence for the first try. By half-time, two

John Fidler and John Orwin bossed the line-outs, whilst Phil Blakeway and Malcolm Preedy scrummaged to great effect. This starved Yorkshire of possession and, although British Lion, Peter Winterbottom, was prominent in loose play, it set the basis for an impressive victory. John Carr took his chances well with two tries in the second half, and Bob Hesford scored another; Stuart Barnes converted one and kicked a penalty. Yorkshire had to feed off scraps, and were unable to engineer many holes in the home defence, so were confined to a brace of penalties by Alan Old. This impressive performance set up a semi-final against Middlesex, also played at Kingsholm, two weeks later.

Gloucestershire 13 Middlesex 12
26th November 1983

THE CROWD WAS certainly up for this match, the Citizen declaring that 'the County's adherent and partisan devotees gave Kingsholm the cup tie atmosphere which visiting supporters secretly admire and outwardly loath'.

Gloucestershire: S Hogg; A Morley, R Knibbs (Bristol), R Mogg, N Price (Gloucester); S Barnes, R Harding (Bristol); M Preedy, S Mills, P Blakeway, J Fidler, J Orwin, J Gadd (Gloucester), M Rafter (captain), R Hesford (Bristol)

Middlesex: N Stringer (Wasps); A Dent (Harlequins), R Gordon (London Scottish), R Cardus (Wasps), S O'Reilly (Metropolitan Police); M Williams, J Cullen (Wasps); P Curtis (Rosslyn Park), J Olver, M Claxton, W Cuthbertson, R Riddell (Harlequins), K Bowring (London Welsh), D Cooke (captain), C Butcher (Harlequins)

Referee: Mr D Thomas (North Midlands)

[Gloucestershire Archives]

Middlesex made the early running with a first minute penalty kicked by Nick Stringer, followed by his conversion of a try by prop Claxton, which was the result of excellent work by Williams, who then popped over a dropped goal. Gloucestershire had been having the better of the game territorially, but found themselves 0-12 down. Then the home forwards began to rumble. Alan Morley started the comeback with a try, and two penalties by Stuart Barnes reduced the deficit to two points by half-time.

In the second half the Gloucestershire pack dominated. John Fidler took the ball at will in the lineout, and Malcolm Preedy probably ran further with the ball in hand than the whole of his three-quarter line. A solitary Barnes penalty brought victory, but it was the fervour and intensity of the forward effort which set Kingsholm alight.

To those who had grown up with the parochial and hotly contested South West group matches at the start of each county season, it seemed strange to find Gloucestershire facing their neighbours, Somerset, in the County Championship final at Twickenham. But perhaps it made it all the sweeter when Gloucestershire prevailed 36-18 in front of 26,000 spectators.

Gloucestershire fielded a full strength side the following season to defend their title, although some counties did not. Nevertheless there was a memorable game against Yorkshire at Kingsholm.

Gloucestershire 30 Yorkshire 19
10th November 1984

LOCAL FANS WERE disappointed that the Gloucester contingent in this County Championship quarter-final was reduced before kick-off by the withdrawal of John Gadd and Steve Mills through injury, but at least this brought in Mike Teague. Four Gloucester players meant their lowest representation in the County side for many a year, but gate receipts still totalled £4,621-90.

Gloucestershire: P Cue: A Morley, R Knibbs, S Hogg (Bristol), A Richards (Gloucester); S Barnes, R Harding (Bristol); M Preedy (Gloucester), K Bogira, A Sheppard (Bristol), J Orwin (captain, Gloucester), A Blackmore (Bristol), M Teague (Gloucester), R Hesford (Bristol), D Pegler (Wasps). Replacements: M Trott (Clifton), S Everall (Cheltenham).

Yorkshire: D Norton (Headingley, captain); M Harrison, B Barley (Wakefield), J Buckton (Saracens), R Underwood (RAF); A Old (Sheffield), N Melville (Wasps); P Huntsman (Headingley), P Lazenby (Morley), J Tinker (Harrogate), M Verhoeven (Morley), A Fraser (Headingley), S Tipping (Sale), P Buckton (Liverpool), S Peacock (Army and Middlesborough). Replacements: P Gray (Roundhay), D Heron (Wakefield).

Referee: Mr R Parker (North Midlands)

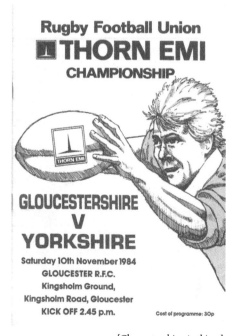

[Gloucestershire Archives]

The Gloucestershire team [Gloucestershire Archives]

Yorkshire started at a tremendous pace, and scored two tries in the first twelve minutes to open a 12-3 lead. John Buckton scored the first thanks to some feeble defence, and Mike Harrison went over for the second; Alan Old converted both. Gloucestershire had only a penalty goal by Stuart Barnes in response, but, with John Orwin and Mike Teague leading the charge up front, they fought back and scored two tries of their own. Ralph Knibbs, who had been shaky in defence, made amends with a solo run for a try which put his side back in contention. Barnes converted, and a pushover try by Bob Hesford, put Gloucestershire ahead 13-12 after 25 minutes. A dropped goal by Barnes and a penalty by Old saw the score progress to 16-15 by half-time.

John Orwin battling for possession at a line-out against Yorkshire [Citizen]

Early in the second half, the Kingsholm crowd roared their disapproval of a forward pass to Rory Underwood, but the referee saw it differently, and there was no stopping the England wing as he dived into the corner to put Yorkshire back in the lead, 19-16. However, Gloucestershire lasted the pace better, and got their noses ahead again with a try by Alan Morley.

With four minutes to go and a tense finish in prospect, there was a loudspeaker announcement that Somerset had won easily in the other group game, so Gloucestershire knew they had to win to stay in the competition. Captain Orwin later confirmed 'the players heard it loud and clear' and it galvanised them into a frenetic finish. Within seconds Mike

Teague went over for a try, and, although Barnes missed the conversion, Knibbs put the seal on their victory by dashing through for his second; Barnes converting.

Despite being hot favourites, Gloucestershire then lost their semi-final at Bristol, 9-14, to Notts, Lincs and Derbys.

This was the last season in which players from the top clubs participated in the County Championship. In February 1985, the Gloucester, Bristol and Bath clubs jointly told the Gloucestershire and Somerset County Unions that unless fixtures between Gloucestershire, Somerset and Devon were arranged for midweek, the major clubs would discourage their players from taking part. This was rather reminiscent of the situation almost a century earlier, when in 1890 the Gloucester Club only agreed to remain a member of the County Club if matches were played on weekdays.

It was recognised that travelling problems meant that fixtures with Cornwall should continue to be played on Saturdays. Gloucestershire and Somerset agreed to fall in line with the clubs' wishes, but Devon dug their heels in and refused to accept midweek fixtures. Consequently Gloucester refused to make Kingsholm available for matches, details of County matches were omitted from the Club's fixture lists, and players were asked not to play for the County.

Since 1984-85, county sides have been drawn largely or entirely from junior clubs, and matches have been played at the grounds of those clubs, the only exception being:

Gloucestershire 12 Cornwall 9
21st November 1987

A CROWD OF 3,500 was attracted to this Saturday match; the Gloucestershire coach was Charlie Hannaford.

Gloucestershire: S James (Lydney); C Howard (Rugby), J Powell (Berry Hill), C Allen (Moseley), M Speakman (Clifton); G Price (Lydney), S Baker (Stroud); G Sargent (captain), G Mann (Gloucester), A Brookes (Malvern), P Wallace (Matson), P Miles (Bath), C Scott (Cheltenham), M Teague, M Longstaff (Gloucester). Replacements: P Howell (Lydney), D Jones (Cinderford)

Cornwall: N Allen (Camborne); B Trevaskis (Falmouth/Bath), T Mead (Saltash/Devon & Cornwall Police), G Champion (captain, Truro/ Devon & Cornwall Police), S Rogers (Camborne); P Bradley (RAF/ Redruth), D Rule (Camborne); J May (Redruth), B Andrew (Camborne), S Lord (Camborne/Royal Navy), M Haag (Bath/St Ives), T Cook (Hayle/ Devon & Cornwall Police), A Curtis (Redruth), A Bick (Penzance-Newlyn), G Williams (St Ives). Replacements: T Willis (Redruth), P Elliott (Redruth/Royal Navy)

Referee: Mr R C Quittenton (London)

Although ahead 9-3 at half-time, the home side was lucky to win. Cornwall was the better side throughout the second half, and at 9-9 with a quarter of the game still to go looked likely winners. But Cornish attacks were repeatedly thwarted by gritty defence, and a fourth penalty by Howard, against two penalties and a dropped goal, was enough to see Gloucestershire home. This victory left them as winners of the South West group, but proved to be the last County game played at Kingsholm, although the ground has continued to host County Cup Finals and North Gloucestershire Combination Cup Finals.

The Divisional Championship

WITH THE WITHDRAWAL of the major clubs from the County Championship in 1985, Gloucester agreed to support a Divisional Championship, which was proposed by Gloucestershire and Kent, and put in place by the RFU for the 1985-86 season. They were immediately rewarded with the selection of Kingsholm to host one of the first Divisional fixtures. Even though these matches were effectively England trials, the competition failed to excite much interest amongst rugby supporters.

South West 9 Midlands 19
14th December 1985

ALTHOUGH PLAYED ON a Saturday, only £3,425-75 was taken on the gates. The small crowd soon turned to jeering the poor showing of the South West team, although the selection of ten Bath players and only three from Gloucester served to heighten the level of scorn which poured forth from the Shed.

[Gloucestershire Archives]

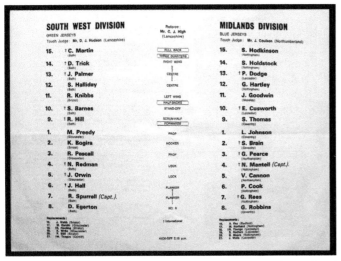

[Gloucestershire Archives]

Selecting so many players from one club was supposed to give the South West an advantage in greater cohesion, but it never materialised, and they went down to their second defeat in the competition. Continually under pressure, the South West scrum kept collapsing, and Simon Hodgkinson kept kicking the resulting penalties. Eventually the referee had had enough and he awarded a penalty try, which put Midlands 15-0 ahead, before Simon Halliday scored a try to register South West's first points. The Citizen predicted the reaction of the watching England selectors: 'as far as the South West players went they would have pencilled no names in, and several were probably crossed out.'

Orwin contests a lineout [Citizen]

In 1987, Kingsholm was due to stage the South West v North match, but the ground was frozen and the game was switched to Torquay. Support at Kingsholm may have been luke-warm, but this was even more of a financial disaster for the South-West, since it was their only home game of the 1987-88 season, and a paltry £1,700 was taken on the gate from 800 spectators.

South West 20 London 13
3rd December 1988

THREE YEARS LATER the Divisional Championship was still struggling to generate much enthusiasm, and only 4,623 turned up for the first match of this season's competition, with gates receipts coming to £9,297-92. Those who stayed away must have known it was going to be a poor quality, dour, bruising contest, notable chiefly for the repeated interventions of the touch judges, Tony Spreadbury and Martin Hill, amidst multiple warnings from the referee.

South West: J Webb (Bristol); A Swift, J Guscott (Bath), S Hogg, R Knibbs (Bristol); S Barnes (Bath, captain), R Harding (Bristol); M Preedy, K Dunn, R Pascall (Gloucester), J Morrison, N Redman, J Hall, A Robinson (Bath), M Teague (Gloucester)

London: S Thresher (Harlequins); S Smith (Wasps), J Salmon (Harlequins), F Cough, M Bailey (Wasps); A Thompson (Harlequins), S Bates (Wasps); P Curtis, J Olver (Harlequins), J Probyn (Wasps), N Edwards, P Ackford, M Skinner (Harlequins), D Pegler (captain), J Ellison (Wasps)

Referee: Mr I Bullerwell (East Midlands)

[Gloucestershire Archives]

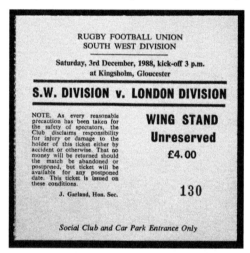

[Gloucestershire Archives]

the score was disallowed for foul play elsewhere on the pitch. The contest boiled down to a dominant South West pack against a more inventive set of London backs. With two minutes left, London led 13-10, but the South West forwards turned up the pressure, and Mike Teague broke from a scrum to burst over for a try, only the television coverage showing that he had managed to touch the ball down. There was still time for Teague and Richard Harding to break from another scrum, then feed Barnes, whose deft kick allowed Swift to sweep in for his second try.

South West 12 London 12
15th December 1990

THE LONDON SIDE came into this encounter as hot favourites to win the Championship, whereas there were by now well-founded doubts about the commitment of the South West to this competition. The local supporters found that they were expected to support a home side packed with Bath players, but, perhaps surprisingly, did so vociferously. John Etheridge was returning to Kingsholm for the first time since moving from Gloucester to Northampton. There were late changes in the centre

[Gloucestershire Archives]

South West seemed to have started well, when Stuart Barnes wriggled through, before chipping ahead to send in Tony Swift for a try, but

Mike Teague leads the charge against London with Richard Pascall alongside
[Citizen]

ADT SECURITY SYSTEMS DIVISIONAL CHAMPIONSHIP

SOUTH WEST DIVISION	Referee	LONDON & SOUTH EAST DIVISION
GREEN JERSEYS; GREEN SHORTS; GREEN SOCKS	Ken McCartney (Scotland)	WHITE JERSEYS; WHITE SHORTS; WHITE SOCKS WITH RED HOOPS
15 *JONATHAN WEBB (Bath)	FULL-BACK	15 STEVE PILGRIM (Wasps)
	THREE-QUARTERS	
14 *TONY SWIFT (Bath)	RIGHT WING	14 *ANDREW HARRIMAN (Harlequins)
13 *JEREMY GUSCOTT (Bath)	CENTRE	13 *WILL CARLING (Harlequins)
12 ABEDAYO ADEBAYO (Bath)	CENTRE	12 DAMIAN HOPLEY (Wasps)
11 PAUL HULL (Bristol)	LEFT WING	11 EVERTON DAVIS (Harlequins)
	HALF-BACKS	
10 MIKE HAMLIN (Gloucester)	STAND-OFF	10 *ROB ANDREW (Wasps) CAPTAIN
9 *RICHARD HILL (Bath)	SCRUM HALF	9 CRAIG LUXTON (Harlequins)
	FORWARDS	
1 VICTOR UBOGU (Bath)	PROP	1 *JASON LEONARD (Harlequins)
2 *GRAHAM DAWE (Bath)	HOOKER	2 *BRIAN MOORE (Harlequins)
3 RICHARD LEE (Bath)	PROP	3 *JEFF PROBYN (Wasps)
4 NIGEL REDMAN (Bath)	LOCK	4 *PAUL ACKFORD (Harlequins)
5 JOHN ETHERIDGE (Northampton)	LOCK	5 SIMON DEAR (Rosslyn Park)
6 *JOHN HALL (Bath)	FLANKER	6 *MICK SKINNER (Harlequins)
7 *ANDY ROBINSON (Bath) CAPTAIN	FLANKER	7 *PETER WINTERBOTTOM (Harlequins)
8 *MIKE TEAGUE (Gloucester)	No. 8	8 *DEAN RYAN (Wasps)

* International

Replacements	Touch Judges	Replacements
16 John Callard (Bath)	Geraint Davies (Liverpool)	16 *John Buckton (Saracens)
17 Steve Knight (Bath)		17 Guy Gregory (Nottingham)
18 Bob Philips (Gloucester)	Michael Edwards (Warwickshire)	18 Rob Glanister (Harlequins)
19 Kevin Dunn (Gloucester)		19 *Paul Rendell (Wasps)
20 Martin Haag (Bath)	KICK-OFF 3.00 p.m.	20 Stewart Davies (Rosslyn Park)
21 Martyn Sweatt (Exeter)		21 Ben Clarke (Saracens)

[Gloucestershire Archives]

for London, with J Buckton (Saracens) and R Lozowski (Wasps) replacing Carling and Hopley. England captain, Will Carling, was left out because he had failed to make the midweek training session, but ate humble pie by turning up to sign autographs.

Mike Teague about to make a tackle [Citizen]

Well-matched packs struggled for ascendancy, and the match turned into a spoiling and niggly encounter. There was plenty of tension, but most of the scoring opportunities came from penalties, with Rob Andrew kicking four out of five, whilst Jonathan Webb managed two from four. But the South West snatched a draw, which was the least they deserved, with the only try right at the end of the match. From a scrum, Mike Teague broke away, fed Richard Hill and the ball was whipped along the line for Tony Swift to live up to his name and race through to complete the move; Webb converted.

South West 9 North 34
19th October 1991

WITH THE COUNTER-ATTRACTION of the Rugby World Cup on the television, only 102 spectators turned up at Kingsholm, and most of them probably wished they had stayed at home. They saw a dismal display by a South West team which seemed not to have been introduced to one another, and in which Gloucester lock, Dave Sims was played out of position at No 8. They received their just desserts with another wooden spoon.

South West: A Lumsden; J Fallon (Bath), R Knibbs, J Redrup, P Hull (Bristol); N Matthews (Gloucester), S Knight (Bath); B Phillips, J Hawker (Gloucester), M Crane (Bath), M Haag (Bath), J Etheridge (Northampton), N Maslin, A Robinson (captain, Bath), D Sims (Gloucester); Replacement: M Preedy (Gloucester)

North: I Hunter (Northampton); S Bromley (Liverpool St Helens), B Barley (Wakefield), K Simms (captain, Liverpool St Helens), D Cooke (West Hartlepool); G Ainscough (Orrell), D Scully (Wakefield); M Whitcombe (Sale), N Frankland (Newcastle Gosforth), S Peters (Waterloo), D Baldwin (Sale), K Westgarth (Newcastle Gosforth), M Greenwood (Nottingham), N Ashurst (Orrell), A McFarlane (Sale)

Referee: Mr S V Griffiths (North Midlands)

The North were dominant in the set pieces, more mobile in the loose, quicker in the backs, and had the best kicker in Gerry Ainscough. Yet the South West started the stronger, but Paul Hull missed two early penalties, and the North scored first with a flying try by Spencer Bromley. An exchange of penalties left it 3-9 at half-time. The floodgates opened in the second half with tries for the North from Bromley again, David Cooke and David Scully, interspersed with three more penalties. Jim Fallon scored a consolation try for the South West in the final quarter.

South West 26 London and South East 24
12th December 1992

THE SOUTH WEST team, coached by Keith Richardson, had won 29-9 the previous week against the North, with Simon Morris, the only Gloucester player selected, scoring a hat trick of tries. The South West went into this game having never previously won more than one game in a Divisional Championship. It was billed as the showdown for the England fly-half position between the incumbent, Rob Andrew, and the challenger, Stuart Barnes.

[Gloucestershire Archives]

A line out between South West and London [Citizen]

The South West were forced to defend for most of the first half, as Andrew racked up three penalties, and Alex Snow scored a try. Andrew hit a post with the conversion and shortly afterwards did the same again with a penalty, narrow misses which were to prove expensive by the end of the game. A solitary penalty by Jon Webb reduced the arrears to 3-14 at half-time.

Another penalty by Andrew seemed to have put the game out of reach for the South West. But their pack found renewed vigour and stormed back to set up a second Webb penalty and tries from Andy Robinson and Nick Beal, which put South West ahead for the first time. Andrew responded with a run round the blindside which split the defence, and he converted his own try. Barnes sent Jeremy Guscott through for a try, and in the final minutes Webb kicked a penalty from a patch of mud

South West in possession [Citizen]

[Gloucestershire Archives]

GLOUCESTER WING, PAUL Holford, experienced his first taste of representative rugby when included as a late replacement in the South West team, and delighted the crowd with some of his silky running. Paul Hull was also a late replacement when the South West captain, Stuart Barnes, dropped out, and Charles Vyvyan started for the North in place of Tim Rodber.

The North had the better of it in the early stages, and Paul Grayson kicked a penalty and a drop goal as well as converting a try by Jim Mallinder. Jonathan Callard kept the South West in touch with three penalties, and they gained the upper hand in the latter stages of the game. Much better quality possession led to three tries. Firstly determined play by Derek Eves set up Paul Hull for a dashing inside break, before Callard set up Adedayo Adebayo on the left wing, and lastly Steve Ojomoh powered round the blindside from a scrum. The South West went on to win the Divisional Championship for the second time.

to clinch the victory. Andrew had scored 19 points and Barnes none, but it was the mercurial brilliance of Barnes which had turned the game in the second half – a microcosm of their different skills and rivalry, which would continue to divide the opinions of spectators and selectors alike.

South West 29 North 16
23rd October 1993

[Gloucestershire Archives]

South West 11 Midlands 16
25th November 1995

[Gloucestershire Archives]

Pete Glanville kicks ahead [Citizen]

TORRENTIAL RAIN MADE the ball and the pitch slippery, but an exciting match unfurled despite the many errors which the conditions induced, and the attention of a sparse crowd was retained right to the end of the match.

South West: P Hull (captain, Bristol); P Holford (Gloucester), S Enoch (Pontypridd), M Denney (Bristol), J Sleightholme (Bath); A King (Rosslyn Park), B Fenley (Gloucester); K Yates (Bath), P Greening (Gloucester), D Crompton (Bath), G Archer (Bristol), C Yandell (Saracens), P Glanville (Gloucester), J Pearson, E Rollitt (Bristol); Replacement: R Fidler (Gloucester)

Midlands: J Quantrill (Rugby Lions); R Subbiani (Bedford), A Kerr (Moseley), B Whetstone (Bedford), H Thorneycroft; P Grayson (captain, Northampton), J Farr (Winnington Park); M Volland, T Beddow (Northampton), N Webber (Moseley), D Grewcock (Coventry), R West (Gloucester), I Skingsley (Bedford), B Pountney, G Seely (Northampton)

Referee: Mr J Pearson (Durham)

Paul Holford made a try-saving tackle before the Midlands opened the scoring with a try by Budge Pountney, created by a run down the right by Rob Sabbiani. The crowd came to life when the South West responded with a break up the left by Phil Greening which resulted in Bruce Fenley wriggling over for a try, but Alex King missed the conversion and a subsequent penalty. A try by Ian Skingsley and a penalty from King brought the score to 8-10 at half-time.

Early in the second half Paul Hull and Pete Glanville combined well to put King in position to drop a goal, which put the home side ahead for the only time in the match. Jim Quantrill kicked two penalties to give the lead back to the Midlands, but the rest of the match belonged to the South West. They ran two penalties chasing the win, and they had their chances. Greening made a good run and put Sleightholme away, but King dropped the final pass; West made a good tackle to deny Sleightholme; and in the closing seconds Glanville was about to run in under the posts for the winning try when he was brought back for an obstruction in midfield.

This was to be the last Divisional game at Kingsholm before an unloved competition was finally put out of its misery.

Rugby World Cup 1991

PRE-TOURNAMENT MATCHES

IN CELEBRATION OF the centenary of rugby at Kingsholm, where the first match was played on 10th October 1891, both England and Ireland came to play against Gloucester in matches which also served as preparation for their forthcoming participation in the Rugby World Cup.

Mike Teague with the ball for England [Citizen]

Gloucester 4 England 34
14th September 1991

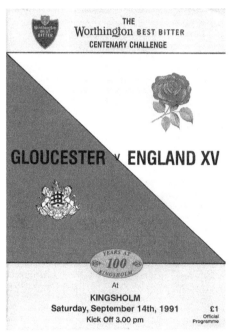

[Gloucester Rugby Heritage]

IN A MATCH labelled as the Worthington Best Bitter Centenary Challenge, Will Carling, the England captain, gave 'Iron' Mike Teague the honour of leading the England side out, which meant that the Kingsholm crowd of 8,200 probably gave their warmest reception ever to a visiting team. This was the second of three warm-up matches for England and they arrived at Kingsholm as Grand Slam Champions and on the back of a 53-0 demolition of the Soviet Union at Twickenham. Extra police

were on duty to control a large crowd.

Gloucester played with fierce commitment and pride, roared on by a passionate Kingsholm crowd. For much of the match they were the equal of England in every phase of the game, even managing to edge it in the set scrum, whilst in the loose Paul Ashmead, Sam Masters and Ian Smith gave as good as they got against a world-class back row of Mike Teague, Dean Richards and Peter Winterbottom. Jon Webb kicked England ahead with a penalty, but when Tim Smith attempted to level the scores with one for Gloucester, his kick hit a post and stayed out. However, the ball bounced just beyond the try line and Derrick Morgan produced a magical moment for the home supporters. He was the quickest to react and touched the ball down to put Gloucester ahead.

Paul Ashmead in possession [Citizen]

[Gloucester Rugby Heritage]

They stayed in the match for an hour, but thereafter England were a different class. They scored four tries in the final quarter, and Jon Webb ended up with 22 points including two tries. David Pears burst through a gap in the Gloucester defence to score one, Webb's second in the 78th minute was the best of the match when he rounded off a move started deep in England territory, and Chris Oti went over in injury time. In the end it was a comfortable and convincing win for England, although Will Carling, the England captain, conceded that 'it was always going to be the

England scrum-half Richard Hill starts a move [Citizen]

Don Caskie chasing back [Citizen]

hardest of our three warm-up games – Gloucester played well, are a well-drilled side and posed us problems'.

Gloucester 14 Ireland 13
21st September 1991

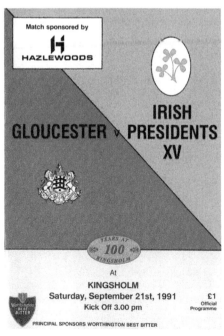

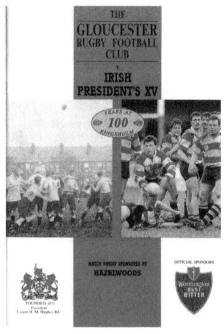

Although labelled the Irish President's XV, this was a virtually full-strength Ireland side, with only two first-choice players omitted. Phil Matthews, born in the Hucclecote area of Gloucester, had been appointed captain of Ireland for their Rugby World Cup campaign, and he led them in this game. It was Ireland's last game before they met Zimbabwe in their first RWC match. Gloucester provided much more serious opposition. They brought in Jerry Perrins for Derrick Morgan, the hero of the previous week, who was on the side-lines with the leg which he had fractured against England in plaster. The only change from the teams in the programme was in the Irish second row, where M Galway (Shannon) replaced Francis.

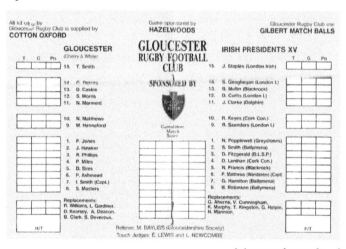

Ireland started strongly, and took the lead after 15 minutes when Jim Staples was sent over for a try after Phil Matthews and Steve Smith had sucked in the Gloucester defence. But the Gloucester pack then took control, with their front row dominating in the scrums and hooker John Hawker taking three strikes against the head, Dave Sims outplaying British Lion, Donal Lenihan in the line-outs, and Ian Smith usually first to the loose ball. When Ireland did have the ball, ferocious Gloucester tackling kept knocking them back. Marcus Hannaford and Ian Smith

Marcus Hannaford bursts away against Ireland with Sam Masters and Ian Smith in support [Citizen]

Ireland gain possession [Citizen]

soon put Jerry Perrins over for an equalising try from a five metre scrum. Full-back Tim Smith added a penalty on the stroke of half-time and three minutes after the interval he kicked Gloucester into a six point lead.

Gloucester on the attack against Ireland [Citizen]

Sam Masters wins a lineout [Citizen]

By this stage the Cherry and Whites were in total control and Paul Ashmead touched down after a wonderful break from Hannaford only for the final pass to be ruled forward. But Gloucester scored the second try they fully deserved when centre Simon Morris picked up and dived over in the corner after Neil Matthews had been held up just short. A delicate chip over the approaching Ireland cover by Don Caskie should have resulted in a try for Tim Smith but he knocked on over the try line. Minutes later Jerry Perrins should have put John Hawker in for a try but his pass went slightly behind the Gloucester hooker. But for these errors, Gloucester would have been out of sight. However, Ireland belatedly found some of their traditional fire in the final five minutes and were rewarded with a penalty from Ralph Keyes and a converted try by centre David Curtis, but it was too little too late.

Gloucester were deserved winners, having produced one of their best ever performances to comprehensively outplay their distinguished opponents. They were confident and utterly committed, whereas Ireland became increasingly desperate as their attacks broke down against Gloucester's mean defence. The only disappointment for Gloucester was that they had squandered several clear scoring opportunities, which would have rendered the final score a better reflection of their superiority.

RUGBY WORLD CUP MATCH

WHEN THE COMPETITION proper got underway, Kingsholm was proud to host a pool game, especially since it involved the mighty All Blacks.

New Zealand 46 USA 6
8th October 1991

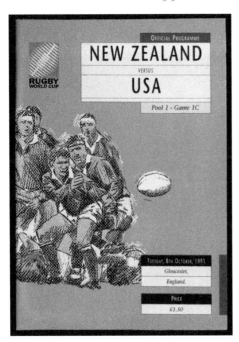

[Gloucestershire Archives]

[Gloucestershire Archives]

US Eagles. A capacity crowd of 12,000, with supporters from around the world, made for a festive occasion. Eagles centre, Mark Williams, claimed that this was 11, 995 more than they were used to. He had previously found

HAVING WON THEIR first match against England at Twickenham, and then come to Gloucester to hold training sessions at Saintbridge and Old Richians, the All Blacks arrived at Kingsholm and crushed the

Mark Pidcock gets the ball away for USA with his captain, Kevin Swords behind him [Citizen]

	NEW ZEALAND		USA
FULL BACK	T. J. WRIGHT	15	P. SHEEHY
RIGHT WING	J. K. R. TIMU	14	G. M. HEIN
RIGHT CENTRE	C. R. INNES	13	M. A. WILLIAMS
LEFT CENTRE	B. J. McCAHILL	12	J. R. BURKE
LEFT WING	V. TUIGAMALA	11	K. G. HIGGINS
OUT HALF	J. PRESTON	10	C. P. O'BRIEN
SCRUM HALF	G. T. M. BACHOP	9	M. D. PIDCOCK
FORWARDS	A. T. EARL	8	A. M. RIDNELL
	M. N. JONES	7	S. LIPMAN
	A. J. WHETTON	6	M. H. SAWICKI
	G. W. WHETTON (CAPT)	5	C. E. TUNNACLIFFE
	I. D. JONES	4	K. R. SWORDS (CAPT)
	G. H. PURVIS	3	N. MOTTRAM
	S. B. T. FITZPATRICK	2	P. W. JOHNSON
	S. C. McDOWELL	1	C. LIPPERT

REPLACEMENTS

16 S. J. PHILPOTT	16 R. B. NELSON
17 W. K. LITTLE	17 M. G. DeJONG
18 J. HEWETT	18 B. DALY
19 M. CARTER	19 A. FLAY
20 R. W. LOE	20 L. MANGA
21 G. DOWD	21 R. FARLEY

[Gloucestershire Archives]

Va'aiga Tuigamala looks unstoppable [Citizen]

Craig Innes scores New Zealand's seventh try [Citizen]

Kingsholm an intimidating place to play when he lost there with both Middlesex and Wasps, but he was now delighted to find the Kingsholm crowd rooting for the underdogs. This was the first run-out at Kingsholm for Ian Jones, who would later be greeted with adulation when he returned as Gloucester player. E Whitaker was a late replacement for Higgins on the wing for the Eagles. The referee was Mr E Sklar (Argentina).

The Eagles were fired up for the occasion, with their captain, Kevin Swords, leading from the front, dominating the lineouts, and deservedly named as man of the match. Their defence was heroic, and they held out for 15 minutes before the All Blacks tide started to engulf them. Jon Preston kicked a penalty and in the 22nd minute Andy Earl crashed over from a 5-metre scrum. Two minutes later, quicksilver full-back Terry Wright scored his first try after a strong run by flanker Michael Jones, and he soon outpaced the Eagles defence for his second. The biggest cheer of the afternoon greeted a penalty for the Eagles by Mark Williams, but one in return by Preston gave the All Blacks a comfortable 20-3 lead at half-time.

Within four minutes of the restart, Graham Purvis crashed over

Terry Wright completes his hat trick [Citizen]

for the All Blacks fourth, and John Timu added the fifth from a well-rehearsed blind side move. After 55 minutes Williams kicked a second penalty for the Eagles, but with the loss of prop Christopher Lippert with a knee ligament injury, they began to struggle. In the final ten minutes, the All Blacks were at their most awesome, scoring three further tries, their sixth registered by Va'aiga Tuigamala who, having bounced off tacklers all afternoon, just strolled over. Craig Innes got number seven and Terry Wright completed his hat trick in injury time. The Eagles had earned much credit and gained many admirers, but points had proved much harder to come by against relentless opponents.

England v Australia Schools

England Schools 30 Australia Schools 3
25th January 1995

THIS UNDER-18 MATCH was the last of the Australian tour, which had seen them unbeaten in the eleven games they had played previously during their progression through Ireland, Scotland, France and England. The star of the Australian team was Elton Flatley playing at centre. The three Gloucestershire representatives in the England squad all came from Colstons Collegiate in Bristol. The evening kick-off was at a wet and windy Kingsholm, but a large and enthusiastic crowd braved the elements to see England become the first European team to defeat Australia at this level since 1974.

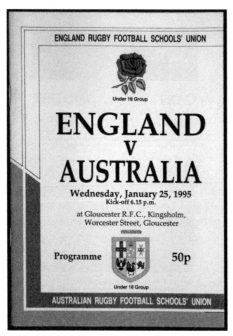

[Gloucestershire Archives]

[Gloucestershire Archives]

Elton Flatley gave Australia the lead with a penalty, but Jeremy Cook equalised with one for England. Australia certainly had the better of the first half, but two last-ditch tackles by Sampson and Cook prevented them from scoring tries and they missed a penalty, before a second by

[Gloucestershire Archives]

Cook gave England a somewhat fortuitous half-time lead, 6-3.

England had the wind behind them in the second half and they scored within three minutes of the restart. Booth outpaced the defence in chasing a chip to the corner by Sampson and he just touched down before the ball crossed the dead ball line; Cook converted from the touch line. England were straight back on the attack and Martyn Wood scored from a scrum by the posts; Cook converted. Joe Ewens then charged down a kick and sprinted to the line to score in the corner; Cook again slotted a difficult conversion. Australia were rocked by these three converted tries in the space of ten minutes, but fought back, only to find the England defence quite impenetrable, although Ewens suffered two injuries in as many minutes as he tackled his heart out. Foul play by Australia allowed Cook to kick a further penalty on the stroke of time to complete the scoring and round off a comprehensive victory.

England Under-19 12 Australian Schools 24
2nd December 2005

AUSTRALIA ARRIVED AT Kingsholm with a reputation for classy backs, and the crowd of 3,057 were ready to endorse this by the end of the match. However, England were only outdone by three tries to two, and showed plenty of quality of their own, most notably through the performances of Dominic Waldouck, the Wasps centre, and Jack Forster, Gloucester's very own loosehead prop from Hartpury.

England U-19: T Arscott; O Dodge, D Waldouck, T Youngs (captain), J Turner-Hall; D Cipriani, J Simpson; J Forster, J Page, T Mercey, D Attwood, S Pitfield, C Pennycook, A Saull, H Ellis; Replacements: G Hughes, A Greendale, D Pointon, D Cole, M Deacon, C Beech

Australian Schools: Q Cooper; A Barrett, R Kellam, B Gillespie, L Turner; K Beale, N Sievert; D Roach, J Hanson, B Daley, D Linde, J Afu, J Lam, D Pocock, P McCutcheon (captain); Replacements: J Salvi, J Egan, B McCalman, G Warren, T Tusitala, S Wykes, P Betham, B Vaaulu

Referee: Mr T Hayes (Wales)

Australia opened the scoring when Nathan Sievert worked quick ball wide, and Rowan Kellam, a powerful centre with a solid boot on him, charged through England's defence to score a try, which Sievert converted. The England pack were dominant in the tight, but a hand in the scrum allowed Sievert the opportunity to extend the lead with a penalty. Forster's supremacy in the scrum earned England two successive penalties, but Joe

Plaques presented by the RFU [Gloucester Rugby]   *Plaque presented by the visitors [Gloucester Rugby]*

Simpson ran the second and the greasy ball was fumbled, and Lachlan Turner seized on the loose ball to dash diagonally across the full length of the pitch to score in the opposite corner. Sievert banged over the conversion and Australia went in at the interval with a commanding 17-0 lead.

The half-time talk by Nigel Redman, the England coach, appeared to have had some impact after the break, when England built up the pressure and closed down the Australian danger men much more quickly. Andrew Barrett was shown a yellow card and from the resulting penalty, quick hands enabled Olly Dodge, the Leicester winger, to dive over for England's first points; Danny Cipriani converted. A period of Australian attack was repelled, and patient approach work by England eventually created a three-man overlap, which culminated in Dodge scoring his second try in the corner. A five-point deficit with 15 minutes remaining made for an exciting finish, despite the torrential rain. However, with a minute to go, the rain eased and the Australian backs struck, Kurtley Beale scoring the decisive try and Quade Cooper converting it.

Rugby League

As the playing strength of Gloucester grew during the 1880s and 1890s, the Club's fixture list expanded to include matches against the strongest clubs in the land. Initially this meant spreading the net more widely in the south of England and the Midlands and many more fixtures against Welsh clubs, but even before the move to Kingsholm the Club was keen to seize opportunities to play against clubs from the north of England. Between 1889 and 1895, games were played against Huddersfield, Swinton, Wigan, Hull, St Helens, Dewsbury, Wakefield, Broughton Rangers, Tyldesley, Runcorn, Morecambe and Salford.

During this time, tensions had been growing between many of the northern clubs and the Rugby Union over what payments were allowable as reasonable expenses. A particular bone of contention was the question of broken time payments, by which players were compensated for loss of earnings during time taken off to play rugby. The RU were uncompromising in their defence of a strict amateur code, and this resulted in a schism in August 1895, when many northern clubs, including all those listed above as opponents of Gloucester, broke away to form the Northern Union. The NU soon decided to change some of the laws of their game as well, such as reducing teams to 13 players and doing away with line-outs, and so Rugby League was born. The Rugby Union imposed draconian penalties for anyone associated with Rugby League – they would never again be allowed to have any association with the Rugby Union game.

However, it was not only the north of England in which many players were suffering financial hardships, earning low wages and having to make substantial sacrifices to play rugby. This certainly applied in Gloucester and it resulted in a steady stream of players from the Club going north to secure contracts with Rugby League clubs. Such negotiations had to be conducted in secret, because even talking to a League club was sufficient to earn a lifetime ban from the Union game. Whilst there may have been dismay at the loss of a good player, there was a great deal of understanding on the part of the Gloucester Club and supporters towards players who decided to improve the wellbeing of their family by securing financial reward for their playing ability. These players could never again play any part within the Gloucester Club, but they were highly regarded and made welcome in Club and City when they returned home.

This position was overturned for the duration of World War Two, when Service sides were selected with no regard to whether the players were Union or League players. So, the Services wartime internationals which were played in Gloucester saw several League players cheered to the rafters as they performed at Kingsholm. But this relaxation did not apply to club games and disappeared altogether as soon as the war was over. It was to be another 50 years before the world changed again, with Rugby Union becoming a professional game, the pariah status of Rugby League a thing of the past, the Gloucester Club starting to recruit players from League clubs, and Kingsholm hosting a match in the 2000 Rugby League World Cup. Where past generations would have expected instant excommunication, all was now sweetness and light.

RUGBY LEAGUE INTERNATIONAL

New Zealand 64 Lebanon 0
29th October 2000

This pool game was played on one of the coldest days experienced at Kingsholm. It featured the official New Zealand team (also in the tournament was a native NZ team called the Aotearoa Maoris). New Zealand were one of the tournament favourites and their opponents were definitely one of the minnows. The Lebanon side, nicknamed 'The Cedars', consisted entirely of Australians of Lebanese origin, who were based in New South Wales, mostly inner-city Sydney. Only two of the team which played at Kingsholm had actually been born in Lebanon. They had played their first competitive match two years previously, but they had thrashed the USA 62-8 to qualify for these World Cup Finals. A Lebanese sports reporter was asked to comment and said 'for Lebanese people this tournament means nothing. They have no association with the sport because they never see it and nobody plays it'. The crowd numbered around 2,500 despite the dreadful weather conditions – cold, gale-force winds and driving rain.

New Zealand: R Barnett (London Broncos); B Jellick (Northern Queensland), T Carroll (Leeds), W Talau (Canterbury), L Vainikolo (Canberra); H Paul (Bradford), S Jones (Auckland); Pongia (Canberra), Swain (Melbourne), Smith (St George Illawarra), Kearney (Melbourne), L Swann (Auckland), R Wiki (Canberra); Substitutes: J Vagana, R Paul, Rua, Cayless,

Lebanon: Hazem El Masri; Najarrin, Katrib, Touma, Saleh; Stanton, Coorey; Maroon, Semrani, Elamad, Chamoun, Khoury, Lichaa; Substitutes: Salem, Nohra, Tamer, S El Masri

Lesley 'Volcano' Vainikolo dives over for one of his tries [Citizen]

Unsurprisingly the Lebanese were well beaten by a New Zealand side which included Henry Paul and Lesley Vainikolo, both of whom would later change codes and play at Kingsholm for Gloucester, Paul signing the following season and Vainikolo in 2007. Paul turned his ankle early in this match and had to go off, but New Zealand rolled on without him. Lebanon made an impressive number of tackles, but New Zealand's greater pace and power overwhelmed them as they ran in twelve tries.

The Kiwi's play-maker, Stacey Jones, collected twenty points, scoring the final two tries and kicking six conversions after Paul had gone off. There were two tries apiece for Vainikolo, Ritchie Barnett, Tonie Carroll and Willie Talau, and one each for Brian Jellick and Logan Swann. Carroll claimed the game's outstanding try, a solo effort from 60 metres out. It was 26-0 at half-time, and as the Lebanese tired so the Kiwis prospered in the second half and it became a rout.

Despite being crushed in this match, in their other pool games Lebanon lost only 22-24 to Wales, and drew 22-22 with the Cook Islands.

England Teams at Kingsholm in Recent Times

ENGLAND UNDER-21

England Under-21 27 Ireland Under-21 19
5th March 2004

A CROWD OF 7,357 turned out on a Friday evening to cheer on England's juniors, and were rewarded with a dogged victory in a messy battle between two well matched sides, who managed very little continuity, thanks in part to a referee who seemed to be whistling constantly.

England: J Clarke (Northampton); M Garvey (Gloucester), C Bell, A Reay, U Monye; A Jarvis (Harlequins), C Stuart-Smith (captain); N Wood (Gloucester), R Hawkins (Bath), D Wilson (Newcastle), J Percival (Worcester), C Day (Sale), B Russell (Northampton), W Skinner (Leicester), B Skirving (Saracens); Replacements: S Friswell (Leicester), T Warren (Worcester), T Parker (Harlequins), M Hopley (Worcester), R Wigglesworth (Sale), B Davies (Gloucester), J Bailey (Bristol).

Ireland: A Finn (Dolphin); R Lane (University College, Cork), J Hearty (Blackrock College), G Telford (Instonians), T Bowe; G Steenson (Queen's University, Belfast), T O'Leary (Cork Constitution); J Wickham (Clontarf), D Fogarty (Cork Constitution), K Doyle (University College, Dublin), D Gannon (Blackrock College), S O'Connor (Cork Constitution), K McLaughlin (University College, Dublin), O Hennessy (Dungannon), J Heaslip (Dublin University); Replacements: C Geoghegan (University College, Dublin), S Bennett (Bath), N McComb (Dundee HSFP), D O'Brian (Old Belvedere), R Shaw (Wasps), M Glancy (Loughborough University), B O'Donnell (UL Bohemians)

Referee: Mr C Damasco (Italy)

Clive Stuart-Smith [Gloucester Rugby]

England were soon behind to a Gareth Steenson penalty, but their pack responded powerfully, and Clive Stuart-Smith and Adrian Jarvis put Andy Reay in for the first try, only to have the conversion charged down. England were playing fast, if not always accurate, rugby, and Marcel Garvey zoomed clear to put Ben Russell in for the second try. As half-time approached, Ireland came into it more, and Hearty scored from close range.

A penalty put Ireland ahead after the break, and England's game grew ever more error-strewn as the penalty count rose against them. Jarvis's angled grubber allowed Chris Bell to slide in for a try, but two penalties by Steenson pegged them back to 20-19, until Bell picked a lovely line from Reay's pass and settled the issue with his second try.

England Under-21 22 Wales Under-21 19
19th March 2004

A CROWD OF 10,065 watched a thriller which kept the Grand Slam hopes of England's junior side alive.

England: J Clarke (Northampton); M Garvey (Gloucester), C Bell, A Reay, U Monye; A Jarvis (Harlequins), C Stuart-Smith (captain); N Wood (Gloucester), R Hawkins (Bath), M Guess (Gloucester), J Percival (Worcester), C Day (Sale), B Russell (Northampton), W Skinner (Leicester), B Skirving (Saracens); Replacements: S Friswell (Leicester), T Warren (Worcester), T Parker (Harlequins), L Narraway (Gloucester), R Wigglesworth (Sale), B Davies (Gloucester), J Bailey (Bristol)

Wales: M Nuttall (Celtic Warriors); J Wellwood(Wasps), G Evans (Llanelli), L Thomas (Pontypridd), F Brillante (Cardiff); N MacLeod (Cardiff Blues), R Rees (Swansea); J Yapp (Cardiff Blues), K Crawford (Ebbw Vale), C Griffiths (Neath), I Evans (Llanelli), L Charteris (Newport), R Dale (Newport), J Merriman (captain, Gloucester), G Quinnell (Llanelli Scarlets); Replacements: I George (Newport), W Kay (Newcastle Falcons), J Mills (Bath), T Brown (Hartpury College), J Ireland (Cross Keys), M Jones (Neath), L Andrews (Cross Keys)

Referee: Mr M Changleng (Scotland)

Marcel Garvey and Nick Wood, Gloucester players who started for the Saxons
[Gloucester Rugby]

England's pack was dominant early on, and Ben Skirving scored the first try only five minutes into the game; Adrian Jarvis converted. Wales mounted their first attack after 15 minutes and scored through Gavin Quinnell, the conversion by Lee Thomas levelling the scores. Back came England, Skirving burrowing over for his second try, and when Ian Evans received a yellow card for battering into Nick Wood, all seemed set fair for the home side. But while Wales were down to 14 men, Richard Rees scored from a long way out, and before the interval, James Merriman, the Wales captain from Gloucester, scored under the posts, and Wales turned round 19-12 to the good.

Luke Narraway and Brad Davies of Gloucester came on at half-time for England, and soon after they were faced by Tom Brown of Gloucester, Saracens and Hartpury College coming on for Wales, all of which added to local interest. Davies converted a try by Andy Reay to level the scores, and England continued to press hard, but three turnovers inside the Welsh 22 foiled them, until Davies kicked a penalty from 40 yards with ten minutes to go to put England ahead. Wales stormed back and came close to snatching victory, but a knock-on right on the English line ended the game.

Luke Narraway and Brad Davies, who came off the bench at half-time [Gloucester Rugby]

ENGLAND A

England A 18 Ireland A 33
17th March 2006

THIS FIXTURE WAS cunningly organised to be played on St Patrick's Day and to coincide with the National Hunt Cheltenham Gold Cup Festival just down the road at Prestbury Park, so there was no lack of Irish support ringing around Kingsholm amongst a crowd of 10,505.

England A: M van Gisbergen; P Sackey (Wasps), J Clarke (Northampton), O Smith (Leicester), C Bell (Leeds); S Drahm (Worcester), S Perry (captain, Bristol); T Payne (Wasps), A Titterell, S Turner (Sale), T Palmer (Leeds), L Deacon (Leicester), A Beattie, M Lipman (Bath), C Jones (Sale); Replacements: M Cairns (Saracens), N Wood (Gloucester), D Ward-Smith (Bristol), T Rees (Wasps), N Walshe (Bath), S Vesty (Leicester), D Armitage (London Irish)

Ireland A: R Kearney (Leinster); T Bowe (Ulster), G Duffy (Harlequins), K Lewis (Leinster), I Dowling; J Staunton, T O'Leary (Munster); R Hogan, J Fogarty (Connacht), B Young (Ulster), M O'Driscoll (captain, Munster), M McCullough, N Best (Ulster), S Jennings (Leicester), J Heaslip (Leinster); Replacements: R McCormick (Ulster), L Cullen (Leicester), R Wilson (Ulster), C Keane, (Connacht),

Referee: Mr C Berdos (France)

Ireland proved to be a cohesive and well-organised outfit, which contrasted with an England side which dithered too often and appeared

to lack structure. However, it started very promisingly for England. For the first 15 minutes, they benefited from Irish mistakes, Shane Drahm kicked a penalty from in front of the posts, and Shaun Perry created the space to send prop Stuart Turner careering through the centre. When he was stopped, Perry recycled the ball quickly and Paul Sackey scooted over in the corner. Two penalties from Jeremy Staunton got Ireland back into the game, and when a third drifted wide, Ireland drove forward from the line-out and Ian Dowling darted over in the corner. Drahm equalised with another easy penalty, but the Irish forwards now had the bit between their teeth and Staunton's try and conversion gave them an 18-11 advantage at the break.

In the second half, a penalty attempt by Staunton hung up in the wind and Kieran Lewis took advantage to snaffle a try and extend the Irish lead. A line-out drive led to Michael Lipman's try on the hour mark, which Drahm converted, but the best had been saved for last. The Irish forwards worked the ball through multiple phases and, when it was finally whipped out along the backs, Rob Kearney saw a gap and cut a wonderful line to score the conclusive try. However, the biggest cheer of the night greeted the arrival on the pitch of the Gloucester loosehead prop, Nick Wood, as a late replacement.

ENGLAND UNDER-20

England Under-20 28 Wales Under-20 15
1st February 2008

THE ATTENDANCE WAS 4,554. England made a late change when injury side-lined Andy Saul; he was replaced by Matt Cox, and Tom Sargeant came onto the bench.

England U-20: G Tonks (Leicester); N Cato (Saracens), L Eves (Bristol), J Turner-Hall (Harlequins), M Benjamin (Worcester); A Goode (Saracens), B Youngs (Leicester); N Catt (Bath), J Gray (Northampton), A Corbisiero (London Irish), G Gillanders (Leicester), S Hobson (Cornish Pirates), J Fisher (London Irish), M Cox (Worcester), H Ellis (captain, Wasps); Replacements: B Moss (Bath), T Sargeant (Harlequins), D Norton (Gloucester), S Stegmann (Harlequins)

Wales U-20: D Evans (Scarlets); L Halfpenny (Blues), G Owen (Ospreys), J Davies (Scarlets), J Norris (Dragons); D Biggar, G Williams; R Bevington (Ospreys), B Roberts (Dragons), P Palmer (Blues), J Turnball (Scarlets), J Groves (captain, Blues), J Tipuric (Ospreys), N Cudd, L Phillips (Scarlets)

The commemorative plaque presented to Gloucester Rugby [Gloucester Rugby]

Referee: Mr J Garces (France)

England made a bright start, with Miles Benjamin, Noah Cato and Luke Eves all threatening, but Wales tightened their grip, narrowly missing a try and a dropped goal, and pressing the England line. But Andy Goode put Cato through a hole in midfield, and his swerve and pace were sufficient to outstrip the defence for a splendid try. Within ten minutes England struck again, Eves and Greig Tonks combining to give Benjamin the space to brush off tackles and keep his balance to get over for the second try. Goode converted both. Leigh Halfpenny and Goode swapped penalties to make the score 17-3 at half-time.

After 50 minutes, England won turnover ball, spun it wide to Cato, and he slipped it inside to Eves, who scored. Goode added a penalty, but there was a Welsh revival when Josh Turnball spun off the side of a ruck to score in the corner, and Halfpenny ran in a try from long range and kicked the conversion to reduce the deficit further. But Goode had the last word with his third penalty to seal a comfortable victory.

England Under-20 43 Ireland Under-20 14
14th March 2008

England U-20: N Cato (Saracens); S Stegmann (Harlequins), L Eves (Bristol), A Goode (Saracens), M Odejobi (Wasps); A Greendale (Leeds), J Simpson (Wasps); N Catt (Bath), J Gray (Northampton), A Corbisiero (London Irish), G Kitchener (Worcester), S Hobson (Cornish Pirates), J Fisher (London Irish), M Cox (Worcester) H Ellis (captain, Wasps); Replacements: S Freer (Leeds), B Moss (Bath), J Cannon (Northampton), A Saull (Saracens), B Youngs (Leicester), G King (Worcester), D Norton (Gloucester)

Ireland U-20: D Kearney; S Scanlon, E O'Malley, C Cleary, C Cochrane; I Madigan, D Moore; P Karayiannis, J Harris-Wright, B Barclay, D Nolan, E Sheriff, K Essex, P Ryan, P Mallon; Replacements: S Douglas, S Archer, I Nagle, T Conneely, I Porter, M Dufficy, E Sheridan.

Matt Cox, who scored for England U-20, and would return to Kingsholm as a Gloucester player [Gloucester Rugby]

Ireland scored an early try when David Kearney burst through a gap forty metres out and ran in unopposed, but England soon responded. Ellis battered his way up to the line before the ball went to Alex Goode, who put Seb Stegmann over in the corner and kicked the conversion. Ireland had England on the back foot for most of the first quarter and retook the lead with an Ian Madigan penalty. After half an hour, England constructed

a glorious sweeping move to score from long range, the ball going through the hands of Joe Simpson, Adam Greendale, Noah Cato, Stegmann and Hugo Ellis, who scored; Goode again converted. England immediately conceded a careless penalty from the restart and Madigan punished them to reduce the deficit to 14-11. England again ran the ball from a long way out, Mark Odejobi breaking tackles and Cato blasting towards the corner, before off-loading for Luke Eves to score. Another Madigan penalty made it 19-14 at half-time, when England suffered a setback, with their captain, Ellis, having to retire injured.

However, they started the second half strongly and again spread the ball wide. Jon Fisher broke down the right and Matt Cox was up in support to claim the try, which was only awarded after a TMO review. Then Goode slipped an inside pass to Cato, who blasted his way past three defenders to score. Suddenly England were running rampant, with Greendale and Goode getting close before Nathan Catt ploughed over. Five minutes from time the job was finished when a length-of-the-field counter-attack resulted in Odejobi scoring the final try. This fine display secured the Junior Grand Slam for England.

England Under-20 41 Wales Under-20 14
5th February 2010

THE ENGLAND UNDER-20 side was coached by former Gloucester player, Mark Mapletoft; the attendance was 4,774.

England U-20: T Catterick (Newcastle); W Hurrell (Leicester), T Homer (London Irish), R Clegg, S Smith (Harlequins); F Burns (Gloucester), S Harrison (Leicester); J Marler (Harlequins), J George (Saracens), S Knight (Gloucester), C Green (Leicester), J Gaskell (Sale), W Welch (Newcastle), J Rowan (captain, Leeds), A Gray (Newcastle); Replacements: R Buchanan (Harlequins), L Imiolek (Sale), C Matthews (Harlequins), J Wray (Saracens), S Stuart (Harlequins), J Joseph (London Irish), J May (Gloucester)

Wales U-20: D Fish; J Loxton, O Williams (Blues), S Williams (Scarlets), K Phillips; M Jarvis (Ospreys), R Downes (Blues); D Watchurst (captain, Dragons), R Williams (Blues), S Gardiner (Scarlets), M Cook (Blues), J King (Ospreys), J Thomas (Dragons), J Navidi (Blues), M Allen (Pontypool); Replacements: I Davies (Glamorgan Wanderers), T Davies (Scarlets), L Peers (Ospreys), T Faletau (Dragons), G Davies, L Rees (Scarlets), M Pewtner (Dragons)

Wales took the lead with an early penalty from Matthew Jarvis, and tried roughing up Freddie Burns, which caused tempers to boil over,

Freddie Burns on the attack against Wales [Citizen]

but it was Burns who slotted an equalising penalty. Wales regained the lead by spinning the ball to the left for James Loxton to race into the corner. However, the English pack was starting to get the upper hand, which set up another Burns penalty to make it 8-6 at half-time.

England made a wonderful start to the second half, Joe Marler, the prop, bursting through tackles at high speed to go over under the posts; Burns converted. Wales came back with a Jarvis penalty, but Burns then took charge on his home ground, tearing through the middle of the field, kicking cross-field for Jamie George to score in the corner, and kicking the difficult conversion. Jarvis landed another penalty, but Shaun Knight, Gloucester's young prop, laid on a scoring pass for his skipper, Jacob Rowan. Burns made way for his team mate, Jonny May, and Tom Homer kicked the conversion. Alex Gray saw a red card for foul play, but it made little difference to an England team which now had all the impetus. Marler ran in his second try, and to the delight of the locals, May battled his way through on the left wing and stretched out an arm to touch down for England's fifth and final try.

ENGLAND SAXONS

England Saxons 41 Tonga 14
12th June 2011

THIS MATCH WAS played as part of a Churchill Cup double-header at Kingsholm and attracted 5,357 spectators. Despite being played during the summer, it was a damp and gloomy day, and the match was similarly dour. England, who had scored 13 tries against USA a few days earlier, took one look at the weather and decided to play it tight. Local supporters had been hoping to see the talents of Charlie Sharples and Henry Trinder being given free reign, but they were ignored as the forwards stuffed the ball up their jerseys and did the job.

- *Charlie Sharples tries to break through against Tonga [Citizen]*

England Saxons: A Goode (Saracens); C Sharples, H Trinder (Gloucester), B Twelvetrees (Leicester), T Ojo (London Irish); R Clegg (Harlequins), P Hodgson (London Irish); M Mullan (Worcester), D Paice (London Irish), M Stevens, M Botha (Saracens), D Attwood (Gloucester), J Gaskell (Sale), T Johnson (Exeter), J Crane (captain, Leicester). Replacements: J Gray (Harlequins), M Brown, J Turner-Hall (Harlequins), M Young, K Brookes (Newcastle), G Kitchener (Worcester), J Gibson (London Irish)

Tonga: E Paea; V Helu, Hufanga, S Fonua, V Iongi; K Morath, D Morath; T Lea'aetoa, S Telefoni, Pulu, S Timani, E Kauhenga, J Afu, P Kolomatangi, P Mapakaitolo; Replacements: Hehea, Havea, Fainga'anuku, Ula

Referee: Mr R Poite (France)

In the first half a dominant England pack was rewarded with two penalty tries when their powerful scrummaging caused the Tongan scrum to disintegrate, and captain Jordan Crane grabbed another from close range. The lineout was a similarly one-sided contest. It was 'old school forward bludgeon' but Tonga had no answer to it. England closed the first half with a Rory Clegg penalty and opened the second the same way.

The ball eludes both Dave Attwood and the Tongan jumper at a lineout [Citizen]

Tonga eventually mounted an attack, and drove Sione Timani over from a lineout, Kurt Morath adding the extra two points. But having lost one of their props to the sin bin for persistently collapsing the scrum, they promptly did it again, and the referee had little option but to award England their third penalty try, a somewhat unusual hat trick. A rare glimpse of the ball for Sharples saw him seize the opportunity, jinking this way and that and back again to go round four defenders, but the try of the match came when Mike Brown attacked from far out, which put Crane into space, and his smart grubber kick allowed Billy Twelvetrees to stroll in for a lovely try. But the last word went to Tonga, with a try for flanker Koloamatangi.

England Saxons 8 Ireland Wolfhounds 14
25th January 2014

ENGLAND CHOSE A team of emerging players only three of whom had previously won caps, whereas Ireland went for much greater experience, including twelve capped players, and this added nous paid off. Local interest in Freddie Burns, Charlie Sharples and Elliott Stooke brought out 8,200 spectators on a stormy evening at Kingsholm, but the high wind and sticky conditions combined to make for an error-strewn game.

[Malc King]

Anthony Watson breaks away for a try [Citizen]

Freddie Burns kicking against the Wolfhounds [Citizen]

England Saxons: E Daly (Wasps); A Watson (Bath), M Hopper (Harlequins), S Hill (Exeter), C Sharples; F Burns (Gloucester), J Simpson (Wasps); A Waller (Northampton), J George (Saracens), T Mercey (Northampton), C Matthews (Harlequins), G Kruis (Saracens), C Clark (Northampton), L Wallace (Harlequins), D Ewers (Exeter). Replacements: D Ward (Harlequins), N Catt (Bath), S Wilson (Newcastle), E Stooke (Gloucester), S Dickinson (Northampton), D Lewis, H Slade (Exeter), R Miller (Sale)

Ireland Wolfhounds: F Jones (Munster); F McFadden (Leinster), R Henshaw (Connacht), D Cave, C Gilroy (Ulster); I Madigan, I Boss (Leinster); D Kilcoyne (Munster), R Herring (Ulster), M Moore (Leinster), I Henderson, D Tuohy (Ulster), R Ruddock (Leinster), R Copeland (Cardiff). Replacements: R Strauss, J McGrath (Leinster), S Archer (Munster), R Diack (Ulster), J Murphy (Leinster), K Marmion (Connacht), I Keatley, S Zebo (Munster)

Referee: Mr I Davies (Wales)

The Irish half-backs, Ian Madigan and Isaac Boss controlled the first half, and each scored a try, both converted by Madigan. In between Anthony Watson scored a runaway try from an interception in his own half.

There were high hopes for the England team when they turned round with the wind behind them in the second half, but they found the Irish defence, aided by a stream of English handling errors, to be impenetrable. A Freddie Burns penalty was the only score, although England finished the game hammering away at the Ireland line.

Other Representative Rugby at Kingsholm in the Professional Era

Gloucester 32 Combined Services 7
5th November 1996

THERE WAS A late replacement for the Combined Services, with Ian Morgan starting on the wing in place of Spencer Brown.

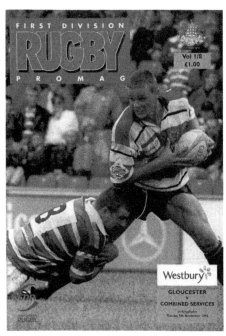

[Gloucestershire Archives]

Both teams more or less ran everything, but the howling gale, which Combined Services had at their backs in the first half, did not help the standard of play, and there were lengthy periods when the fireworks shooting up from gardens around Kingsholm were more entertaining than the rugby. Gloucester scored three first half tries against the elements – a tapped penalty led to Paul Holford diving over in the corner; the same player then fielded a kick out of defence and scored from a lovely jinking run; and Mike Lloyd finished off a move started by Andrew Stanley and carried on by Bullock, Hart, Caskie and Holford, which made the score 15-0 at half time.

Paul Holford, who scored a hat trick of tries against Combined Services
[Gloucester Rugby]

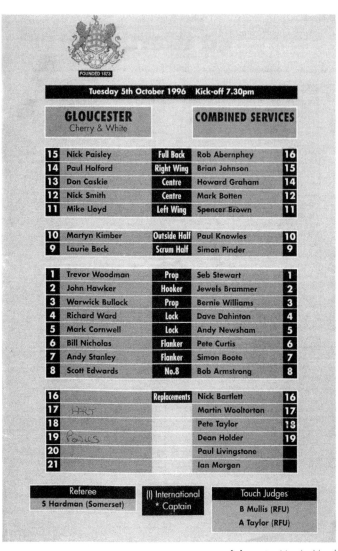

Tuesday 5th October 1996		Kick-off 7.30pm	
GLOUCESTER Cherry & White		**COMBINED SERVICES**	
15 Nick Paisley	Full Back	Rob Abernphey	16
14 Paul Holford	Right Wing	Brian Johnson	15
13 Don Caskie	Centre	Howard Graham	14
12 Nick Smith	Centre	Mark Botten	12
11 Mike Lloyd	Left Wing	Spencer Brown	11
10 Martyn Kimber	Outside Half	Paul Knowles	10
9 Laurie Beck	Scrum Half	Simon Pinder	9
1 Trevor Woodman	Prop	Seb Stewart	1
2 John Hawker	Hooker	Jewels Brammer	2
3 Warwick Bullock	Prop	Bernie Williams	3
4 Richard Ward	Lock	Dave Dahinton	4
5 Mark Cornwell	Lock	Andy Newsham	5
6 Bill Nicholas	Flanker	Pete Curtis	6
7 Andy Stanley	Flanker	Simon Boote	7
8 Scott Edwards	No.8	Bob Armstrong	8
16	Replacements	Nick Bartlett	16
17 HART		Martin Wooltorton	17
18		Pete Taylor	18
19 POLES		Dean Holder	19
20		Paul Livingstone	20
21		Ian Morgan	21

Referee	(I) International	Touch Judges
S Hardman (Somerset)	* Captain	B Mullis (RFU) A Taylor (RFU)

[Gloucestershire Archives]

The Gloucester forwards came close to scoring early in the second half, but it was only when the ball went wide that Holford got in for his hat trick. Combined Services struck back immediately, Ian Morgan scoring wide on the left and Paul Knowles kicking the difficult conversion. Hart picked the ball off his toes to start a move, which Smith and Paisley carried on, but the chance seemed to have been lost when the pass to Lloyd went wide, but he kicked the ball ahead and won the chase; Paisley converted. Rather unluckily, Morgan was over the line again for Combined Services when he was called back for a penalty to his own side, and when Holford was stopped just short, Mark Cornwell was up in support to score the final try.

Combined Services 26 Barbarians 45, 9th November 1999

THIS WAS THE third Remembrance Match played between these teams, and Kingsholm was chosen as the venue because it was also the home of Royal Air Force rugby at the time, thanks to the proximity of RAF Innsworth. Proceeds went to the Royal British Legion. Scottish

Amicable, sponsors of the Barbarians, agreed to donate £300 to English youth rugby for every try they scored in the match, so that raised £2,100.

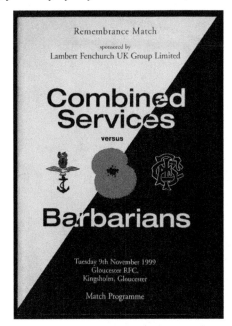

[Gloucestershire Archives]

Combined Services: K Bovadra; B Johnson (captain), R Greenslade-Jones, T Osman, G Kyle; H Graham, B Walder; J Thorpe, F Bibby, C Budgen, L Francis, D Cross, A Dawling, C Cadwallader, H Parr; Replacements: C Carmichael, M Roberts, G Cassidy, N Bartlett, I Laily, P Taylor, L McCormick

Barbarians: S Swindells (Manchester); H Thorneycroft (Northampton), C Joiner (Leicester & Scotland), S Hastings (captain, Watsonians & Scotland), P Saint-André (Gloucester & France); S Vile (Bristol), B Fenley (Worcester); J Mallett (Bath & England), D Addleton (Coventry), A Sharp (Bristol & Scotland), R Fidler (Gloucester & England), D Sims (Worcester & England), C Vyvyan (Wharfedale), M Venner (Henley), M Schmid (Rotherham & Canada); Replacements: T Walsh (Henley), P Hull (Bristol & England), P Whittaker (Bristol), R Elliott (Bedford), G Prosser (Pontypridd & Wales), W Bullock (Birmingham Solihull), L Hewson (Manchester)

Referee: Mr N Whitehouse

Philippe Saint-André, the Gloucester player-coach, Dave Sims, the former Gloucester captain, and Rob Fidler, the Gloucester international, who all turned out for the Barbarians [Gloucester Rugby]

The Barbarians scored first, Dave Sims taking the ball on from a lineout and David Addleton scoring from the forward drive. Philippe Saint-André was greeted with a roar every time he touched the ball, even though his first action was to kick the ball dead behind his own goal-line to save a try. But Combined Services maintained the pressure and Howard Graham ran in to the right of the posts and converted his own try. The

Barbarians started to settle down, Saint-André had his first run after 25 minutes, and from a Combined Services defensive scrum, Charlie Vyvyan charged down the ball and scored. Mark Venner was driven over from a lineout, and Steve Swindells converted both of these tries, which gave the Barbarians a 17-9 lead at half-time.

This was stretched early in the second half with a Steve Vile try, converted by Swindells. But Combined Services struck back when Rory Greenslade-Jones charged over from the back of a ruck. The loudest roar of the evening greeted a try by Saint-André, which made the score 33-12. Play then swept from one end of the field to the other. Combined Services reduced the deficit when Kittione Bovadra slipped through the defence for a try, but this was cancelled out by one in reply from Scott Hastings. Likewise a try by Combined Services number 8, Howard Parr, was matched by Venner diving over in the left corner to round off the game.

Barbarians 14 Ireland 39
27th May 2008

IRELAND USED THIS match as a final warm-up a fortnight before they played the All Blacks on a short tour of New Zealand and Australia. On behalf of the Barbarians, Mickey Steele-Bodger said 'we are most fortunate that we have approval to play the match at Gloucester, this rugby-orientated city which has a magnificent team and heritage of its own. We are grateful for being permitted the use of their splendid facilities.' This contrasted nicely with a story told by Mike Teague of a pre-match meal before he played for the Barbarians at Leicester, when David Campese came in and sat down next to him. Micky Steele-Bodger came over and guided 'Campo' to another table with the comment 'You can't sit with him, he's from Gloucester.'

Barbarians: P Hewat (London Irish); I Balshaw (Gloucester & England), G Thomas (Cardiff & Wales), J Pretorius (Lions & South Africa), L Vainikolo (Gloucester & England); S Larkham (Ricoh & Australia), M Claassens (Bath & South Africa); O le Roux (Leinster & South Africa), S Bruno (Sale & France), C Visagie (Saracens & South Africa), R Skeate (Stormers), S Dellape (Biarritz & Italy), M Molitika (Cardiff & Tonga), D Croft (Reds & Australia), P Wannenburg (Blue Bulls & South Africa); Replacements: M Regan (Bristol & England), P Collazo (Gloucester & France), F Pucciariello (Munster & Italy), K Chesney (Saracens), A Gomersall (Harlequins & England), G Jackson (Saracens), T Delport (Worcester & South Africa)

Ireland: R Kearney (UCD & Leinster); S Horgan (captain, Boyne & Leinster), B O'Driscoll (UCD & Leinster), L Fitzgerald (Blackrock College & Leinster), T Bowe (Belfast Harlequins & Ulster); P Wallace, I Boss; B Young (Ballymena & Ulster), R Best (Belfast Harlequins & Ulster), M Ross (Harlequins), R Casey (London Irish), M O'Kelly (St Marys College & Leinster), S Ferris (Dungannon & Ulster), S Jennings (St Marys College & Leinster), J Heaslip (Clontarf & Leinster); Replacements: B Jackman (Clontarf & Leinster), T Court (Malone & Ulster), R Caldwell (Dungannon & Ulster), N Best (Belfast Harlequins & Ulster), F Murphy (Leicester), J Sexton (St Marys College & Leinster), G Dempsey (Terenure College & Leinster)

Shane Horgan stood in as captain of Ireland for the absent Brian O'Driscoll, led from the front and scored twice in the early stages of the match. Tommy Bowe added another from the opposite wing. Paddy Wallace had his kicking boots on, and in no time the Barbarians were 0-24 in arrears and chasing the game. The Barbarians did manage a massive hit by Ollie Le Roux, which put Michael Ross out of the game, and Craig Newby put the first points on the board for the Barbarians. This was in first half injury time, an unfortunately accurate description, since Newby was carted off to hospital on a stretcher as a result of his effort.

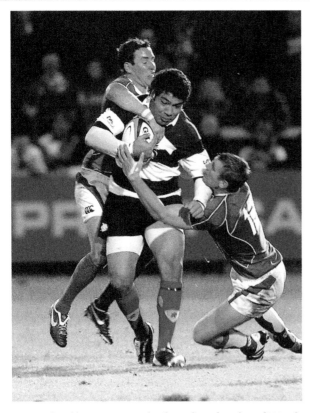

Two Irish tacklers are not enough to bring down the Volcano [Citizen]

Thereafter the second half had less structure. Wallace kicked a penalty goal and Malcolm O'Kelly's powerful running set up a try for Jamie Heaslip. Neil Best came on as a replacement and promptly dispatched Cobus Visagie from the field with a punch; the referee took no action, but the Barbarians soon exacted their revenge. Indeed they seemed fired up by this incident and scored their second try through Pedrie Wannenburg, but the last word went to Ireland with another try for Heaslip just before the final whistle.

Gloucester 5 Australia 36
3rd November 2009

HAVING HAD TO turn down a possible fixture against the All Blacks, because the financial guarantees being demanded would have crippled the Club, Gloucester were pleased to sign a deal to bring the Wallabies to Kingsholm for a sum which was challenging but viable. They were rewarded with a packed stadium, and they pushed the boat out to entertain not only the visitors but also a host of people influential at Twickenham. The success of the evening was to prove important in sustaining the bid for matches at Kingsholm in the 2015 Rugby World Cup.

The Australians came into this game three days after playing the All Blacks in Tokyo, and used the occasion to put out some of their brightest young talents in Lachie Turner, Ryan Cross, Drew Mitchell, Luke Burgess and Tatafu Polata-Nau.

Gloucester: F Burns; C Sharples, H Trinder, T Molenaar, T Voyce; C Spencer, D Lewis; P Doran-Jones, D Dawidiuk, P Capdevielle, W James, A Eustace, J Boer (captain), A Qera, D Williams: Replacements: J Simpson-Daniel, J Pasqualin, R Harden, D Attwood, A Satala

Australia: K Beale; L Turner, R Cross, T Smith, D Mitchell; Q Cooper, L Burgess; R Brown, M Hodgson, M Chapman, D Mumm, D Dennis, S Ma'afu, T Polata-Nau, S Kepu; Replacements: M Dunning, P Cowen

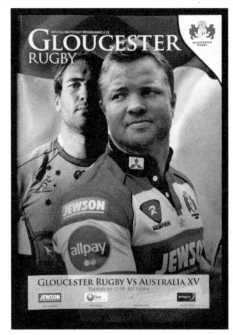

[Gloucestershire Archives]

Referee: Mr A Small

Quade Cooper opened the scoring with a penalty, before the pace of Burgess and Plata set up Cross for the first try, which Cooper

Paul Doran-Jones and Akapusi Qera pack down against Australia [Citizen]

Henry Trinder tackled by Luke Burgess [Citizen]

converted. Gloucester responded with a fine try of their own, started by a clever cross-field kick by Carlos Spencer, which was superbly gathered by Charlie Sharples, who then threw a wonderful pass over his shoulder to Freddie Burns, who dived over to score. Australia came straight back, Cooper and Cross combining to send Tyrone Smith over for a try which established a 15-5 lead at half-time. During the break, entertainment was provided by the Royal Marines Commando Display Team.

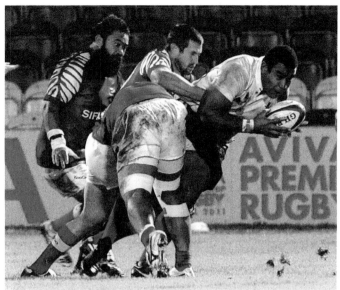

Joe Kava, the Combined Services No 8, with the ball [Citizen]

Sekope Kepu and Tatafu Polata-Nau get to grips with Jake Boer [Citizen]

Gloucester came out refreshed and had a fine third quarter, the introduction of Apo Satala adding some extra oomph. But their best efforts faltered against a resolute Wallaby defence, and in the final quarter Australia ran in three more tries with two from Mitchell and one from Cooper. The first was the pick of the three, lock David Dennis running 50 yards before making a peach of an inside pass to Mitchell to put him in under the posts; all three were converted by Cooper.

Combined Services 25 Samoa 66
17th November 2010

THE SOUTH SEA Islanders found conditions very alien at a freezing Kingsholm, and this was sufficient for them to shy away from a planned training session on the evening before the match. A commentary on the match was broadcast on Services radio across the world.

Combined Services: S Douglas; J Marlin, P Nacamavuto, A Evans, S Rokoduguni; J Prasad, D Pascoe (captain); M Lewis, M Dwyer, K Dowding, D Ball, M Cormack, M Lee, G Barden, J Kava; Replacements: B Priddey, C Budgen, D Bates, D Chambers, I Martin, W John, J Reid

Samoa: M Pesamino; F Otto, U Setu, J Helleur, S Sinoti; L Lui (captain), J Poluleluligaga; R Muagututia, F Selesele, M Timoteo, D Leo, C Slade, L Mulipola, T Paulo, S Lemalu; Replacements: M Schwalger, N Leleimalefaga, F Levi, A Aiono, U Mai, B Vaaulu, G Williams

Referee: Mr R Debney (RFU)

Dave Pascoe kicked a penalty before the Samoans had warmed up, but once they found their rhythm, Sinoti Sinoti cut a great line before Iosefa Tekori spun out of a tackle to go over for the first try, which Lolo Lui converted from the touchline. A harsh sin binning did not help the Services cause, and by half-time the Samoans were out of sight at 35-13.

The highlight of the match came when Services overthrew at a lineout and substitute loose forward, Falamiga Selesele, rocketed away to score from 60 metres out. The final tally was ten tries to Samoa, with

Daniel Leo responds for Samoa [Citizen]

Misioka Timiteo, Fautua Otto and Selesele scoring two apiece, and Tekori, Richard Muagutula, Mikaele Pesamino and Sinoti adding one each; Lui kicked eight conversions. The Combined Services never gave up with three tries from Greg Barden, Jamie Reed and a penalty try resulting from their dominance in the scrums; Pascoe added two conversions and two penalties.

Mikaele Pesamino touching down for Samoa [Citizen]

British Army 17 Georgia 30
23rd March 2011

THE GEORGIA TEAM was coached by former Gloucester player, Don Caskie.

British Army: M Magnus; B Seru, N Nacavamutu, P Gittins, G Qasavakatini; J Prasad, G Slade-Jones; R Reeves, M Dwyer, M Lewis (captain), B Hughes, R Cooke, P Llewellyn, M Bowman, B Bolodua; Replacements: C Budgen, A Whittaker, K Dowding, J Kava, M Koriayadi, D Delietamani, I Martin, G Ferguson, B Bakaso, J Reed, S Speight

The Army team [Citizen]

The Georgia team [Citizen]

Georgia: Players' names not known

Georgia dominated the first half, regularly turning the screw up front and showing plenty of invention and precision amongst the backs. Running straight lines they regularly threatened and would have scored but for a knock-on, before loosehead prop Karlen Asieshvili bundled over from short range. Right wing George Shkinin scored the second, latching on to the loose ball from an Army knock-on, and another forward drive saw Asieshvili go over for his second. Their flame-haired full back Kiasashvili slotted a penalty to secure a convincing 20-0 lead at half-time.

The Army looked a beaten side, but showed a lot more grit in the second half, although Kiasashvili registered the first points with another penalty. Then the Georgian captain, Zviad Maisuradze, blasted through, and a score seemed certain when the ball went loose and the Army pounced. Flying wing Ben Seru scooped the ball up and raced 50 metres, and when he was stopped, centre Naca Nacavamutu was on hand to steal round the ruck and saunter under the posts for a splendid try. Spirits

Melvin Lewis, the Army captain, hits a Georgian wall [Citizen]

raised, the Army were transformed, and Fijian International fly-half Jack Prasad put on a virtuosos turn, cutting through on the blind side and having arms just long enough to stretch over. A lengthy injury changed the tempo of the match again, and replacement hooker Jaba Bregvadze bulldozed his way over to score the deciding try, but there was still time for Denny Delietamani to strike back with the Army's third try, converted by Ian Martin.

Italy A 24 Russia 19
12th June 2011

TWO FORMER CAPTAINS of Gloucester featured in this match – the Russian side was coached by Kingsley Jones, and Marco Bortolami came off the bench to play for Italy. The match was played as a curtain raiser for the England Saxons v Tonga match, which followed.

Italy A: R Trevisan; G Toniolatti, A Pratichetti, M Pratichetti, M Sepe; R Bocchino, T Tebaldi; M Vosawai, M Bergamasco, F Minto, V Bernabo (captain), J Furno, F Staibano, T D'Apice, A De Marchi. Replacements: A Mancini, M Aguero, D Chistolini, M Bortolami, D Gerber, G Venditti, N Belardo

Andrey Bykanov evades the clutches of Ruggero Trevisan [Citizen]

Russia: I Klyuchnikov; V Artemiev, M Babaev, S Trishin, R Yagudin; Y Kushnarev, A Bykanov; V Grachev (captain), M Sidorov, V Gresev, D Antonov, A Panasenko, A Chernyshov, V Tsnobiladze, G

Tsnoiladze. Replacements: V Korshunov, A Travkin, I Prischepenko, A Garbuzov, A Shakirov, A Ryabov, I Galinovsky

Referee: Mr D Pearson (RFU)

An undistinguished match was won by forward power in conditions which made handling difficult. Italy A were 18-6 ahead at half-time, with tries by Pratichetti and Tonialetti, Tebaldi kicking two penalties and a conversion. Kushnarev kicked two penalties for Russia.

Olly Morgan on his way to a try [Citizen]

Andrea Pratichetti hands off Igor Klyuchnikov [Citizen]

In the second half, the Russian backs saw a bit more of the ball, and Yagudin scored a try, which Kushnarev converted and added two penalties, but penalties kicked by Tebaldi and Bocchino saw Italy A home.

Gloucester 47 Russia 7
26th August 2011

THIS PRE-SEASON MATCH was played as a testimonial for James 'Sinbad' Simpson-Daniel and as a World Cup warm-up for Russia. The heavens opened and thunder rumbled round the ground, but even that was not enough to dampen the spirits of the 4,951 Kingsholm faithful, there to salute and say farewell to their favourite son. Russia put out what was thought to be just about their strongest side, but they became such a shambles that their RWC pretensions looked rather feeble.

Gloucester: O Morgan; J Simpson-Daniel, J May, L Vainikolo, T Voyce; T Taylor, D Lewis; N Wood, D Dawidiuk, D Chistolini, W James, A Brown, P Buxton, A Hazell, G Evans; Replacements: K Britton, D Murphy, Y Thomas, T Heard, D Lyons, T Savage, M Cox, D Robson, N Runciman, F Burns, R Mills

Russia: I Klyuchnikov; V Artemyev, M Babaev, A Makovetskiy, V Ostroushko; Y Kushnarev, A Yanyushkin; S Popov, V Korshunov, A Travkin, D Antonov, A Byrnes, A Ostrikov, A Fatakhov, V Grachev; Replacements: V Tsnobiladze, A Khrokin, V Botvinnikov, I Prischepenko, A Voytov, M Sidorov, V Gresev, A Shakirov, K Rachkov, D Simplikevich, A Garbuzov

Referee: Mr G Garner

The Gloucester pack simply blew Russia away in the set scrums, and also enjoyed dominance in the lineouts, so there was a plentiful supply of good ball for the backs. Jonny May in particular scared the wits out of the Russian defence with his searing pace. However, it was the forwards who struck first, Gareth Evans, on his debut for the Club, driving over on the back of the obliteration of a Russia scrum. This domination up front also allowed Dario Chistolini to make an impressive debut for Gloucester.

Nick Wood congratulates Jonny May on his try [Citizen]

The plaque presented by the Russian Rugby Union to mark their appearance at Kingsholm [Gloucester Rugby]

Sinbad then set up a try for Olly Morgan, but despite some trademark mazy runs, he never got the chance to score himself. Rather it was the new pretender to the title of fastest man at Kingsholm, Jonny May, playing at inside centre, who scorched in for the next try. Darren Dawidiuk showed great mobility to escape the clutches of the fringe defence and plenty of pace in sprinting home, before May added his second. That made it 33-0 at half-time.

Russia were doubtless given an inspirational speech in their dressing room by their coach, Kingsley Jones, the former Kingsholm favourite and Gloucester captain. They came out firing on the resumption and kept battling to the end of the game. Nevertheless it was Gloucester who added further tries from Tim Taylor and Lesley Vainikolo, before Alexander Khrokin, to popular acclaim, managed a consolation try for Russia, converted by Klyuchnikov. A minute before the final whistle, Sinbad was substituted so that he could receive the rapturous reception from his devoted following which his sparkling career so deserved.

Barbarians 29 Ireland 28
29th May 2012

IRELAND USED THIS match to warm up for their forthcoming tour of New Zealand, although no Leinster players were available. With past and present Gloucester players featuring in the Barbarians side, 11,654 turned up to watch on a sun-drenched evening.

Barbarians: C Haymans (Bayonne); P Sackey (Stade Francais); M Tindall (Gloucester); D Traille, I Balshaw (Biarritz); F Contepomi (Stade Francais), R Lawson (Gloucester); D Jones (Ospreys), B August (Biarritz), J Afoa (Ulster), M O'Driscoll (captain, Ulster), C van Zyl (Treviso), F Louw (Bath), M Gorgodze (Montpellier), R Lakafia (Biarritz). Replacements: A de Malanche (Stade Francais), N Tialata (Bayonne), P Taele (Biarritz), A Qera (Gloucester), R Rees (unattached), S Donald (Waikato), C Lualua (Leinster).

Ireland: K Earls (Munster); C Gilroy, D Cave, P Wallace (Ulster), S Zebo; R O'Gara, C Murray (Munster); B Wilkinson (Connacht), M Sherry (Munster), D Fitzpatrick, D Tuohy (Ulster), D Ryan (Munster), J Muldoon (Connacht), C Henry (Ulster), P O'Mahoney (Munster). Replacements: R Best (Ulster), R Loughney (Connacht), D O'Callaghan, J Coughlan (Munster), P Marshall, N Spence, A Trimble (Ulster)

Referee: Mr J Garces (France)

Mike Tindall scoring for the Barbarians [Citizen]

The match was played with all the intensity of a full international, with the physical confrontation threatening to boil over on several occasions, although the Barbarians kept to their tradition of running

penalties rather than kicking for goal. Breaks by Mike Tindall and Makuma Gorgodze created the position from which Iain Balshaw ghosted in for the first try. Craig Gilroy then resisted being bundled into touch and wriggled, spun and fought his way over the line. To and fro it went with another Tindall break putting in Cornelius van Zyl from short range, only for Keith Earls to finish off a length-of-the-pitch move in reply. The Barbarians finished the first half strongly, with Paul Sackey scoring from a quick tap which caught the Irish defence napping and unable to lay a finger on him. Balshaw was then held up over the line, which restricted the Barbarians lead to 19-14 at the interval.

The second half started with equal frenzy, Simon Zebo zipping in for a try, which was matched by a smashing effort by Mike Tindall, which brought the house down. Ireland were facing defeat, but rallied strongly and squeezed Gilroy over in the corner. Ronan O'Gara's touchline conversion looked as though it had won the spoils at 28-26, only for the Barbarians to fight their way into the Irish 22, where a hand in the ruck allowed Felipe Contepomi to kick a last gasp penalty and snatch the win for the Barbarians. Everyone, on and off the field, was breathless by the end of it.

Gloucester 31 Fiji 29
13th November 2012

THIS WAS FIJI'S first visit to Kingsholm for 42 years, their previous visit being on their Independence Day. The ground held some happy and some sad memories for Fiji's Timoci Matanavou, who had scored two tries when playing there for Toulouse earlier in the year, even though that game ended in a famous victory for the Cherry and Whites. With Gloucester facing three games in eight days, there was a fair amount of squad rotation for this game, and a considerable physical challenge for some of the younger players from a typically robust Fiji side. The crowd of 8,147 enjoyed a cracking game of rugby and gave a rousing reception to Fiji performing the I Bole before kick-off.

[Malc King]

Gloucester: M Thomas; S Reynolds, D Locke, T Molenaar, I Clark; D Robson, D Lewis; Y Thomas, K Britton, D Chistolini, W Graulich, H Casson, R Moriarty, M Cox, P Buxton; Replacements: T d'Apice, D Murphy, T Heard, B Sparks, B Field, G Boulton

Fiji: M Talebalu; T Matanavou, S Wara, J Matavesi, W Votu; J Ralulu, K Bolatagane; S Samoca, T Tuapati, M Ramumu, A Ratuniyarama, S Qaraniqio, J Domolailai, M Volau, N Nagusa; Replacements: S Naureure, D Manu, R P Makutu, A Naikatini, I Ratuva, N Matawalu, R Fatiaki, A Natoga

Referee: Mr J P Doyle

Fiji's backs ran riot in the first half and stretched out to an 18-0 lead, their big powerful runners threatening to overwhelm their smaller, nippy opponents. Jonetani Ralulu started the scoring with a penalty before hooker Talemaitoga scored a fine opening try. Ralulu added a second penalty before Matanavou finished off a midfield break in style. Gloucester were rocked but they fought back and Matt Cox bullied his way over from short range. Dan Robson converted and kicked a penalty to reduce the arrears to 18-10 at half-time.

Peter Buxton with the ball [Citizen]

Fiji came out rejuvenated and scored another cracker as Watisoni Votu latched onto a superb cross-kick to score his side's third try. But then, to the surprise and delight of the home supporters, the Gloucester pack took control. Twice they muscled their way to a penalty try, and twice Ralulu responded with a penalty. The crowd was loving it, and

Koree Britton leads the charge against Fiji [Citizen]

erupted with excitement when Koree Britton peeled off a rolling maul to touch down. Dan Robson' conversion edged Gloucester ahead 31-29, and although Ralulu had a late chance to win the match with a penalty from within his own half it fell short and wide. Nerves were jangling when Gloucester needlessly conceded a 5-metre scrum, but they held out for a famous win.

Gloucester 14 Barbarians 62
17th November 2015

A SHORT TOUR BY the Barbarians formed part of their 125th anniversary celebrations. A side composed of Southern Hemisphere players, many of whom had stayed on in England after the Rugby World Cup, came to Gloucester for their first match, before travelling to Twickenham to meet Argentina. Gloucester had played a Premiership game three days previously and had a European Challenge Cup two days later, so it was largely an Academy side which took the field against very strong opposition, although Tim Molenaar made a guest appearance back in cherry and white after his transfer to Harlequins. The Barbarians were coached by Michael Cheika of Australia, boasted 573 international caps, and included 12 players who had been involved in the Rugby World Cup. The attendance was recorded as 8,087, but for most of the match they occupied only three sides of the ground, because the game was played in gale force winds which caused the evacuation of the Worcester Street stand.

[Gloucestershire Archives]

Gloucester: M Protheroe; H Robinson, O Thorley, T Molenaar, S Reynolds; L Evans, B Vellacott; N Wood (captain), D Dawidiuk, N Thomas, J Latta, T Hicks, E Stooke, D Thomas, L Ludlow; Replacements: H Walker, D Murphy, J McNulty, W Safe, H Randall, J Evans

Barbarians: N Milner-Skudder (Hurricanes & New Zealand); J Tomane (Brumbies & Australia), F Venter (Cheetahs) R Crotty (Crusaders & New Zealand), N Nadolo (Crusaders & Fiji); P Lambie, C Reinach (Sharks & South Africa); J Mackintosh (Chiefs & New Zealand), J Hanson (Reds & Australia), T Smith (Rebels & Australia), L De Jager (Cheetahs & South Africa), V Matfield (captain, Northampton & South Africa), S Hoiles (Waratahs & Australia), A Savea (Hurricanes), J Butler

Ollie Thorley and Harry Robinson confront Nehe Milne-Skudder [Citizen]

((Brumbies); Replacements: S Moore (Brumbies & Australia), T du Toit (Sharks), C Faumuina (Blues & New Zealand), B Botha (South Africa), S Fardy (Brumbies & Australia), T Kerr-Barlow (Chiefs & New Zealand), L Sopoaga, W Naholo (Highlanders & New Zealand)

Referee: Mr D Richards (Berkshire)

The Barbarians opened the scoring when Nemani Nadolo battered his way over, but Pat Lambie's attempted conversion almost blew back to the 22. Dan Thomas snaffled the ball at the back of a Barbarians scrum and sprinted under the posts for an opportunistic try. The conversion by Lloyd Evans briefly put Gloucester ahead, but Nehe Milner-Skudder soon scored on the end of a sweeping move. Nadolo then scattered Gloucester players like skittles, which resulted in a try for Joe Tomane. He soon scored again after slick handling by Milner-Skudder. Gloucester then held their opponents for a lengthy period, but just before half-time Ryan Crotty went over to make the score 31-7.

The Barbarians struck repeatedly early in the second half, a quick tap setting up Lood de Jager to drive over from close range, Crotty making a sharp break before slipping the scoring pass to Ardie Savea, Waisake Naholo scoring with his first touch of the ball, and Tomane scything through to send Tawera Kerr-Barlow racing away for another. But Gloucester refused to lie down and, despite Molenaar being sin-binned, they enjoyed a period of pressure. Dan Thomas came agonisingly close to a second try and the referee awarded a penalty try to Gloucester at the ensuing scrum; Evans converted. At the death, the Barbarians lived up to their reputation for attacking rugby by launching a move from their own line which ended in a try for Lambie and conversion by Savea.

Rugby World Cup 2015

PRE-TOURNAMENT MATCHES

FOLLOWING THE ANNOUNCEMENT that Kingsholm would be the venue for four matches during RWC 2015, three matches were organised to allow teams who would play there to familiarise themselves with the ground.

Gloucester 40 Japan 5
12th November 2013

JAPAN ARRIVED IN Gloucester fresh from playing Scotland at Murrayfield, and keen to experience the delights of playing at Kingsholm. Their team was a mix of experienced internationals and up-and-coming players. About 7,000 turned out to watch the match under floodlights.

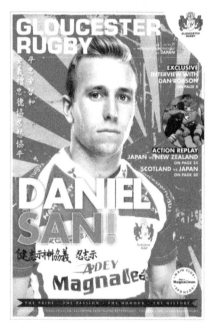

Charlie Sharples, Tom Savage and Jonny May hunting [Citizen]

Jimmy Cowan makes a break [Citizen]

Gloucester: R Cook; C Sharples, J May, M Tindall, J Simpson-Daniell; R Mills, J Cowan; Y Thomas, D Dawidiuk, R Harden, E Stooke, J Hudson, T Savage (captain), A Hazell, M Cox. Replacements: K Britton, J Gibbons, S Knight, L Ludlow, R Moriarty, D Robson, B Burns, S Reynolds

Japan: Y Fujita; A Yamada, S Shimomura, Y Hayashi, Y Imamura; Y Tamura, A Hiwasa; Y Nagae, Y Aoki, H Yamashita, S Makabe, S Ito, J Ives, K Horie, T Kikutan. Replacements: S Horie, H Hirashima, T Asahara, H Ono, M Broadhurst, K Ono, K Matsushima, K So

Referee: Mr I Tempest

Japan started well and, getting quickly to a breakdown, were rewarded with a try after only two minutes. Gloucester soon struck back, and had scored four tries by half-time, including a hat trick by Charlie Sharples, and one from James Simpson-Daniell. Although Japan engineered further scoring opportunities in the second half, the Gloucester defence held firm, and their finishing was more accurate. Steph Reynolds raced in from the half-way line, and the biggest cheer of the night came when flanker Matt Cox received the ball wide on the right inside his own half, and set off down the line. A powerful hand-off and a jinking run resulted in a memorable try to round off proceedings.

Tonga 40 USA 12
15th November 2014

BY THIS TIME it was known that these teams would be playing at Kingsholm during RWC 2015. Tonga, ranked 13th in the world, were marginal favourites against the USA with a ranking of 16th, but both had the confidence of victories the previous week. They attracted a crowd of 8,949.

Tonga: Vungakoto Lilo; David Halaifonua, Siale Piutau, Hemani Paea, Fetu'u Vainikolo; Kurt Morath, Sonatane Tukulua; Tevita Mailau, Aleki Lutui, Paea Fa'anunu, Lua Lokotui, Joe Tu'ineau, Sione Kalamafoni, Nili Latu (captain), Viliame Ma'afu. Replacements: Elvis Taione, Sione Lea, Sila Puafisi, Lisiate Fa'aoso, Hale T Pole, Taniela Moa, Latiume Fosita, Otulea Katoa

[Malc King]

[Gloucestershire Archives]

USA: Folau Niua; Tim Maupin, Seamus Kelly, Andrew Suniula, Tim Stanfill; Shalom Suniula, Mike Petri; Nick Wallace, Phil Thiel, Mate Moeakiola, John Cullen, Greg Peterson, Scott LaValla (captain), John Quill, Matt Trouville. Replacements: Tom Coolican, Angus MacLellan, Benjamin Tarr, Tai Tuisamoa, Kyle Sumsion, Todd Cleaver, Thretton Palamo, Roland McLean

Lua Lokotui wins a lineout for Tonga [Citizen]

Referee: Mr M Fraser (New Zealand)

Both sides contributed to an entertaining and open game, with slick handling, fast running, scintillating breaks, thunderous hits and exciting flair. The USA took an early lead when Niua looped round to put Stanfill in for the first try. The next, from far out by Vainikolo, and three penalties gave Tonga a comfortable lead, but a try by Quill from a strong maul put the Eagles back in contention before half-time.

Hugs all round for the final try by the Tongan captain, Nili Latu [Citizen]

In the second half, Tonga proved the more powerful side, which enabled them to take control of the game, and they scored three tries in quick succession to settle the contest. Ma'afu barged over from close range and Lilo, benefiting from a sharp break and well-timed offload from Halaifonua, ran in from long range. Latu dived over gleefully from a rolling maul just before the end to complete a handsome victory.

Japan 13 Georgia 10
5th September 2015

A FORTNIGHT BEFORE THE start of RWC 2015, Japan, who would be playing both Scotland and USA at Kingsholm in one group, and Georgia, who would be playing Tonga at Kingsholm in another group, met for a warm-up game. These teams had played one another less than a year previously and Georgia had prevailed by dominating in the scrum and maul. It was a more even contest up front this time.

Japan: A Goromaru; Y Fujita, M Sau, C Wing, H Tui; H Tatekawa, F Tanaka; M Mikami, S Horie, H Yamashita, L Thompson, H Ono, M Leitch (captain), M Broadhurst, R Holani; Replacements: T Watanabe, T Kizu, K Hatekeyama, S Makabe, A Mafi, A Hiwasa, K Ono, K Matsushima

Georgia: M Kvirikashvili; M Giorgadze, D Kacharava, M Sharikadze, G Aptsiauri; L Malaguradze, V Lobzhanidze; M Nariashvili, J Bregvadze, D Zirakashvili, G Nemsadze, K Mikautadze, S Sutiashvili, V Kolelishvili, M Gorgodze (captain); Replacements: S Mamukashvili, D Kubriashvili, L Chilachava, L Datunashvili, G Chkhaidze, G Begadze, T Mchedlidze, G Pruidze

Referee: Mr J Lacey (Ireland)

Japan had the brighter start and took the lead with a penalty kicked by Ayumu Goromaru. It took Georgia a quarter of the game to make their first foray into the Japanese half, but they seized their chance. Winger Muraz Giorgadze kicked a grubber through the defence and went over in the corner for a try which Merab Kvirikashvili converted. Goromaru narrowed the deficit with his second penalty, but Lasha

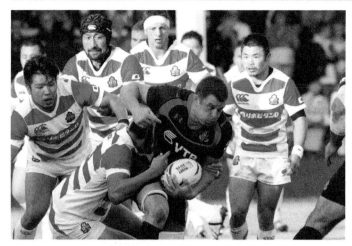

Action from Japan v Georgia [Citizen]

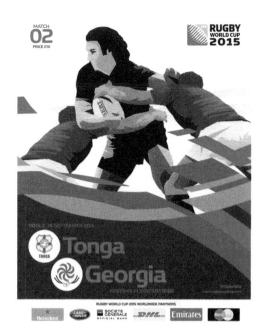

[Gloucestershire Archives]

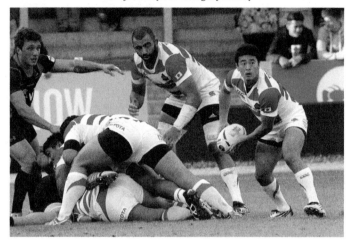

Malaguradze restored the four-point lead with one for Georgia. It looked as though the solid Georgian defence would then win them the game, but two minutes from time Amanaki Lelei Mafi went over from a rolling maul to score the winning try, converted by Goromaru.

RUGBY WORLD CUP MATCHES

Tonga 10 Georgia 17
19th September 2015

TONGA HAD QUALIFIED directly for the RWC finals as a result of their performances in previous tournaments, which included a 19-14 victory over France, the eventual losing finalists, in the 2011 tournament. Georgia, known as the Lelos, earned their place on the big stage by winning the 2012-14 European Nations Cup, going unbeaten through that 10-match campaign. The sides had met twice previously, with each winning once, both matches being played in Tbilisi.

Tonga: V Lilo; T Veainu, W Helu, S Piutau, F Vainikolo; K Morath, S Tukulua; T Mailau, E Taione, H Aulika, L Lokotui, S Mafi, S Kalamafoni, N Latu, V Ma'afu. Replacements: S Piukala, S Taumalolo, P Ngauamo, S Puafisi, H T-Pole, J Ram

Georgia: M Kvirikashvili; T Mchedlidze, D Kacharava, M Sharikadze, G Aptsiauri; L Malaguradze, V Lobzhanidze; M Nariashvili, J Bergvadze, D Zirakashvili, G Nemsadze, K Mikautadze, G Tkhilaishvili, V Kolelishvili, M Gorgodze. Replacements: G Begadze, K Asieshvili, S Mamukashvili, L Chilachava, L Datunashvili, S Sutiashvili

Referee: Mr N Owens (Wales)

Tonga took an early lead with a penalty kicked by Morath,

Tonga and Georgia take to the field [Malc King]

The Tongans get in the mood before kick-off [Citizen]

but Georgia soon responded in kind through the boot of Kvirikashvili, and a Gorgodze try scored under the posts, converted by Kvirikashvili, established a half-time lead of 10-3. In the second half, Kvirikashvili made useful ground with a break down the right, from which the ball was worked across the field, where Tonga appeared to have spoiled Georgian possession, but Giorgi Tkhilaishvili scooped up the loose ball, shook off a despairing tackle and dived over in the left corner. The conversion by Kvirikashvili from the touchline sailed over. The game appeared safe at 17-3, but the Tongan backs were showing flashes of greater speed and inventiveness and came close when Siake Piutau was first to a grubber kick over the line, but he failed to control the ball and the chance was gone. Their endeavour was finally rewarded when Fetu'u Vainakolo went over in the corner and the conversion by Morath left them only one score behind with eight minutes left on the clock. But the Georgian brick wall of a defence remained solid and Tongan hopes perished upon it.

Mamuka Gorgodze, the Georgian captain, has help in celebrating his try [Citizen]

Man of the match was the Georgian No 8, captain and try-scorer, Mamuka Gorgodze, nicknamed Gorgodzilla, who led by example, turning up to good effect all over the field. Not far behind him, both figuratively and literally, was scrum half Vasil Lobzhanidze, at aged 18 making history as the youngest player to appear in a Rugby World Cup. At the end of the match, Georgian celebrations were exuberant and well deserved. They knew that they had just won the greatest victory in their nation's rugby history.

Scotland 45 Japan 10
23rd September 2015

[Gloucestershire Archives]

THIS WAS SCOTLAND'S first match in the tournament, but Japan came into it only four days after an historic win over South Africa. Kingsholm was packed out and vociferous. Greig Laidlaw, a Gloucester player at the time, may have encouraged many to support Scotland, but the Japanese cherry and white jerseys and their under-dog status persuaded many a local to cheer them on.

Scotland bin outside Kingsholm [Malc King]   *Japan bin [Malc King]*

Scotland: S Hogg: T Seymour, M Bennett, M Scott, S Lamont; F Russell, G Laidlaw (captain); A Dickinson, R Ford, W P Nel, G Gilchrist, J Gray, R Wilson, J Hardie, D Denton; Replacements: S Maitland, R Grant, F Brown, J Welsh, R Gray, J Strauss

Japan: A Goromaru; K Matsushima, M Sau, Y Tamura, K Fukuoka; H Tatekawa, F Tanaka; K Inagaki, S Horie, H Yamashita, L Thompson, J Ives, M Leitch (captain), M Broadhurst, A Mafi; Replacements: K Hesketh, A Hiwasa, M Mikami, K Hatakeyama, S Ito, S Makabe, H Tui

Referee: Mr J Lacey (Ireland)

Greig Laidlaw kicked two early penalties, but Japan responded when Ayumu Goromaru put a lovely spiral kick from his own half into touch in the corner and from the lineout the ball was slipped quickly sideways into a rolling maul which rumbled over the line thanks to the weight of the Japanese pack being supplemented by several of their backs; Goromaru added the conversion. Laidlaw responded with two more penalties to give Scotland a 12-7 lead at half-time, which rather flattered them, since Japan had missed penalty kicks at goal and had suffered a reduction in numbers when Matsushima was sent to the sin bin, a seemingly harsh decision

Japan and Scotland scrum down [Malc King]

Japan drive over for a try [Citizen]

when he appeared to have legally stripped the ball from an opponent.

Japan had visibly tired towards the end of the first half, but the break revived them and they were rewarded with a penalty from Goromaru to reduce the deficit. However, Amanaki Lelei Mafi was stretchered off and John Hardie ran a try into the corner. Goromaru struck the post with a penalty attempt, but it stayed out, and in the last quarter the exertions

Mark Bennett scoring for Scotland [Citizen]

of their previous match clearly caught up with Japan. They faded badly, Scotland took full advantage, and it became a rout as Mark Bennett scored under the posts and Tommy Seymour intercepted to race most of the length of the field for another. The icing on the cake came with Bennett's second try and one from Finn Russell; Laidlaw's deadly accurate kicking converted all four.

Argentina 54 Georgia 9
25th September 2015

GLOUCESTER SUPPORTERS WERE disappointed that local favourite Mariano Galarza was unable turn out for Argentina because he had been suspended following the Pumas clash with New Zealand in their previous match.

Argentina: J Tuculet; S Cordero, M Bosch, J M Hernandez, J Imhoff; N Sanchez, T Cubelli; M Ayerza, A Creevy (captain), N T Chaparro, M Alemanno, T Lavanini, J M Leguizamon, J M F Lobbe, F Isa; Replacements: L G Amorosino, J De La Fuente, P Matera, M Landajo, J Montoya, R Herrera, J O Desio

Georgia: M Kvirikashvili, T Mchedlidze, D Kacharava, M

[Gloucestershire Archives]

Argentina and Georgia bin [Malc King]

Sharikadze, G Aptsiauri; L Malaguradze, V Lobzhanidze; M Nariashvili, J Bregvadze, D Zirakashvili, G Nemsadze, K Mikautadze, G Tkhilaishvili, V Kolelishvili, M Gorgodze; Replacements: M Giorgadze, G Pruidze, G Begadze, K Asieshvili, S Mamukashvili, L Chilachava, L Datunashvili, S Sutiashvili

Referee: Mr J P Doyle (England)

Argentina took the lead when Nicolas Sanchez chipped over an unconvincing drop goal from short range, and they quickly built on this when Tomas Lavanini bundled over for a try. But Georgia were not to be intimidated and fought their way back into the game, reducing the deficit with three penalties from the boot of Merab Kvirikashvili against a further two by Sanchez. Georgia were pressing again when a forward pass brought the half-time whistle at 14-9.

Early in the second half, a yellow card effectively ended the match as a contest. It was shown to the Georgian captain and inspiration, Mamuka Gorgodze, and with his departure the heart seemed to go out of his team. Whilst he sat on the naughty step, Argentina scored three tries from Tomas Cubelli, Juan Imhoff and Santiago Cordero; Sanchez converted all three and Gorgodze came back onto the field facing a deficit

Tomas Cubelli scores for Argentina [Citizen]

of 9-35. There was no way back and by the end Argentina had run in three more tries from Martin Landajo, Cordero and Imhoff, with Bosch adding two conversions.

USA 18 Japan 28
11th October 2015

A SPECTACULAR SUNSET GREETED the early arrivals at Kingsholm, which looked brilliant in the floodlights. Yet again a sell-out crowd rose to the occasion and gave a noisy and appreciative welcome to both teams. This vibrant level of support was maintained throughout the match.

[Gloucestershire Archives]

USA: C Wyles; T Ngwenya, S Kelly, T Palamo, Z Test; A J MacGinty, M Petri; E Fry, Z Fenoglio, T Lamositele, H Smith, G Peterson, A McFarland, A Durutalo, S Manoa; Replacements: P Thiel, C Dolan, J Quill, D Barrett

Japan: A Goromaru; Y Fujita, H Tatekawa, C Wing, K Matsushima; K Ono, F Tanaka; K Inagaki, S Horie, H Yamashita, L

[Neil Edwards]

Thompson, J Ives, M Leitch, M Broadhurst, R K Holani; Replacements: K Hesketh, A Hiwasa, M Mikami, T Kizu, K hatakeyama, S Makabe, A Mafi

Referee: G Jackson (New Zealand)

The Americans threw themselves into the fray from the start and were rewarded with a penalty kicked by Alan MacGinty after five minutes. The Japanese soon struck back, and a couple of minutes later Kosei Ono slipped through the defence and chipped ahead; it looked as though Yoshikazu would score, but when he failed to make it over the line, Kotaro Matsushima was on hand to burst over; Ayuma Goromaru converted. The game swung again when a long pass set the lightning-quick Takudzwa Ngwenya free to score for the USA. But they failed to secure possession from the restart and Japan made them pay; although

Lule Thompson wins a lineout for Japan [Citizen]

their backs were brought down, their forwards set up a powerful maul from which Yoshikaza Fujita jumped out to score under the posts. Goromaru converted and then kicked a penalty to stretch the half-time lead to 17-8.

Goromaru and MacGinty exchanged penalties before Eric Fry was caught sticking his boot out for a trip and, whilst he was in the sin bin, Amanaki Lelei Mafi forced his way over from the back of a lineout. That settled the outcome, but the Eagles refused to lie down and a fine pass from MacGinty put Chris Wyles in for the final try; MacGinty added the conversion. Goromaru rounded things off with his third penalty.

Japan thoroughly merited their victory and had much to celebrate from a tournament in which they had played fast and entertaining rugby and had snatched the most famous win of the pool stages against South Africa. Nevertheless they suffered the misfortune of being the first team in any RWC to win three of their four group matches yet fail to qualify for the knock-out stages.

Gloucestershire Archive References

LISTED HERE ARE the images in this book which have been copied from material held at Gloucestershire Archives, but which need to be requested for public viewing as they are kept in secure and climate-controlled storage. For each item this list records the page in the book on which the illustration appears, a short description of the illustration, and the reference number in the Gloucestershire Archives catalogue.

Not included in this list are images copied from sources available in the public search rooms at Gloucestershire Archives. This includes images from the Cheltenham Chronicle and Gloucestershire Graphic, which are available in hard copy in bound volumes. It also includes images from various newspapers, notably the Gloucester Citizen, the Gloucestershire Echo and the Journal, which can be viewed on microfilm at the Archives. Each image in the book copied from these sources is identified next to the image as CC&GG, Citizen, Echo or Journal.

Page	Description	Reference
8	H V Page – Magpie	DY15/12007GS
13	T B Powell – Magpie	DY15/12007GS
14	Walter Jackson –	D10800/5/2/3
15	W H Taylor – Magpie	DY15/12007GS
15	George Whitcomb – Magpie	DY15/12007GS
16	Gloucestershire v Devon – Magpie	DY15/12007GS
17	Gloucestershire v Somerset – Magpie	DY15/12009GS
19	Budd, referee – Magpie	DY15/12008GS
21	Halifax advert – Magpie	DY15/12010GS
21	Gloucestershire team	D10800/4/5/1
22	John Hanman	D10800/5/2/1
25	Stout brothers	D10800/5/2/1
28	England team	D10800/4/5/2
28	Wales team	D10800/4/5/3
32	Whacker Smith	D10800/5/2/1
32	George Hall	D10800/5/2/1
48	F Welshman	D10800/3/4/1
49	Four internationals	D10800/5/2/1
54/55	England Schools Trial programme	D11873/103/1/1
86	Roberts v Voyce programme	N29.54GS
88	Invitation to Fred Wadley	D10800/6/2/3/45
95	Hampshire programme	JQ21.9GS
95	Invitation to Wadley	D10800/6/2/3
95/96	Warwickshire programme	D10800/6/2/1/1
96	Commiseration card	D10800/6/4/7
106	England v Wales team lists	D10800/3/4/1
109	England v Wales programme	N29.72GS
112	RAF v NCDS programme	GA N29.64.GS
113	Comb Serv v NZ programme	D10800/6/2/1/5
114	G & S v Australia programme	D11873/50/1/9
116	England trial programme 1949	D11873/37/1/18
116/117	England trial programme 1962	D10800/3/2/2/4
117	S&SW v Midlands U-23 programme	D11873/50/1/145
118	England trial programme	D11873/50/1/173
122	England v France U-18 programme	D10800/6/2/1/15
128	England v Australia Schools programme	D11873/81/1/9
130	Poster for G'shire v Middlesex	JZ21.5GS
130	Middlesex programme	D11873/50/1/8
131	Lancashire programme	D11873/25/1/5
133	Cornwall programme	D11873/50/1/10
134	Middlesex programme	D11873/50/1/11
137	East Midlands programme	D11873/25/1/34
139	Somerset programme	D11873/50/1/14
140	Devon programme	D11873/50/1/22
141	Somerset programme	D11873/50/1/30
142	Durham programme	J21.48 GS
144	Somerset programme	D11873/50/1/47
145	Devon programme	D11873/82/1/1
146	Warwickshire programme	D11873/50/1/48
148	Somerset programme	D11873/102/1/11
149	Oxfordshire programme	GA D11873/4/1/7
153/154	Centenary programme and ticket	D11873/35/1/2
156/157	International XV programme	D11873/81/1/1
163	British Police v RAF programme	D11873/18/1/2
163	Gloucester v British Police programme	D11873/42/1/83
164	England v Wales Police programme	D11873/50/1/83
164/165	Gloucester v British Police programme	D11873/50/1/93
165	England v Wales Police programme	D11873/50/1/130
165/166	Gloucester v British Police programme	D11873/50/1/160
166	Gloucestershire Police 150th programme	D10800/3/2/1/8
167	W Counties v S Africa programme	D11873/50/1/42
168/169	W Counties v Fiji programme	D11873/50/1/70
169	W Counties v NZ programme	D11873/50/1/9
170	W Counties v NZ action	D 11873/35/3/3
171	Gloucester v S Counties programme	D11873/42/1/101
171/172	PSW v Belgrano programme	D11873/42/1/107
172/173	S&SW v Australia programme	D11873/6/1/168
173	S Africa Barbarians programme	D11873/19/1/10
174	England Emerging v NZ programme	D11873/19/1/12
175	England A v S Africa A –programme	D11873/39/1/44
177/178	Japan match programme	D11873/35/1/39
178	Japan tour programme	D11873/50/3/3
179	Japan - Voyce and Watkins	D11873/42/2/1
179	USA tour programme and letter	D11873/50/3/4
179/180	Civil Service v USA programme	D11873/81/1/7
180/181	Zimbabwe programme	D11873/35/1/66
182	England v Wales Colts programme	D11873/81/1/40
182/183	S&SW v Romania programme	D11873/6/1/247
184	Portuguese President's programme	D11873/19/1/24
185	England A v Italy A programme	D11873/19/1/42
185	SW v W Samoa programme	D11873/19/1/58
189	Surrey programme	D11873/50/1/71
191	Somerset programme	D11873/35/1/4
191	Cornwall programme	D11873/50/1/78
192	Devon programme	D11873/35/1/9
192	Oxfordshire programme	D11873/50/1/82
193	Devon programme	D11873/35/1/13
194	England U-23 programme	D11873/42/1/161
195	Warwickshire programme	D11873/35/1/22
196	Eastern Counties programme	D11873/50/1/143
196/197	Monmouthshire programme	D11873/50/1/161
197	Somerset programme	D11873/35/1/40
198	Oxfordshire programme	D11873/35/1/42
199	Devon programme	D11873/35/1/48
200	Somerset programme	D11873/35/1/57
201	Middlesex programme	D11873/35/1/58
201	Somerset programme	D11873/35/1/67
202	Buckinghamshire programme	D11873/35/1/68
202/203	Northumberland programme	D11873/35/1/71
203	Devon programme	D11873/6/1/156

204	Lancashire programme	D11873/35/1/77	216	NZ v USA programme and ticket	D11873/35/1/191
205	Kingston	NQ.29.37GS	218	Australia Schools programme	D11873/19/1/40
205	Yorkshire programme	D11873/6/1/216	226	Combined Services programme	D11873/39/1/41
206	Middlesex programme	D11873/6/1/218	227	Comb Serv v Barbarians programme	D11873/39/1/95
206	Yorkshire programme	D11873/6/1/238	228	Australia programme	D11873/39/1/281
207	Gloucestershire team	D11873/50/3/8	233	Barbarians programme	D11873/88/1/8
208	SW v Midlands programme	D11873/50/1/426	235	Japan programme	D11873/78/1/6
209	SW v London & SE programme and ticket	D11873/35/1/121	236	Tonga v USA programme	D11873/78/1/24
209	SW v London & SE programme	D11873/50/1/464	237	Tonga v Georgia programme	D11873/88/1/1
210	SW v London & SE programme	D11873/35/1/212	238	Scotland v Japan programme	D11873/88/1/2
211	SW v North programme	D11873/59/1/13	239	Argentina v Georgia programme	D11873/88/1/3
211	SW v Midlands programme	D11873/19/1/56	240	Japan v USA programme	D11873/88/1/4
214	Gloucester v Ireland programme	D11873/43/1/54	240	Japan v USA ticket	D11873/88/3/1

Index

Penn, K 138
Penney, H 36
Penygraig 9, 190
Percival (schoolboy) 121
Perks, D 177
Perrins, G 214
Perrins, J (Jerry) 184, 214-15
Phelps, D (Dave) 140-1
Phelps, D 19
Phelps, E L 6
Phelps, K 195
Phelps, T 12-13
Phillips Petroleum 127
Phillips, E L Rev (Bill) 101-2, *101*
Phillips, F W 4-5
Phillips, R (Bob) 209, 213-14
Pickles, R C W (Reg) 66, 68-9, 71-2, 74-5, 78, 82
Pinkney, E A (Eddie) 156-7, 166, 171, 178, 195, 198
Pitt, R G (Ron) 143-4, *144*, 147, 150-1, *151*, 159, 161
Plaza 122
Plummer, R (Reg) 58
Plymouth 49
Pocock 4-5
Pointon, D (Dave) 157, 192-4, 197, 218
Police Athletic Association 163
Pollard, B 150
Polledri, P 178
Pomphrey, N (Nigel) 158, 181, 197-200, 202-4
Poole, F O 19, 21-2
Porter, R 141
Portuguese Presidents XV 184
Possibles 17, 22, 28, 88-9, *88*, 116-7, 123
Potter, M J (Mick) 162, 192
Powell (schoolboy) 90
Powell, G 139
Powell, J 207
Powell, R 178, 197-8
Powell, T B 13, *13*
Pratten, D G 133-4, *133-4*, 136-7, *137*
Preece, S 74
Preece, W 78
Preedy, M (Malcolm) 166, 173, *173*, 181, 204-6, *205*, 208, 210
President's XV 157
Press, E P 16
Price, B 123, *123*
Price, C (Cliff) 87, *114*, 135, 138
Price, G 207
Price, J R 21, 23
Price, M 123
Price, N 206
Price, R 93
Price, T W (Tom) 101-3, 114, *114*, 116, 129, *129*, 133, *133-5*, 135-6, *137*
Probables 17, 22, 82, 88-9, *88-9*, 116-7, 123
Probert, R/W 79, 82-3, *83*
Protheroe, D V 194
Protheroe, M 233
Protherough, D A 150
Protherough, V D 195-6, *196*
Prowse, A S 74, 78-9
Pruen, G G 1, 3
Public School Wanderers 171, 273
Pugh (schoolboy) 54
Pugh, Sgt Maj 60, 65
Pullin, J V (John) 118, 147, 150-1, 157, 160, 169, 187-90, 192-4, 197
Pumas 239
Purcell, Tpr 56
Purton, A 36

Qera, A (Akapusi) 228, *228*, 232
Quixley, H 46

Rabbits 42
Racing Club de France 45, 120
Radford, J (John) 141-2
RAF 62, 64-5, *64*, 111-12, *111-12*, 119-20, 163
RAF Innsworth 226
Rafter, M J (Mike) 158, *173*, 181, 197-204, *203-4*, 206
Ram Hotel 22, 24, 49
Randall, H 233
Reade, B 177
Red & Whites 147
Red Cross 56, 105
Redco 117-18
Redding, A 42, 46, 49, 51-3, 60, 64-5
Redding, M A (Mike) 126
Redman, R 134, *134*
Redruth 46, 187
Redwood, B 142-3
Redwood, P W 101-2, *101*
Redwood, R L (Bob) 151-3, 155, 160, 163, 167, 190-2, 194
Reed, Fred 157, 162, 178, 199
Reed, J 79
Rees, K 135
Rest of County 36
Reynolds, J 60, *63*, 64-5
Reynolds, S (Steph) 232-3, 235
Richards, A 206
Richards, C A L 99
Richards, G B 123
Richards, T J 41
Richards, W 83
Richardson, E A 78
Richardson, K (Keith) 153, 155-6, 160-1, 166, 171, 174, 210
Rickards, A R 74
Rickerby, Lt 56
Ricketts, A M 25
Rigby (schoolboy) 54
Ritchie, R B 2
Robbins, A 51, 53
Robbins, H 65
Robbins, L 60, 64-5
Robbins, W 58, 60
Roberts 92
Roberts, H 76, 82, 83
Roberts, M (Martin) 173-4
Roberts, R A 94
Robert, W's XV 86
Robertson, Pte W S 56
Robinson, Andy 175
Robinson, H (Harry) 133
Robson, D (Dan) 231-3, 235
Roderick, Maj 71-2
Rogers 90
Rogers, A J (Tony) 151, *152*, 169, 187-8, 190, 194
Rollitt, D M (Dave) 147-2, 157, *158*, 169, 187-90, 192-8, 199, 199
Romania 177, 182-3, *177, 183*
Romans, G (George) 25-6, 30-3, 36, 36-7, 59, *59*, 86, *86, 96*
Romans, George's Gloucester XV 36
Rooke, F 36
Rose, C 24
Rose, J W 5
Rose, T 129, *129*
Rowles, V 10
Rowsell, B 137
Royal Gloucestershire Hussars 56-7

Royal Marines 229
Royal Naval Depot 58, *59-61*, 60-2
Runciman, N 231
Runcorn 220
Russell, F 53
Russell, F J (Frank) 192-3
Russia 230-2, *230-1*
Rutherford, D (Don) 117, 148-53, *149*, *151-2*, 156, 159, 161
Ryland, W R 151

Sables 119
Safe, W 233
Saint-André, P (Philippe) 227
Saintbridge 216
St Helens 220
Salford 220
Salmon, K 86, 95, 96, 98-9
Samoa 185-6, *186*, 229, *229*
Sanders, H A 3, 5-9
Sargent, G A F (Gordon) 178, 181, 190, 192, 197-8, 200-1, 203-4, 207
Satala, A 228-9
Savage, T (Tom) 231, 235, *235*
Savory, F 3
Saxby, L E (Les) 83, 85, 94-6, *94, 96-97*, 98-9
Saxons 221, 224-5, 230
Scotland (19 Group) 128
Scotland 177, 185, 195, 235-6, 238-9, *238*
Scotland Schools 125, 218
Scotland Under-19 126
Scott, C 207
Scottish Borderers 104
Scottish Schools' RU 126
Scrivens 166, 213
Seabrook, F J 82-3, *83*
Searle, E H 23
Seymour, A C 2
Shannon, F 26
Sharp, A 184
Sharples, C (Charlie) 224-5, *224*, 228-9, 235, *235*
Shaw, M V 74, *74*, 76, 78, 82-3
Sheen, I (Ian) 119, 139-42, 177
Sheppard, A (Austin) 158, *173*, 178, 181, 201-3, 206
Sheppard, W V 100
Shirer, J A 8
Short, M 79, 82, 83
Sibery, C H *151*
Simmonds, J 92
Simmons, P J 188-9
Simonett, J F (John) 156, *157*, 158, 197
Simpson, H S 6-10, 13, 16
Simpson, S G 12
Simpson-Daniel, J (James) ("Sinbad") 228, 231, 235
Sims, D (Dave) 173-4, *174*, 185, 210-11, 213-14, 227, *227*
Sloman, H B 3-5, 8, 10
Smart, R 55
Smart, S (Sid) 51-3, *52*, 64, 65-9, *70*, 72, 86
Smith (schoolboy) 54, 90, 121-2, *121-2*
Smith 121
Smith, C A (Whacker) 26, 30-3, *30, 32*, 36, 38, 41
Smith, Claud 31
Smith, Cpl 56
Smith, D 144-6
Smith, D W 36-7
Smith, E 9, 12
Smith, F (Frank) 45-7, *45*
Smith, G H 25, 30, 36
Smith, I (Ian) 166, 173, 184, 213-14, *215*
Smith, J 13

Lightning Source UK Ltd.
Milton Keynes UK
UKOW07n2357071217
314060UK00003B/23/P

9 781906 978464